China–Europe Relati

"This book fills an important gap in its treatment o
hensive, full of insights, invaluable in bringing toget.   ... and Chinese
scholars on an equal footing. Required reading for a   ... practitioners alike."

Sir Christopher Hum KCMG, Master of Gonville and Caius College, Cambridge,
and British Ambassador to China 2002–5.

"This book about the China–EU relationship appears at a good time, when both China and
the European Union are considering ways to further develop their ties. This collection of
assessments by leading scholars on the subject from China, Europe and the United States is
unique – demonstrating the benefits of scholarly cooperation."

Wu Jianmin, President, China Foreign Affairs University
and former Chinese Ambassador to France.

"This study provides an in-depth review of the history, background and issues in the
[China–Europe] relationship. The political and economic dimensions, but also the role of
academic and expert circles as cultural intermediaries, are described here as nowhere else."

François Godement, Professor and Directeur Sciences Po/Asia Centre (Paris)

The fast-developing relationship between China and Europe has become one of the most
important in international affairs. *China–Europe Relations* takes an innovative and
insightful look at this phenomenon, examining:

- the state of Chinese studies in Europe and European studies in China;
- the decision-making behind the EU's China policy, and what the Chinese perceptions
  and assessments are of Europe that shape China's Europe policy;
- the recent rapid growth of bilateral commercial and technological relations;
- the global context of the bilateral Sino-European relationship, in particular the interaction of China, the EU and the United States;
- prospects for the future evolution of these relationships.

The most systematic and comprehensive study on the subject to date, written by a stellar team
of international contributors from China, Europe and the United States, *China–Europe Rela-*
tions will appeal to students, academics and policy-makers alike who are interested in
international relations, comparative foreign policy and Chinese and European politics.

David Shambaugh is Professor of Political Science and International Affairs and Director
of the China Policy Program at the George Washington University. He is also a nonresident
Senior Fellow in the Foreign Policy Studies Program at the Brookings Institution in Washington, DC.

Eberhard Sandschneider is Otto Wolff Director of the German Council on Foreign Relations (DGAP).

Zhou Hong is Professor of European Politics and Modern History, and Director of the Institute of European Studies at the Chinese Academy of Social Sciences (CASS).

China–Europe Relations

Perceptions, policies and prospects

**Edited by
David Shambaugh,
Eberhard Sandschneider
and Zhou Hong**

Routledge
Taylor & Francis Group

LONDON AND NEW YORK

First published 2008
by Routledge
2 Park Square, Milton Park, Abingdon, Oxon OX14 5RN

Simultaneously published in the USA and Canada
by Routledge
270 Madison Avenue, New York, NY 10016

Routledge is an imprint of the Taylor & Francis Group, an informa business

Typeset in Times New Roman by
Bookcraft Ltd, Stroud, Gloucestershire
Printed and bound in Great Britain by
Antony Rowe Ltd, Chippenham, Wiltshire

British Library Cataloguing in Publication Data
A catalogue record for this book is available from the British Library

Library of Congress Cataloging in Publication Data
Shambaugh, David L.
China–Europe relations: perceptions, policies and prospects / David
Shambaugh, Eberhard Sandschneider and Zhou Hong.
   p. cm.
   Includes bibliographical references and index. 1. Europe–Relations–
   China. 2. China–Relations–Europe. 3. Europe–Foreign relations–China.
   4. China–Foreign relations–Europe. I. Sandschneider, Eberhard,
   II. Zhou, Hong. III. Title.
D1065.C5S52 2007
327.5104–dc22   2007011520

ISBN 978-0-415-43198-9 (hbk)
ISBN 978-0-415-43199-6 (pbk)

Contents

Tables

Illustrations

Contributors

Franco Algieri is Senior Research Fellow and directs the EU–China research project at the Center for Applied Policy Research (CAP), Ludwig-Maximilians-University Munich. He teaches political science at the Ludwig-Maximilians-University and he is a guest professor at Renmin University of China in Beijing. Before joining CAP, he was a research fellow at the Institute for European Politics (IEP) in Bonn. He has published widely on EU–Asia (especially EU–China) relations and on the EU's foreign and security policy. His forthcoming books include *Die Chinapolitik der Europäischen Union. Formulierung, Ausgestaltung und Institutionalisierung im Rahmen europäischer Außenpolitik* (Baden-Baden 2007).

Robert Ash is Professor of Economics with reference to China and Taiwan at the School of Oriental and African Studies (SOAS), University of London. Since 1999 he has been Director of the SOAS Taiwan Studies Programme, and he is currently an Associate Dean in the Faculty of Law and Social Sciences. From 1986 to 1995 he was Head of the Contemporary China Institute at SOAS; and in 1997–2001 he was Director of the EU–China Academic Network. His research interests embrace a wide range of issues relating to China's social and economic development. He has held visiting research and teaching positions in Australia, Hong Kong and, most recently, at Sciences-Po in Paris. His most recent books are *China, Hong Kong and the World Economy* (co-authored, 2006); *China Watching: Perspectives from Europe, Japan and the United States* (co-edited, 2007); and *Taiwan in the Twenty-First Century* (co-edited, 2007).

Kjeld Erik Brødsgaard is Professor and Director at the Asia Research Centre, Copenhagen Business School. He is also Senior Editor of the *Copenhagen Journal of Asian Studies* and a member of the Advisory Board of the EU–China Academic Network (ECAN). His most recent publications in English include *The Chinese Communist Party in Reform* (2006) and *Bringing the Party Back In: How China is Governed* (2004).

Dai Bingran is Emeritus Director and Jean Monnet Chair in economics of the Centre for European Studies, Fudan University. He is Vice Chairman and Secretary General of the Chinese Society for EU Studies, and has been guest professor and research fellow to a number of Chinese and European universities and research institutes. His current research interests include the EU's economic restructuring and reforming, EU–China relations, and his book in preparation is *Fundamentals of European Integration: History, Institution and Policies.*

Jean-Pierre Cabestan is Professor and Chair of the Department of Government and International Studies at Hong Kong Baptist University. He was previously Senior Researcher at the French National Centre for Scientific Research (Centre national de la recherche scientifique) and affiliated with the Institute of Comparative Law of the University of Paris and also associate researcher at the Asia Centre, Paris. His most recent books include *Chine–Taiwan: la guerre est-elle concevable? La sécurité extérieure de Taiwan face à la menace de la Chine populaire* (2003); and (with Benoît Vermander) *La Chine et ses frontières. La confrontation Chine–Taiwan* (2005). He has also published numerous articles and contributions in English on China's political system and reform, Chinese law, Chinese foreign policy, relations across the Taiwan Strait and Taiwanese politics.

Bates Gill is Director of the Stockholm International Peace Research Institute (SIPRI). He previously held the Freeman Chair in China Studies at the Center for Strategic and International Studies in Washington, DC. from 2002–7. He previously served as a Senior Fellow in Foreign Policy Studies at the Brookings Institution, and as the inaugural director of the Brookings Center for Northeast Asian Policy Studies. His other affiliations include membership on the Board of the National Committee on US–China Relations, the Council on Security and Cooperation in the Asia Pacific (US Committee), and the China-Merck AIDS Partnership. His most recent books include *Rising Star: China's New Security Diplomacy* (2007) and *China: The Balance Sheet: What the World Needs to Know Now about the Emerging Superpower* (co-authored, 2006).

Ruan Zongze is currently Minister–Counselor in the Chinese Embassy in Washington (2007–). He was previously Vice President and Senior Fellow at the China Institute of International Studies (CIIS) 2002–7. He holds a PhD in International Relations from China Foreign Affairs University. He was a visiting scholar at the University of London's School of Oriental and African Studies from 1992–3. From 1996–2000, he served as second and first secretary in the Chinese Embassy in the UK. His research interests are mainly concerned with US foreign policy, Sino-American relations, major power relations, and East Asian integration. His latest book is *The Transition of the International Order and Peace in East Asia* (2006).

Eberhard Sandschneider is Otto-Wolff-Director of the Research Institute of the German Council on Foreign Relations (DGAP). He completed his PhD and "habilitation thesis" in Political Science at the Saar University in Saarbrücken. He was Professor of International Relations between 1995 and 1998 at the University of Mainz, before being appointed as Chair in Chinese Politics and International Relations at the Freie Universität (Free University) of Berlin in 1998. His research interests concern all aspects of contemporary China,

European security and transatlantic relations, international politics in Asia, and foreign policy decision-making processes. His most recent book is *Global Rivals – China's Astounding Rise and the Paralysis of the West* (2007).

David Shambaugh is Professor of Political Science and International Affairs, and founding Director of the China Policy Program at the George Washington University. He is also a nonresident Senior Fellow in the Foreign Policy Studies Program at the Brookings Institution, and previously served as the editor of *The China Quarterly* and Reader in Chinese Politics in the University of London. His research concerns the domestic politics, foreign relations, military, and security policy of contemporary China, as well as the international politics of Asia and Europe. His most recent books are *China's Communist Party: Atrophy and Adaptation* (2007); *China Watching: Perspectives from Europe, Japan, and the United States* (2006); *Power Shift: China and Asia's New Dynamics* (2005); and *The Odyssey of China's Imperial Art Treasures* (2005).

Song Xinning is Jean Monnet Professor of European Studies and Director of the Centre for European Studies at Renmin University of China. He is also the (Co-) Executive Director of the Brussels Institute of Contemporary China Studies jointly established by Renmin University of China and Free University of Brussels (VUB). Since April 2007 he has been a Senior Research Fellow of Comparative Regional Integration Studies at the United Nations University in Bruges, Belgium, and took up a professorship there in 2007. His recent books include *Political Economy of European Integration* (2007), *Europeanization and Conflict Resolution: Case Studies from the European Periphery* (2006), *Environmental Policy and Economic Development: The EU Environmental Policy and Its Implication for China* (2002), and *Handbook of European Union and European Integration* (2002).

Volker Stanzel is Political Director in the German Federal Foreign Ministry. He previously served as the German Ambassador to China from 2004–7. He has been with the German Foreign Service since 1979, serving as Director for Asian and Pacific Affairs from 2001 to 2002 and Director-General for Political Affairs from 2002 to 2004. His publications in English include: *China's Perception and Possibilities of its International Role* (1997); *NATO after Enlargement* (1998); *New Problems in Transatlantic Relations* (1999); *Remembering and Forgetting* (2001); *Asia's Role in the World* (2002); *The Experiment of Afghanistan* (2005); *Thoughts on Germany's China Policy* (2005). Books in German: *Japan: Head of the Earth* (1982); *Winds of Change: East Asia's New Revolution* (1997); *China's Foreign Policy* (2002).

Michael Yahuda is Professor Emeritus of International Relations at the London School of Economics. Since retiring in 2003 he has been a Visiting Scholar at the Sigur Center for Asian Studies at George Washington University until June 2006. From 2006 to 2007 he was a Fellow at the Woodrow Wilson International Center for Scholars. He enjoys an international reputation as a specialist on China's foreign relations and the international politics of East Asia. He has published six books and more than 200 scholarly articles and chapters in books. His most recent book is *The International Politics of the Asia-Pacific Since 1945* (2005).

Zhang Zuqian is Senior Researcher at Shanghai Institute for East Asian Studies (SIEAS). He is also Deputy Secretary General and Director of the Department for Research and Consultation at Shanghai Institute for European Studies (SIES). Between 1982 and 2005 he worked as postgraduate, junior researcher, and senior researcher at the Shanghai Institute for International Studies (SIIS), where he served as Editor of the *Yearbook of International Affairs* and *SIIS Internal Reports*, Director of Department for Comprehensive Studies and Director of Department for European Studies. In 2005 he retired from SIIS and began to work at SIEAS. He has published numerous articles on European affairs and China–Europe relations.

Zhou Hong is Professor of European Politics and Modern History, and Director of the Institute of European Studies at the Chinese Academy of Social Sciences (CASS). She is an elected Member of the Academic Divisions of CASS, the elected Deputy Director of the Division of International Studies and she chairs the nationwide Chinese Association for European Studies. Her recent publications include *Donors in China* (2007); *Whither the Welfare State?* (2006); *The EU and American Models Compared* (2003); and *Foreign Aid and International Relations* (2002).

Zhu Liqun is Professor of International Studies and Vice-President of China Foreign Affairs University (CFAU). She is also Director of European Studies Center at CFAU and Vice Editor-in-Chief of *Foreign Affairs Review*. She was a 2003–4 visiting Fulbright Scholar at George Washington University's Sigur Center for Asian Studies. Her most recent book is *Security Organizations and Security Structure in the Post-Cold War Europe* (2002), and she has published numerous articles on the United Nations, US–China relations, the ASEM process, East Asian regional institutions, China–Europe relations, and European affairs.

Part I
Introduction

1 Introduction

Assessing the China–Europe relationship

David Shambaugh, Eberhard Sandschneider and Zhou Hong

The development of China over the past thirty years is fascinating and is arguably *the* most important international development of our era. China – it seems to many Western observers – is on its way to becoming a new superpower with the potential to threaten the dominant position of the United States, not only in the Pacific theatre but maybe also in the whole world. It is not surprising, therefore, that the rise of China and its implications for the world's only superpower are portrayed and discussed widely within the political and academic community both inside and outside the United States. An overwhelming array of books and articles has been published on these issues, and numerous conferences are convened to analyse the implications.

However, this is not the case when it comes to relations between China and Europe. These relations have been discussed to a much lesser degree. Only one edited book has appeared on the subject in recent years,[1] although the periodical literature is a bit more plentiful. While the Sino-European relationship has blossomed – even boomed – since the mid-1990s, the academic world has failed to keep up with it. This volume is intended as a significant effort to fill this void in the literature and to bring to bear on the burgeoning Sino-European relationship some of the best minds and analysis from China, Europe, and the United States. It is truly a trilateral partnership, among the fifteen contributors, the three co-editors and their respective institutions – the China Policy Program of the Elliott School of International Affairs at the George Washington University, the German Council on Foreign Relations (DGAP), and the Institute of European Studies of the Chinese Academy of Social Sciences (CASS). Both the editors and the contributors of this book are convinced that the publication of this volume is important at this point in time for several reasons.

First, it provides a comprehensive assessment of the current state of, and the prospects for, China–Europe relations. The fifteen chapters herein cover a wide range of topics, assessing the Sino-European relationship from a number of angles. The subtitle of the volume – Perceptions, policies and prospects – illustrates the emphasis in the pages to come. It provides historical perspective on the relationship; it assesses the state of Chinese studies in Europe and European studies in China; it explores how the European Union goes about making its China policy and what the Chinese perceptions and assessments are of Europe that shape

China's Europe policy; it exposes the significant bilateral commercial and technological relationship that has grown apace in recent years; it places the bilateral Sino-European relationship in a global context and particularly looks at the interaction of China, the EU, and the United States; and it assesses the prospects for the future evolution of these relationships. It is the most systematic and comprehensive study on the subject to be published to date.

Second, this volume is important because it fills a gap in Western debates about how to manage China's rise. With this book, we hope to fuel academic and political discussions and highlight several issues and topics that have not been deeply discussed up to this point. In particular, the study exposes the alternative ways in which the European Union states think about and deal with China – in contrast with the United States. This volume illustrates the very different philosophical, political, and strategic perspectives that exist with respect to China on the two sides of the Atlantic Ocean.

Thirdly, the volume provides insight into Chinese thinking about Europe and – to a lesser extent – the United States. While there is a robust community of "Europe Watchers" active in China today (as Dai Bingran's chapter reveals), the views and writings of this community are virtually unknown outside China (and not even that widely within China's broader international relations community). Thus, really for the first time, this volume gives voice to some of China's leading Europe specialists, illuminates their domestic discourse, and makes their views known to the wider world.

The editors and contributors of this volume are, of course, well aware of the challenges that the publication of such a book poses. Everybody involved in the project has done their best in order to make this a high-quality publication, which will prove to be useful for both students and scholars of international relations, as well as the interested public who want to know more about the current state of Chinese–European relations and their prospects for the future. The study took shape over a three-year period, beginning in 2004 with several reflective and probing discussions among the editors. In 2005 the decision was made to formally collaborate and commission a number of papers to be included in the volume. These first drafts were written and first presented at a three-day conference "China and Europe: Integrating Continental Powers," held at the DGAP in Berlin in July 2006 (in the midst of the World Cup!). This conference was notable particularly for its collegiality and the spirit of partnership among all the contributors, but it was also characterized by intensive discussion of each of the draft chapters – illustrating the best of the "peer review" (*tonghang pingyi* in Chinese) process. This experience revealed just how far Chinese scholarship in international relations has come and how comfortable and confident Chinese scholars are today interacting with their Western counterparts in serious scholarly settings. Following the conference, and based on detailed suggestions from the editors and a second set of peer reviewers arranged by Routledge Press, all chapters were revised (often several times) for publication. Thus, the publication of this volume in 2007 reflects three years of hard work, but also tremendous collegiality.

Highlights of the volume

Michael Yahuda of George Washington University opens the discussion with a wide-ranging and thoughtful historical retrospective on the evolution of the Sino-European "encounter." His skilful overview identifies two main factors that have shaped these relations from the outset. The first is the geographic circumstances of both continents, which he describes as "the tyranny of distance." Physical distance has contributed to perceptual distance in Yahuda's view, as Chinese and Europeans have misunderstood each other for a very long time. The second major influence, he suggests, is the importance that trade had as the main conduit for and substance of relations between the two for almost two thousand years. Despite the importance of distance and trade, China and Europe mutually influenced each other in other fields as well, especially after the Middle Ages in Europe. Yahuda expertly demonstrates the impact that European thought had on successive generations of Chinese intellectuals, from the Enlightenment to the present – but he also shows that such ideational and cultural influences have flowed in reverse as well, as generations of Europeans have been fascinated by things Chinese. Yahuda does not confine himself solely to the relations between China and Europe, but also shows the effects that relations between China, the United States, and the former Soviet Union had on Sino-European relations during the Cold War. He argues that, during this long period, China and Europe were never really able to develop their own autonomous ties, independent of the superpowers – and it was not until the end of the Cold War that the relationship could really begin to develop on its own.

The third section of the volume focuses on European perceptions of and approaches to China. Kjeld Erik Brødsgaard of Copenhagen Business School opens with a comprehensive analysis of Chinese studies in Europe. This is a very ambitious undertaking since, as noted above, every European country has its own approach and policy towards China. Therefore, it is not surprising that the landscape of China studies in Europe is equally diverse. Brødsgaard's chapter is fully up to the challenge, though, as he has authored one of best studies ever undertaken on the subject.[2] He starts with an overview of the historical evolution of Sinology in Western Europe. He notes the famous figures in the development of the field in England, France, Germany, Holland, and Scandinavia. The study of Chinese philology, philosophy, religon, ancient literature, archaeology, and ancient history dominated the discipline – and consequently made it difficult for the social sciences to become established and shift focus to the study of contemporary China. This Sinological tradition continues to cast a long shadow over European China studies to this day. However, Brødsgaard traces the development of the study of contemporary (post-1949) China from the late 1970s. He shows how the field grew fairly rapidly in Scandinavia, Germany, and the UK – although this was really due to a handful of key scholars, such as Jürgen Domes, Stuart Schram, Kenneth Walker, Christopher Howe, Oskar Weggel, Brunhild Staiger, Marie Claire Bergere and Lucien Bianco. With this cohort, however, social science analysis of China commenced in Europe. Brødsgaard then goes on to detail the current state of contemporary China studies and he describes considerable growth in individuals and institutions. He also discusses pan-regional organizations such as ECAN (the European China Academic Network) and EACS (the European Association of Chinese Studies) that link scholars together. Finally, he provides a lengthy and fascinating description of the types of subjects that European scholars have focused on – in the process tracing the evolution of three generations of scholars and scholarship.

"It's the system that matters," argues Franco Algieri of the University of Munich. He explains in his chapter how the European Union bureaucracy in Brussels goes about making its policy towards China. The EU, particularly its executive arm the European Commission, has been among the most active of all governmental institutions across Europe in fashioning and articulating a strategy and policy towards China. While attention has been paid to the *output* of Commission policy, Algieri is really the first to focus on the *input* side of the equation. A specialist in the EU institutional architecture, he understands better than most the arcane and complex bureaucratic machinery operating in Brussels. In this chapter he brings his knowledge to bear on China policy. In focusing on how the EU's institutional structure influences the shaping and conduct of its relationship with China, he focuses on four key areas of cooperation: the political dialogue, trade policy, human rights policy, and the arms embargo. Algieri suggests that the EU's China policy is fashioned between the various institutions in Brussels, the capabilities that can be used for effective policy-making, and the interests of individual European member states. In some areas policy coherence has come at the cost of competition among various bureaucratic interests and countries. Particularly in the field of human rights, these systemic aspects threaten the coherence and credibility of European China policy.

In his chapter Jean-Pierre Cabestan of Hong Kong Baptist University and formerly the French National Centre for Scientific Research, explores the role of Taiwan in European relations with China, but he also details the nature and dynamics of European relations with the island in the economic, educational, cultural, and political realms. This is probably the most thorough summary of European–Taiwan ties available. His analysis shows how EU–Taiwan relations have afflicted European policy towards the People's Republic of China over time, although not nearly to the same extent as in the United States. As Cabestan describes, Taiwan has never had the presence or lobbying impact in European capitals that it has had in Washington – although he describes earnest efforts by the Taiwan government in recent years to lobby the European Parliament in Brussels and to establish a better beachhead in the main European capitals. He also notes that the expansion of the EU to incorporate the new twelve members from the former communist states in Eastern Europe has proven beneficial for Taipei, as a number of them (particularly the Czech Republic and Poland) are politically sympathetic to Taiwan's anti-communist cause. Arguing that Taiwan has proved to be "more an irritant than leverage" for the EU in its relations with China, he also addresses the question of whether the EU might adopt a more active role in the future settlement of the political impasse across the Taiwan Strait.

In Section IV of the volume, Fudan University Professor Dai Bingran turns the tables by taking a look at European studies in China. At first, he reflects on the development of European studies in China, which began only during the 1970s, in which he was personally involved at Fudan University. Europe, in those days, was seen as part of the "second world" – to be mobilized in a common united front against the former Soviet Union. The other prism through which Chinese analysts looked at Europe then was as a "state-monopoly capitalist" system. But specific knowledge of European societies, economies, and politics was minimal. The field only really began to develop in the 1990s, and largely as a result of three factors. The first was the building of an independent relationship between the two sides after the Cold War – and the Chinese government had need for more expertise and information about the EU. The second factor was the impetus provided by the European Commission Delegation in China that provided funding for the creation of European studies centres across China. A third factor that Dai identifies has to do with the Chinese desire to learn from and adapt various aspects of the "European model" that may be of use to China's reform process. Finally, Dai discusses the government and private sector "consumers" of research produced by China's Europe Watchers. His chapter also includes comprehensive appendices that catalogue all the main European studies centres in China, as well as the main journals published in the field.

The next chapter by George Washington University Professor David Shambaugh also focuses on China's Europe Watchers, as he undertakes a systematic analysis of the content of books and articles written since 2001 about Europe's and the EU's role in world affairs. Shambaugh notes that to date in the West much more has been written about European views of China than vice versa, and his chapter (as well as the following ones by Zhu Liqun, Song Xinning, and Ruan Zongze) begin to rectify this deficit. Shambaugh delves into more than twenty Chinese journals and a number of books to elucidate Chinese perceptions of Europe in three areas: Europe's role in world affairs and the EU as an international actor; China–Europe relations; and the EU–US–China "triangle." In all three areas, but particularly the first, Shambaugh finds a high degree of what he describes as "cognitive dissonance," i.e. Chinese analysts have a strong propensity to project their own ambitions and preferences onto Europe and European actions. Chinese (like others) have certain core beliefs about world affairs and the kind of international order they would like to see emerge – as a result, they are quick (and often overly quick) to find confirmation of their inclinations in European actions. Thus, for example, there is a strong proclivity to view Europe as a "pole" in the emerging multipolar global order that China seeks. When it comes to assessing China–Europe relations, China's Europe Watchers are almost uniformly upbeat and optimistic. They praise EU policy as being enlightened and farsighted (in contrast to the "hedging" or alleged neo-containment policies of the United States) – and they take great satisfaction in the China–EU "comprehensive strategic partnership" (proclaimed in 2003). Nonetheless Chinese analysts (like the Chinese government) remain dissatisfied with the EU arms embargo and failure to grant China Market Economy Status. In terms of the so-called China–Europe–US "triangle,"

Chinese analysts are constantly looking for faultlines across the Atlantic, which can possibly be exploited by China. Some see numerous such transatlantic tensions, while other analysts identify greater solidity of ties. Some see the US and EU trying to collectively manipulate or pressure China – for example, on questions of human rights, trade policy, political liberalization, and civil society development. Others, though, view the triangle in more positive-sum terms. In sum, while there are differences of opinion within China's Europe watching community, there remains a high degree of agreement on many issues. Also, despite a tendency towards cognitive dissonance, one is struck by the depth of understanding of the EU and European affairs, as well as the straightforward, non-ideological nature of Chinese analyses.

In the next chapter, Zhu Liqun of China's Foreign Affairs University carries forward the analysis of the previous chapter by examining Chinese perceptions of the EU and Europe on two levels. First she examines scholarly journals and the assessments provided by Chinese scholars. She also finds China's Europe Watchers to be generally positive about Europe's role in world affairs – particularly as a normative model for multilateralism and non-coercive behaviour. In fact, she notices a recent shift in Chinese assessments away from the previous realist school that emphasized Europe as a pole in an emerging multipolar world, towards viewing Europe more as a "civilian and normative power." She also finds that Chinese scholars believe that there is substantial convergence between China and the EU in their respective views of global governance, which bodes well for future cooperation. The second half of Zhu's chapter reports the findings of a survey of Chinese university students' perceptions of various aspects of the EU and Europe. This survey data is some of the first to be systematically undertaken in China, and is therefore most interesting – even if it is impressionistic and problematic in methodological terms. Overall, one sees many positive perceptions.

The last chapter in this section, by Song Xinning of Renmin University in Beijing, examines Chinese views specifically of European integration and enlargement processes. Chinese analysts have followed these twin processes very carefully over the years. Generally speaking, he finds surprise among European analysts concerning the pooling of sovereignty and the scope and pace of EU integration. Given the high premium that Chinese place on sovereignty, this is not surprising. Yet Chinese analysts have also been interested in these processes as a possible model for Asian integration. He also notes various aspects of the "European Model" that have intrigued Chinese analysts. Finally, he notes that the incorporation of twelve new East European states into the EU may cause more problems than opportunities for China – in both political and commercial terms.

Section V of the volume turns to the commercial, economic, and technological domain – containing twin chapters by a European and a Chinese contributor. Robert Ash of the University of London's School of Oriental and African Studies examines Europe's commercial relations with China, while Zhang Zuqian of the Shanghai Institute for East Asian Studies does so in reverse.

Ash's chapter is a *tour de force*. It is probably the best single assessment of the Europe–China economic relationship in print. It begins with a discussion of the evolution of the EU's economic strategy towards China since 1978, tracing the shifts and growth in the bilateral trade and investment relationship. Next, Ash focuses closely on the FDI inflows and outflows to/from China, and exposes some very interesting patterns from unique data not previously examined. This is followed by a careful study of the bilateral trade patterns between China and the EU. Finally, Ash goes "beyond the numbers" by drawing attention to the European corporate experience in China. Again, this is not something that has been written about previously, and his discussion adds some interesting comparisons to the American and Asian experiences.

Zhang Zuqian next looks at the bilateral trade and investment relationship from China's perspective. He provides a number of case studies of successful European joint ventures in China and indicates general Chinese satisfaction with European investment. Zhang then looks at Chinese investment in the EU, a subject about which not much is known. He provides a number of interesting examples of successful Chinese firms operating in Europe. He also looks at technology transfer from Europe to China. Finally, Zhang lists a number of difficulties and problems China has had with Europe in the trade realm, notably anti-dumping duties and the failure to grant China Market Economy Status.

The final section of the volume places the China–Europe relationship in global context, and does so in three particular ways. First, Volker Stanzel (former German Ambassador to China) examines the interaction of the two sides in terms of global governance, largely in the international institutions. He argues that the post-Cold War order has opened up a Pandora's Box of pressing and complicated issues on the international agenda – many of which require Sino-European efforts to effectively address them. Much of the remainder of his contribution examines the degree to which Chinese and European orientations are or are not compatible on a range of global governance issues. Not surprisingly, he finds some overlap – but the differences he exposes are not to be trivialized or ignored, as they fester beneath the surface of the relationship and will act to limit cooperation in certain areas. But on big issues, like strengthening the United Nations and upholding international law, Stanzel finds considerable congruence. Energy policy may be another such commonality. He concludes with a list of important global issues that the two sides will confront in the years to come – but he remains somewhat agnostic about the ability of China and Europe to effectively tackle these problems owing to what he identifies as differences in values. Stanzel asks whether China, as a rising centre of gravity in the international system, will exert its new role not only in the sense of co-determining the global rules, but also as a responsible partner for multilateral solutions.

In his chapter, Bates Gill of the Stockholm International Peace Research Institute, looks into the complex triangular relations between the United States, Europe and China – which have seen increasing, but still insufficient, American interest over the past few years. He begins with an instructive introduction to American understanding (or lack thereof) of China–Europe relations. His data and arguments are not encouraging, as Americans tend to be rather oblivious to this important relationship. It was only the arms embargo imbroglio that briefly caught the attention of the US

Government, but once that issue was shelved, the interest quickly faded. Gill's findings are a clarion call for more investment into transatlantic dialogue about China. His analysis of the differing US views of EU–China relations interestingly shows that there are strong American concerns about the tightening of China–Europe cooperation, stoking fears about possible constraints for the United States' freedom of action on the global stage. Thoroughly discussing both bilateral and trilateral problems and tensions between the US, the EU and China, Gill identifies six key areas a cooperative agenda should focus on: regional stability in Asia (and elsewhere); counter-terrorism; nonproliferation; transnational challenges in the areas of public health, law enforcement, resource depletion, environmental degradation, energy, etc.; strengthening global economic institutions; and assisting China in meeting its internal socio-economic challenges. This is a useful menu and roadmap for trilateral cooperation.

In his chapter, Ruan Zongze of China's Foreign Ministry, contributes a thoughtful chapter on the triangular interaction of China, Europe, and the United States on the world stage. He is optimistic about the potential for collaboration on a number of issues of global governance. He believes that China is increasingly a "responsible stakeholder" in the international arena, and that this will allow for more and more collaboration on global problem-solving. He also examines the main elements and dynamics of relations along each leg of the triangle, offering some very interesting comparisons. On balance, Ruan rejects the thinking that the triangle is inherently zero-sum – rather identifying numerous areas for joint cooperation among all three sides.

Finally, in the conclusion of the volume, the editors take stock of the overall relationship and offer their observations about its likely trajectory in the future.

We know that the range of topics in this volume is by no means comprehensive. Nor is the above summary of the chapters comprehensive. Nevertheless we are convinced that this book at least covers the most important issues in the relations between China and Europe (and, in some case, the United States), and we encourage readers to carefully delve into each one, as they are all rich in data and analysis. The value of the chapters lies in their detail. The Sino-European relationship is exceedingly complex, and thus superficial journalistic "snapshots" of the relationship are no replacement for serious scholarship. We have attempted in this volume to provide such analytical breadth and depth. In the end, we hope to make a significant contribution to the study of the relations between both powers and we hope to stimulate subsequent research by others.

Notes

1   The only book on China–Europe relations published in the West in recent years is Richard Louis Edmonds (ed.), *China and Europe Since 1978: A European Perspective* (Cambridge: Cambridge University Press, 2002).
2   For another set of recent evaluations of China scholarship in Europe, see the chapters by Ash, Cabestan, and Moller in Robert Ash, David Shambaugh, and Seiichiro Takagi (eds.), *China Watching: Perspectives from Europe, Japan and the United States* (London: Routledge, 2007).

Part II
Historical context

2 The Sino-European encounter

Historical influences on contemporary relations

Michael Yahuda

The history of relations between Europeans and Chinese can be traced back at least as far as the beginning of the Christian era. The value of the goods brought from China on the famous Silk Road (which also included the route by sea via the Middle East and India) that bore silk and other luxuries to Rome is known to have been so significant as to lead to a "serious adverse balance which was made up by bullion or species payment."[1] There was little of comparable value and volume that Rome had to offer that was acceptable in China. This was a pattern that was to repeat itself throughout most of the eighteenth century until the introduction of opium turned the scales heavily the other way. The contemporary adverse balance of trade between the countries of the EU and China, however, is dissimilar as it is due less to China's self-sufficiency than to the nature of its role in the globalized chain of production. However, the main point to be made about the earlier trade is that it was indirect and that, being conducted through the agency of "middle men" in central and southern Asia, there were no direct relations between Europeans and Chinese at this time.

Two major factors that have continued to shape relations between Europeans and Chinese down to the present may be seen to have operated from the outset. The first is the tyranny of distance, which has been partially overcome by modern technology and transportation. With the exception of the hundred years or so from the first Anglo-Chinese War of 1840, neither China nor Europe impinged much on each other's geopolitical concerns. The second is the primacy of trade as the main conduit for and substance of their relationship.

Direct relations between European states and China did not begin until 1514, when the Portuguese first reached China from Malacca. However, it is important to bear in mind that well before that date European civilization and development had been greatly influenced by the transmission of inventions and discoveries first made in China. Interestingly, the provenance of these inventions was unknown even in 1620 when the English philosopher Francis Bacon identified three discoveries:

> Unknown to the ancients, and of which the origin, though recent, is obscure and inglorious; namely printing, gunpowder, and the magnet. For these three have changed the whole face and state of things throughout the world, the first

in literature, the second in warfare, the third in navigation; when have followed innumerable changes; insomuch that no empire, no sect, no star, seems to have exerted greater power and influence in human affairs than these mechanical discoveries.[2]

Of course it was these "discoveries" which enabled the more martial, mercantile and industrializing European states to reach out to China in the nineteenth century and to bring China into the modern age by force of arms.

As the European 'moment' in China receded and as the Europeans were absorbed and weakened by their two world wars, they paid less attention to China, although Chinese continued to call upon expertise from Europe. The establishment of the People's Republic in 1949 ushered in a new era in the politics and economics of Sino-European relations that was dominated by the effects of the Cold War. Ironically, however, the ideology and organizational principles that underpinned the rise of communism in China and that gave expression to China's new national identity were of European origin, but that fact was not to play a significant part in their new relationship. Despite indications of some differences over its policy towards China with their chief ally, the United States, the policies of the West European states in the final analysis were a product of their dependence on the United States in this period of bipolarity. The same applied to the East European states as their relations with China were a product of their relations with the Soviet Union. With the end of the Cold War and the changes that took place in both China and Europe, the two sides were able to establish a more independent relationship.[3]

In order to identify the main themes that have shaped the historical experience of Sino-European relations I shall look at four broad periods: 1500–1800, when Europeans were influenced by China; the nineteenth and early part of the twentieth centuries when the Europeans forcibly broke into China and shaped the modernization of the country; 1949–89, the Cold War period, when their relations were dependent on the two superpowers; and finally, 1990–2006, when the two sides developed relations that were largely independent of third parties. I shall argue that the long and varied history of Sino-European relations casts a shadow over the present, even as the two sides seek to establish a close and equitable relationship. They are still affected by the geopolitical distance between them, by their different sets of values and by misunderstandings. Yet there can be no question that they are currently experiencing the best stage of their relationship.

The Chinese contribution to the modernization of Europe, 1500–1800

The reason for beginning in the sixteenth century is because it is from this time on that there were continuous and direct relations between Europeans and Chinese. Clearly there were many points of contact before then, but they were not continuous. Additionally, as Joseph Needham's monumental study, *Science and Civilization*, has shown, there were many examples of the passing of influence from the one civilization to another in ancient and medieval times that need not have involved direct transmission.[4] My concern here, however, is with the direct experiences the two have had of each other and how that may have shaped subsequent relations.

Geoffrey Hudson described this period as one of "China Besieged" by which beginning with "the first penetration of the Portuguese to the coasts of China in 1514 to the close of the eighteenth century the nations of Europe drew a cordon around China both by sea and land, so that by the end of the period the country bore a resemblance to a walled city in a state of siege, a siege wherein the invaders coming from afar have occupied the open country but are not strong enough to storm the walls, while the defenders make no serious effort to drive them away."[5] However, that is not the way these encounters were perceived by the Chinese or the Europeans at the time. Foreign traders were restricted to one or two ports, where their activities were strictly regulated and those few Europeans, mainly Catholic missionaries, who were allowed into China proper had a tenuous existence which did not last long. Although the Jesuits introduced higher levels of mathematics and astronomy, which resulted in a more accurate calendar, better cartography and the cannon, their residual influence seems to have been slight and seldom acknowledged. Qian Long's famous epistle to King George III of England in 1793 typified the Chinese approach. Explaining the character of his universal dominion, the role of tribute bearers and the futility of posting permanent envoys in Beijing, the Son of Heaven concluded, "there is nothing we lack, as your principal envoy and others have observed. We have never set much store on strange or ingenious objects, nor do we need any more of your country's manufactures..."[6] Contemporary Chinese have tended to date the beginning of the European imprint upon China in 1840 with China's defeat in the Opium War.

Although China may have been besieged during these 300 years, it was Europe that was more influenced by China than vice versa. The thirteenth century reports of the marvels of Chinese civilization and of its superior achievements in standards of living, urbanization, technology and governance were confirmed and amplified after a gap of some 400 years by reports of Portuguese and others who had lived in China. The most notable of these were the reports of the Jesuits, some of whom had lived within access to the court for twenty or thirty years. By no means blind to Chinese faults, these reports were by and large positive and were to have a major impact on Europe at the time of the Enlightenment.[7]

Key thinkers of the Enlightenment such as Leibniz and Voltaire were much impressed by what they had read about Confucianism and Chinese philosophy. The philosopher Leibniz, who has been described as "a monumental European figure whose understanding of Chinese culture was remarkably sophisticated for his age," argued that while the Europeans surpassed the Chinese in certain respects, the Chinese in turn were superior in the adaptation of ethics and politics to practical life.[8] Voltaire, who also took an interest in the reports about China, but not to the extent of Leibniz, was especially impressed by the secular nature of Confucianism and by the absence of clergy within government. Idealizing the Yong Zheng Emperor, Voltaire wrote:

He was always concerned with alleviating the plight of the poor and putting them to work. He observed the law carefully, he curbed the ambitions and deceits of the bonzes, maintaining peace and prosperity, encouraging all useful skills and arts, and above all the cultivation of the land. From his time public buildings, large scale highways, canals joining all the rivers of this great empire, were maintained with a splendor and thrift which has no equal other than among the ancient Romans.[9]

To be sure, Voltaire was not simply a disinterested observer. He was using the example of China as a stick with which to beat the *ancien régime* at home. An idealized view of China has also been used by others as a means of criticizing the present regime. A more recent example was the use in the late 1960s by Western student revolutionaries of Mao's Cultural Revolution in their protests against their home establishments.

Not all examples of China's intellectual influence at this time should be seen in terms of a countermodel to the existing order. Others, also at one remove from the Chinese scene, saw the Chinese example as an inspiration for positive theories and indeed action. Thus Francois Quesnay, the leader of the French physiocrats, regarded as the first scientific school of economics, was much influenced by Chinese classical philosophy and he favoured something called the "natural order." Applied to economics, he argued that all wealth was ultimately derived from land, which he called the "net product," and care of the state should be devoted to encouraging primary production, leaving manufacture and commerce to adjust themselves according to demand. He argued that the latter two did not create wealth and asserted that state attempts to control them would only interfere with the natural order. It was from this unlikely source that the doctrine of *laissez faire* was derived.[10]

A phenomenon that became true of later times developed in this early period, by which views of China derived from the same sources could diverge widely. If Voltaire and Quesnay admired Chinese 'despotism' and the despots' adherence to timeless laws, Montesquieu saw nothing good in despotism. He declared, "China is a despotic state whose principle is fear."[11] Rousseau, picking up on a point made by Matteo Ricci about the lack of martial spirit among the Chinese, also attacked the then fashionable cult of China by arguing that all the virtues and wisdom claimed on the country's behalf failed "to protect this realm against subjection by ignorant and rude barbarians [i.e. the Manchus]"[12] These disagreements mark yet another characteristic of the European discourse about China, namely that the main thrust of the argumentation had to do with matters within Europe itself. Thus Rousseau, for example, heralding the incipient nationalism of the French Revolution, held that man's highest virtue was his willingness to die for his country in war.[13]

The eighteenth century was indeed the time when the cult of China was at its height. Chinese porcelain, which had already found imitators in Europe, was in high demand and had led to the manufacture in China of porcelain with what were thought to be European designs for export to Europe. Meanwhile in Europe a craze for things based on the more whimsical patterns of Chinese design led to the fashion of *chinoiserie*, which spread beyond the wealthy and the aristocracy to reach the new rising middle classes in Europe.[14] Similarly the export of tea from China helped to establish not only the practice of drinking tea, but a new social custom of drinking it, especially in England. Chinese influence in the arts and culture of the time was extensive. Perhaps its most lasting contribution was in government through the emulation of its selection of government service through open examinations. The first to do so was Frederick William, the elector of Brandenburg, who in the mid-seventeenth century was judged to have created an efficient civil administration staffed by civil servants chosen on a competitive basis. In France similar reforms preceded the Revolution and Britain followed suit in 1870 and even then it was said to have been influenced by the Chinese example with its emphasis on the classics as the preferred curriculum.[15]

In retrospect, however, it is clear that the admiration for things Chinese owed much to the perception of the superiority of China, but by the end of the eighteenth century that period was drawing to a close because of the growing ascendancy of Europeans over the rest of the world as the voyages of discovery and the expansion of trade were followed by the Industrial Revolution. China meanwhile was in decline and Europeans stopped admiring a "timeless China" and instead began to see it as a country resistant to change and indeed backward. Lord MacCartney, whose mission had been so imperiously dismissed by the great emperor Qianlong, foretold this change when he compared China to an enormous drifting ship in danger of going aground.

The European imprint on the modernization of China 1800–1949

Rather than trace the familiar story of the forcible breakdown of China's self-exclusion by Europeans and others in the nineteenth century, which led to the collapse of the Qing Dynasty and the chaotic years of the first half of the twentieth century including the invasion by Japan and the civil war, I shall try to identify some of the more enduring imprints made by the Europeans in the course of China's painful embrace of the modern world.[16]

Perhaps the most profound and most enduring legacy of the European-led "century of shame and humiliation" that was imposed on China was less the tangible consequences of successive military defeats than the more intangible psychological and intellectual effects. China had been conquered many times before in its long history, but never before by bearers of a civilization that could transcend that of China itself. Until then Chinese intellectuals had taken pride in the superiority of their civilization, which had been able to "Sinify" their barbarian conquerors. In fact the ruling Qing dynasty from Manchuria was itself an example of such a transformation after its triumph over the Ming in 1644. The Chinese self-conscious sense of superiority in both the material and spiritual dimensions was suddenly shattered by the Europeans who came from the sea unlike previous conquerors who had come on horseback from the north and the west. In many respects modern Chinese history may be seen as a continuing struggle to come to terms with the challenges of modernity first posed by the Europeans from the first Anglo-Chinese War of 1839–42, better known as the Opium War.

It was not until the Chinese were defeated in the Second Anglo-Chinese War of 1858–60 that they finally recognized that they were encountering a challenge unlike anything their people had ever encountered before in their long history. Even then they thought that European superiority was merely the product of better technology and that they could restore the Confucian system if only they could master that technology. As the scholar-official Feng Guifen put it, "what we … have to learn from the barbarians is only one thing, solid ships and effective guns."[17] To this end, Chinese were sent to study in Europe and Europeans were hired in China to help manufacture a modern arsenal and a modern navy.

This first attempt at "self-strengthening" ended in failure, in part because of the immensity of the problems in a project designed to impose modern manufacture on a deeply entrenched traditional society and in part because of the continuing predatory challenges of the Europeans.[18] Arguably, the experiment was doomed to fail as the Confucian system could not survive in its traditional form in the modern world that the Europeans were spreading throughout the globe. Yet even as China was to undergo several attempts at modern transformation the abiding goal has been similar to these Confucian reformers, namely to adapt as much as possible to modernity in order to preserve an authentic Chinese way. This is as true of China's contemporary communist rulers as it was true of Mao and of Republican China before him. Thus contemporary Chinese arguments about globalization carry echoes of those much earlier debates about how to ensure that Western alien influence does not undermine Chinese (communist) values – or as the Confucian scholars of the nineteenth century put it, "Western learning for practical purposes and Chinese learning for the fundamentals" (*Xixue wei yong, Zhongxue wei ti*).[19]

However, according to Chinese history textbooks of the Republican era as well as post-1949 textbooks, the most significant impact of the "century of shame and humiliation" is the image of their imperialistic attacks upon China's sovereignty and territorial integrity. Although Britain, France and Germany (then as now, the key European powers) did not seek to annex territory like Russia and Japan, they nevertheless are regarded as having taken the lead in imposing unjustifiable harm upon the country. In addition to the treaty ports, rights of extra-territoriality and other infringements on Chinese sovereignty, they also threatened China's periphery, preparing the ground for attempts at secession.

Chinese anger at the century of "shame and humiliation" initiated primarily by the Europeans is no longer directed at Europe, but is targeted more at the US and Japan, who in effect began to supersede the Europeans from roughly the beginning of the twentieth century. As we shall see, the deflection of nationalist anger away from the Europeans facilitated the emergence after 1949 of an altogether more equal relationship based on practical calculations of national interest.

Rather than retread familiar territory it may be of greater interest to reflect on the broader impact of the Europeans, beyond the legacy of their attacks upon China.

At issue is how far the Europeans contributed to the transformation of Chinese life and civilization towards modernity.

Perhaps the most significant impact of the Europeans on Chinese history was in the political realm – both in the sense of theory and of practice by bringing about the modernization of the Chinese state. This first took place in the realm of theory. Chinese students who went to Europe in the 1870s and 1880s to study naval technology and other scientific and applied technologies took an interest in British, French and German societies around them and realized that the advances of the Europeans had deeper social and philosophical mainsprings. One of the most significant of these returned students was Yan Fu, who translated into classical Chinese the key writings of John Stuart Mill, Montesquieu and Adam Smith, which profoundly changed the outlook of the new generation of students at the end of the century.[20] His translation of Thomas Huxley's *Evolution and Ethics* helped to popularize theories of social Darwinism by which the "survival of the fittest" was applied to social groups and nations and which greatly alarmed Chinese youth in particular, who at the turn of the century feared that China itself might perish through its own backwardness, divisions and foreign attacks. In the early 1900s some Chinese influenced by Bakunin and Kropotkin were drawn towards anarchism. But the main intellectual influences that were to shape the evolution of Chinese political thought and action were variants of liberalism and socialism, bearing in mind that all were driven by the nationalist ideals of curing the country's ills so that it could be strong and rich enough to stand up to China's adversaries and allow China to assume what was seen as its rightful place as one of the great powers. These ideals have remained in one form or another as the bedrock of Chinese aspirations to the present day.

The European liberal democratic persuasion was highly influential in China up until the end of the First World War, when it seemed to Chinese that the Western powers set aside their professed vision of a liberal world order in favour of power politics as they bequeathed the German concessions in China to Japan in the peace treaty signed in Versailles in 1919. Indeed it was the receipt of that news on 4 May 1919 that sparked the huge new cultural and political movement among the young in China to transform their country along democratic and scientific lines. It also brought to a head the debate between liberalism and socialism, with liberalism losing ground to those who favoured a socialist alternative that sought to address China's problems in a holistic and programmatic way and in which the interests of the collectivity were put ahead of the individual.

Given the intense preoccupation with national survival, Marxism, which had hitherto been regarded as a theory of interest only to countries with advanced capitalist systems, suddenly gained appeal with the success of the Bolshevik revolution in Russia in 1917. As explained by one of the founders of the Chinese Communist Party, Li Dazhao, the Bolsheviks had been successful precisely because Russia was backward. They had been able to call upon the hitherto suppressed energies of Russia's 'backward' population and were able therefore to sweep away the smaller classes that held them back. The implication was that if Russia was backward, China was even more so and hence its revolutionary potential was even greater.

Chinese revolutionaires also took heart from the failure of the Western interventions in Russia's civil war in 1921. Thus it was the Leninist version of Marxism that found favour in China and to this day it is the Leninist form in the shape of the CCP that has harnessed Chinese nationalism to its name. But for a while in the 1920s all the forms of European thought, culture and theatre flourished in China, especially in the treaty ports, notably Shanghai, where Chinese intellectual life flourished under the ironic protection of the laws and police of the foreigners' extraterritorial concessions.[21]

Europeans also influenced the practice as well as theories of politics in China. That may be seen as having operated at two related levels, the international and the domestic. The Chinese had to abandon their claim to universal dominion headed by the Son of Heaven and accept that they constituted a state among other states. This involved accepting the laws and practices inherent in the European system of states, known as the Westphalian system. Interestingly, the Chinese were able to adapt to that fairly well before the end of the nineteenth century and indeed by this stage their leaders were recognized to be skilful in the practice of diplomacy, bearing in mind China's inherent weaknesses at that time.[22] Although Chinese have their own distinctive traditions of realism, the impact of the power politics practised by the European powers and their successor Japan has played an important part in contributing to the realist thinking that has shaped much Chinese foreign policy subsequently. The embrace of the Westphalian system also meant that Chinese were no longer concerned about frontiers and the management of nomadic barbarians, instead they began to focus on their territorial integrity, on their sovereign rights and on where precise borders might be drawn. None of these concepts had existed before in their political lexicon.

Meanwhile, China had to address threats from more powerful European states who were able to impose their will on China as a result of their naval strength. Never before in Chinese history had the country been subjugated from the sea. Chinese attempts to construct their own naval forces in the nineteenth century with British and other European advisers foundered in defeat first by France in 1885 and then by Japan ten years later. It was not until the second part of the twentieth century that China was able to establish the beginnings of a modern navy.[23] But the Chinese also had to face threats on land from Russia and from Japan, especially towards the end of the nineteenth century, and from then until more contemporary times most of China's military effort was essentially land-based.

Another question arose: what was legitimate Chinese territory? Under the Qing, Chinese rule was expanded beyond the traditional 18 provinces to include Manchuria, Inner and Outer Mongolia, Tibet and the vast areas beyond the Gansu Pass. But much of that had come under Qing rule through peculiar feudal arrangements involving lines of authority inherent in Tibetan Buddhism. The peoples in these regions were largely non-Han Chinese. But the modern Chinese claim was based on the European right of succession, traceable to European dynastic rule in the seventeenth and eighteenth centuries rather than to the newer nationalist basis of the consent of the governed.[24] The contradictions inherent in these two bases of territorial claims, derived ultimately from the Europeans, continue to provide problems for Chinese to the present day, both with regard to Taiwan and with regard to the fear of secessionism voiced by the contemporary Chinese government.

The domestic dimension of statehood has perhaps been even more troublesome. By the nineteenth century Europeans tended to see sovereignty as residing among the people rather than with dynastic rulers. That involved the transformation of people from subjects to citizens and the idea that legitimate government required the consent of the governed.

The direct European impact upon the domestic development of statehood in China has been less significant than on the external dimension. The Europeans were influential in the period of self-strengthening when the objective was to carry out reforms to save the dynastic state. European advisers were instrumental in helping to establish armaments manufacturing, military schools and the training of a modern army. The British government in particular was keen to support the Qing state, even to the extent of clashing with British merchants and their claim that only Chinese obstructionism was denying them access to a vast Chinese market of 400 million that would allow the cotton mills of Lancashire to "go on spinning forever."[25] The myth of the Chinese market has continued to grip the European (and American) imagination down to the present – despite the balance of trade being overwhelmingly the other way. Be that as it may, after the collapse of the Qing, the British looked for a kind of "strongman" to hold the country together. The Europeans on the whole were not sympathetic to the new generations of young nationalists. Although the Europeans, notably the British and the French, held on to their concessions in the treaty ports, where Chinese intellectuals were able to flourish, notably in Shanghai, free from the reach of warlords, the Europeans were of declining importance in shaping China's future.

Nevertheless, Chinese continued to be fascinated by European models as perhaps offering ways in which Chinese could overcome their immediate problems and establish a strong and modern state. The Communist Party even under Mao's leadership was much more closely modelled on that of the Soviet Union than Mao chose to admit in his lifetime.[26] But at the time of its ascendancy in the 1930s, elements in the Kuomintang professed admiration for Mussolini's fascism as a model that could be suitable for China, where the scope for democracy was limited and here a supreme leader had been able to revive the national spirit of the country. During this time Germany was even more influential. The KMT had its own "Blue Shirts," a German-inspired proto-fascist youth organization, and Chiang Kai-shek relied on German military advisers for a brief time in his campaign against the communist forces in the mid-1930s.[27] Yet, in general, the Europeans were too absorbed in their intramural problems in the inter-war period to be effective players in China from this time on. Once again, the tyranny of distance meant that neither China nor Europe was vital to the other in its respective geopolitical theatre.

In the course of the hundred years or so after the Opium War, Europe was both directly and indirectly enormously influential in the bringing of modernity to

China in terms of science, technology, ideas and social change. The Europeans in the nineteenth century brought with them not only guns and the desire to trade, but they were the bearers of the Industrial Revolution. This meant railways, industrial factories, the telegraph, capitalism, etc. It also meant the spread of European-style education, the practice of modern medicine, a turn to writing in the vernacular with new literature, newspapers, new modern ways of writing about history and new kinds of cities and the birth of new social classes. It gave rise to the emancipation of women. Arguably, this modernity was universal in its appeal and despite its European provenance little that was specifically European survived, except perhaps for European buildings in some of the key treaty ports. Typical perhaps is how few inroads European missionaries made into China despite enormous effort and dedication on their part.[28]

A dependent relationship: the Cold War 1949–89

Relations between China and Europe during this period were dominated by Cold War issues and in particular by each side's relations with the United States and the Soviet Union. That did not mean that some of the Europeans and the Chinese did not try at different times to forge distinctive relations with each other, but it did mean that in the final analysis their policies were subordinated to, or were derivative of, their relations with the two superpowers.[29] The most obvious indication of this is how the Iron Curtain in Europe divided the relations of the East European states with China from those of the West Europeans. The relations of the East Europeans with China were completely determined by their relationship with the Soviet Union. This was as true of the East Europeans who deviated from the Soviet Union – Yugoslavia, Albania and Romania – as it was for the others who were subordinate to the Soviet Union. The West European states enjoyed more freedom from their superpower ally, yet the relations of the NATO countries with China broadly followed the pattern set by the United States. They were relatively frosty until the rapprochement between China and the US of 1971 and then, like the US, Europe cultivated China while being wary of being lured into anti-Soviet positions at the cost of détente.

However, within these broad guidelines individual European states sought to forge particular sets of relations with China, while China at different times sought to cultivate Europeans at first to circumvent the American embargo and then to gain access to European technology (both military and civil) in the 1970s and 1980s, as well as to stiffen their opposition to the Soviet Union. This period may therefore be subdivided into two parts:

From the end of World War II to 1971

In the immediate aftermath of the establishment of the PRC several European states including Denmark, Sweden, Switzerland, Norway, Britain and the Netherlands recognized the new government, unlike the United States, which continued to recognize the KMT government that had retreated to Taiwan. Britain in particular had economic interests in China, which it hoped to protect, and above all it sought to retain the colony of Hong Kong. British diplomats argued that recognition would place the West in a better position to exploit any differences between the Soviet Union and China that would appear because their national interests were not identical and the diplomats held that the American policy on recognition was too ideological. The apparent difference between the two allies helped to sow the seeds for later Chinese attempts to cultivate the West Europeans and to exploit what they saw as transatlantic differences.

The outbreak of the Korean War consolidated the Cold War divide in East Asia and put a seal on any attempts by the Europeans to develop new approaches towards China at that time. Six European countries participated in military operations in Korea and a further four provided medical units.[30] However, the Korean War did not damage European relations with China as much as it did those with the US. The Geneva Conference of 1954 that was convened ostensibly to settle matters in Korea is remembered most for the agreements reached on Indo-China. Those agreements were reached primarily through the diplomatic efforts of China, Britain and France and they had only the grudging support of the American side.[31] By the terms of the Geneva agreement the French withdrew altogether from Indo-China and the only European forces left in the region were British, but they were focused on defeating first the Malay communist insurgency and then on resisting the Indonesian low-key military challenge to the creation of Malaysia. The Geneva Conference proved to be the last time that the Europeans played a decisive role in shaping strategic issues concerning China. They did so in effect by being a restraining influence on the American side. Indeed the British government thought it had restrained the Americans from using nuclear weapons in the course of the Korean War.[32] Interestingly, none of the European governments was willing to assist the US with military forces in the second Vietnam War (1965–73).

The West Europeans also took a different position on questions of trade as from 1952 onwards they began to trade with China in defiance of the American trade embargo. Although that trade was not of great significance for either side, the fact that it carried on at all was not without symbolic significance.[33]

Nevertheless, the West Europeans sided with the United States on most of the key issues in its relations with China. Whatever misgivings they might have had on the recognition of the ROC (i.e. Taiwan) or on the voting at the United Nations on the China question, they nevertheless toed the American line. Even the French recognition of China in 1964 with its incipient suggestion of a new approach to the international politics of the Cold War mattered little in the end because the onset of the Cultural Revolution soon brought to an end any thoughts of the Chinese being willing to cultivate the Europeans as a kind of "second world" between the Americans and the "third world."[34]

The East Europeans developed different relations with China, notionally because of their membership of the socialist camp, but in practice because of their relations with the Soviet Union. China forged close relations with them and benefited from the industrial technology they transferred to China. Yugoslavia was an early exception from whom the Chinese distanced themselves at first because it had been stigmatized by Stalin for its insubordination and then in the 1960s as it was deemed to be more revisionist than the Soviet Union. As relations with the East Europeans as a whole deteriorated in step with the deterioration of relations with the Soviet Union, Albania and Romania were embraced by the Chinese because of their new-found distaste for Soviet dominance.

Interestingly, in the realm of ideas, it would be true to say that if anything the Europeans (or at least some on the left of the political spectrum) looked to China for inspiration rather than the other way round. This was especially true of the Cultural Revolution during the late 1960s when European students and some French intellectuals including Sartre claimed to see in Mao's assault on established institutions something in common with their own aspirations in the so-called revolution of 1968. But in retrospect it is clear that yet again this was an example of dissatisfied European intellectuals using an imagined view of China with which to castigate their respective domestic establishments. If anything the episode illustrated European ignorance of the true situation in China, but interestingly, it also attested to a new respect for a China whose people, in Mao's words, "had stood up."

From tripolarity to the end of the Cold War (1971–89)

The Sino-American rapprochement of 1971 brought about an alignment between the two against the Soviet Union. It also brought about a change in China's relations with the West Europeans. But just as the United States did not wish to be seen as bound with the Chinese in anti-Soviet alliance, so the West Europeans did not wish to sacrifice their prospects of détente with Moscow by taking as hard a line as Beijing would have wished.

Since détente was most prized by the West European social democratic parties, the Chinese tended to favour the more conservative West European leaders such as Edward Heath and Margaret Thatcher of the UK and Franz Josef Strauss of West Germany. The Chinese were particularly interested in military exchanges with the West Europeans, but despite much interest in buying advanced weaponry little was purchased, perhaps because of problems of absorption. For example, a plant for manufacturing the Rolls Royce Spey jet engine was purchased for GBP 200 million in 1975 and completed in 1980, but to no avail, as the Chinese did not have a suitable airframe.[35]

The first step in the early 1970s saw the establishment of full diplomatic relations with all the West European countries, which had not yet occurred. Trade then grew apace, quadrupling in value between 1971 and 1975 from a very low base. But even in 1980 China ranked only as 31st as a destination for exports from the European Community and it ranked 29th as a source of imports. The EEC was more important to China as it ranked 4th in China's overall trade. Trade had doubled in value between 1975 and 1980, but as a proportion of China's trade the value of the EEC contribution had fallen from 18 to 11 per cent. The rate of growth of China's regional trade had grown even faster – a pattern that was to be sustained into the future.

It was in the 1970s that China sought to accommodate Europe (East and West) in their Theory of "the Three Worlds." They were designated as belonging to the "second world" as opposed to the two superpowers in the first world and the developing countries in the third world. The Europeans were deemed to be struggling against the overweening dominance of the two superpowers and therefore they were seen as worth courting. But the Chinese were particularly keen to line them up against the Soviet Union, which was said to be threatening them more than China. But, in truth, China and Europe were geopolitically too distant from each other to be able to exert significant strategic influence in their respective parts of the world.[36]

This context changed somewhat in the 1980s, first because of the transformation of China through the policies of economic reform and opening-up that were linked to the establishment of diplomatic relations between China and the United States and second because of the softening of China's hostility to the Soviet Union. Europeans began to see China not only as a potentially huge market, but also as a place where their experience could be useful in helping China meet the massive tasks of reform and renewal. The Chinese too began to look at West Europeans as partners for trade and development in a relationship that would be comfortable to both sides and that would be free of the strategic complications involved in their relations with Japan or the United States. In that sense the very distance between the two sides could be said to have become a positive factor. In 1985 relations had improved to the extent that the EEC and China were able to sign their first agreement. It focused primarily on trade facilitation, but it also looked forward to deepening their relationship.

Relations with the East European countries also changed significantly, as China began to take an interest in their experiences with reform communism. After all, the organization of the Chinese economy and of its state enterprises was much more similar to those of the East than of the West Europeans. Perhaps for the same reason China's leaders were less enamoured with some of the political changes taking place first in Poland in the early 1980s with the emergence of an independent trade union determined to introduce more democracy. Second, the emergence of Gorbachev in the Soviet Union in 1985 and his promotion of *Glasnost* and *Perestroika* were a mixed blessing as far as Deng Xiaoping and his close colleagues were concerned. They were happy enough with the winding down of Soviet involvement in Vietnam and Afghanistan and with the proposed troop reductions to the north of China, but his political reforms were seen as potentially challenging to their style of rule in China itself.

The closer ties with the Europeans came to an abrupt end with the "Tiananmen massacre" of 4 June 1989. The shock and outrage in Europe led to the imposition of sanctions on China by the European Council that included a ban on meetings with senior leaders, military exchanges and military sales. Later that year all the East European communist governments collapsed as the Cold War came to an end. The European expectation was that the Chinese communist government would follow suit before long. That expectation was strengthened when the Soviet Union disintegrated in 1991. China's leaders for their part were also shocked by these events and took the view that part of the reason for these developments was what they called the Western policy of "peaceful evolution," that is, long-standing Western attempts to undermine communist systems by peaceful means. It seemed as if a burgeoning Sino-European relationship had been brought to an abrupt halt.

Independent relations since the end of the Cold War

The end of the Cold War brought to an end the bipolar structure of international politics which had shaped and constrained the character of relations between Chinese and Europeans in the previous four decades. To be sure, that structure had become less clear-cut in the last few years of the 1980s as the Soviet Union under the leadership of Gorbachev had begun to loosen its attachment to long-held Cold War positions and as Chinese policies of economic reform and opening up to the outside world were beginning to change the basis of China's relationship with the capitalist world. Nevertheless, the actual end of the Cold War brought about fundamental changes to world politics and economics that opened up new opportunities for China and Europe to deepen and expand their relationship on terms that owed little to third parties.

The immediate focus of the two sides was coming to terms with what might be termed the "domestic after-effects" of the Cold War, with the fortuitous result that each side was better placed to deal with the other. As China's leaders reestablished tight control over their country and began to improve relations with immediate neighbours, Deng Xiaoping's "Southern Tour" in 1992 overrode most of his colleagues to press ahead still further with rapid economic growth based on economic reforms and opening-up. The Europeans, for their part, began to firm up some of the political dimensions of their union, which had hitherto been dominated by the economic and trade dimensions. The European Community had been making progress in developing common positions on foreign policy especially towards the end of the 1980s, but the end of the Cold War bloc in Europe, the unification of Germany and the appearance of post-communist governments in the former Eastern Europe injected new momentum that found expression in the Treaty of Maastricht of 1992 that gave institutional form to a Common Foreign and Security Policy (CFSP) of what was now called the European Union.

For their part, China adapted rapidly to the end of the Cold War in Europe by reestablishing diplomatic relations with the post-communist states of Eastern Europe. Although Beijing's principal objective was to forestall Taipei from making diplomatic inroads into the new Europe, China's quick acceptance of the new realities facilitated the improvement of relations with the EU once the immediacy of Tiananmen had begun to fade. In any event trade relations had not been broken off and by 1990 European leaders were beginning to appear in Tiananmen Square, notably the British Prime Minister, whose visit was deemed vital to securing a Chinese agreement on Hong Kong matters, whose impending transfer back to China had been agreed in 1984.

In response to the international impact of the fast-growing Chinese economy and to the emergence of East Asia as a new centre of the international economy, the European Commission, as the executive arm of the EU, issued its first policy paper in 1993 on an Asian strategy that was in fact centred on China. Although the paper was produced at the initiative of Germany and France it expressed a common EU view. Free of the difficulties and divisions that beset the Europeans nearer to home, distant China offered new opportunities primarily for trade and commerce, but also as a place where the EU could put into practice many of the policies which were emerging as part of its CFSP. Namely, encouraging the development of good governance through the rule of law, assistance in tackling environmental problems, poverty alleviation, training and assistance in management and in technology transfers, promoting democracy and the expansion of civil society, and so on.

Collectively and separately the Europeans have devoted significant resources to these endeavours. The ultimate goal was to deepen China's participation in the international system and to promote its emergence as a responsible great power that observed the norms and principles of international society. In so far as the Europeans had a larger goal for world order it was for a system that would be characterized by observance of international law and regulations as agreed in multilateral institutions. In that sense the EU approach towards China has been reasonably consistent as one of the key places where a distinctive EU voice would emerge. Meanwhile relations between the Europeans and the Chinese took place both at the level of the EU and at the level of the separate states. As in earlier periods, the three major states – France, Germany and Britain – were the key players in the relationship. The successful handover of Hong Kong by Britain to China in 1997 helped to reduce lingering Chinese suspicion of British (and by implication European and Western) sincerity regarding their professed support for China's rise as a major player in world affairs. The handover of Macau by Portugal in 1999 brought to an end the remaining European imperial toehold in China. Although these matters were settled on a bilateral basis by China with each of the two European states, it was at the EU level where negotiations of terms of trade took place and where the key points of the relationship with China were defined for all members of the EU.

The EU and the Chinese have since been able to institutionalize the easier and less problematic dimensions of their relationship, which by 2004 both agreed to call a "strategic partnership." But that was only after what the Chinese found were surprisingly tough negotiations with the EU over the terms of its entry into the World Trade Organization in 2001. The following year the Chinese government published a "White Paper" on their relations with Europe, the first time they had done so with regard to any country or region. By 2004 the value of EU–China trade exceeded both that of China's trade with the US and with Japan, and China ranked as the EU's second most valuable trading partner after the US. As to be expected, there were some disagreements about trade – as in fact is common between all major trading partners – but they did not dent the progress of relations.

It took the issue of the lifting of the arms embargo to bring to the fore some of the underlying limits on the character of the new EU–China relationship. Two factors in particular came into play: first, the weakness of the EU as a coherent international actor and second, the difference in the Chinese and the European approaches to the global role of the United States as the world's only superpower. The EU may have the institutional mechanisms to operate as a unitary actor in negotiating terms of international trade, but that does not apply as yet to broader foreign and security policy. Yet reminiscent of their view of the role of Western Europe in the Cold War in the 1970s and early 1980s, China saw the EU as an independent political centre that could help them to check the policies of the dominant power in the international system that they saw as an adversary, actual or potential. China's leaders portrayed the world as undergoing economic globalization while becoming politically multipolar. The burgeoning economic relations with the EU were seen as part of the process of globalization, but what the Chinese sought was EU acceptance of China's multipolar vision in which the EU would become a separate pole, independent of the US.[37]

France shared this view, as did Germany under Chancellor Schroeder to a certain extent, and together they were the most important advocates for lifting the embargo. Many in the EU bureaucracy also shared this view insofar as they held that the EU should articulate an independent voice in world affairs, coupled with its own defence force, that would inevitably be separate from, if not opposed to, the United States. However, Britain, the Netherlands, Sweden and some of the new EU members objected sometimes for different reasons – reflecting the diversity of the priorities in foreign policy by European states. Britain and some others objected in principle to the vision of a multipolar world with the EU as a separate pole. Others such as Sweden objected to lifting the arms embargo on the grounds that China had not yet done enough to improve its human rights record. Interestingly, the Chinese side did not proceed to ratify the UN Covenant on Civil and Political Rights even though many in the EU suggested that that would have eased the way to lift the embargo.

Meanwhile, a new source of friction has developed in Sino-European relations as the depth of their economic relationship is beginning to hurt vested domestic economic interests in Europe. The rapid development of Chinese exports in certain consumer goods has given rise to demands that they be curtailed. But perhaps more importantly, they have accentuated fears of the malevolent effects of globalization in some European countries – fears that were a factor in the rejection of the European constitution in referendums in France and the Netherlands in 2005. Additionally, the European emphasis on the promotion of good governance, especially in Third World countries, is encountering new difficulties as a consequence of the different approach adopted by their Chinese partners. Professing the principle of non-interference, a resurgent China has cultivated regimes in developing countries in its pursuit of energy and other raw materials without regard to the character of the regimes or their treatment of their own citizens.

Thus, despite forging an independent relationship, which both sides continue to see as vital to their interests, the Europeans have found themselves constrained by their obligations to allies whose national security interests are more directly affected by China's rise. In many respects it may be argued that up until this point Sino-European relations enjoyed a free ride as there was no clash of major interests between them. But now in addition to the problem over the arms embargo, the difficulties of adjusting to some of the effects of globalization in Europe are also causing problems in Sino-European relations. Perhaps it may be argued that these apparent setbacks are signs of the mature stage reached by the relationship. In a world in which issues of security and economic change cannot be confined to any of its individual regions without affecting the others, it is to be expected that EU–Chinese relations could be free of friction.[38] The next stage of their relationship should show how their strategic dialogue, begun in 2005, and new Framework Agreement negotiations begun in 2006, can deal with these problems.

Conclusion

This historical overview suggests that there are both continuities and discontinuities between the past and the present. One of the continuities is the impact of the vast and largely inimical physical distance between China and Europe. Until the Europeans arrived on Chinese shores five hundred years ago the contact between the two sides was indirect and trade depended on the uncertain degree of order between warring peoples of Central Asia and the Middle East. Even today the prospects of a much-vaunted overland link between China and Europe are held back by the disorder and insecurity in these intervening regions.

However, apart from the century of European ascendancy, the 'tyranny of distance' has meant that neither the Europeans nor the Chinese have impinged on the other's geopolitical security concerns. Once China was united under a central and effective government in 1949 a new and more equal relationship became possible. But the full development of the potentialities of this factor was delayed until the end of the Cold War. The four decades of the Cold War saw each side subordinate the character of their relations to the priorities of their relations with the two superpowers. It was only after the end of the Cold War that the two sides were able to establish an independent relationship. It is clear that the rapid development of that relationship as measured in terms of trade, educational exchanges, institutionalized political exchanges across the board and the ready acceptance of European aid, including that to help in the development of a more civic society, all benefited from the absence of the kind of security concerns that bedevil China's relations with Japan and the United States.

Yet globalization, which has been a positive factor in driving the new relationship between the two sides has also, more recently, acted as a constraint. The arguments about the lifting of the arms embargo (which ultimately reflected differences in approach from the United States) and about the potential loss of European jobs show that Europeans cannot separate themselves from the problems of regional security in East Asia, nor can Chinese look at economic globalization as a cost-free enterprise. Beyond that, globalization has brought the domestic societies of both sides into closer interaction with each other for the first time.

The physical distance between China and Europe is also mirrored in the cultural and what might be termed the psychological domains. Neither constitutes familiar territory to the other and that has led to misunderstandings from the past to the present. That has not prevented either side from being influenced by the other, but not perhaps in ways that could have been anticipated. As noted earlier, China exerted a major influence on developments in Europe in establishing the foundations on which much of modernity was developed in Europe, in both the technological sense leading up to the Industrial Revolution and in political and philosophical senses leading to the European Enlightenment. Later, when Europeans broke down the doors of China's self-exclusion, the main lessons China derived from the exercise were concerned with building a modern state that in turn was able to stand up to the West.

The gap in knowledge and understanding between the two is still very great. For example, few Europeans would be able to name a single Chinese author of fiction or a Chinese painter. Some have become familiar with recent Chinese films, but, apart from a few specialist scholars, probably not a single European could claim knowledge of the intellectual debates that have been conducted in China since the Tiananmen tragedy of 1989. China remains remote to most Europeans. Many may recognize it as a budding superpower, but there is no debate in Europe, as in America, as to what possible implications may arise from that. China, like India, fits increasingly into European concerns about the downside of globalization in terms of the loss of jobs. China also appears on the European global radar screen in concerns about global warming and illegal migration, but it is still not central to those concerns. On the Chinese side, Europe does not loom large in the political imagination, except as a possible pole in a multipolar world that could constrain American power. It is true that specific aspects of the social policies of certain European countries are seen as possible exemplars from which the Chinese might draw lessons, but there is little general understanding of the deeper European debates about these problems or about the future evolution of the EU. As David Shambaugh's chapter in this volume illustrates, even the writings of China's European specialists tend to see their subject matter through the prism of China's foreign policy agenda, rather than in its own terms.

As China and Europe have reached a new stage in their relationship in which they have found that they cannot avoid the difficult problems inherent in the arms embargo issue or the downsides of globalization, they also have to address more of the difficulties that stem from their different values and political systems. This is a new challenge in which past history cannot serve as a useful guide. That applies to how they can manage the problems arising from the interactions of their domestic societies and from their relations with third countries including those in Third World as well as the US and Japan.

The EU and China may share something in common by being newly emerging entities of global significance in the twenty-first century, but the EU's emphasis on democratic accountability and the rule of law is very different from the Chinese concern with preserving Communist Party rule. The divergences between the two will require careful management, and handling of the new difficulties will be a test of the significance of the institutions that the two have built between them in the previous decade. Nevertheless, the historical experience of the series of encounters between Chinese and Europeans should suggest that there is a profound reservoir of mutual respect that should facilitate a successful evolution to the next stage.

Notes

1 G.F. Hudson, *Europe and China: A Survey of their Relations from the earliest times to 1800* (London: Edward Arnold & Co, 1931) p. 98.
2 Joseph Needham, *Science and Civilisation in China, Volume 1: Introductory Orientations* (Cambridge: Cambridge University Press, 1961) p. 19.
3 David Shambaugh, *China and Europe: 1949–95* (London: SOAS, Contemporary China Institute, 1995).
4 Needham, op. cit., p. 244.
5 Hudson, op. cit., p. 235.
6 Ssu-yu Teng and John K. Fairbank, *China's Response to the West* (Cambridge, MA: Harvard University Press, 1963) p. 19.
7 For accounts and discussion of these reports, see among others, D.E. Mungello, *The Great Encounter of China and the West, 1500–1800* (Lanham, MD: Rowman & Littlefield, 1995); Hudson, op. cit.; Adolph Reichwein, *China and Europe: Intellectual and Artistic Contacts in the Eighteenth Century* (London: Kegan Paul, Trench, Trubner & New York: Alfred A. Knopf, 1925); Jonathan D. Spence, *Chinese Roundabout* (New York: W.W. Norton, 1993); and Colin Mackerras (ed.) *Sinophiles and Sinophobes* (Oxford: Oxford University Press, 1995). The most famous and influential thirteenth-century account remains that of Marco Polo despite recent doubts as to whether he had actually set foot in China. See Frances Wood, *Did Marco Polo Go to China?* (Oviedo, Florida: Waterview Press, 1995).
8 Mungello, op. cit., p. 67.
9 Mackerras, op. cit., p. 39.
10 Hudson, op. cit., pp. 322–6.
11 Mackerras, op. cit., p. 43.
12 Hudson, op. cit., p. 321.
13 Ibid., p. 321.
14 Mungello, op. cit., pp. 78–80.
15 See E.N. Gladden, *Civil Services of the UK 1855–1950* (London: Cass, 1967) and Roy MacLeod (ed.), *Government and Expertise: Specialists, Administrators and Professionals, 1860–1919* (Cambridge University Press, 1988). It is worth noting that senior civil servants in Britain are still referred to as "Mandarins."
16 For an outstanding account of that history, see the relevant chapters in Jonathan D. Spence, *The Search for Modern China* (London: Hutchinson, 1990). See also Immanuel Hsu, *The Rise of Modern China* (Oxford: OUP, 1995).
17 Cited in Jonathan D. Spence, *The Search for Modern China* (London: Hutchinson, 1990) p. 197.
18 The standard study of this period is still Mary Wright, *The Last Stand of Chinese Conservatism: The T'ung Chih Restoration, 1862–74* (Stanford: Stanford University Press, 1957).
19 For contemporary debates, see Chaohua Wang (ed.), *One China, Many Paths* (London and New York: Verso, 2003).
20 Benjamin Schwartz, *In Search of Wealth and Power: Yen Fu and the West* (Cambridge, MA: Belknap Press, 1964).
21 For detailed accounts, see Vera Schwarcz, *The Chinese Enlightenment: Intellectuals and the Legacy of the May Fourth Movement of 1919* (Berkeley: University of California

Press, 1986) and Chow Tse-tsung, *The May Fourth Movement: Intellectual Revolution in Modern China* (Cambridge, MA: Harvard University Press, 1960).

22　Gerrit W. Gong, "China's Entry into International Society," in Hedley Bull and Adam Watson (eds.), *The Expansion of International Society* (Oxford: Clarendon Press, 1985) pp. 171–83.

23　For an extended discussion, see Wang Gungwu, *Anglo–Chinese Encounters Since 1800* (Cambridge: CUP, 2003) pp. 14–42.

24　For discussion of these competing claims to statehood, see James Mayall, *Nationalism and International Society* (Cambridge: Cambridge University Press, 1990), especially pp. 18–34.

25　Nathan A. Pelcovits, *Old China Hands and the Foreign Office* (New York: Octagon Books, 1969), the quote is on p. 3.

26　See for example the recent biographies of him by Philip Short, *Mao: A Life* (New York: Henry Holt, 1999) and by Jung Chang and Jon Halliday, *Mao: The Untold Story* (London: Jonathan Cape, 2005).

27　For a brief survey, see Spence, op. cit., pp. 396–7. For more extensive coverage, see William Kirby, *Germany and Republican China* (Princeton University Press, 1984) and Bernd Martin (ed.), *The German Advisory Group in China: Military Economic and Political Issues in Sino–German Relations, 1927–38* (Dusseldorf: Droste, 1981).

28　Kenneth S. Latourette, who had been sympathetic to the missionary cause in China, estimated that on the eve of the establishment of the PRC the number of professed Christians was less than 1 per cent of the population and that Christianity had made "but slight impress" upon the religious life of the great masses of non-Christians. See his *The Chinese: Their History and Culture* (New York: Macmillan, 1951) p. 656.

29　For a clear account of these distinctions, see David L. Shambaugh, *China and Europe, 1949–95*, op. cit.

30　The first category included Belgium, France, Greece, Luxembourg, the Netherlands and the UK. The second included Denmark, Italy, Norway and Sweden.

31　For an account of the Geneva Conference, see Robert F. Randle, *Geneva 1954: The Settlement of the Indo-China War* (Princeton: Princeton University Press, 1969).

32　D.C. Watt, "Britain and the Cold War in the Far-East 1945–58" in Yonusuke Nagai and Akira Iriye (eds.), *The Origins of the Cold War in Asia* (Tokyo: University of Tokyo Press and New York: Columbia University Press, 1977).

33　Alexander Eckstein, *Communist China's Economic Growth and Foreign Trade* (New York: McGraw Hill, 1966).

34　Michael B. Yahuda, *China's Role in World Affairs* (London: Croon Helm, 1978) pp. 217–8.

35　Michael Yahuda, *China's Foreign Policy after Mao* (London: Macmillan, 1983) p. 191.

36　Ibid., pp. 188–96.

37　See the chapter in this volume by David Shambaugh, "China eyes Europe in the world: real convergence or cognitive dissonance?"

38　For an exploration of these themes, see the chapter in this volume by Volker Stanzel, "The EU and China in the global system."

Part III
Europe's approaches to China

3   China studies in Europe

Kjeld Erik Brødsgaard *

Writing a comprehensive survey of European China studies is a Herculean task – even for a European. There are at least four sets of challenges in such an undertaking: cultural, geographic, institutional and definitional.

Culturally, there are about thirty countries – each with its own history, culture and, not least, language. Most scholarship in the major European countries is actually conducted in each national language. While there is a trend towards publishing (especially cutting-edge) journal articles in English, books are still more frequently published in the national language in many European countries, notably in France and Germany. Even in the Scandinavian countries scholars have an obligation also to occasionally publish in their own native language. The language barrier makes it very difficult to create a comprehensive picture of the field. It also makes it difficult to measure the impact of scholars and research milieus in a uniform way since the major qualitative indices measuring the impact of individual scholars are all in English, meaning that most European scholars, except UK-based scholars, are disadvantaged.

There is also a practical challenge in the sense that there is no consensus about how to define Europe in a geographical sense. The continent was split by the Cold War for half a century and is only slowly beginning to integrate within an EU framework. Although Russia will probably never join the EU, for historical reasons it is often regarded as part of Europe. Turkey was historically never part of Europe, but for political reasons the question of Turkey's admission to the EU is seriously being debated.

A third, and perhaps the most serious, challenge is the fragmented institutional nature of European China scholarship. There are a number of major centres – notably in Leiden, London, Paris, Munich, Copenhagen, Berlin – but most research is conducted in scattered small research environments, often consisting of only one or two scholars. In fact, the general picture is one of fragmentation rather than unity and cooperation. This naturally affects efforts at systematization.

Finally, there are definitional disagreements about what constitutes China studies. The traditional centres of Sinology will argue that real China scholarship must have a strong orientation towards language and culture.[1] There is thus a basic inclination to leave contemporary political, social and economic studies out of the picture as ephemeral preoccupations. However, during the last two decades considerable change has occurred, so that the curriculum and the composition of university staff has shifted in a more modern, if not contemporary, direction in many universities. Yet it is telling that a survey on China studies in the UK commissioned by the European Association of China Studies did not even mention some of the most well-known, respected and well-published scholars in British China scholarship – namely Peter Nolan of Cambridge University, and Robert Ash and Christopher Howe at SOAS.

This chapter focuses on West European China studies.[2] It is structured in the following way. First, there is a general overview of the development of Sinology in Western Europe, beginning with the establishment of the first chair in Chinese at the College de France in 1814 and ending with the situation in the 1970s when, under the influence of the Cultural Revolution, pressures to expand into contemporary China studies began to increase in West European universities. Second, the chapter will sketch the emergence of contemporary China studies in Europe, focusing on institutional developments and new forms of research cooperation.[3] In this section a case study of the Scandinavian scene will be included. Third, we will attempt to analyse the field in terms of research themes and issues and in terms of three generations of scholars. Fourth, some thoughts on the future of European China scholarship will be offered. Fifth, and finally, some concluding observations are offered.

The beginning of European China studies

The beginning of Sinology as an academic discipline in Europe dates back to 1814, when a *"chaire de langues et littéeratures chinoises et tartares-mandchoues"* was established at the Collège de France.[4] The chair was filled by Jean-Pierre Abel-Rémusat. Rémusat and his successor Stanislas Julien founded the so-called Paris School which dominated European Sinology almost until the Second World War. The Paris School included Édouard Chavannes, who commented on and translated the *Shiji* and historical works; Paul Pelliot, who studied the Dunhuang manuscripts; and Henri Maspero, a student of Chinese pre-Qing history and religion and Chinese phonology.

In the UK, it took some time before regular academic positions in Sinology were established. In the second half of the nineteenth century, Oxford and Cambridge gave professorial rank to former diplomats such as Thomas Wade and Herbert Allen Giles and the missionary James Legge. But their appointments did not lead to any firm tradition and was not much more than "an exotic ornament in these universities" – to quote the words of Herbert Franke.[5] In London, the School of Oriental and African Studies was established in 1916, but a regular professorship in China was only put in place in 1932.[6]

In Germany, the first chair in Sinology was established as late as 1909 in Hamburg. It was given to the historian Otto Franke. Franke later moved to Berlin (1923) to succeed the Dutch Sinologist J.J.M. de Groot, who in 1912 had "accepted a call" (the way that professorial appointments have traditionally occurred in Germany) from the University of Berlin. In Berlin, Franke was an inspiration to a number of young students who were to become famous sinologists in their own right: Stefan [Étienne] Balazs, Karl Bünger, Wolfram Eberhard, Walter Fuchs, Walter Simon, etc. In Leipzig the first chair was opened in 1922. From 1925 Eric Haenisch held the chair until he moved to Berlin in 1932, where he served for thirteen years. German Sinology suffered greatly during the 1930s and 1940s. Journals and institutes were closed and many scholars left the country. This was of great benefit to American universities, where Europeans largely dominated Sinology until the Second World War. Herbert Franke interestingly observed that "when in the US in May 1937 a group of Sinologists published a memorandum on the necessity to promote Chinese studies, the document was signed by James R. Ware, George A. Kennedy, Ferdinand Lessing and Peter A. Boodberg. Among these, Kennedy had a PhD from Berlin University, Lessing was a German immigrant and Boodberg had a Russian background."[7]

When J.J.M. de Groot left Leiden in 1912 to take up the new chair of Sinology in Berlin, the chair of Chinese languages and literature in Leiden was left vacant until 1930, when J.J.L. Duyvendak took up the position. The same year Duyvendak convinced the university authorities to establish the Sinological Instituut at Leiden. Duyvendak also argued that the Chinese books of the university should be located under the roof of the Sinological Instituut. The result was the creation of an institute cum library which were to have great impact on Chinese studies in Europe.[8]

After World War II a major expansion of Sinology occurred. This first took place in the UK, where the so-called "Scarborough Report" of 1947 recommended a series of measures to be taken to strengthen the study of the languages of Asia, Africa and the Slavonic world.[9] As a result a series of new posts were created and funds set aside for young aspiring scholars to spend a few months or perhaps a year in Asia. At SOAS, for example, the Scarborough Report allowed for the establishment of new lectureships in Chinese philosophy, law, history, art and archaeology.

The expansion spread to the continent. In Leiden it was spearheaded by Erich Zürcher, who in 1961 was appointed to a Chair for the History of the Far East in the Sinological Instituut. Zürcher managed to centralize all expansion in the field in terms of funding and position in his own institute. In Germany the field was reorganized after World War II. Some of the major centres of Sinological research, such as Leipzig, became part of the communist German Democratic Republic (GDR) and atrophied as a result. However, from the 1950s and 1960s new Chairs of Sinology were established in West Germany, including in Bochum, Erlangen, Göttingen, Heidelberg, Tübingen and Köln. In Germany the development of Sinology took a much more decentralized course than in Holland. A common pattern was that Chinese studies developed within an area studies structure, most usually being a subsection of an Institute or Department of East Asian Studies with its focus – in terms of tenured faculty and state-allocated financial resources – in more traditionally oriented studies. This common north European pattern can be illustrated by the Scandinavian case below.

Another common pattern was a focus on the written language. Most of the empire builders in the field were accomplished within classical Chinese, but few could actually speak modern Chinese. To the extent modern texts were used in teaching, these would normally be in complicated characters rather than the simplified characters used in mainland China. This was increasingly being perceived as anomalous by the students and became a point of contention when the student revolution broke out in 1968.

The emergence of China studies in Scandinavia

Chinese studies as a scholarly discipline in Scandinavia began with Bernhard Karlgren's (1898–1978) studies of Chinese phonology. Karlgren was appointed Professor of East Asian Philology and Culture at the University of Gothenburg in 1918, where he taught Chinese as well as Japanese. In 1939 he moved to Stockholm to take up the position as Director of the Museum of Far Eastern Antiquities and Professor of East Asian Archaeology.[10]

Karlgren had an enormous role in the establishment of Sinology as an academic discipline in Scandinavia. This was not only because of his own pioneering philological studies, but also because the American-based Rockefeller Foundation (in order to strengthen Chinese studies in Scandinavia) entrusted him with the task of educating a group of young Sinologists. It was intended that these students should take up the responsibility of developing Chinese studies in their respective countries. It all worked according to plan. Søren Egerod became Professor of East Asian Languages at the University of Copenhagen in 1958 and established the university's East Asian Institute in 1960. Henry Henne was appointed professor at Oslo University in 1966 and headed the development of Chinese studies in Norway and Malmqvist succeeded Karlgren in Stockholm in 1965. A fourth student, Else Glahn, became Associate Professor at the University of Aarhus in 1973 and established Denmark's second Institute of East Asian Studies.

Although Karlgren also wrote some popular works on modern Chinese history, his main scholarly contribution was in the tradition of European Sinology, with a strong emphasis on classical studies. His students upheld this tradition and focused their institution-building on aspects of Sinology such as historical phonology, classical religion and philosophy and linguistics. Historical studies benefited from Karlgren's contributions to a lesser degree and studies of Chinese modern history and society were not among the disciplines that had the attention of his students.[11] Thus the establishment of the East Asian Institute with a focus on modern studies in Aarhus were very much the result of Egerod's reluctance to allow modern studies to develop in his own institution. The first tenured position within this field appeared in Norway in 1970. Only in 1986 was a similar tenure-track position established in Copenhagen, and in Stockholm it came even later.

In sum, Chinese studies in Europe began as studies of Chinese philology, philosophy, religion, ancient literature, archaeology and ancient history. The university departments and institutes that sprang up during the 1950s and 1960s were all formed by powerful individuals that had a strong view on what constituted true Sinology. Among this group of scholars there was surprisingly little disagreement as to the general direction European Sinology ought to take. In 1975 they even formed a European Association of Chinese Studies (EACS) where they would meet among like-minded colleagues and graduate students. Sinology lived in the ivory tower and was totally unprepared for the 1968 revolution that suddenly brought contemporary politics into the maelstrom of university politics and stimulated the interest in contemporary China studies.

The emergence of contemporary China studies in Europe

From the late 1970s contemporary China studies began to emerge. In many countries it fragmented the field and resulted in the creation of new institutes and centres, as the traditionally oriented departments refused to take up contemporary studies. This was the case in Britain, France, Italy, the Scandinavian countries and, to a certain extent, in Germany. Only in Leiden did Erik Zürcher, by a masterstroke, prevent fragmentation from occurring. His saving grace was the creation of a Documentation Centre for Contemporary China within the Sinological Instituut at Leiden University. It was equally fortunate for the development of Dutch contemporary China scholarship that the economic historian E.B. Vermeer was put in charge of the Documentation Centre. In the early 1980s the young British scholar Tony Saich joined the Documentation Centre and in 1986 he was appointed Professor of Chinese Government and Politics at Leiden. Together with Stefan Landsberger and Frank Pieke, they created one of the most active and dynamic centres of contemporary China studies in Europe.

In the UK, London University's renowned School of Oriental and African Studies (SOAS) took the lead. Stuart Schram in politics, Elisabeth Croll and Hugh Baker in anthropology, and Kenneth R. Walker, Robert F. Ash and Christopher Howe in economics created an environment of great scholarship. This research milieu became the home of *The China Quarterly*, which was established in 1960 under the founding editorship of Roderick MacFarquhar. For more than 45 years *The China Quarterly* has maintained its pre-eminence as the leading journal of the field. When Stuart Schram and Kenneth Walker were on the eve of retirement, the SOAS group was joined by the younger American scholar David Shambaugh, then fresh from his PhD at the University of Michigan. Shambaugh joined the SOAS faculty as a Lecturer in Chinese politics, but quickly rose through the ranks to Reader in Chinese politics at the University of London. In 1991, SOAS also appointed him Editor of *The China Quarterly*, a job he did admirably for five years before his return to a professorship in the United States. Unfortunately, SOAS never managed to fill the professorships in politics that Schram's retirement and Shambaugh's departure left vacant. Similar to the Sinological Instituut in Leiden, the central role of SOAS was boosted by a fine collection of contemporary Chinese source material.

The development of contemporary studies in the UK was stimulated by a number of official government reports and grants which paved the way for the establishment of new academic posts and the expansion of Sinological library collections.[12] By the end of the 1990s, Departments of East Asian Studies/Chinese Studies were located in Cambridge, Durham (from 1989), Edinburgh (1965),

Leeds (1963), London, Oxford, Sheffield (1996) and Westminster (1992).[13] Cambridge and Oxford continued to concentrate on traditional subjects, whereas the new departments built strong competencies in modern and contemporary studies. It may be noted that Joseph Needham, the scholar who did the most to bring the achievements of China and Chinese civilization to the notice of the educated public, never held a chair at a British university. Needham made Cambridge the home of the Needham Research Institute, but the institute was independent of the university and Needham was never offered a chair at Cambridge. The Cambridge Chair at the Faculty of Oriental Studies was held by great scholars such as the linguist E.G. Pulleyblank, historian Dennis Twitchett, and their successors, but retrospectively none of them measured up to Needham's enormous contributions to western China scholarship.

In Germany, Jürgen Domes succeeded in establishing a contemporary Asia programme called Research Unit for Chinese and East Asian Politics at the University of Saarbrücken. What was remarkable was that this unit was established within the Faculty of Law and Social Sciences, and thus broke with the European pattern of having East Asian studies confined to an area studies structure. Domes had an important influence on the development of contemporary studies by publishing a number of important books and articles and by training a few select students later took up chairs in Berlin (Eberhard Sandschneider), Trier (Sebastian Heilman) and Rotterdam (Barbara Krug). However, the research unit in Saarbrücken did not survive the retirement of its founder.

Another important development in Germany was the establishment of the Institut für Asienkunde in 1956. It was located in Hamburg on the initiative of the German Parliament and the Federal Foreign Office. The institute's objective was to conduct scholarly research of the political, economic and social development in Asia with particular emphasis on China, Japan and Southeast Asia (as well as India). For many years it was the only research institute outside the university structure that worked exclusively on Asia. The Institut für Asienkunde rapidly built up one of the best libraries on contemporary Asian affairs in Germany. It also launched a publications series as well as the influential journal *China Aktuell*. Well-known German China scholars such as Oskar Weggel, Rüdiger Matchetski and Brunhild Staiger worked in the institute for many years.

In Scandinavia, the development of contemporary China studies in Copenhagen was to a large extent identical with the rise of the Centre for East and Southeast Asian Studies (CESEAS) and the reorganization of the Nordic Institute of Asian Studies (NIAS). CESEAS grew out of the activities of a working group appointed by the university president in 1981 to prepare a new two-year area studies programme. CESEAS acquired its own premises in 1989 and became the home of an increasing number of research projects dealing with contemporary Chinese affairs. Many of these later resulted in doctoral dissertations. The Centre paid great attention to publication activities and established an international journal *The Copenhagen Journal of Asian Studies* (formerly *Copenhagen Papers in East and Southeast Asia Studies*) as well as a series of working papers (*Copenhagen*

Discussion Papers). Within a couple of years the Centre had grown into a major research institution with approximately eight research fellows, the majority of whom worked on China.

For bureaucratic reasons the University of Copenhagen in 1994 decided to close down the various interdisciplinary centres in the university or merge them with existing institutes/departments. This decision also implicated the CESEAS, which was closed down in 1994. The various research projects and activities have been moved back to the institutes, in particular to the Department of Asian Studies and the Nordic Institute of Asian Studies (NIAS).

NIAS was originally established in 1967 by the Nordic Council of Ministers under the name of the Scandinavian Institute of Asian Studies (SIAS).[14] The stated purpose of the institute was to stimulate Asian studies in the humanities and the social sciences in the Scandinavian countries and to act as a channel of communication between Scandinavian and foreign scholars. However, the initial emphasis in the institute's projects and appointments was on philological Oriental studies, thereby reflecting the first director Professor Søren Egerod's own interests. By the mid-1980s it was felt that even more of the research capacity of SIAS should be devoted to social science study of contemporary Asian affairs and a major reorganization of the institute took place. One of the stated aims of the reorganization process was that the institute, renamed NIAS, in the future should concentrate its attention on East and Southeast Asia and downgrade work on the Near East and South Asia. All academic posts became of limited duration, a special information unit was established, and a research professorship along with a research assistant was added to the research staff.[15]

Recently, NIAS was reorganized once again. As a result a consortium comprising the University of Copenhagen, the Copenhagen Business School and Lund University has agreed to take over (from the Nordic Council of Ministers) the responsibility to continue NIAS as an academically independent research institute with a responsibility to further Asian studies in the Nordic region. The University of Copenhagen was appointed to be the host institution for the new NIAS.[16] NIAS is currently headed by Dr Jørgen Delman.

The current situation

According to a survey conducted by the International Institute for Asian Studies (IIAS) on behalf of the European Science Foundation's Asia Committee, in the 1990s there were around 8,000 European Asianists.[17] Around one-fifth of these (approximately 1,600) were estimated to be an "active China expert." This number has probably increased by a few hundred. The European Association of Chinese Studies (EACS) has a membership of around 700. But many of the scholars working in the contemporary China field in Europe are not members of EACS.

In the UK there are about 100 academic China specialists. The above-mentioned survey of British China studies lists a full-time staff of 51 and a part-time staff of 39. In addition, one finds the occasional China specialist at various research institutions, such as the Royal Institute of International Affairs (Chatham House), International

Institute of Strategic Studies, etc. Most of the expansion in contemporary China studies in recent years has taken place outside the traditional centres of Sinology. Manchester, Bristol, Leeds, and Nottingham universities have all experienced a growth spurt of late. The University of Nottingham has established a China Policy Institute which has recruited a number of China specialists including Zheng Yongnian. Zheng worked for a number of years as a senior researcher at the East Asian Institute of the National University of Singapore (NUS). The University of Manchester has also invested heavily in setting up a new Centre for Chinese Studies and has appointed Liu Hong, also previously at NUS, to a Chair in Chinese Studies. The University of Leeds is also experiencing an expansion of its Asia-related programmes. The China programme is headed by Professor Flemming Christiansen. Even the traditional Sinological centres have seen some significant new additions of staff, the most important being the appointment of Vivienne Shue to the new Leverhulme Chair of Contemporary Chinese Studies at Oxford University. These and other appointments as well are all a good sign of the revival of contemporary China studies in the UK.

In Germany, by 2004, there were around forty Chairs in Sinology at eighteen various universities – including Thomas Heberer in Duisburg, Eberhard Sandschneider in Berlin, Thomas Scharping in Köln, and Sebastian Heilmann in Trier.[18] At present there are probably twice as many associate and assistant professorships, as well as a number of researchers at research institutions such as Institut für Asienkunde in Hamburg, Stiftung Wissenschaft und Politik (SWP) in Berlin, etc. In 1994 the Institute for East Asian Studies was established at the University of Duisburg-Essen. With two professors, two associate professors and a number of research associates in contemporary Chinese studies, the institute has developed a strong profile in the China field.[19]

In the Scandinavian countries there are an estimated 100 active China scholars, including a number of PhD students and doctoral researchers. Currently the most dynamic research environment is in the Copenhagen area, which benefits from the combined resources of NIAS, the Chinese section at the Department of Cross-cultural and Regional Studies at the University of Copenhagen and the Asia Research Centre of the Copenhagen Business School.[20] This research environment also benefits from the nearby presence of the Centre for East and Southeast Asia at Lund University, which has several scholars, including postdoctoral positions,[21] working on contemporary China, and possesses a strong library. However, it is difficult to arrive at a precise number of Scandinavian China specialists since a considerable number (especially in Denmark and Norway) are employed only temporarily and may have several years between their research grants. In between these grants they still do research and publish. Thus there is a whole cohort of people who are not on a regular career path, yet do serious research on China. The only reason why this can function is the comparatively decent economic compensation given to unemployed scholars in Scandinavia by the government.

The situation in France is complicated, with contemporary China scholars dispersed throughout a number of research institutes rather than universities. The most important ones are the Centre for International Studies and Research (Centre d'études et de recherches internationales) of the French National Foundation for Political Sciences (Fondation National des Sciences Politiques) and the Research Centre on Modern and Contemporary China (Centre sur la Chine Moderne et Contemporaine or Centre Chine) of the Higher School of Social Sciences (Ecole des Hautes Etudes en Sciences Sociales).[22] The Centre for International Studies and Research is host to five scholars on contemporary China, including Jean-Luc Domenach and Jean-Philippe Béja. Centre Chine was established by Jacques Guillermaz, a former military attaché and a specialist on the history of the Chinese Communist Party. Centre Chine currently has five scholars working on China, including Isabelle Thireau, Michel Bonnin and Yves Chevrier. However, most scholars working on contemporary China in France seem to be associated with the Centre Chine some way or another – most of these associated are actually on the payroll of other organizations such as CNRS, the French National Centre for Scientific Research (Centre National de la Recherche Scientifique). They include Jean-Philippe Béja and the Taiwan specialist Jean-Pierre Cabestan, who spent many years in Taiwan and Hong Kong as director of the Hong Kong-based Centre for Research on Contemporary China (Centre d'études français sur la Chine contemporaine) and editor of the centre's academic journal China Perspectives (in 2007 Cabestan moved back to Hong Kong's Baptist College). There are also a few contemporary China scholars working in Lyons and Aix-en-Provence-Marseilles. At the Aix-Marseille University most research related to contemporary China takes place in the Institute for Southeast Asian Studies and has a focus on Taiwan.

Leiden University has lost its position as the dynamic centre of contemporary European China research. The Documentation Centre for Contemporary China still exists, but Tony Saich took a professorship at Harvard University's Kennedy School of Government and Frank Pieke moved to Oxford University.[23] Currently Leiden has no chair in contemporary Chinese affairs.

Contemporary China studies began relatively late in Spain and Portugal. In 1992 the Centro de Estudios de Asia Oriental was established at the Universidad Autonoma de Madrid under the leadership of Taciana Fisac, and now has more than a dozen faculty members. The Universidad Autonomo de Barcelona has also initiated research on contemporary China and started a Master's Programme in East Asian Studies from September 2006. In Portugal, the first Master's Programme in Chinese Studies started at the University of Aveiro in 1998. This initiative was followed by the establishment of an Oriental Institute at the Institute of Social and Political Sciences at the Technical University of Lisboa. The institute has also launched the journal Revista Portuguesa de Estudos Asiáticos.

An interesting new phenomenon is the emergence of contemporary China studies in European business schools. This is very much the case in Scandinavia where three professorships in International Business with particular reference to China now exist. As mentioned above, a major research environment focusing on contemporary China is developing at the Copenhagen Business School (CBS). At CBS there is also a rapidly expanding Asia Studies Programme which focuses on China. The programme has a very strong language dimension with up to 20 hours of language training during the first preparatory year. Later economics, sociology and business studies are added. At Leeds University there is strong cooperation between scholars in international business at Leeds University Business School and the China experts in the Department for East Asian Studies. This cooperation has resulted in the establishment of the Centre for Chinese Business and Development, headed by Delia Devin, and the Institute on Contemporary China, headed by Flemming Christiansen. At SOAS in London the establishment of the Centre for Finance and Management is also the result of a growing interest in Chinese business and management. Also of importance is the dynamic research environment on Chinese business studies at the Judge School of Business at Cambridge University.[24] This particular research environment, directed by Peter Nolan, has produced a considerable number of PhD dissertations – many of them authored by Chinese students studying at Cambridge.

Cooperation among individuals and institutions

For years the European Association for Chinese Studies (EACS) was the only vehicle for bringing together European scholars and researchers on China. The prehistory of EACS dates back to 1948 when the first Conference of Junior Sinologues was held.[25] The primary aim of the "Junior Sinologues" was the reestablishment of contact among European China scholars interrupted by the war. Another objective was to stimulate East–West cooperation in Chinese studies. For a quarter of a century the Junior Sinologues met every year, except for 1960 and 1968.

In 1975 some of the members of the Junior Sinologues took the initiative to form the EACS. The new organization elected a board and a president. The first president was Søren Egerod. He was succeeded by Göran Malmqvist, Piet van der Loon, Erik Zürcher, Marianne Bastid-Bruguiere, Rudolf Wagner, Glen Dudbridge and Alain Peyraube. The list reads like a "Who's Who" in classical European Sinology. The EACS has not been able to significantly move into the contemporary field and the association's biannual conferences still focused on traditional Sinology in terms of the themes and contents of the panels organized. The EACS produces a Newsletter and occasional conference volumes with papers presented at the biannual conferences. The association also has a library travel grant programme funded by the Taiwan-based Chiang Ching-kuo Foundation.

There are also national and regional associations. One example is the British Association of Chinese Studies (BACS), which was founded in 1976 and has a membership of about 200. Another example is the Nordic Association for China Studies (NACS), which was formed in June 1991 with the aim of "promoting research and teaching on China within the social sciences and the humanities and to stimulate exchange of information and contacts between scholars and students studying Chinese affairs." The NACS has around 50 members and is oriented towards modern and contemporary China studies.

During the late 1980s and early 1990s, the ERASMUS network (supported by the EU Commission) played a major role in stimulating European China scholarship. ERASMUS was designed to promote student exchange and was rather decentralized in its operation. Thus the operation of the ERASMUS programme in

Chinese studies was entrusted to a network of universities, which included all the major centres of European China scholarship. Representatives of these centres and institutes would meet twice a year to coordinate student exchange among their various universities. The representatives would often be the heads or chairpersons of Chinese studies in these centres. Even though the focus was on student exchange, there was also a certain degree of staff mobility involved and the biannual meetings formed the platform of exchange of important information and ideas. The great advantage of the ERASMUS network was that it engaged the people directly involved in teaching and research in European universities. For some reason the European Commission in Brussels decided to change ERASMUS into SOCRATES – which shifted the focus of operation away from the research and teaching environment to the university bureaucrats. This happened at a time when the ERAMUS network was beginning to recognize the importance of contemporary studies.

In recent years a number of research school networks have sprung up. In Sweden the Swedish School of Advanced Asia-Pacific Studies (SSAAPS) was established in 2001 with the aim of providing support for the research training of PhD students in Asian studies and stimulating interaction between the Swedish and the international research community in the field. In Finland there is a University Network for East and Southeast Asian Studies established in 1996 which aims to promote education and research relating to East and Southeast Asia. All twenty universities in Finland are members of the Network. On a European level a European Research School Network of Contemporary East Asian Studies has been formed based in Duisburg with seven participating institutions.[26] These research networks represent a promising new development since they promote one of the most crucial factors in the development of the field: the recruitment and training of new research talent.

ECAN

A significant event in the development of contemporary China studies in Europe was the creation in 1996 of the EU–China Academic Network (ECAN). ECAN was the brainchild of David Shambaugh, an initiative developed over his last three years at SOAS. The rationale behind ECAN was to create a community of European scholars on contemporary China and to foster closer cooperation between scattered European research institutions within the field of contemporary China studies. As Editor of *The China Quarterly*, Shambaugh travelled widely across the European continent, became impressed by the range of academic expertise on China, but was struck by the almost total lack of horizontal interaction and cooperation among European China specialists and their institutions. ECAN was created to rectify these deficits, particularly in the wake of the then popular "Maastricht Spirit" of EU transnational cooperation. Shambaugh was also concerned that a successor generation of academic China experts in the social sciences were not being trained in sufficient numbers across Europe, and thought there needed to be an EU-wide scholarship initiative. Another important goal of ECAN was to inform and to help define the EU Commission's strategy and policy with regard to China. For all of these reasons and following numerous lobbying trips to Brussels, Shambaugh was able to persuade the EU Commission to financially support ECAN, which commenced its activities in early 1997 and operated for five years.

ECAN was designed as a network of collaborating European institutions that would act as "nodes" for the network within the various member countries. The original seven collaborating institutions were Centre de Recherches et de Documentation sur la Chine Contemporaine (Paris), Institut für Asienkunde (Hamburg), Sinological Institute, University of Leiden, Centre for Pacific-Asia Studies, University of Stockholm, Department of Asian Studies, University of Copenhagen, Centro de Estudios de Asia Oriental, Universidad Autonoma de Madrid, School of Oriental and African Studies, London University. SOAS served as the institutional secretariat of the network, and it was coordinated by Professor Robert Ash.

ECAN's core activities consisted of a series of relatively small policy workshops attended by academic specialists and policy-makers from the EU and from individual European governments. Another important activity was holding large annual conferences with more than a hundred academics, government officials and representatives of the European business community participating. The proceedings of the workshops as well as papers presented at the annual meetings were edited and published in a publications series.[27] No fewer than five edited books were published in five years. Finally, ECAN administered the EU–China Research Fellowship Fund (ECRFF). Grants from ECRFF provided financial support to a number of young scholars, in the final year of the PhD study or in the early stages of their subsequent academic careers, conducting field research or archival studies in China, Taiwan or Hong Kong.[28]

ECAN clearly functioned as a catalyst for stimulating and encouraging contemporary China studies in Europe. However, in 2002, ECAN's activities came to an abrupt halt as funds for the first phase ran out and the EU Commission had trouble finding a new budget line for its continuation. In 2004 the institutions behind ECAN were encouraged to submit a proposal for the re-launching of the network. At the beginning of 2006, almost two years later all the technicalities were finally in place, and Phase II began. The EU Commission awarded the project to the European Institute of Asian Studies in Brussels, to be implemented by a team headed by EIAS Director Willem van der Geest. An advisory board composed of Professors Robert F. Ash, Kjeld Erik Brødsgaard, Francois Godement and Thomas Heberer was formed to advise on the choices and direction of the network.[29]

The objective of Phase II of ECAN continues to be to foster closer cooperation between the scattered European research institutions and the sources available within the contemporary China field. More specifically, Phase II is supposed to develop a number of tailored briefing papers to be presented to staff of EU institutions. A limited number of these briefs will form the basis of workshops with EU policy-makers and officials. There will also be an annual Network Meeting held in Brussels. All ECAN members will be invited to attend this meeting, where there will be keynote addresses from leading scholars and officials.

Whereas membership of the original ECAN network was based on institutions, the new ECAN primarily aims to attract members on an individual basis. However, distressingly, in early 2007 EIAS (the institutional home of ECAN) collapsed under financial pressure. At the time of writing, ECAN's future remains in doubt.

The commitment of the European Commission to ECAN should be commended. However, the impact on the further development of European China studies in an academic sense will be limited. Funds are allocated to stimulate cooperation in the form of workshops and meetings, but there are no funds to generate new research in terms of funding of research projects or research fellowships. The knowledge provided to EU officials and policy-makers in the form of briefing papers presented at workshops will have to draw on existing competencies within the various universities and research institutions in the member countries. The new ECAN is also more policy-oriented than during Phase I and aims to disseminate rather than generate new knowledge and insight. In this sense the new ECAN does not involve an upgrading or expansion of European China scholarship. It is clear that the EU bureaucracy can benefit enormously from ECAN. It is less clear how ECAN will stimulate contemporary China studies as an academic pursuit.

Research materials

There has always been a close relationship between the development of European China scholarship and the establishment of major library holdings. The largest holdings of materials pertaining to China, in Chinese as well as in Western languages, are found in Cambridge, Oxford, Heidelberg, Munich and Leiden. If contemporary China materials are included, London (SOAS) and Copenhagen should also be added to the list.

The foundation of the Chinese collection at Cambridge was laid in 1886 with the donations by Sir Thomas Wade, the first Professor of Chinese in the university. Systematic acquisition of Chinese materials began in the years immediately following World War II and has continued ever since. The Chinese collection currently contains over 100,000 titles of printed books. Current accessions cover Chinese history, geography, archaeology, social sciences and law, language, literature, philosophy and religion, fine arts, science and technology. Japanese Sinology is also well represented. Over 1,000 current Chinese serials are subscribed to.[30] Cambridge is also home to the library of the Needham Research Institute. The library holds about 30,000 titles, focusing on Chinese science, technology and medicine. The library also holds a valuable collection of off-prints, many of them unpublished. Joseph Needham's personal archives are deposited in the Cambridge University Library.[31]

As in Cambridge, the Chinese library collection in Oxford began to emerge in the nineteenth century. The development of a modern Sinological collection began after World War II, following the recommendations of the Scarborough Report. It has steadily expanded over the last five decades to the point where Oxford now hosts one of the largest Sinological collections in Europe. There are now over

130,000 titles in the Chinese language collections, with over 2,000 new titles added each year, and more than 750 current Chinese periodical titles taken annually. More recently, the Library has begun to systematically acquire materials relating to the study of modern and contemporary China. As is the case in other major European libraries, the Chinese language collections are reinforced by the extensive holdings of publications in Western and other Asian languages.[32]

The third major collection of library material on China in the UK is held by SOAS. The collection consists of some 170,000 volumes of printed material and many items in microfilm and some 5,000 periodical and newspaper titles. The strengths of the collection are in politics and government, foreign relations, anthropology and ethnic minorities, business, finance and economics, law, modern Chinese literature, modern Chinese language, military, overseas Chinese and the Chinese Communist Party. Thus, in comparison with Oxford and Cambridge, the SOAS library is much more oriented towards modern and contemporary China, as well as the social sciences. Professors Schram, Walker, Howe, Shambaugh, Ash and Croll had much to do with building the contemporary social science holdings of the SOAS collection (the collection also includes material in English as well as other European languages).[33]

In Germany the two most important library collections are in Heidelberg and Munich. The older collection is located in Munich, where the library of the Institute for Sinology at the Ludwig Maximilian University in Munich holds more than 110,000 volumes. Similar to the other major libraries mentioned above, the library also holds an important collection of *collectanea* (*congshu*) and subscribes to a large number of Western and Chinese periodicals. The collection is focused on traditional Sinology, mainly in the areas of philosophy, religion, literature and history. This reflects the institute's history and its past and present research activities. The library facilities in Munich are further strengthened by the Sinological holdings of the Bavarian State Library, which is located close to the university and has the largest collection of works in classical Chinese found in Germany.[34] The collection in Heidelberg has been rapidly expanding in recent years. The library of the Instiute for Sinology now holds more than 80,000 monographs, including 1,100 volumes of *separata* and 31,750 volumes of *collectanea*. The library also subscribes to 420 journals and 12 daily newspapers (including one of the world's only complete runs of *Liberation Army Daily*). Also valuable is the collection of microfilms and especially the ambitious Digital Archive for Chinese Studies which can be accessed from partner libraries in other universities.

In Scandinavia the main collections are located in Copenhagen. The library of the Department of Asian Studies has several thousand volumes of books relating to Chinese language, history, art, religion, philosophy, literature, and society. The library cooperates with the Royal Library, which has about 40,000 volumes in Chinese, and the library of the Nordic Institute of Asian Studies, which contains 34,000 books and a total of 1,500 periodical titles of which about 500 are received currently. The Asia Research Centre of the Copenhagen Business School has a small library with statistical material focusing on social and economic developments. In addition, the main library of the Copenhagen Business School holds a large collection of Western language books and journals within the social sciences.

In sum, impressive European library collections for Chinese studies have been built after World War II. It is no coincidence that the major centres for China studies are found where the library facilities are located and vice versa. This continues to be the case even though electronically based library resources are becoming increasingly important. This is especially the case in contemporary studies. Much important Chinese material, including major newspapers, is now available on the internet. Major university libraries now also subscribe to databases, where most of the relevant Western language research journals can be accessed. However, the library still constitutes the heart of most research institutes and cannot be wholly substituted by individual access to electronic databases.

Three generations of European China scholarship

Early European contemporary China studies were characterized by a number of factors. They had their origin in academic circles outside the traditional Sinological institutes and there was often a fine line between academic research and more journalistic (newspapers and magazines) and popular work (school textbooks). Members of these circles constituted a peculiar group of development economists, political scientists, journalists and intellectuals of often left-wing persuasion. Many studies were heavily influenced by the Cultural Revolution and tended to structure the analytical framework according to official Chinese self-characterizations, which divided Chinese politics and economic and social development according to a "two-line struggle" model – pitting the "revisionist line of Liu Shaoqi" against the "revolutionary line of Mao Zedong."[35] Works on China that were introduced and quoted in the debate mostly consisted of studies by scholars from the European continent, especially from France and West Germany, and to a much lesser extent of works produced by American scholars.[36] In the middle of the 1970s the debate on the nature and development trajectory of the so-called transitional societies dominated the social science discourse and here China played an important role as an alternative to Soviet development models.

The first generation

The most influential scholar within this field in the late 1960s and early 1970s was Charles Bettelheim, a professor of economics at the Sorbonne. Bettelheim's works originally focused on the Soviet planning system.[37] He believed that a centralized planning system would guarantee a socialist development process. Nevertheless, events in the Soviet Union and in Eastern Europe, especially the Soviet invasion of Czechoslovakia in 1968, caused him to re-evaluate his position and he became increasingly critical of the Soviet Union.[38] The final results of this re-evaluation appeared in *Calcul économique et formes de propriété*, which is generally considered Bettelheim's major theoretical work.[39] Here he elaborates the basic concept of a grand theory of the transitional society. The book won him the

reputation of being the central theorist in the intensified discussion of the beginning of the 1970s on the basic questions confronting societies in transition from
capitalism to socialism.

In 1973 Bettelheim published *Révolution culturelle et organisation industrielle
en Chine*, which was based on a short trip to China in 1971.[40] The book aimed to
apply the very abstract analysis contained in *Calcul économique et formes de
propriété*. Whereas the former work conceptualized the fundamental contradictions behind the facade of socialist planning and ownership and the movement
towards capitalist restoration, *Révolution culturelle et organisation industrielle en
Chine* offered an illustration of a socialist development of the transitional society.

Following the death of Mao, the ascendancy of Hua Guofeng and the arrest of
the Gang of Four in October 1976, Bettelhem argued that China now was heading
in the Soviet "revisionist" direction and could no longer serve as a model for
socialist development.[41] At about the same time, he resigned from the presidency
of the French–Chinese friendship association and his letter of resignation revealed
his disagreements with the newly-pragmatic post-Mao leadership of Deng
Xiaoping.[42]

Although Bettelheim was not a Sinologist, he influenced the field in ways few
could rival. This was the case not only in France where several monographs were
published directly under his aegis,[43] but also in the rest of the continent the class
struggle variant of the two-line model became highly influential. In the United
States the works of Bettelheim and the class struggle interpretation of Chinese
politics inspired the works of the very active group of young scholars in the
Committee of Concerned Asian Scholars.

In the UK one of the more important early contributions within the class
struggle approach to Chinese politics was Joan Robinson's *The Cultural Revolution in China*.[44] The book was the result of a short visit to China in November
1967. In her introduction Robinson claimed that at the outset of the Cultural Revolution there was an organized group within the party and the state administration
who were preparing to take power. These "rightists" were accused of "taking the
capitalist road" and obstructed socialism. Therefore the aim of the Cultural Revolution was to root out "all remnants of bourgeois ideas and a bourgeois way of
life," so that socialism could be carried out in China.

In Germany we also find examples of studies written from a class struggle
perspective. A good example is Giovanni Blumer who maintained that the Cultural
Revolution was caused by a conflict between two opposing leadership groups, led
by Mao Zedong and Liu Shaoqi respectively.[45] There are many more examples of
works written within the two-line paradigm.[46] Nevertheless, the works discussed
in this context are believed to be representative of this particular type of analysis.
The authors dominated the public discourse and there were only a few dissenting
voices.[47]

At about the same time as Bettelheim sidelined himself in the China field,
Jürgen Domes published a path-breaking article in *The China Quarterly* dealing
with the intra-elite conflicts during the 1975–6 period, which led to the ouster of
the Gang of Four and the rise of Hua Guofeng.[48] Domes put forward the novel idea

that the political process in China was dominated by the existence of functional/ opinion groups which might solidify into factions. Domes further refined his views in the seminal book *Politische Soziologie der Volksrepublik China*.[49] In 1985 he published *The Government and Politics of the PRC*, which further demonstrated Domes' detailed knowledge of Chinese politics.[50]

Domes defined opinion groups as issue-based coalitions which are usually limited to short-term cooperation, where factions are programme-oriented coalitions of opinion groups formed on the basis of alternative policy platforms and competing claims for political power. Domes posited that opinion groups solidify into factions when consensus on issues as well as procedures breaks down among the elite. Domes claimed that the Chinese political system could be defined as a "transitional crisis system" characterized by repeating cycles of group formation – action condensation – conflict resolution – group formation. In positing there are more than two groups operating in the Chinese political system, Domes broke away from the two-line paradigm and also disassociated himself from official Chinese self-charaterizations.

Another German scholar who devoted himself to rigorous detailed analysis in studying China was the economist Willy Kraus. His study of China's economic and social development between 1949 and the late 1970s was extremely useful and, at the time of its publication, perhaps the most detailed analysis available.[51]

In the UK, classical studies dominated at Oxford and Cambridge, but at SOAS in London Stuart Schram and Kenneth Walker provided a platform for contemporary studies.[52] Schram's research on Mao was path-breaking and he became the world's leading expert on the Chairman. His colleague, the economist Kenneth Walker, is widely regarded as the founder of modern Chinese economic studies in Britain.[53] His three PhD students (Christopher Howe, Robert Ash and Peter Nolan) have exercised an enormous influence on the field. Christopher Howe actually began to publish in the early 1970s and must be considered to belong to the first generation.[54]

In France, a few Sinologists, including Claude Aubert, Lucien Bianco, Claude Cadart and Jean-Luc Domenach, published a book that sought to "open a road of serious discussion" on China. They documented the various ways the Chinese authorities would use to make European China specialists adopt official Chinese self-characterizations of developments in China.[55] The book also shows that *Le Monde*, the authoritative French newspaper, was very reluctant to publish anything critical of China and Mao. This substantiates my basic argument that the views of Bettelheim and other two-line struggle adherents of the Cultural Revolution dominated public opinion through easy access to publishing houses and important national newspapers.

Traditional Sinology watched from the sidelines. Most Sinologists continued their philological studies or concentrated on philosophy, religion, classical literature and ancient history. Getting involved in analysis of current events was out of the question. Contemporary Chinese affairs were not included in the core curriculum of the study programmes and the language training concentrated on classical Chinese and complicated characters. However, the students' interest in contemporary affairs was growing, causing increased pressure on faculty to change curriculum and textbooks.[56]

The second generation

The second generation is the generation that began their studies during the 1970s under the impact of the Cultural Revolution and the subsequent "reform and opening" process. In the immediate post-Mao period, Chinese society entered a period of liberalization of Chinese society and it became easier to travel and study in China. There was a significant increase in the number of European students studying in Chinese universities and they were allowed to study not only at the usual languages schools and universities in Beijing, Tianjin, Nanjing, Shanghai and Shenyang, but also in places such as Canton, Chengdu, Jinan, Qufu, etc. Some students even went to China two or three times on official exchange programmes and were able to do some initial field research. By the mid-1980s, one or two years of studies in China became a *sine qua non* for anyone seriously considering to do research on contemporary China at the graduate or postgraduate level.

Returned students brought new perspectives into the traditional Sinological institutes. The majority were interested in modern and contemporary studies and put pressure on their teachers and professors to modernize their curricula and teaching materials accordingly. An increasing number of students from the social science disciplines went to China to study Chinese. This phenomenon further stimulated the growth of more modern social science-oriented studies. However, due to the particular institutional structure of Chinese studies in Europe, the impetus for change had to come from within. The traditional Sinological institutes began to actively promote research within the field and contemporary studies were finally allowed to establish themselves within the formal university structure, although some of the senior professors continued to drag their feet.

The themes studied and the framework for analysis underwent a paradigmatic change during the second generation. Thus research went beyond official Chinese self-characterizations and began to question basic assumptions underlying the work of the first generation. The two-line struggle was rejected and there was a growing awareness of the factional and ideological complexities of Chinese politics. There was also a new stress on social forces and dissident phenomena such as the Chinese democracy movement of 1978–9.[57] There was also an interest in studying central–local relations, highlighting the spatial dimension of Chinese politics and examining in detail economic and political developments in individual provinces.[58] A few scholars focused on the policies towards the national minorities.[59] On a more general level, economic studies, including the politics of economic reform, received new attention, stimulated by the emergence of much new statistical material coming out of China.[60] But a number of scholars inspired by the first generation continued to uphold the importance of systematizing and understanding the Chinese economic discourse rather than just describing the unfolding of factual events.[61] Some economists also developed an interest in comparing

China and the Soviet Union or China with India.[62] Others focused on specific sectors, for example agriculture or grain yields.[63]

Research on science and technology and technology transfer and acquisition was strengthened considerably after China adopted an open-door policy from 1978 onwards. In contradistinction to the work of the first generation, second generation scholars regarded science and technology acquisition as having a positive influence on China's economic development. In 1978 Lund University even established an institute, The Research Policy Institute, which focused on science- and technology-related issues with a focus on China, India and Vietnam.[64]

Research on Chinese foreign policy mostly dealt with China's relations to the two superpowers and its Asian neighbours.[65] Related to this was an emerging interest in China's defence establishment and defence capabilities.[66] The works of the late Gerald Segal are especially noteworthy, although Segal never studied Chinese and in this sense is atypical of the second generation of China scholars.[67]

From the mid-1980s there was an increasing interest in methodological issues and some work appeared sorting out and evaluating the different approaches being used and discussing the reliability and usefulness of available data and ways of interpreting them.[68] This preoccupation with the theoretical framework and empirical foundation for academic research in the field intensified in the late 1980s and was carried into the 1990s.[69]

Many second generation European China scholars renewed their interest in social protest and dissident movements in the wake of the Tiananmen debacle in 1989.[70] After the crackdown there was a tendency to focus on the centrifugal forces in Chinese society rather than forces that seemed to keep China together.[71] This tendency was reinforced after the breakdown of the Soviet bloc after 1989.[72]

The third generation

The third generation of contemporary China scholars in Europe have benefited from much more rigorous methodological training. They have all taken courses relating to theory and methodology – such as fieldwork and techniques of interviewing – and most of them have supplemented their study trips to China with longer visits to major European and American research centres. In the 1980s a new system was instituted in Scandinavian universities, according to which a PhD degree or equivalent research would be a prerequisite for entering the three-phase career pattern of Assistant Professor–Associate Professor–Full Professor, similar to the American system. It was no longer possible to become a university Professor based on an MA thesis alone.[73] The PhD reform had a great impact on Chinese studies. In the past, many books were actually revised versions of MA theses. But as a consequence of the new stress on doctoral training, more and more works were either revised PhD dissertations or spin-offs from doctoral work. This picture already began to emerge in the late 1980s, but it became even more pronounced in the 1990s.

In terms of the themes studied there are changes compared to the 1980s, although not on a scale to qualify for a paradigmatic change. The third generation is not particularly interested in macroeconomic issues and the former stress on economic development and economic reforms is no longer present. Instead more limited issues and themes such as the role of political institutions and local government in economic development or policy formulation and implementation in certain policy arenas are taken up.[74] These themes also entail studies of cadre management, the role of the party and the relationship between the party and new social groups,[75] corruption,[76] and how the political system works at various levels and in various sectors.[77] Other new themes are ethnicity and identity among ethnic minorities and cultural identity in China as well as among overseas Chinese.[78] Issues concerning land problems and related policies, especially as they relate to ownership and property rights[79] and rural–urban migrations and interactions[80] are also being studied, and there is a renewed interest in state–business relations and the changing economic-social relationship between the state and the workers.[81] Finally, an increasing number of works on China in the European business schools are being published by scholars with a background in Chinese studies.[82]

The second generation is, of course, still active in the field. Some continue to work within their original research interests,[83] while others focus their attention on new areas of research. Examples of new topics include centre–regional relations,[84] civil society,[85] private entrepreneurs and the private sector,[86] the Cultural Revolution,[87] the role of the Communist Party,[88] institutional reform,[89] population policy and demography,[90] and China's relations with Western Europe.[91]

Transatlantic debates

During the 1960s and early 1970s there was a clear distinction between American and European China scholarship in terms of research themes and agendas. US scholarship focused on the authoritarian, if not totalitarian, aspects of the Chinese system, whereas European China scholarship had a more sympathetic view of China's developmental trajectory. Over the years there has been a convergence between American and European scholarship. Thus in the 1990s, in the wake of the Tiananmen debacle, European scholars focused, similarly to their American colleagues, on the centrifugal tendencies in Chinese society, resulting in a plethora of studies on civil society, social organizations, private entrepreneurs and other forms of non-governmental development. However, contemporary European China scholarship has never totally rejected the view that, except for the Cultural Revolution chaos, China has enjoyed steady economic development and a political system that was able to deliver a certain degree of political and social stability. The realization that the system probably will hold has grown stronger in recent years and has resulted in the contours of a new research agenda built on an interest in how the system works rather than predictions on when it will break down. Important initiatives such as ECAN are also predicated on an assumption that China is holding together and will become increasingly important in economic, political and cultural aspects. American contemporary China scholarship has a different focus and is more concerned with "the coming collapse of China," "the China threat," "China's governance crisis," etc.[92]

In the foreign policy arena one may also detect a slight divergence between European and American scholarship in evaluating the implication of China's rise. Europeans tend to stress the Bismarckian rather than the Wilheminian aspects of China's foreign policy behaviour. This divergence was at the centre of the EU–US controversy on whether or not to lift the European arms embargo against China instituted in the wake of the Chinese military's crackdown on the student demonstrations in June 1989.

In sum, an overview of the field reveals that the contours of an interesting debate across the Atlantic are appearing. An increasing number of studies relate to how the Chinese political, ideological and economic system works in specific arenas and fields, how ordinary Chinese participate in grassroots political and social reform, how the Chinese Communist Party maintains its power over selected groups of personnel in the power system, etc. In the foreign policy area there also is an increasing interest in the rationale behind the Chinese policies rather than the prospect of a rising revisionist China set on altering the power balance in the world.

Conclusion

Contrary to widespread belief, contemporary China studies in Europe did not grow naturally out of Sinology. In fact, European Sinology was, until the 1960s, almost exclusively dominated by classical pursuits and was not receptive to modern and contemporary studies. The result was that it was left to journalists, diplomats and social scientists without language training to try to meet the growing public interest in contemporary affairs. Only from the mid-1980s did major Sinological university departments and institutes begin to open positions in modern and contemporary China studies. By now contemporary studies have grown strong and in many universities classical studies are on the defensive. But, unlike in the United States, most research is still embedded in an area studies structure most usually being a sub-section of an Institute or Department of East Asian Studies. This appears to be a common West European pattern. It means that positions in contemporary China studies are only slowly starting to emerge within the disciplines, although a number of the more prominent third generation European China scholars have been able to marry solid language skills with appropriate training in a social science discipline. However, in order to truly solidify the development of contemporary studies, European universities have to learn from the US and bring Chinese studies out of the confinement of area studies. This is fortunately already occurring in a number of European business schools and hopefully the social science disciplines will soon follow.

As was the case twenty years ago, Chinese studies in Europe are concentrated in France, the UK, the Netherlands, Germany and the Nordic countries. The rest of Europe provides a picture of scattered small research environments with only one or two researchers and no associated study programmes. The EU Commission has taken an initiative to bring the scattered research institutions and individuals together by launching ECAN. However, this will not necessarily enhance the quality of research conducted and will therefore not necessarily enhance European China scholarship's competitiveness in relation to American China scholarship. For this to happen, the EU would need to stimulate scholarship by launching major research programmes and by facilitating the recruitment of a new generation of scholars. This would also make it possible to escape the confinement of the comparatively small national funding systems for research that tend to reinforce the parochialism caused by the fact that much research continues to be done and reported in one of the many national languages of Europe. Currently the European China scholarship field is still dominated by the second generation, and the third generation is only slowly beginning to take over. It is difficult to see more than the dim contours of a new fourth generation on the horizon.

In recent years contemporary studies have grown considerably. New departments and centres have been formed, a number of new chairs have been established and considerable external funding secured. Clearly the dynamics in Chinese studies have evolved from classical to contemporary studies, and this is bound to become even more pronounced as the third generation consolidates their position in the field. In conclusion, it can be said that contemporary China scholarship has finally broken through the barrier and the field is currently in a healthy and solid state.

Notes

* I am grateful to Jan-Willem Blankert, Jean-Pierre Cabestan, David Shambaugh, Volker Stanzel and Michael Yahuda for their very useful critiques and suggestions on earlier drafts of this chapter.

1 I use Sinology and Chinese studies interchangeably, although I am aware that in some circles, particularly in the United States, Sinology has a slightly negative connotation. This is certainly not the case in Europe, where many still would claim that Sinology is what China research should be all about. Strictly speaking, Sinology does imply a certain command of the Chinese language, whereas Chinese studies primarily refer to the object under study, namely China. For example, Franke claims that Sinology must be based on the study of texts. See Herbert Franke, *Sinologie an deutschen Universitäten* (Wiesbaden: Franz Steiner Verlag, 1968), p. 1. In contrast, the late Joseph Levenson argued that studying the texts is a useful methodology, but Chinese studies must aim further: "The Sinology that means control of texts is a wonderful means, but a weak end .... The time is past for texts to be used for spiritual athletics, ascetic proofs of honesty, and thoroughness in the abstract. We need to be honest and thorough not in marching and counter-marching through the literature 'because it is there', but because it relates to intellectual problems, to more than methodology." See Joseph R. Levenson, "The Humanistic Disciplines: Will Sinology Do?" *Journal of Asian Studies*, Vol. 23 (1963–4), pp. 507–12.

2 By now a considerable number of surveys on European China studies have been published. In 1992 more than 40 Sinologists met in Taiwan for a conference on European Sinology, which was sponsored by the Chiang Ching-kuo Foundation. Most of the senior professors of traditional Sinology took part, including: Herbert Franke (Germany), Jacques Gernet (France), Lionelle Lanceotti (Italy), Christopher Harbsmeier (Norway), Göran Malmqvist (Sweden), Søren Egerod (Denmark), Michael Loewe (UK), Erik Zürcher (Holland). The subsequent conference volume is one of the

few published introductions to European Sinology – see Ming Wilson and John Cayley (eds.), *Europe Studies China* (London: Han-Shan Tang Books, 1995). Another useful, albeit short, piece is Thomas Kampen's review article, "China in Europe: A Brief Survey of European China Studies at the Turn of the Century," in *China Review International*, Vol. 7, No. 2 (Fall 2000). For a discussion of European China scholarship informed by the ongoing debate on Orientalism, see Hans Hägerdal, *Väst om Öst: Kina-forskning og kinasyn under 1800-tallet och 1900-tallet* (Lund: Lund University Press, 1996). Most recently, three studies in a book on international China studies analyse contemporary European China studies within the fields of economics, politics and foreign policy studies respectively. See Robert F. Ash, "Studies of China's Economy in Europe," Jean-Pierre Cabestan, "Studies of Chinese Politics in Europe" and Kay Möller, "Studies of China's Foreign and Security Policies in Europe," all in Robert F. Ash, David Shambaugh, and Seiichiro Takagi (eds.), *China Watching: Perspectives from Europe, Japan, and the United States* (London: Routledge, 2006). In the 1990s, under the editorship of David Shambaugh, *The China Quarterly* also published a series of surveys on China studies in various parts of the world, including one on French China scholarship and one on Scandinavian scholarship. See Lucien Bianco, "French Studies of Contemporary China," *The China Quarterly*, No. 142 (June 1995), pp. 509–20, and Kjeld Erik Brødsgaard, "Contemporary China Studies in Scandinavia," *The China Quarterly*, No. 147 (September 1996), pp. 938–61. On contemporary China studies in Northern Europe see also Tony Saich, "Contemporary China Studies in Northern Europe," *Asian Research Trends*, No. 4 (1994), pp. 11–128. In the 1990s, the European Association of Chinese Studies also commissioned a number of surveys on Chinese studies in a number of European countries. The survey on UK scholarship has proven useful in this context. See *Chinese Studies in the UK*, European Association of Chinese Studies Survey, No. 1998, p. 34.

3 I realize that there may be contrasting views on the definition of "contemporary." In this context, the term "contemporary" is to be understood as the post-1949 period, i.e. the period covering the People's Republic of China.

4 See Herbert Franke, "In Search of China: Some General Remarks on the History of European Sinology," in Ming Wilson and John Cayley (eds.), *Europe Studies China,* op. cit., pp. 11–25.

5 Ibid., p. 14. In fact Legge's appointment at Oxford was the result of strong pressure from personal friends who actually as private benefactors collected the funds needed to pay for the stipend of the professor. See Hans Hägerdal, *Väst om Öst: Kina-forskning og kinasyn under 1800-tallet och 1900-tallet* (Lund: Lund University Press, 1996), p. 129.

6 *Chinese Studies in the UK*, European Association of Chinese Studies Survey, No. 1998, p. 34.

7 See Franke, *Sinologie an deutschen Universitäten,* op. cit., p. 16.

8 See Wilt L. Idema, "Dutch Sinology: Past, Present and the Future," in Wilson and John Cayley (eds.), *Europe Studies China*, op. cit., pp. 88–110.

9 *Chinese Studies in the UK*, op. cit.

10 For a description of Karlgren's activities and contributions see Søren Egerod, "Bernhard Karlgren," *Årsboken* (Yearbook) (Lund: Vetenskapssocieten, 1980), pp. 112–28. On Bernhard Karlgren and the history of Swedish Sinology, see Göran D. Malmqvist, "On the History of Swedish Sinology," *Europe Studies China: Papers from an International Conference on the History of European Sinology* (London: Han Shan Tang Books and The Chiang Ching-kuo Foundation for International Scholarly Exchange, 1995), pp. 161–74. See also Torbjörn Lodén, "Towards a History of Swedish China Studies," in Joakim Enwall (ed.), *Outstretched Leaves and His Bamboo Staff. Studies in Honour of Göran Malmqvist on his 70th Birthday* (Stockholm: The Association of Oriental Studies, 1994), pp. 5–25.

11 The only dissertation in history produced under Karlgren's supervision was Hans Bielenstein's *The Restoration of the Han Dynasty* (1953). For a discussion of historical

studies of China past and present in Scandinavia, see Leif Littrup, "Chinese History and Scandinavia – Developments and Problems," *Scandinavian Journal of History*, Vol. 11, No. 1 (1986), pp. 41–53.

12 The Scarborough Report (1947), Hayter Report (1961), the Parker Report (1986) and the Higher Education Funding Council Report (1997).

13 *Chinese Studies in the UK*, op. cit.

14 Annual Newsletter of the Scandinavian Institute of Asian Studies, 1985 (Copenhagen, 1986).

15 See Kauko Laitinen, "Scandinavian Institute of Asian Studies – A Form of Nordic Research Cooperation," *Newsletter for Research in Chinese Studies* (December 1989), pp. 247–9.

16 Jørgen Delman and Leena Höskuldsson (eds.), *NIAS Annual Report 2004/2005* (Copenhagen: Nordic Institute of Asian Studies, n.d.).

17 See IIAS, *Guide to Asian Studies in Europe* (Richmond, Surrey: Curzon Press, 1998). The directory lists 5,000 Asianists, but it is admitted that the directory is far from exhaustive and that the listed number of 5,000 probably only constitute about 60 per cent of the total number of European Asianists.

18 See Thomas Kampen, (compiler), "Professorinnen, Professoren und Institute der deutschsprachigen Sinologie (1945–2004)", http://www.sino.uni-heidelberg.de/staff/kampen/sinologie.htm.

19 The senior professor in Duisburg working on contemporary China is Thomas Heberer.

20 The Asia Research Centre was established in 1995 as a virtual centre within the Department of International Economics and Management at the Copenhagen Business School. In 2003 it was allocated its own office space. The Asia Research is now a permanent institution with its own budget. It has nine researchers, including a professorship in Chinese studies and three associate professors and two PhD students focusing on international business and management with particular reference to China. The centre also publishes Scandinavia's only regularly published academic journal on China, *The Copenhagen Journal of Asian Studies*. The centre is directed by Professor Kjeld Erik Brødsgaard.

21 Associated scholars include Maria Svensson, an expert on human rights-related issues in China, and Michael Schoenhals, a leading scholar on the Cultural Revolution. The centre is directed by Professor Roger Greatrex.

22 See Jean-Pierre Cabestan, "Studies of Chinese Politics in Europe," op. cit.

23 Frank Pieke's works include *The Ordinary and the Extraordinary: An Anthropological Study of Chinese Reform and Political Protest* (Dissertation, 1992).

24 The China Big Business Programme directed by Peter Nolan has resulted in a number of important studies, in particular Nolan's path-breaking opus *China and the Global Business Revolution* (Houndsmill: Palgrave, 2001). See also his *Indigenous Large Firms in China's Economic Reform: The Case of Shougang Iron and Steel Corporation* (London: SOAS, Contemporary China Institute, 1998).

25 See EACS Newsletter, No. 32 (June 2004).

26 Institute of East Asian Studies, University of Duisburg-Essen; Department for East Asian Studies, Leeds University; Centre for East and Southeast Asian Studies, Lund University; Asia Research Centre, Copenhagen Business School; Nordic Institute of Asian Studies, Copenhagen; the Asia Programme, *Universitat Autonoma de Barcelona*; Department of East Asian Studies, University of Lyons.

27 The publications of ECAN include Werner Draguhn and Robert Ash (eds.), *China's Economic Security* (Richmond, Surrey: Curzon Press, 1999); Robert Ash (ed.), *China's Integration in Asia: Economic Security and Strategic Issues* (Richmond, Surrey; Curzon Pres, 2002); Heike Holbig and Robert Ash (eds.), *China's Accession to the World Trade Association: National and International Perspectives* (London: RoutledgeCurzon, 2002); Kjeld Erik Brødsgaard and Bertel Heurlin (eds.), *China's Place in Global Geopolitics: International, Regional and Domestic Challenges* (London: RoutledgeCurzon, 2002); Taciana Fisac and Leila Fernández-Stembridge (eds.), *China*

Today; Economic Reforms, Social Cohesion and Collective Identities (London: RoutledgeCurzon, 2003).

28 Robert Ash, "The EU–China Academic Network (ECAN), 1997–2001" (unpublished paper).

29 See the webpage of ECAN at http://www.ecanet.eu.

30 http://www.lib.cam.ac.uk/readershandbook/D6.html.

31 http://www.nri.org.uk/library.html.

32 http://www.bodley.ox.ac.uk/dept/oriental/chi.htm.

33 http://www.soas.ac.uk/library/index.

34 http://www.fak12.uni-muenchen.de/sin/.

35 For a discussion of the relationship between Western scholarship and Chinese political ideas and developments in the 1966–76 period, see Kjeld Erik Brødsgaard, "China Through the Looking Glass: The Effects of Chinese Self-Characterizations on West European China Scholarship," *Issues and Studies*, Vol. 22, No. 7 (July 1986), pp. 129–53.

36 Notable exceptions include Mark Selden's *The Yenan Way in Revolutionary China* (Cambridge, Mass.: Harvard University Press, 1971); and Franz Schurmann's *Ideology and Organization in Communist China* (Berkeley: University of California Press, 1968).

37 E.g. *La planification soviétique* (Paris: Marcel Riviere, 1939); *Problèmes théoriques et pratiques de la planification* (Paris: P.U.F., 1946); *L'économie soviétique* (Paris: Recueil Sirey, 1950).

38 See Paul M. Sweezy and Charles Bettelheim, *On the Transition to Socialism* (New York: Monthly Review Press, 1971).

39 Charles Bettelheim, *Calcul économique et formes de propriété* (Paris: Francois Maspero, 1970).

40 Charles Bettelheim, *Révolution culturelle et organisation industrielle en Chine* (Paris: Francois Maspero, 1973).

41 See Charles Bettelheim, *Questions sur la Chine après la mort de Mao Tsé-tung* (Paris: Francois Maspero, 1978).

42 See *Le Monde*, July 6, 1977.

43 Most notably Edouard Poulain, *Le mode d'industrialisation socialiste en Chine* (Paris: Francois Maspero, 1977); and Patrick Tissier, *La Chine: Transformations rurales et développement socialiste* (Paris: Francois Maspero, 1976).

44 Robinson, *The Cultural Revolution in China* (Harmondsworth: Penguin Books, 1969).

45 Giovanni Blumer, *Die chinesische Kulturrevolution* (Frankfurt am Main: Europäische Verlagsanstalt, 1968).

46 Other examples than those mentioned in the text and in the notes, include the titles below. In France: Jean Chesnaux, *La Chine: Un Noveau Communisme, 1949–76* (Paris: Haitier Université, 1977); in Germany: Rainer Hoffman, *Kampf Zweier Linien; Zur politischen Geschichte der chinesischen Volksrepublik, 1949–77* (Stuttgart: Ernst Klatt Verlag, 1978); Ulrich Menzel, *Wirtschaft und Politik im modernen China* (Opladen: Westdeutcher Verlag, 1978); Cheung-Lieh Yu, *Der Doppelkharacter des Sozialismus: Zur politischen Ökonomie der Volksrepublik China*, I–II (Berlin: Verlag Klaus Wagenbach, 1975), Peter Hennicke (ed), *Probleme des Sozialismus und der Übergangsgesellschaften* (Frankfurt am Main: Suhrkamp, 1973); in the UK: Jack Gray, "The Two Roads: Alternative Strategies of Social Change and Economic Growth in China," in Stuart R. Schram (ed.), *Authority, Participation and Cultural Change in China* (London: Cambridge University Press, 1973), pp. 109–53; in Italy: Maria Antonietta Macciochi, *Dalla China: dopa la rivoluzione culturale* (Milan: Giangiacomo Feltrinelli Editore, 1971); in Scandinavia: Kjeld Allan Larsen, Kai Bundgaard Madsen, Ida Munk Nielsen, and Knud Erik Skouby, *Kina et land i socialistisk udvikling* (China: A Country in Socialist Development) (København: Akademisk Forlag, 1973); Göran Leijonhufvud; *Mao Zedong och den ständiga revolutionen* (Mao Zedong and the Permanent Revolution) (Stockholm: Aldus, 1975); Bjørn Hettne, *Utvecklingsstrategier i Kina*

och Indien (Development Strategies in China and India) (Studentlitteratur, 1971); Preben Sørensen, *Vejen til Folkekommunen* (The Road to the People's Communes) (Kongerslev: GMT, 1975). Jan Myrdal; *Kina: revolutionen går vidare* (China: The Revolution Continued) (Stockholm: Pan/Norstedt, 1970).

47 Pierre Ryckmans writing under the pseudonym of Simon Leys described the special "technique of hospitality" the Chinese authorities at the time used to lead foreigners visiting China to believe that they saw the "real China," although they were in fact taken on a guided tour of the country. See Simon Leys, *Chinese Shadows* (Harmondsworth: Penguin Books, 1978). As pointed out by Simon Leys, the image of the country the foreigner brought home from such a visit was often an image, shaped by smiling inter-preters, and helpful tour guides, which closely resembled the official Chinese image. It was in fact China seen through the looking glass. Simon Ley's book created quite a furore when it was published. Many newspapers and journals ignored it and in the public debate it had little impact. In Denmark the newspaper *Information* published translated excerpts of the book in early 1978. The newspaper was flooded by angry letters to the editor complaining about this "smear campaign" against China.

48 Jürgen Domes, "'The Gang of Four' and Hua Guofeng: Analysis of Political Events in 1975–6," *The China Quarterly*, No. 71 (September 1977), pp. 473–97.

49 Jürgen Domes, *Politische Soziologie der Volksrepublik China* (Wiesbaden: Akademische Verlagsgesellschaft, 1980).

50 Jürgen Domes, *The Government and Politics of the PRC* (Boulder, CO: Westview Press, 1985).

51 The English version appeared as *Economic Development and Social Change in the People's Republic of China* (New York: Springer, 1982).

52 Stuart R. Schram was Professor of Politics with reference to China at SOAS. He was head of the Contemporary China Institute from its establishment in 1968 until 1972. His early works include *Mao Tse-tung* (Harmondsworth: Penguin Books, 1967); *The Polit-ical Thought of Mao Tse-tung* (Harmondsworth: Penguin Books, 1969) and *Mao Tse-tung Unrehearsed* (Harmondsworth: Penguin Books, 1974).

53 See especially his *Planning in Chinese Agriculture: Socialisation and the Private Sector* (London: Frank Cass & Co. Ltd., 1965); and *Food Grain Procurement and Consumption in China* (Oxford: Oxford University Press, 1984). For a portrait of Kenneth Walker, see Robert Ash (collected and ed.), *Agricultural Development in China, 1949–89: The Collected Papers of Kenneth R. Walker (1931–89)* (Oxford: Oxford University Press, 1998), pp. 1–8.

54 His early publications include *Employment and Economic Growth in Urban China, 1949–57* (Cambridge; Cambridge University Press, 1970) and *Wage Patterns and Wage Policy in Modern China, 1919–72* (Cambridge; Cambridge University Press, 1973); *China's Economy. A Basic Guide* (London: Elek Books, 1978).

55 In the case of Lucien Bianco it even amounted to an attempt to pressure him into not reporting on a trip to China in September 1974. Personal information from Professor Bianco.

56 When, in 1974, I searched for a faculty member to supervise my MA thesis on Chinese foreign policy, I was referred to an Associate Professor in the Department of History who had once taught a one-semester course on China based on Franz Schurman's *Ideology and Organization in Communist China*. This was the best expertise the University of Copenhagen could offer at the time (sic!).

57 In France, an important group of returned students including Beja, Bonnin and Andrieu translated and published many important documents related to the democracy move-ment. See for example Liu Qing, *J'accuse devant le tribunal de la société* (Paris: Editions Robert Laffont, 1982) and Victor Sinade (penname for Michel Bonnin). In Denmark a group of students who had been studying in China during the 1978–9 period also published commented texts concerning the democracy movement: Flemming Christiansen, Susanne Posborg, and Anne Wedell-Wedellsborg, *Den demokratiske*

bevægelse i Kina. Kommenterede tekster fra den kinesiske undergrundsbevægelse (The Democracy Movement in China: Commented Texts from the Chinese Underground Movement) (Copenhagen: Hans Reitzel, 1980). In the UK, David S.G. Goodman also translated and published material on the Chinese democracy movement after his return from China. See his *Beijing Street Voices: The Poetry and Politics of China's Democracy Movement* (London: Marion Boyers, 1981). In Scandinavia, see also Kjeld Erik Brødsgaard, "The Democracy Movement in China, 1978–9: Opposition Movements, Wall Poster Campaigns, and Underground Journals," *Asian Survey*, Vol. XXI, No. 7 (July 1981), pp. 747–74.

58 See Eduard Vermeer's *Economic Development in Provincial China: The Central Shaanxi since 1930* (Cambridge: Cambridge University Press, 1988) and David S.G. Goodman, *Centre and Province in the People's Republic of China. Sichuan and Guizhou 1955–65* (Cambridge: Cambridge University Press, 1986).

59 Thomas Heberer, *China and Its National Minorities: Autonomy or Assimilation* (Armonk, New York: M.E. Sharpe, 1990).

60 Gordon White, *Riding the Tiger: Politics of Economic Reform in China* (London: Palgrave Macmillan, 1993).

61 See, for example, Søren Clausen, "Chinese Economic Debates After Mao and the Crisis of Official Marxism," in Stephan Feuchtwang and Athar Hussein, (eds.), *The Chinese Economic Reforms* (London: Croom Helm, 1983), pp. 53–73; Jørgen Delman and Peer Møller Christensen, "A Theory of Transitional Society," *Bulletin of Concerned Asian Scholars*, Vol. 13, No. 2 (1981), pp. 2–15.

62 See T.J. Byres and Peter Nolan, *Inequality: India and China Compared, 1950–70* (Milton Keynes: Open University Press, 1976). See also Nolan's comparative study of the Russian and Chinese economies in transition: *China's Rise, Russia's Fall: Politics and Economics in the Transition from Stalinism* (Basingstoke: Macmillan, 1995). On contrasting paths of agricultural development in China and the Soviet Union, see Nolan's *The Political Economy of Collective Farms* (Cambridge: Polity Press, 1988).

63 See Robert F. Ash, "Prospects for China's Grain Sector: a Chinese Perspective," in Wolfgang Klenner (ed.), *Economic Trends in East Asia* (Berlin: Springer Verlag, 1989), pp. 419–31. See also his Y.Y Kueh and Robert Ash (eds.), *Economic Trends in Chinese Agriculture: The Impact of Reform* (Oxford: Clarendon Press, 1993). See also Jørgen Delman, Clemens Stubbe Østergaard, and Flemming Christiansen, *Remaking Peasant China* (Aarhus: Aarhus University Press, 1990). This is the first publication of the European Conference on Agricultural and Rural Development in China (ECARDC), established in 1989.

64 In its most active years, the institute was headed by Jon Sigurdson. See his *Technology and Science in the People's Republic of China* (Oxford: Pergamon Press, 1980); "Technology and Science – Some Issues in China's Modernization," in Joint Economic Committee, *Chinese Economy Post-Mao*, Vol. 1: *Policy and Performances* (Washington, D.C.: US Government Printing Office, 1978), pp. 476–534. See also Erik Baark, "Commercialized Technology Transfer in China, 1981–6: The Impact of Science and Technology Policy Reforms," *The China Quarterly*, No. 111 (September 1987), pp. 390–406; and "Fragmented Innovation: China's Science and Technology Policy Reforms in Retrospect," in *China's Economic Dilemmas in the 1990s: The Problems of Reforms, Modernization, and Interdependence* (Washington, D.C.: U.S: Government Printing Office, 1991), Vol. 2, pp. 531–45. On technology acquisition see also Henry N. Geraedt, *The People's Republic of China: Foreign Economic Relations and Technology Acquisition, 1972–81* (Lund: Research Policy Institute, 1983) and Jørgen Delman, *The Role of Training in Technology Transfers to China – A Case Study of the Danish Experience*, Copenhagen Discussion Papers, No. 4 (March 1989).

65 E.g. Jean-Pierre Cabestan, *La politique asiatique de la Chine* (Paris: Fondation pour les études de défense nationale, 1986).

66 See Eberhard Sandschneider, *Militär und Politik in der Volksrepublik China, 1969–85* (Hamburg; Institut für Asienkunde, 1987).

67 Segal's many publications include *The Great Power Triangle* (London: Macmillan, 1982); *Defending China* (London: Oxford University Press, 1985); *Sino-Soviet Relations after Mao* (London: International Institute of Strategic Studies, Adelphi Papers, No. 202, 1985); *The Soviet Union and the Pacific* (Oxford: Oxford University Press, 1990). See Barry Buzan and Rosemary Foot (eds.), *Does China Matter? A Reassessment: Essays in Memory of Gerald Segal* (London: Routledge, 2004). Clemens Stubbe Østergaard is also an example of someone who never studied in China, but nevertheless belongs to the European contemporary China circles. See, for example, his "Multipolarity and Modernization: Sources of China's Foreign Policy in the 1980s," *Cooperation and Conflict*, Vol. 18 (1983), pp. 245–67.

68 David Goodman (ed.), *Groups and Politics in the People's Republic of China* (Armonk, New York: M.E. Sharpe, 1984); Michael B. Yahuda (ed.), *New Directions in the Social Sciences and Humanities in China* (Houndmills, Basingstoke: Macmillan, 1987). Eberhard Sandschneider conducted comparative work on systemic change with interesting perspectives on political stability and transformation in China. See, for example, his *Stabilität und Transformation politischer Systeme. Politikwissenschaftliche Aspekte einer Theorie der Systemtransformation* (Opladen: Leske und Budrich, 1995).

69 See Kjeld Erik Brødsgaard, "Models of the Chinese Policy-Making Process: Beyond the Two Lines," in Leif Littrup (ed.), *Analecta hafniensia. 25 Years of East Asian Studies in Copenhagen* (London: Curzon Press, 1988), pp. 29–39 and "Indfaldsvinkler til studiet af kinesisk samtidshistorie" (Approaches to the Study of Chinese Contemporary History), *Historisk Tidsskrift*, Vol. 89, No. 3 (1989), pp. 300–23. See also Ole Bruun, Søren Poulsen, and Hatla Thelle (eds.), "Modern China Research: Danish Experiences," *Copenhagen Discussion Papers* (September 1991); and Søren Clausen, "Current Western Perceptions of Chinese Political Culture," in Søren Clausen, Roy Starrs and Anne Wedell-Wedellsborg (eds.), *Cultural Encounters: China, Japan and the West* (Aarhus: Aarhus University Press, 1995), pp. 446–86.

70 See for example Tony Saich (ed.), *The Chinese People's Movement: Perspectives on Spring 1989* (Armonk: New York, 1990). See also Jean-Philippe Béja, Michel Bonnin and Alain Peyraube's translation into French of many of the written documents written by the main players of the 1989 Beijing Spring: *Le tremblement de terre de Beijing* (Beijing's Earthquake) (Paris: Gallimard, 1991).

71 See Kjeld Erik Brødsgaard, "Civil Society and Democratization in China," in Margaret L. Nugent (ed.) *From Leninism to Freedom: The Challenges of Democratization* (Boulder: Westview Press, 1992), pp. 231–58.

72 Gordon White, *The Chinese State in the Era of Economic Reform: The Road to Crisis* (London: Palgrave Macmillan, 1991).

73 Sweden already instituted the Fil.Dr. (PhD) in the early 1970s.

74 See, for example, Oscar Almén, *Authoritarianism Constrained: The Role of Local People's Congresses in China* (Göteborg: Department of Peace and Development Research, Göteborg University, 2005), and Mattias Burrell, *The Rule-Governed State: China Labour Market Policy, 1978–98* (Uppsala: Department of Government, University of Uppsala, 2001).

75 See Heike Holbig, "The Party and Private Entrepreneurs in the PRC," in Kjeld Erik Brødsgaard and Zheng Yongnian (eds.), *Bringing the Party Back in: How China is Governed* (Singapore: Far Eastern University Press, 2004), pp. 239–68; Maria Heimar (formerly Edin), "State Capacity and Local Cadre Control in China: CCP Cadre Management from a Township Perspective," *The China Quarterly*, No. 173 (2003), pp. 35–52; id., "The Cadre Responsibility System and the Changing Needs of the Party," in Kjeld Erik Brødsgaard and Zheng Yongnian (eds.), *The Chinese Communist Party in Reform* (London: Routledge, 2006), pp. 122–38.

76 Flora Sapio, "La corruzione in Cina: campagne e 'retizzazione del fenomeno'," *Mondo Cinese*, No. 124 (2005), pp. 5–15.

77 Sebastian Heilmann, *Das politische System der VR China* (Wiesbaden: VS, second updated version, 2004); *Das politische System der VR China im Wandel* (Hamburg: Institut für Asienkunde, 1996); and "Regulatory innovation by Leninist Means: Communist Party Supervision in China's Financial Industry," *The China Quarterly*, No. 181 (March 2005), pp. 1–21.

78 Mette Thunø, "The Use of Chinese Sources for the Study of Chinese Emigration to Europe," *Revue Européenne des Migrations Internationales* (March 1996); "Reaching Out and Incorporating Chinese Overseas: The Trans-territorial Scope of the PRC by the End of the Twentieth Century," *The China Quarterly*, No. 168 (December 2002), pp. 910–29; Mette Halskov Hansen, *Lessons in Being Chinese: Minority Education and Ethnic Identity in Southwest China* (Seattle: University of Washington Press, 1999); id., *Frontier People: Han Settlers to Minority Areas in China* (Vancouver: University of British Columbia Press, 2005), id., "Fostering 'Love of Learning': Naxi Responses to Ethnic Images in Chinese State Education," in Kjeld Erik Brødsgaard and David Strand (eds.), *Reconstructing Twentieth Century China: State Control, Civil Society, and National Identity* (Oxford: Clarendon Press, 1998), pp. 280–309.

79 Peter Ho, *Institutions in Transition: Land Ownership, Property Rights and Social Conflict in China* (Oxford: Oxford University Press, 2005); (ed.), "The Clash over State and Collective Property: The Making of the Grass Land Law," *The China Quarterly*, No. 161 (March 2000), pp. 348–95.

80 Rachel Murphy, *How Migrant Labour is Changing Rural China* (Cambridge: Cambridge University Press, 2002). Rachel Murphy is a recent recipient of *The China Quarterly's* "Gordon White Prize". She was awarded the prize for "Turning Peasants into Modern Chinese Citizens: Population Quality Discourse, Demographic Transition, and Primary Education," *The China Quarterly*, No. 177 (March 2004), pp. 1–20.

81 Jane Duckett, *The Entrepreneurial State in China* (London and New York: Routledge, 1998); and "State, Collectivism and Worker Privilege: A Study of Urban Health Insurance Reform," *The China Quarterly*, No. 177 (March 2004), pp. 155–73.

82 Tony Fang, *Chinese Business Negotiating Style* (Thousand Oaks: Sage, 1999); Susan Aaagaard Petersen, "Culture's Influence on Performance Management: The Case of a Danish Company in China" (PhD dissertation, Copenhagen Business School, 2006).

83 E.g. Stig Thøgersen, *A County of Culture. Twentieth Century China Seen from the Village Schools of Zouping, Shandong* (Ann Arbor: University of Michigan Press, 2002).

84 See Harald Bøckman, "China Deconstructs? The Future of the Chinese Empire-State in a Historical Perspective," in Brødsgaard and Strand, *Reconstructing Twentieth Century China: Social Control, Civil Society, and National Identity*, pp. 310–46.

85 See Gordon White, et al., *In Search of Civil Society: Market Reform and Social Change in Contemporary China* (Oxford: Clarendon Press, 1996); Clemens Stubbe Østergaard, "Citizens, Groups, and a Nascent Civil Society in China: Towards an Understanding of the 1989 Student Demonstrations," *China Information*, Vol. IV, No. 2 (Autumn 1989), pp. 28–41. See also Kjeld Erik Brødsgaard, "State and Society on Hainan: Liao Xun's Ideas on 'Little Government Big Society'," in Brødsgaard and Strand, *Reconstructing Twentieth Century China: Social Control, Civil Society, and National Identity*, pp. 189–215.

86 See Ole Bruun, "Political Hierarchy and Private Entrepreneurship in a Chinese Neighborhood," in Andrew G. Walder (ed.), *The Waning of the Communist State: Economic Origins of Political Decline in China and Hungary* (Berkeley: University of California Press, 1995), pp. 184–214. Thomas Heberer, *Unternehmer als strategische Gruppen. Zur sozialen und politischen Funktion von Unternehmern in China und Vietnam* (Hamburg: Institut für Asienkunde, 2001); Thomas Heberer, "Ethnic Entrepreneurship

and Ethnic Identity: A Case Study Among the Liangshan Yi (Nuosu) in China," *The China Quarterly*, No. 182 (June 2005), pp. 407–27.

87 See Michael Schoenhals, "The CCP Central Case Examination Group, 1966–76," *The China Quarterly*, No. 145 (March 1996), pp. 87–111; Schoenhals (ed.), *The Cultural Revolution Reader* (Armonk: M.E. Sharpe, 1996); and Roderick MacFarquhar and Michael Schoenhals, *Mao's Last Revolution* (Cambridge, MA: Belknap Press, 2006).

88 See Brødsgaard and Zheng, *Bringing the Party Back in: How China is Governed*, op. cit.; Brødsgaard and Zheng (eds.), *The Chinese Communist Party in Reform* (London: Routledge, 2006).

89 Kjeld Erik Brødsgaard, "Institutional Reform and the *Bianzhi* System in China," *The China Quarterly*, No. 170 (June 2002), pp. 363–86. For an early comprehensive discussion of administrative reform in China in Deng's Era, see Jean-Pierre Cabestan, *L'administration chinoise après Mao: les réformes de l'ère Deng Xiaoping et leurs limites* (China's Administration after Mao: The Reforms of the Deng Xiaoping Era and Their Limits) (Paris: Editions du Centre National de la Recherche Scientifique, 1992).

90 Thomas Scharping, *Birth Control in China, 1949–2000: Population Policy and Demographic Development* (London: RoutledgeCurzon, 2003); (ed.), *The Evolution of Regional Birth-Planning Norms, 1954–97* (Armonk, New York; M.E. Sharpe, 2000).

91 See special issue of *The China Quarterly* (March 2002) with articles by, *inter alia*, Eberhard Sandschneider ("China's Diplomatic Relations with the States of Europe"); Kay Möller ("Diplomatic Relations and Mutual Strategic Perceptions: China and the European Union") and Markus Taube ("Economic Relations between the PRC and the States of Europe").

92 See, for example, Gordon G. Chang, *The Coming Collapse of China* (New York: Random House, 2001); Bruce Gilley, *China's Democratic Future. How It Will Happen and Where It Will Lead* (New York: Columbia University Press, 2004); Minxin Pei, *China's Trapped Transition: The Limits of Developmental Autocracy* (Cambridge, MA: Harvard University Press, 2006).

4 It's the system that matters

Institutionalization and making of EU policy toward China

Franco Algieri

China is one of the most prominent topics on the EU's external relations agenda. The intensity with which EU–China relations have been developed, especially since the 1990s, clearly indicates that Europeans do react to the rise of China – be it in economic, political or security political terms. However, in the political as well as in the academic debate there is an ongoing dispute whether there exists something that can be called an "EU China policy" or not. Looking at the sum of the multitude of different forms of relations that are conducted between the EU and China, it *can* be claimed that there *is* a China policy of the EU. This policy is determined by a variety of interests, from the governments of the EU member states, from interest groups, from the EU institutions (the European Commission, the Council and the European Parliament) and from the legal framework of the EU/EC Treaties.

This chapter examines one aspect of the EU's China policy – its institutionalization and the way in which it is conducted in the overarching context of European foreign policy. In a normative way my basic argument is that EU–China relations are determined to a large extent by the forms for regulating and structuring the Union's external relations. These forms have been developed over time by the member states in the context of the European integration process. In order to understand how the China policy of the EU is formulated and works, the first part of this chapter gives an overview on the EU China policy process. This will be followed in the second part by looking at the EU's China policy at work. For this purpose we examine the political dialogue, trade relations, human rights policy, and the issue of the arms embargo will be used for illustration.

The EU China policy process

In order to understand the making of the EU's China policy some preliminary perspectives are needed in order for readers to understand how to analyse the EU as a foreign policy actor. It has to be taken into consideration that the Union is not an actor which can be compared to a state. The policy-making process in such a unique political actor is a complex and interwoven process of formulating a common interest that spans different levels, i.e. the supranational, the national and the subnational. Different actors with specific interests cooperate horizontally (between the institutions of the EU as well as among the member states) and vertically (between the supranational, national and subnational levels) to commonly agree on problem-solving mechanisms and how to use them.

In such a multi-level system, common interests have to be defined and resources for external action have to be put together in order to meet the challenges of the international system.[1] While a transfer of sovereignty from the national to the supranational level takes place in the field of trade policy, in the security and political arena only gradual agreement amongst the member states of the EU can be observed. European foreign policy is understood as comprising all policies of the EC and EU, directed at third actors, mainly states, but also regions or international organizations. In the framework of these policies, specific procedures are agreed upon and instruments developed for conducting relations with third parties. This is further underlined when we look at what the European Commission lists as the three principal components of the EU's external action, i.e. trade policy, development policy and the political dimension.[2] Thus, to understand the EU's policy-making we have to see a system with a great diversity of levels and actors and a complex institutional setting that influences the behaviour of the actors involved.[3]

The main actors concerning the formulation and implementation of European foreign policy are the Council (of Ministers), the European Commission, and the European Parliament. The European Council (the heads of state and government) has to be considered as defining the overarching goals and direction of European foreign policy. These actors have different competencies in the single policy areas that determine European foreign policy. Trade policy is organized on the supranational level, with the European Commission as the most important actor and, as such, the member states have transferred their respective competencies to a supranational body which is supposed to harmonize national interests. Yet in the foreign and security policy domain, the member states are reluctant to transfer competencies and stick to the intergovernmental method. Consequently, a coexistence of different legal frameworks and of a different distribution of power characterizes the foreign policy process of the EU.

This system of the EU is also reflected in the China policy process. It is impossible to exactly identify the number of persons and units involved in this process in the single EU institutions. There is, for example, little institutional memory to be found in the European Commission. It depends on the issue at stake as to how many actors are directly or indirectly involved in the coordination and policy-making process. However, several key players can be mentioned and they are shown in the following simplified graphs.

European Commission Directorate General (DG) External Relations

Inside the Commission's DG External Relations, DG A-3 and Directorate H (DG/H) are of central importance. It is here, especially in H/2, where the core for formulating the Commission's China policy can be found – but also DGA-1, which is

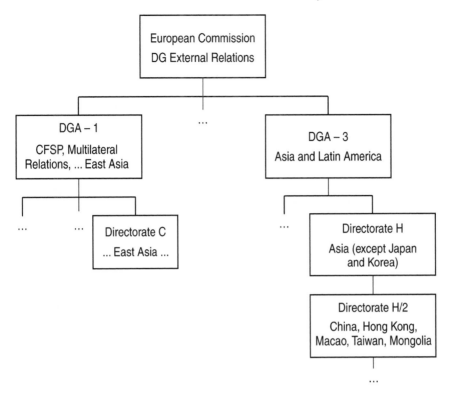

Figure 4.1 European Commission External Relations

responsible for CFSP and multilateral relations, and here Directorate C (DG/C) dealing with East Asia are of relevance. The China desk in DG External Relations (DG/E) is involved in a permanent unit for cross-institutional coordination.

European Commission cross-DG and Delegation interaction

Inside the Commission cross-DG interaction takes place. As concerns China, of special relevance are parts of DG External Relations, DG Trade, DG Humanitarian Aid (ECHO) and the European Aid Cooperation Office. A special role is played by the Commission Delegation in China. Almost half of the personnel in the Beijing Delegation deal with questions of development cooperation and programmes that contribute to improving the profile of the EU in China. Cooperation between the Commission in Brussels and the Delegation in Beijing is crucial in order to grasp the multitude of problems and interests in Europe, in China, as well as for European business in China. For the latter, the European Chamber of Commerce in China plays a necessary role for supplying the Commission with the respective information.

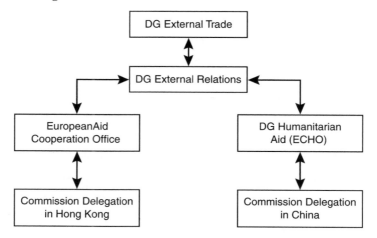

Figure 4.2 European Commission and Delegations

Council Secretariat and European Parliament

Apart from the Commission, the Council Secretariat and the European Parliament need to be included in the institutional policy-making process. Inside the Council Secretariat the Directorate Asia/Oceania in DG/E, as well as the Asia Task Force in the Policy Unit, must also be considered. In the case of the European Parliament, it is the Foreign Affairs Committee which has China most centrally on the agenda.

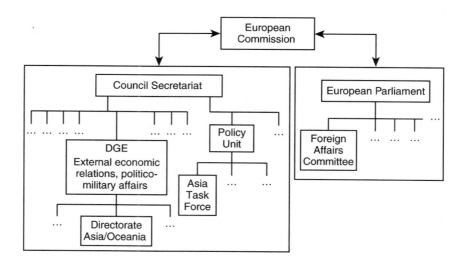

Figure 4.3 European Commission, Council and European Parliament

Apart from these actors, nongovernmental actors and interests have to be taken into consideration. Lobbies and interest groups, be they pan-European or national, try to influence the EU's China policy-making. To be sure, lobbying and influence by the Chinese embassy on the EU and its member states is also part of this process, be it directly in Brussels or in China. All these particular interest actors (the term comprises in this context governments as well as business or other non-governmental actors) choose different channels on the national and supranational levels for articulating their interests. They get involved in different ways (for example when the Commission is drafting a new "Communication" on China), but it is not just a one-way street, in the sense that those actors and interest lobbies try to influence each other as well as the EU agencies. It is especially necessary for the European Commission to get the most accurate and comprehensive picture of all actors and interests concerned.

This policy-making process is difficult to manage because of its high complexity and multitude of diverging interests. Furthermore, one big obstacle to be considered is that the interaction between different bureaucratic structures is extremely cumbersome at times. There is a kind of mutual suspicion not just between the European Commission and the Council, but also inside single institutions of each. For example, open and effective coordination and communication between DG/E in the Council and the Policy Unit in the Council turns out to be quite difficult to achieve. Moreover, while the Commission is relatively equipped with personnel dealing with China, the Council appears to be quite understaffed.

Understanding the making of the EU's China policy thus necessitates considering this complex structure with all its attendant bureaucratic difficulties. Against this background the multi-faceted dialogue structures of EU–China relations have to be analysed.

European China policy at work

European foreign policy is put into practice by using specific instruments and capabilities. Those are, on the one hand, conventional ones like diplomacy; trade, aid, and offering of economic benefits; threatening with or using sanctions or restrictive measures; and available technologies, human capital or political tools.[4] The EU can rely on and use the whole range of such capabilities, even though they are not equally strongly developed and often are used in a non-coherent way.[5] The following discussion will explain some features of how EU–China relations are conducted using different examples and where incoherence occurs.

The political dialogue

The political dialogue with third countries and/or regions is a permanent element of the EU's external relations, and it has increased over time since the 1970s. Already then, via the European Political Cooperation (EPC) mechanism, European interests could be articulated with foreign entities. By 2003, the EU had official dialogues with 61 states or state groupings (like ASEAN). The Europeans use

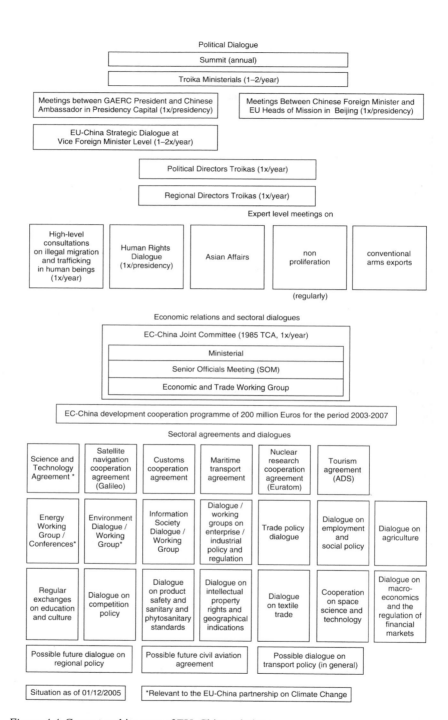

Political Dialogue

Summit (annual)

Troika Ministerials (1–2/year)

Meetings between GAERC President and Chinese Ambassador in Presidency Capital (1x/presidency)	Meetings Between Chinese Foreign Minister and EU Heads of Mission in Beijing (1x/presidency)

EU-China Strategic Dialogue at Vice Foreign Minister Level (1–2x/year)

Political Directors Troikas (1x/year)

Regional Directors Troikas (1x/year)

Expert level meetings on

High-level consultations on illegal migration and trafficking in human beings (1x/year)	Human Rights Dialogue (1x/presidency)	Asian Affairs	non proliferation	conventional arms exports

(regularly)

Economic relations and sectoral dialogues

EC-China Joint Committee (1985 TCA, 1x/year)
Ministerial
Senior Officials Meeting (SOM)
Economic and Trade Working Group

EC-China development cooperation programme of 200 million Euros for the period 2003-2007

Sectoral agreements and dialogues

Science and Technology Agreement *	Satellite navigation cooperation agreement (Galileo)	Customs cooperation agreement	Maritime transport agreement	Nuclear research cooperation agreement (Euratom)	Tourism agreement (ADS)	
Energy Working Group / Conferences*	Environment Dialogue / Working Group*	Information Society Dialogue / Working Group	Dialogue / working groups on enterprise / industrial policy and regulation	Trade policy dialogue	Dialogue on employment and social policy	Dialogue on agriculture
Regular exchanges on education and culture	Dialogue on competition policy	Dialogue on product safety and sanitary and phytosanitary standards	Dialogue on intellectual property rights and geographical indications	Dialogue on textile trade	Cooperation on space science and technology	Dialogue on macro-economics and the regulation of financial markets

Possible future dialogue on regional policy	Possible future civil aviation agreement	Possible dialogue on transport policy (in general)

Situation as of 01/12/2005	*Relevant to the EU-China partnership on Climate Change

Figure 4.4 Current architecture of EU–China relations
Source: http://ec.europa.eu/comm/external_relations/china/docs/architecture.pdf

the political dialogue mechanism to express their common position concerning different topics, whether in a broader sense concerning events in international relations or in a narrower way concerning specific issues in a state or a region with which the EU keeps relations. Most importantly, the parties involved can use this forum to improve mutual understanding.

The political dialogue with China can be traced back to the first half of the 1980s. In 1983 the Council decided to establish, in the framework of the EPC, biannual consultations between the political director of the Foreign Ministry of the country representing the EC presidency and the Chinese ambassador in each respective capital city. The first meeting at the ministerial level took place in 1984 in Paris and, starting in 1986, the EPC Troika at ministerial level and the Chinese Foreign Minister met for the first time on the margins of the UN General Assembly.[6]

These meetings and the high-level political consultations between representatives of the Commission and the Chinese government were integrated into the new framework for the political dialogue in 1994. Additionally there are *ad hoc* meetings between the Foreign Ministers, annual meetings between the Chinese Foreign Minister with the EU ambassadors in Beijing, and a yearly meeting of the Chinese ambassador in the capital city of the country holding the EU presidency with the Foreign Minister of that country. Furthermore, meetings of high officials in different functional policy fields take place.[7] At the first EU–China Summit in 1998 the political dialogue was upgraded, including now also the level of heads of states and governments. The first Troika meeting of the political directors of the EU with their Chinese counterpart was held in 2000.[8]

In 2001 the Commission proposed, in an evaluation of the 1998 China strategy, a list of measures that should lead to an improvement of the intensity/regularity of consultations and an expansion of topics for the agenda of such dialogue. Finally, in 2002 the framework for a strengthened political dialogue was approved by both sides and it commenced thereafter. Today the political dialogue comprises a wide range of topics – from human rights to international security, as well as from international terrorism to environmental questions.

The political dialogue went through different phases and, at times, experienced discontinuity, e.g. after June 1989, as a result of the controversies in the UN Human Rights Commission, and the bombing of the Chinese Embassy in Belgrade in 1999. But both sides always showed great interest in a rapid reestablishment and intensification of the dialogue. On the European side, the Council and the Commission are the primary actors in shaping the dialogue. Additional effect is given by the inter-parliamentarian meetings between the European Parliament and the National People's Congress, which has taken place since 1980.[9]

The political dialogues of the EU with other nations have improved the role of the EU as an international actor and have contributed to dispelling misperceptions and improving cooperation. However, there is a permanent danger of overstretching dialogue structures, which could result in a loss of quality. The high trade, political and economic interdependence between the EU and China, as well as the fact that there are no major conflicts between the EU and China or fundamental differences of interests will, for the time being, keep the political dialogue between the two sides relevant.

Trade policy, sectoral dialogues and the Commission's role in context of China's WTO accession

China is the EU's second-largest trading partner and a number of sector-specific dialogues have been developed and new ones are anticipated (see Figure 4.4). These dialogues comprise competition policy, consumer product safety, customs cooperation, education and culture, energy (including nuclear energy), environment, space cooperation, Galileo global satellite navigation services, information society, intellectual property rights (IPR), maritime transport, regulatory and industrial policy, food safety and sanitary and phytosanitary issues, science and technology, trade policy dialogue, textile trade dialogue, macro-economic and financial sector reforms, employment and social affairs, regional policy, agriculture, civil aviation, and transport. The diversity of these dialogues reveals the important fact that inside the Commission almost every DG is somehow linked to EU–China relations.

The institutionalization of trade relations with China can be traced back to the late 1970s. The trade agreement between the EC and China established the first Framework Agreement in 1978. Due to the expansion of trade relations in the years that followed, the Commission was authorized by the Council in July 1984 to negotiate a new agreement with China. Ten years after the first trade agreement the Agreement on Trade and Economic Cooperation between the European Economic Community and China entered into force on 1 October 1985. Different from the first agreement, it further elaborated that, apart from the economic dimension, European–Chinese relations have political implications. Both agreements can be evaluated to be more than just a regulating framework for European–Chinese trade relations. Moreover, they are a reflection of the deepening of trade and economic relations and, at the same time, are the basis on which these relations are built.

With the agreement of 1978 a Joint Committee was created to oversee the entire commercial relationship. Comprising representatives from both sides this committee has three main functions: (1) a supervisory function; (2) an examination function; and (3) a recommendation function. It became the main body for accompanying and developing European–Chinese trade relations. In the agreement that followed in 1985 these functions were further elaborated in detail. Normally, meetings alternate between Brussels and Beijing, and extraordinary meetings convened as needed. The chair of the committee rotates between the two parties. On the European side, the Community is represented by the European Commission, assisted by representatives of the member states.

The Joint Committee has gained in importance over time, and also became politically more important due to the fact that, since 1988, it can also be convened at the ministerial level. One of the main topics on the committee's agenda was the accession of China to the GATT/WTO. Already from the early days when China showed efforts to join the GATT, the EC showed a positive and generally supportive attitude. On the Commission side, efforts were increased to better understand the economic reform process in China. The European Parliament called on the Council and the Commission to support China's efforts.[10] The support for China's admission in an international regime like the WTO also reflected the context of the EU's market access strategy.[11] The Commission approach was in line with the interests of member states and national enterprises.[12]

From the perspective of a Commission official who was closely involved in the negotiations, there were two main reasons why the Commission supported China's WTO accession.[13] First, managing and regulating world trade in a multilateral framework finds the support of the EU. Second, the Europeans hoped that the integration of China in such a framework would support China's transition from a state-trading country to a market economy and, linked herewith, that the reform-oriented politicians in China would be supported.

The European–Chinese negotiation process turned out to be a long endeavour. Often it seemed like there would be a breakthrough, but then it still took time. From a European perspective, it was believed that China should benefit from transition periods due to its economic development stage. However, this did not mean that rules of the multilateral framework should be changed in favour of China. The then Commissioner for Trade, Sir Leon Brittan, expressed in 1996: "the WTO is a rules-based organization, and we can't engineer China membership on false terms."[14] After the US and China had finished their bilateral WTO negotiations in November 1999, expectations on the European side grew that the Euro–Chinese negotiations would also come to a successful end. Especially on the working level, the intensity of number of meetings increased and finishing the negotiations was, from the Commission's perspective, the highest political priority.[15]

The Council allowed the Commission to react in a flexible manner to the Chinese position, if the Chinese themselves would show flexibility. The final breakthrough was reached in May 2000 after "five days of blunt and sometimes testy negotiations,"[16] and in the final phase the Commissioner for Trade Pascal Lamy and the Chinese minister Shi Guangsheng were intensively involved in reaching an agreement. The foreign ministers of the EU meeting in the Council framework accepted the results of the negotiations. Pascal Lamy explained its negotiation mandate as follows: "The mandate I had this week was (having tested the depth of their resistance) to say to the Chinese: we need you to go as far as you can to the red line you have identified. But if you can't cross it, then we must have compensation, both inside and outside the particular sector concerned. We told the Chinese that we are not going to try to go into your political no-go-zone [...] A great deal of what we have achieved has been offered by the Chinese to compensate us for what they were unable to deliver."[17]

The Commission had to respect the overall community interest, the interests of the member states, the industrial sectors concerned and many interest groups – but also the results of the bilateral negotiations of China with other states, especially the United States. Consequently, there was a high degree of interdependence of European, Chinese and American interests. And for the Europeans there were also security and political implications to be considered. This can be deduced from the following statement by Pascal Lamy: "This deal is not just good for China, but for Asia, for the region as a whole. China's entry into the WTO will contribute to the steady and sustainable path of growth and economic development, not just in China, but also for her neighbours in Asia, and for the rest of the world. This deal, when implemented as part of the multilateral system, will boost the rule of law in China. The fundamental WTO principles of transparency, non-discrimination, administrative independence and independent judicial review, which the WTO holds up, will contribute to the positive evolution of China's economic, legal and social systems."[18]

To conclude, the main role in the bilateral negotiations on the European side was with the Commission, due to the legal provisions laid down in the EC Treaty. Already in 1988 the Commission had asked the Council for authorization to start negotiations with China on the latter's accession to the GATT. With the Council's authorization, inside the Commission the central role was played by the Directorate General for Trade. Further Directorate Generals were involved when topics that affected their responsibilities were touched on. These concerned mainly those from External Relations, Industry, Internal Market and Telecommunication. During the whole negotiation process the Commission coordinated its position closely with the member states and respective industrial sectors like the banking and insurance sector, the automobile sector, or the telecommunications sector. Furthermore, the Commission's delegation in China and representatives from European companies in China were involved. At decisive stages of the negotiation process it turned out that most helpful was to have high-level meetings at the ministerial level and including the responsible Commissioner.

The human rights dimension in European foreign policy

The external policy of the EU is supposed to reflect an approach driven by values. Democracy, human rights, and the rule of law are essential parts of the member states' understanding of how social communities and states should be organized. These are motives by which the European integration process has been and will continue to be driven. Reference can be found for example in Article 11(1) Treaty on European Union:

> The Union shall define and implement a common foreign and security policy covering all areas of foreign and security policy, the objectives of which shall be: to safeguard the common values, fundamental interests, independence and integrity of the Union in conformity with the principles of the United Nations Charter … to develop and consolidate democracy and the rule of law, and respect for human rights and fundamental freedoms.

Another example can be found in Article 181a(1) EC Treaty:

the Community shall carry out, within its spheres of competence, economic, financial and technical cooperation measures with third countries. [...] Community policy in this area shall contribute to the general objective of developing and consolidating democracy and the rule of law, and to the objective of respecting human rights and fundamental freedoms.

Furthermore, these guiding principles are also reiterated in the European Security Strategy (ESS):

The quality of international society depends on the quality of the governments that are its foundation. The best protection for our security is a world of well-governed democratic states. Spreading good governance, supporting social and political reform, dealing with corruption and abuse of power, establishing the rule of law and protecting human rights are the best means of strengthening the international order. Trade and development policies can be powerful tools for promoting reform. As the world's largest provider of official assistance and its largest trading entity, the European Union and its member states are well placed to pursue these goals.

The topic of human rights has an external and an internal dimension for the EU. In the Preamble of the Treaty of the European Union the member states state their commitment to freedom, democracy, human rights and the rule of law. Reference to the importance of human rights was made in the Preamble of the Single European Act and in 1987 the foreign ministers of the EC agreed to establish a working group on human rights in the framework of EPC. Thereafter, several declarations followed through which the member states reiterated their commitment to support the strengthening of human rights and democracy.

In agreements with third countries the human rights dimension has increasingly gained in importance. Many agreements with third countries are based on these values and consequently have a conditionality clause. Karen Smith underlines that it is important for the credibility and acceptance of conditionality that it is supported by all member states: "That the EU is applying 'multilateral' conditionality ... may be considered more acceptable and legitimate than conditionality applied by a single state."[19] By applying conditionality and promoting human rights and democratization objectives, the EU has developed a wide range of instruments and considers their coherent use as essential for European foreign policy.[20]

Democracy promotion and the promotion of human rights are not stand-alone aspects, but have to be seen in context with other guiding values that are fundamental for the EU's functioning as a social entity. The form in which the values are expressed comprises a wide spectrum of instruments like political declarations, demarches, dialogue structures or strategies towards and agreements with third countries and regions. The instruments are used in different ways and differ with respect to their effectiveness. It has been realized, for example, that preferential trade agreements are more effective than human rights agreements.[21] In most cases the EU applies not just one of these instruments but combines them according to the situation and necessity. Nevertheless, discrepancies and incoherence become obvious when one looks comparatively at the EU's different relations with third countries (contrast, for example, the EU's human rights policies in Burma and China). Assuming that European foreign policy is following a *Leitmotiv*, like that described above, these discrepancies and incoherence are weakening the *Leitmotiv*. Furthermore, if a policy of unequal treatment of third countries can be proved, then the question arises of whether democracy promotion as such is at stake?

As concerns relations with China, the form, content and effect of the EU's human rights approach in the context of European foreign policy merits examination. Since the first political dialogue at ministerial level in 1984, this forum promoting European foreign policy values has been steadily upgraded, and in 1998, with the first EU–China summit, the level of heads of states and governments has been included. The topics of prior interest in this dialogue include human rights and questions linked to the political and societal development in China. Of course, the extension of the political dialogue of the EU with third partners can be interpreted as an indicator for the Union's growing importance as an international actor. Connected herewith is the danger of overstretching the dialogue capacities of the EU and, as such, causing a weakening of their impact. Apparently there are differences in quality concerning the importance the dialogue partner gets from the EU. The European–China dialogue can be described as one of those dialogues that is estimated by both sides to be of such importance that its further deepening is continuously considered.[22] Even though the political dialogue between the EU and China witnessed times of discontinuity, such as after the Tiananmen events in June 1989 or following the controversial debate in the UN Human Rights Commission in 1997, both sides always showed a clear interest in reestablishing and intensifying the political dialogue.

Measures for suspending, reducing or stopping economic relations can be decided by the Council, according to Article 301 of the EC Treaty, and have to be based on a common position or a joint action in the framework of CFSP.[23] Before the Treaty on European Union entered into force, a different procedure was applied, i.e. after having found an agreement in the framework of EPC the respective measures could be applied through the Community's trade policy. Sanctions that are taken in the EU context are expected to prove to be more effective than those taken by member states on their own – not least due to the fact that the political symbolism is stronger.

As concerns China, the European Council, in reaction to the events in June 1989, decided on a number of restrictive measures.[24] But it did not take long before individual member states started to argue in favour of an early lifting of the sanctions. The then French Council President Edith Cresson expressed it as follows: "It is quite obvious that all the states were not exactly on the same wavelength as regards the measures to be taken against China."[25] Quite obviously, the perspectives of securing shares in the China market were a guiding interest for some member states.[26] Apart from the economic considerations, the fact that China is a permanent member of the UN Security Council played a decisive role during the Gulf crisis in 1990 and the settlement of the Cambodian question.[27]

The growing weight of China as an international economic, security and political actor has thus been influencing the European position concerning the rapid normalization of relations with the People's Republic. It is also instructive to observe the incoherent European actions at the UN Human Rights Commission in Geneva, as China was able to manipulate and influence the EU member states. In 1998 the then EU Commissioner for External Relations, Chris Patten, described the Chinese strategy as follows: "The Chinese government believes that all it has to do is to crack the whip – threaten a blocked order here, a purchase from a rival there, a withdrawal of its goodwill, a cancellation of good relations until further notice – and we will jump back into line. And by and large we actually do, especially the Europeans."[28]

In the Commission's China Country Strategy Paper of 2002, one of the priorities for cooperation projects with China concerns the support for the transition to an open society based on the rule of law and respect of human rights, through the promotion of good governance, democracy and human rights-related policies.[29] Several instruments are used to promote the values of European foreign policy – amongst them, development aid (ODA). Thirty per cent of all official development aid that goes to Asia comes from the EU.[30] The European cooperation strategy with China runs alongside the goals of the Community's guidelines for development policy published in the year 2000, as well as the corresponding China communications of the European Commission.[31] From the Commission's "Communications" of 1998 and 2001, respectively, it can be deduced that the support of cooperation projects has to be linked more closely to the other policies of the EU which are directed at China.[32] From the Commission's perspective, it has become evident that involving the cooperation partner in developing specific measures is helpful: "The best cooperation form seems to focus on policy advice and support to the reform process, as this strategy is in line with the top-down approach of Chinese reforms and government practice in general."[33] Through this form of cooperation, the development and stabilization of the Chinese reform process are intended to be supported. China's EU Policy Paper of October 2003 also notes development aid and the cooperative approach of the EU towards China as an essential part of the relationship.[34]

In sum, China has become one of the most important countries for the EU and its member states. And this importance is still growing. However, European foreign policy towards China is, when it comes to democracy promotion and the human rights dimension, clearly incoherent. The EU argues that a policy of cooperative engagement of China is most suitable for European interests – but behind this approach lies the very pragmatic conviction that the costs of non-cooperation with China cannot be afforded. In China's EU Policy Paper it is mentioned that there are "no fundamental differences of interests between the EU and China." Differences in respective views of human rights are justified in terms of the differences in historical development, cultural heritage, political systems and the level of economic development.

Without any doubt the EU and its member states are facing a credibility problem. Andrew Nathan explains this with respect to EU–China relations as follows:

> The difference between a China and a Vietnam, a Zaire, or a Saudi Arabia … is not the international standards applied to it, but the country's potential impact on Western and global interests. China should be held to the same standards as other countries, but its international importance justifies giving its rights violations more urgent and sustained attention than the world can afford to spend in every offending country.[35]

It can be argued that there is a deliberate policy of unequal treatment of third countries in the EU's foreign policy as concerns democracy promotion. The more comprehensive bilateral relations have been established between a third state and the EU and its member states, in economic and/or political terms, the more European foreign policy will be reluctant to use negative political instruments. Furthermore, the EU is using a policy of double standards when it comes to democracy promotion, according to the importance of the third state for European foreign policy interests.

Controversy about the arms embargo

Since the second half of the 1990s, China has requested that the EU lift its arms embargo. These calls first found a certain attention in France. The Chinese position was reiterated in the Chinese EU policy paper of 2003, which stated: "The EU should lift its ban on arms sales to China at an early date so as to remove barriers to greater bilateral cooperation on defence industry and technologies." Not long after the publication of this paper, at the Sixth EU–China Summit in Beijing, the European side expressed that it would work towards this end. In the aftermath of the Summit contradictory arguments were used by the Commission, the High Representative for CFSP, and the member states, as to whether a decision on lifting the embargo should be taken or not. The then German Chancellor Gerhard Schroeder demonstrated a positive attitude on lifting the embargo during his visit to China in December 2003, and French President Jacques Chirac emphasized the topic at the European Council in the same month.[36] The European Council called on the Council to work on the topic and in January 2004 the foreign ministers had a first debate, handing the work over to COREPER and the Political and Security Committee.[37]

The positions continued to diverge. While then French Foreign Minister Dominique de Villepin pointed to the privileged partnership with China and consequently supported the lifting of the embargo, the then German Foreign Minister Joschka Fischer still saw need for debate and expressed this during his visit to China in July 2004. In both countries there are strong interests to remain close to China. France intends to close the gap with Germany as the biggest trading partner for China inside the EU. Apart from that, the French defence industry is a factor, as

France is the leading EU state exporting armaments abroad. However, there are no clear indications whether European defence companies would really have a remarkable profit from the lifting of the embargo. Former EU Commissioner Chris Patten argued that because of the Code of Conduct and national restrictions a respective increase could not be expected, "Nobody should think that if EU governments were to decide to lift the embargo, it would lead to a flood of sales of weapons to China."[38]

A clear "no" to the lifting of the embargo came from Scandinavian countries, Ireland, the Netherlands, the European Parliament and new Central European member states. The latter recalled, in a resolution in December 2003, that without any improvement in China's human rights policy the embargo could not be touched.[39] Strong opposition to the lifting of the embargo also came from the United States, as Washington referred to the consequences for the security of Taiwan as well as to the fact that the modernization of the People's Liberation Army would be enhanced.[40]

For the time being the debate seems to have cooled down. The governmental constellation in Germany under the "Grand Coalition" guided by the conservative Chancellor Angela Merkel, as well as a rather silent France, means that the two major countries that once favoured the lifting are now rather reluctant. It is important that the respective control mechanisms for arms exports be strengthened – since the debate about lifting the embargo might again become a topic on the EU's agenda. If and when it does, a new and decisively strengthened Code of Conduct needs to be agreed upon by the member states and put in place.

Conclusion

The present quality of the EU's China policy reflects the development path of European foreign policy. Apart from the interests of single member states, it is the EU's policy-making and institutionalization pattern that matters. From the description of the making of EU China policy outlined in this chapter the following ten conclusions can be drawn:

1   The complex multi-level system of the EU has grown over time and disciplines the behaviour of actors. Those actors involved are forced to cooperate more closely in different policy fields. With the extension of the policies which are coordinated on the supranational level, the China policy has become more and more "Europeanized."
2   The development path of the European integration process matters. According to the pace and form by which integration has stretched from the economic to the political dimension, the more European China policy, as part of European foreign policy, could be deepened.
3   Through supranational cooperation states can reduce the costs of disruptive relations with China. As the example of WTO accession negotiations show, member states had a stronger position as a result of cooperation than if they had been negotiating on their own. By bringing China into a multilateral and institutionalized forum the predictability and stability of EU–China relations increases.

4   The Commission is the most central actor on the supranational level. Most of the initiatives and the formulation of a policy are coming from this supranational institution. Over time it has developed a conceptual framework in order to channel and support interests of the member states and the different business sectors. The Commission is furthermore a kind of transmission belt for bringing European and Chinese interests into the agreed and regulating framework. The desk-level coordination inside the Commission is a precondition for a functional European China policy. Moreover, the Commission has to keep a steady exchange of information with the member states and the Council.

5   With the CFSP (and the inclusion of ESDP) the Council's role was upgraded. Next to the Commission, the Council is the other most central actor. With the extension of the political dialogue, and the more the EU is improving capabilities to be a comprehensive international actor, the Council, the Secretariat General of the Council with the respective units (like the Policy Unit) and the High Representative for CFSP have to deal with China topics. The latter also takes part at the EU–China summits and supports the EU presidency according to Article 18 Treaty on European Union. Furthermore, the Council is also co-ordinating member states' interests in line with Article 16 of the Treaty on the European Union.

6   Even though the Council is, according to Articles 11 and 13.3 of the Treaty on European Union, responsible for the coherence of European foreign policy, the particular interests of and competition among member states is often weakening the "common" position. Without any doubt, there is a group of member states (mostly noticeably Germany, France and the UK) that are the most influential in defining the European China policy.

7   There is also evident competitive behaviour between the EU institutions – the Commission, the Council, and the European Parliament – and a kind of mistrust that can be observed at times. This can be explained, not least, with the different competencies and the discrepancy of how policy fields are legally regulated. Whether the Commission and Council are "two rival cultures" can be disputed, but nevertheless the mixture of community and intergovernmental procedures in overlapping policy fields is a burden for the making of a coherent foreign policy.[41]

8   The European Parliament is, from a Commission as well as a Council perspective, regarded as a rather marginal actor. Due to non-existing rights the Parliament has in CFSP, it has to concentrate on those rights it has in the Community sector. Even though the Parliament regularly stresses the importance of improving the human rights dimension in EU–China relations, its influence is not strong enough to change the political direction of the European China policy significantly.

9   The agenda of the EU's China policy is steadily extended and involves new policy fields. As a consequence of 9/11, for example, the topic of international terrorism has also become part of the Europe–China dialogue. As such, the field of Justice and Home Affairs will gain importance. Further transnational challenges, like illegal migration, will increasingly become topics on the agenda.

10 The EU's China policy will remain characterized by a tension between the state of their institutionalization, the capabilities that can be used for the making of the policy, and the competing interests of member states. In the years to come, European China policy will face the difficulties of incoherence as a consequence of the above-mentioned systemic aspects.

Notes

1 See Michael Smith, "The European Union, foreign policy and the changing world arena," in *Journal of European Public Policy*, Vol. 1, No. 2 (1994), pp. 283–302, p. 291.
2 Commission of the European Communities, *Communication from the Commission to the Council and the European Parliament, The European Communities development policy*, COM(2000) 212 final (Brussels, 26 April 2000), p. 4.
3 For more theoretical considerations on institutions see James G. March and Johan P. Olsen, "The New Institutionalism: Organizational Factors in Political Life," in *The American Political Science Review*, Vol. 78, No. 3, pp. 734–49.
4 This categorization has been made by Christopher Hill, "Closing the Capabilities-Expectations Gap?" in John Peterson and Helene Sjursen (eds.), *A Common Foreign Policy for Europe? Competing visions of the CFSP* (London and New York, 1998), pp. 18–38.
5 Franco Algieri, "The Coherence Dilemma of EU External Relations. The European Asia policy," in *Journal of the Asia Pacific Economy*, Vol. 4, No. 1 (1999), pp. 81–99.
6 Simon Nuttall, *European Political Co-operation* (Oxford: Oxford University Press, 1992), p. 287.
7 Commission of the European Communities, *A Long-Term Policy for China–Europe Relations*. Communication from the Commission, COM(95) 279 final (Brussels, 5 July 1995).
8 Commission of the European Communities, *EU Strategy Towards China: Implementation of the 1998 Communication and Future Steps for a More Effective EU Policy*, COM(2001) 265 final (Brussels, 15 May 2001).
9 21 meetings were held between June 1980 and March 2004, http://www.europarl.eu.int/meetdocs/delegations/chin/5eme_legislature_CHIN.htm (download 18 August 2004).
10 See Bulletin EC 6–1987, 2.2.25; 2.4.19.
11 Commission of the European Communities, Communication from the Commission to the Council, the European Parliament, the Economic and Social Committee and the Committee of the Regions, *The Global Challenge of International Trade: A Market Access Strategy for the European Union*, COM(96) 53 final, (Brussels, 14 February 1996).
12 See e.g. Bundesverband der Deutschen Industrie (BDI), *Der Beitritt der Volksrepublik China zur WTO, Positionspapier,* (Berlin 2000), p. 4. François Godement and Regine Serra, "French Policy Towards China: A Redefinition", in: Miquel Santos Neves and Brian Bridges (eds.), *Europe, China and the Two SARs: Towards a New Era*, (Houndmills and New York: Palgrave, 2000), pp. 4–28; Marta Dassù, "Italian Policy Towards China: The Trading State Approach," ibid, pp. 70–102.
13 Hans-Friedrich Beseler, "The EU–China Negotiation: Breaking the Deadlock," in Heike Holbig and Robert Ash (eds.), *China's Accession to the World Trade Organization: National and International Perspectives* (London, 2002), p. 4. Beseler was inside the Commission Directorate General for Trade in those days.
14 Sir Leon Brittan quoted in *International Herald Tribune*, 8 May 1996, p. 19.
15 Report from the Commission to the Council and the European Parliament on the implementation of the communication *Building a comprehensive partnership with China*, COM(2000) 552 final, C1, 9 (Brussels, 8 September 2000).

16 James Kynge, "EU Trade Deal Clears China's Way into WTO," *Financial Times*, 20/21 May 2000, p. 1.
17 "EU Trade Commissioner Pascal Lamy Informs EU Member States on China WTO Deal," http://europa.eu.int/comm/trade/bilateral/china/wto.htm (download 25 May 2000).
18 Pascal Lamy press conference on 19 May 2000, http://europa.eu.int/comm/trade/bilateral/china/prc.htm (download 25 May 2000).
19 Karen E. Smith, "The Use of Political Conditionality in the EU's Relations with Third Countries: How Effective?" in *European Foreign Affairs Review*, Vol. 3, No. 2 (1998), pp. 253–74, p. 257.
20 Commission of the European Communities, Communication from the Commission to the Council and the European Parliament, *The European Union's role in promoting human rights and democratization in third countries*, COM(2001) 252 final, (Brussels, 8 May 2001).
21 Emilie M. Hafner-Burton, "Trading Human Rights: How Preferential Trade Agreements Influence Government Repression," in *International Organisation*, (Summer 2005), pp. 593–629.
22 See Report from the Commission to the Council and the European Parliament on the implementation of the communication *Building a comprehensive partnership with China*, COM(2000) 552 final (Brussels, 10 September 2003). Ministry of Foreign Affairs of the People's Republic of China, *China's EU policy paper*, (Beijing, 10 October 2003).
23 See Raffaello Fornasier, "Quelques refléxiones sur les sanctiones internationales en droit communnautaire", in *Revue du Marché Commun et de l'Union Européenne*, No. 402 (1996), pp. 670–7. Frédéric Naud, "L'embargo. Une valse à trois temps Nations Unies, Union Européenne et Ètats membres", in *Revue du Marché Commun de l'Union Européenne*, No. 404 (1997), pp. 25–33.
24 See *European Political Cooperation Bulletin*, 89/190; *Bull. EG 6-1989*, 1.1.24.
25 *European Political Cooperation Bulletin*, 89/204.
26 Institute of International Economics, Case studies in sanctions and terrorism, Case 89-2, http:www.iie.com/research/topics/sanctions/china.htmchronology (download 11 May 2004).
27 See *European Political Cooperation Bulletin*, 91/122, 91/481; Desmond Dinan, "European Political Cooperation", in Leon Hurwitz and Christian Lesquesne (eds.), *The State of the European Community: Policies, Institutions and Debates in the Transition Years* (Boulder: Lynne Reinner, 1991), p. 413.
28 Christopher Patten, *East and West: China, Power, and the Future of Asia* (London, 1998), p. 268.
29 European Commission, Working Document, *Country Strategy Paper China* (Brussels, 1 March 2002).
30 http://europa.eu.int/comm/external_relations/asia/rel/prog.htm (download 5 November 2004).
31 Commission of the European Communities, Communication from the Commission to the Council and the European Parliament, *The European Community's Development Policy*, COM(2000) 212 final (Brussels, 26 April 2000).
32 Commission of the European Communities, Communication from the Commission, *Building a Comprehensive Partnership with China*, COM(98) 181 final (Brussels, 25 March 1998). Commission of the European Communities, Communication from the Commission to the Council and the European Parliament, *EU Strategy Towards China: Implementation of the 1998 Communication and Future Steps for a More Effective EU Policy*, COM(2001) 265 final (Brussels, 15 May 2000).
33 European Commission, Working Document, *Country Strategy Paper China*, (Brussels, 1 March 2002), p. 20.

34 Ministry of Foreign Affairs of the People's Republic of China, *China's EU Policy Paper* (Beijing, 10 October 2003), Part III.
35 Andrew J. Nathan, *China's Transition* (New York: Columbia University Press, 1997), p. 255.
36 See *Bulletin Quotidien Europe*, 8604, 2003, p. 4.
37 See *Bulletin Quotidien Europe*, 8631, 2004, p. 4.
38 Chris Patten quoted in David Murphy et al., "The Thin End of the Wedge for the United States," *Far Eastern Economic Review* (12 February 2004), p. 29.
39 See *Bulletin Quotidien Europe*, 8631, 2004, p. 7.
40 See Roger Cliff and Evan S. Medeiros, "Keep the Ban on Arms for China," in *International Herald Tribune*, 23 March 2004, p. 7. David Shambaugh, "European and American Approaches to China: Different Beds, Same Dreams?" *Sigur Center Asia Papers*, No. 15, The George Washington University (Washington 2002), p. 9.
41 David Allen, "Who Speaks for Europe? The Search for an Effective and Coherent External Policy," in: Peterson and Sjursen (eds.), op. cit., pp. 42–58, here p. 51.

5 The Taiwan issue in Europe–China relations

An irritant more than leverage

Jean-Pierre Cabestan

Opinions in the European Union about the importance of the Taiwan issue in EU–China relations differ radically.[1] Some are tempted to an assessment that this issue has been well managed and is gradually being marginalized by the growing importance of China and the diversity of European interests with it. Others are more cautious: concerned about the growing military tension and imbalance across the Taiwan Strait, they draw our attention to the intricacies of the sovereignty issue and the nationalist passions that, on both sides of the Strait, may disrupt the current awkward and uneasy status quo. In their eyes, the EU cannot ignore this potential "hot spot" and should, in coordination with the United States, initiate a more active policy aimed at helping Beijing and Taipei to narrow their differences and open a more constructive dialogue.

At the same time, the EU has continued to develop, in parallel to its official relations with China, non-official links with Taiwan that have contributed to integrating the Taiwanese reality into the China policies of the EU and most member states. To what extent might these denser EU–Taiwan relations influence EU China policy? Conversely, has the rise of China imposed stricter limits on the EU's relations with Taiwan? More economically and politically present on both sides of the Strait, might the EU contemplate playing a more active role in any future settlement of cross-Strait relations?

This chapter is organized into five sections: (1) a historical overview of Europe–Taiwan relations; (2) the emergence of more substantive Europe–Taiwan relations since the 1990s; (3) the dynamism of economic, educational and cultural relations between the EU and Taiwan; (4) the political limits to Europe–Taiwan relations (the "one-China policy"); and (5) the European debate over the status and future of Taiwan and its impact on policies.

Historical overview

The non-peaceful coexistence of two Chinese states – both claiming to be the only legal representative of the Chinese nation – directly affected the China policy of European countries as early as 1949, dividing the Old Continent into two rather incoherent groups. On the one hand, all the Central and Eastern European republics of the Soviet Bloc (from Albania to Romania), a few neutral democratic nations (such as Denmark, Finland, Norway, Sweden and Switzerland) and the United Kingdom (because of Hong Kong) granted official diplomatic recognition to the newly-established People's Republic of China (PRC). On the other hand, other Western European countries, initially hesitant, followed the decision of the United States after the outbreak of the Korean War in June 1950, and maintained diplomatic relations with the Republic of China (ROC) on Taiwan. There were also some special cases: the recognition extended by Yugoslavia was not reciprocated by the PRC until 1955, because of Mao's decision to side with Stalin in his feud with Tito. London kept a consulate in Tamshui, near Taipei, which was an obstacle to the establishment of diplomatic relations with Beijing at the ambassadorial level until the consulate was closed in 1972 (at the time the PRC made a clear distinction between recognition and the establishment of diplomatic relations, in particular for countries such as Britain which did not support its entry into the United Nations). While freshly created East Germany (the Democratic Republic of Germany) quickly recognized the PRC, West Germany (the Federal Republic of Germany) did not open official links with the ROC despite US pressure, instead opting for neutrality, probably because of the division of the German nation.[2]

This complex picture gradually changed in the 1960s. First France normalized ties with the PRC in January 1964, which was followed later (both before and after Taiwan's expulsion from the United Nations in 1971 and Nixon's trip to China in February 1972) by other major members of the European Community, such as Italy in November 1970 and Germany in October 1972.

In each case, Taiwan's status was finessed. There were many more variations than is often assumed. For instance, the normalization of ties between France and the "government of the People's Republic of China" (an exception to the Gaullist principle according to which only *states* can be recognized) included no allusion to the Taiwan issue or the unity of China, in other words that Taiwan was part (or not part) of China.[3] Of course, Paris did not try, despite US pressure, to move towards a "two-China" policy, to maintain diplomatic relations with Chiang Kai-shek, who conveniently took the initiative of cutting these relations immediately. In any case, Beijing would have opposed such a policy even at that time. More isolated internationally then than today, Beijing was more flexible. This flexibility persisted in the early 1970s with regard to countries that had never had official links with the ROC, such as West Germany, Austria and Luxembourg. Probably because of the delicate status of Berlin, a subject on which Beijing did not want to anger East Germany, the PRC authorities agreed with West Germany on a communiqué that simply announced the establishment of diplomatic relations at the ambassadorial level.[4] Austria and Luxembourg were only asked to recognize that the government in Beijing was the "sole legal government of China."

But for countries that had been inclined towards a "two-China" policy, the PRC authorities imposed a "Taiwan clause," in particular after it replaced Taiwan in the UN in 1971. Again, however, this clause could be formulated differently. Most West European governments "took note of the statement of the Chinese government" that "Taiwan is an inalienable part of the People's Republic of China" (for instance Italy, in exchange for the acknowledgment by China that Alto Adige – formerly Austrian South Tyrol – was part of Italy). The United Kingdom went even further: "acknowledging the position of the Chinese government that Taiwan was part of the People's Republic of China," Britain decided to withdraw her official representative from Taiwan.[5]

In other words, the PRC always opposed a "two-China policy" but could not force third countries to recognize that Taiwan was part of the PRC. Even Britain, the most extreme case of concessions made that time by a West European country, simply acknowledged this fact – when it normalized with Beijing in 1979, Washington only admitted that "Taiwan was part of China," not the PRC. European countries did not challenge Beijing's claim but neither did they formally endorse it. For them, Taiwan was a reality with which only non-official links could be established and developed.

In the 1970s and 1980s, relations between European countries and Taiwan remained very discreet. Following Nixon's trip to Beijing, China had become a major diplomatic partner for the whole world, including Europe. Although the PRC's foreign trade was still minuscule, relative to its population, Western Europe and Japan became its main trading partners in the 1970s, way ahead of the Soviet Bloc. In 1975, the European Economic Community established diplomatic relations with China. In 1979 Portugal became the final European state (with the noticeable exception of the Vatican which has kept a representative in Taipei) to normalize official relations with the PRC.

After Deng Xiaoping initiated reforms in 1979, the rapid development of Europe–China economic, political and sometimes military relations contributed to marginalizing Europe–Taiwan political links even further. Yet, in this decade, Europe's trade with the latter remained larger than its trade with the former.[6] And on the basis of its economic success, Taiwan managed to increase the number and enhance somewhat the profile of its non-official representations abroad, including in Western Europe.[7]

However, the fascination that China's opening, reforms and development exerted on most Western European elites until Tiananmen in 1989 prevented them from taking into account the rapidly changing Taiwanese reality. Moreover, the harsh reaction of the PRC to the sale by the Netherlands of two Zwaardvis diesel submarines to Taiwan in 1980 – bilateral relations between Beijing and Amsterdam were downgraded to the level of *chargé d'affaires* for a few years – discouraged other European arms exporters from selling any heavy military equipment to Taiwan until the emergence of new circumstances.[8]

Finally, until the end of the Soviet era, although their relations with China had become difficult after 1960, no Central or Eastern European country dared open even non-official links with Taiwan. The speculation about a Soviet interest in the early 1970s in establishing some sort of anti-PRC connection with the island-state never really materialized.

The emergence of more substantive Europe–Taiwan relations since the 1990s

1989 was a turning point in world history. It also heralded a rather important change in Europe's relations with China and Taiwan. On the one hand, the Tiananmen Incident put an end to the rosy view then dominant in Europe that the PRC would evolve smoothly towards more freedom and democracy – precisely at a time when Taiwan was embarking on constitutional revisions that would move the country peacefully towards institutional democracy in 1991–2. On the other hand, the collapse of the Soviet Bloc, the reunification of Germany and the gradual apparition on the European map of newly independent and democratic countries, all opened a window of opportunity for Taiwan on the Old Continent.

This new environment convinced most European governments to develop more substantive relations with Taiwan and tempted some of them even to re-normalize ties with Taipei. However, these latter moves proved exceptional and short-lived. The re-launch of the reforms by Deng Xiaoping himself in 1992 triggered the economic and diplomatic rise of China that rapidly imposed some powerful limits on the "love affair" between Europe and Taiwan, despite the more dynamic "pragmatic diplomacy" practised by Taipei and growing military tension in the Taiwan Strait following the missile crises of 1995–6.

To be sure, the main trigger for this "love affair" was not, at least as far as Western European countries were concerned, the dramatic changes in Taiwan's political system. The new shared political values – democracy and human rights – did indeed play a part in the upgrading of non-official links. However, both sides quickly realized that common interests lay elsewhere. Taiwan only moderately supported the Chinese dissidents, because it was more focused on its own democratization and nation-building process than on the highly uncertain democratization on the mainland. Ironically, Taipei was actually busy developing trade and economic relations with its former arch-enemy just as the West was boycotting it. Western European countries were mainly attracted by the potential of Taiwan as a market, an investment location, a weapons purchaser and a springboard for conquering another market: China.

On the first three targets, Taiwan was keen to deliver. In the 1990s, European trade with and investments in the island-state increased very rapidly. For instance, trade with France increased from US$500 million in 1982 to US$3.5 billion in 2000. The EU invested six times more in Taiwan during this decade (1990–2000: US$3.7 billion) than it had in the four previous ones (1952–89: US$619 million), including US$1.46 billion from Britain, US$1.18 billion from the Netherlands and US$448 million from Germany.

France took advantage of Taiwan's defence needs to position itself in an arms market almost completely monopolized by the United States. As early as late 1989, Paris proposed the sale of six LaFayette stealth frigates – first the hulls, then the fully equipped ships. Then in 1992, it agreed to sell 60 Mirages-2000-5 (again, first unarmed, then armed with Mika missiles), a sale that convinced US president George H.W. Bush to sell 150 F-16s to Taiwan. China's initial protests after the ships deal, and then sanctions after the sale of the fighters, convinced France to put an end to this newly established relationship (see below) and dissuaded other European arms exporters from trying to open up this market. However, financial reasons also discouraged Paris: there were not enough prospects for new arms deals in Taiwan, and probably also more potential in the PRC, for it to continue to confront Beijing on this issue.

In any case, in the early 1990s, taking advantage of the development of non-official contacts between Beijing and Taipei, most Western European countries upgraded their non-official relations with Taiwan. For instance, in 1989, the French Association for the Promotion of Cultural and Scientific Exchanges with Asia (Association française pour le développement culturel et scientifique en Asie), France's de facto representation in Taiwan, was renamed the French Institute in Taipei (Institut français de Taipei), a choice inspired by the American precedent (American Institute in Taiwan, or AIT, set up in 1979 after the "de-recognition" by the USA). Since 1993 the French Institute has been directed by a career diplomat, who remains on the Foreign Ministry payroll, and has operated as an embassy. Conversely, the Taiwan representation in France, known as ASPECT (Association pour la promotion des échanges culturels et touristiques) was renamed the Taipei Representative Office in France (Bureau de représentation de Taipei en France).[9] Similar changes took place in the first half of the 1990s in Germany and other Western European countries (as in the US).[10]

After 1989, newly democratized Central and Eastern European nations developed another perspective on China (often neglected or poorly explained by outside observers). Despite the Sino-Soviet rift, the PRC had been a close partner of the now defunct socialist regimes of these countries. After 1979, the ideological dispute between the two communist giants had come to an end and been replaced by a "renormalization" process which led in May 1989 to the historic visit by Mikhail Gorbachev to Beijing, overshadowed by the Tiananmen demonstrations. But in 1989, China and Eastern Europe were taking opposite paths. In such circumstances, a number of democratically elected Central and Eastern European governments not only felt a natural affinity with Taiwan, and instinctive antipathy for China, but were tempted to establish diplomatic relations with the island-state at the risk of severing links with the PRC. Lech Walesa's Poland and Vaclav Havel's Czechoslovakia represent the two best-known examples of these temptations.[11] However, both shivered on the brink and eventually pulled back.

As far as formal relations were concerned, China therefore guaranteed its position both in Central and Eastern Europe and in the former Soviet Union, with a couple of provisional exceptions. This has not prevented many of the new regimes or countries established in Central Europe from developing substantial non-official links with Taiwan and sometimes trying to push back the limits of non-officialdom.

The hesitations displayed by Central and Eastern European countries after 1989 led the PRC, in 1991–2, as the USSR was being dismantled, to quickly recognize the newly created states across the former Soviet Union. All of them normalized ties with the PRC immediately after their independence and recognized that

Taiwan was part of China. True, Taiwan managed in 1992 to open a consulate in Riga, the capital city of one of the three newly independent Baltic states, Latvia, which managed to maintain diplomatic relations with the PRC (although the latter withdrew its ambassador shortly afterwards). Nevertheless, this exception did not last long, and it was over by 1994.

Later in the decade, taking advantage of the dismantlement of Yugoslavia, Taiwan succeeded in 1999 in opening an embassy in Macedonia. But again, this new breakthrough on the Old Continent did not survive long either, and it too died two years later. Highly vigilant, China had secured diplomatic relations with all the former republics of Tito's federation, including Montenegro in July 2006, as it had with Slovakia when it became independent in 1993.

Nonetheless, taking advantage of the fierce anti-communism, pro-Americanism (and pro-NATOism), as well as the wariness towards Russia and the close Sino-Russian partnership evident in Eastern Europe, Taiwan has become very active in several countries, in particular those that joined the EU in 2004: the Czech Republic, Hungary, Poland, Slovakia and the Baltic states.

In the mid-1990s, Taiwan's Chiang Ching-kuo Foundation (a government-affiliated foundation that provides grants to scholars and academic institutions for Chinese and Taiwan studies) decided to establish its European headquarters in Prague, probably its friendliest partner in Central Europe. This new office has allowed a growing number of Central and Eastern European students and scholars to study or conduct research on China or on Taiwan as well as often in Taiwan. Well treated by the Czech authorities, the Taiwan Representative Office in Prague is one of the most active in Europe.

Many of these European countries have opened representative offices in Taiwan (in particular the Czech Republic, Hungary, Poland and Slovakia), making the European and, in particular, the enlarged EU presence on the island-state much more visible and comprehensive than it was before 1989: today 16 out of 27 EU member states are unofficially represented in Taiwan. After much caution and many postponements, the European Union itself eventually opened its own representative office in Taipei in 2003 – completing this gradual recognition of the Taiwanese reality without questioning whatsoever the EU's "one-China policy." Officially, this office is aimed at "contributing to the strengthening of communications with the Taiwanese authorities and other economic and social interlocutors. It promotes opportunities for collaboration in areas of mutual interest."[12]

How did the private visit of former ROC President Lee Teng-hui to the USA in June 1995 and the missile crisis of 1995–6 play in Europe–Taiwan relations? European diplomats posted in Taipei were aware that the democratization of the ROC was having dramatic international consequences in terms of Taiwan's identity, nation-building and relations with the PRC. The priority given by Lee Teng-hui to elevating Taiwan's international profile (UN bid, non-official visits to Southeast Asia and the United States) and to reaching out to new allies, also in Europe, was received with some sympathy among European countries and helped convince most of them to upgrade their representation in Taipei, if they had not already done so. The new path that Taiwan was taking as well as its economic opening persuaded the governments of key European nations to agree to dispatch technical or junior ministers to Taiwan on private visits for the first time. In return, their Taiwanese counterparts have been received more frequently in Europe. Taiwanese foreign ministers have sometimes even been discreetly received in countries such as France, Britain and Germany. Typically, however, members of European governments would visit Taipei in order to secure some important economic deal.[13]

The missile crisis itself had an ambiguous impact on Europe–Taiwan relations. On the one hand, it mobilized key EU member states and the European Commission to address a strong statement of concern to the PRC authorities. In addition, the French and British governments sent a clear message to the US administration indicating that they were at its disposal if need be. And European public opinion was clearly on the side of small, democratic Taiwan against giant, authoritarian and bullying China. But at the same time, the emphasis that Beijing placed on Taiwan, its "one-China policy" and its fight against "Taiwan separatism," in a context of rapid economic development on the mainland, led most European governments to shy away from pushing their pragmatic approach to the island-state too forcefully.

The changing map of Europe since 1989, and in particular since the enlargement of the EU from 15 to 25 countries in 2004 to also include eight former socialist republics, has played a part in modifying Europe's relations with China as well as the EU's approach to Taiwan. However, as we will see below, China's negative reaction to the new path pursued by Taiwan has imposed important limits on Europe's "love affair" with the "other China," and this in spite of Taiwan's lobbying efforts (see below). This said, the upgrading of non-official links initiated in the early 1990s has both accompanied and spurred very dynamic economic, educational and cultural relations between Europe and Taiwan.

The dynamism of economic, educational and cultural relations between the EU and Taiwan

In 2005, Taiwan was the EU's 14th largest trading partner overall and 4th most important partner in East Asia, with total trade amounting to €36.5 billion.[14] The EU is Taiwan's 4th most important trading partner, accounting for 10.6 per cent of Taiwan's total foreign trade (behind China and Japan, both accounting for 16 per cent, and the US with 13 per cent). This trade may represent only 1.6 per cent of total EU foreign trade (outside of the Union), but it corresponds to more than one-fifth (17.5 per cent) of EU–China trade and to over two-thirds (68 per cent) of the trade between the EU and South Korea, a country with twice the population. Moreover, Taiwan enjoys a steady surplus with the EU: €10.9 billion in 2005 (exports: €23.7 billion; imports €12.8 billion).

Within the EU, Taiwan's main trading partners are Germany (27 per cent of overall EU–Taiwan trade), the Netherlands (16 per cent, primarily because it is the entry point into the EU for many imports), Britain (12 per cent), France (10 per cent) and Italy (8 per cent). Although much smaller, trade between Taiwan and East European countries – such as the Czech Republic, Hungary, Poland and

Slovakia – has increased very rapidly in the last few years. Overall, in 2005, the share of EU–Taiwan trade taken by the ten new member states has increased from 5 to 7 per cent of Taiwan's exports to the European Union.

However, the EU's trade with Taiwan is stagnating somewhat, despite the dynamism of the European Chamber of Industry and Commerce.[15] In 1999, although the EU consisted of only 15 countries, trade already amounted to €33.25 billion (imports: €21.26 billion; exports: €11.99 billion). And the total amount of trade remained unchanged between 2004 and 2005. This is partly due to the relocation to China of a number of Taiwanese exporters. Between 1999 and 2005, Chinese exports to the EU increased from €52.41 billion to €157.72 billion. But this has also been caused by the slowdown in Taiwan's economic growth and the lack of direct air links with China.

The EU's foreign direct investments (FDI) in Taiwan have continued to increase. With FDI stock in Taiwan worth €6.27 billion, accounting for 0.3 per cent of the total EU stock of outward FDI at the end of 2002, the EU was Taiwan's largest provider of investments (US$1 billion) in 2004. These investments are concentrated in the retail, electronics and semiconductors, transport and power generation sectors. Greater than the stock of the EU's FDI in India (€5.4 billion), these investments corresponded at the end of 2002 to half of the EU stock of FDI in South Korea and 8 per cent of its FDI stock in China.

Accounting for about 17 per cent of the FDI stock in Taiwan, the EU is the third most important foreign investor in the island-state behind the United States (22 per cent) and Japan (20 per cent). In 2005, the EU invested US$677 million (16 per cent of FDI inflow) in Taiwan, compared with US$799 million from the US and US$723 million from Japan.

Taiwan is the 16th largest foreign investor in the EU, with a stock of investments worth €2.2 billion at the end of 2002. This corresponds roughly to the share held by South Korea (2.8 per cent). However, it represents just 0.2 per cent of the total stock of foreign investments in the EU and 1.5 per cent of Taiwan's total outward stock of investments. At the end of 2004, the main recipients of Taiwan's investments were the Czech Republic (US$870 million), Britain (US$483 million), Italy (US$300 million) and the Netherlands (US$196 million). Taiwanese FDI in the new EU member states is concentrated mainly in manufacturing in the electronics and consumer products sectors. In "old" EU countries, the FDI is targeted on R&D centres, logistics, and trade-related facilities.

Educational and cultural exchanges between the EU and Taiwan have been very dynamic since the early 1990s. Attracted by cheaper tuition fees, one-third of Taiwanese students who want to study abroad now go to Europe. In 2004, 10,895 out of 32,525 Taiwanese students looking to study abroad applied for visas to study in the EU (including Switzerland), a large majority in the United Kingdom (9,207), compared with 14,054 applying to the United States. Nevertheless, there has been a significant decrease in the number of Taiwanese students studying abroad since 1999. That year, 16,771 Taiwanese students out of 61,257 applied for a visa to study in the EU, including 13,000 in Britain, compared with 31,043 who applied to the USA.[16] This decrease is due both to the stagnating standard of living in the island-state since the early 2000s and the growing number of Taiwanese students studying in mainland China (estimated at around 2,000, as no exact figures can be provided by the Taiwan government).

Conversely, the number of European students studying in Taiwan remains very small: in 2004, they accounted for less than 10 per cent of the total (940 out of 9,616), just behind the Americans (1,252) but far behind Asians (6,359, including 1,879 Japanese).[17]

Cultural exchanges, although they are hard to quantify, have also developed rapidly since the early 1990s. European cultural events such as exhibitions, concerts and film festivals today constitute a steady feature of Taiwan's cultural life, in particular in Taipei and Kaohsiung. The attraction of European products and way of life has been spurred by these events as well as by the language and cultural activities of the British Council, the Goethe Institut, and the Alliance Française, among others.

Taiwanese cultural activities in Europe have also expanded. Taiwanese movies probably remain the best cultural export, although Chinese movies have now taken over a bigger share of the market. Exhibitions of Chinese art from Taiwan still take place from time to time but, under pressure from the Chen Shui-bian government, Taiwanese representative offices in Europe, as elsewhere, tend to give priority to promoting cultural events that are supposedly typically Taiwanese. For this reason, aboriginal cultural and art events have become more frequent, to the detriment of traditional Chinese performances from Taiwan.

Finally, a growing number of tourist visits have taken place in the last few years between Europe and Taiwan. In 2005, the EU issued 300,000 visas to Taiwanese visitors (+10 per cent over 2004). However, this is still a small proportion of the 8 million Taiwanese who travel abroad every year, including half of them to China, 1 million to Japan and 600,000 to the United States. Conversely, in 2005, around 172,000 Europeans went to Taiwan in 2005 (+4.5 per cent over 2004), 60 per cent on business trips (against 390,000 US citizens).[18]

The political limits to Europe–Taiwan relations: the "one-China policy"

The "one-China policy," today adhered to by all European states (except the Holy See), has placed a crucial limit on the development of more official relations with Taiwan. It is true that there has been a better awareness in Europe of the growing tension in the Taiwan Strait and, indeed, this policy has been complemented by two other principles – the peaceful resolution of the Taiwan issue and the maintenance of the status quo in the Taiwan Strait – that make the policy of both the EU and of its member-states on this question very similar to that of the USA.

On the whole, however, absent any security responsibility in the Asia-Pacific region, Europe is less concerned by the increasing military build-up in the Taiwan Strait and the rapid modernization of the People's Liberation Army. For one thing, Asia is not a foreign policy priority for most European countries. And in Asia, China, identified as one of the three "strategic partners" of the EU (with India and

Japan), is clearly perceived by most EU members as an opportunity more than a threat. In other words, relations with Taiwan have remained a variable directly dependent on the China policy of each country. Moreover, China's growing economic weight and Taiwan's transfer to the mainland of large portions of its production lines, in a context of lingering political and military tension between Beijing and Taipei as well as increasing diplomatic isolation of Taiwan, have played a part in diminishing the EU's interest in Taiwan. While Chen Shui-bian's election in 2000 prolonged Europe's attention to Taiwan's specificity and consolidating democracy, the reluctance of the Taipei government to open direct cargo and passenger air links with China and more generally to face up to and better manage economic integration across the Strait has gradually led this interest to cool. Chen's contested re-election in 2004 and the growing problems of bad governance and corruption that his administration is facing have convinced most European governments to look forward to the next presidential election in 2008 and the probable victory of the new chairman of the Kuomintang (KMT) Party, Ma Ying-jeou.

Recognizing this, some important nuances, and even genuine differences, have emerged in the interpretation of the "one-China" policy among European governments as well as between the EU Commission and the EU Parliament. The various understandings of this policy have evolved over time, affected both by the degree of pressure exerted by Beijing and the individual priorities and worldviews prevalent in the European capitals. While in this respect France has always been a special case in one way or another, Germany and to some extent Britain have witnessed some changes which have underscored the impact of the pressure from both China and the USA on their European partners.

The French connection or the French exception?

France's relations with China and Taiwan have always been perceived as exceptional by all three corners of this triangle.[19] The early recognition of China by France under de Gaulle, its Gaullist approach to world order, and in particular its opposition to any alignment on the United States have, since the 1960s and the beginning of the Sino-Soviet dispute, seduced Beijing. It is true that in the 1970s, Mao's China was disappointed by the lack of firmness exhibited by France (and other European countries) vis-à-vis the Soviet "Polar Bear," but the end of the Cold War re-established a true affinity between China and France focused around the objective of creating a more multipolar world order in which the "hyperpower" (USA) would be better balanced.

Yet, as we have seen, in the years 1989–94, France developed with Taiwan a very close relationship – spurred by a number of large civil and military contracts. Tiananmen played a crucial role in this change but domestic factors in France, such as the 200th anniversary of the French Revolution and the attempt by the French Socialist Party to develop a more human rights-based foreign policy also had an impact on the Paris–Taipei rapprochement. Yet no real strategic vision lay behind this policy. The lack of opportunities for China in the years 1990–1 and the dearth of new markets for the French weapons industry after the end of the Cold War go a long way to explaining the choices made by then President Mitterrand.

Legislative elections in 1993 brought the political right back to power and the foreign policy priority of new Prime Minister Edouard Balladur, strongly pressured by the French business community, was to put an end to the ostracism of France and French companies imposed by the Chinese authorities. In January 2004, France signed a *communiqué* with China in which the former promised "not to authorize any more French companies to participate in the armament of Taiwan" (*bu bizhun Faguo qiye canyu wuzhuang Taiwan*) and, for the first time, recognized that "Taiwan was an integral part of the People's Republic of China" – a commitment that, as we have seen, it had managed to avoid in 1964 when France diplomatically recognized China.[20]

This new accord did not bring to an end the long-term French–Taiwanese military cooperation initiated by the large arms sales approved in 1989–92. The technical section of the French Institute in Taipei continues to supervise the delivery of spare parts and other equipment to the Taiwanese Navy and Air Force as well as the training of Mirage pilots at the Hsinchu air base. Paris has reserved its right to continue to sell defensive weapons to Taipei in moderate quantities, and Beijing has not protested these sales.

However, since 1994 and in particular since the election of Jacques Chirac as president in 1995, France has developed with China a "special relationship" in which Taiwan has been perceived as a troublesome shadow that does not fit with the neo-Gaullist worldview that France has tried to put forward. Yet this has not prevented Paris from concluding deals with Taipei that have sometimes been perceived as sensitive by Beijing (such as the sale of a Matra Marconi observation satellite ROCSAT 2 in 2000). But on the whole, President Chirac has moved closer and closer to China on the Taiwan issue. For instance, in January 2004, when hosting Chinese President Hu Jintao in Paris, Chirac put all the blame for the tension in the Taiwan Strait on the referendum initiative announced by Chen Shuibian in November 2003.[21] And on a visit to China in April 2005, Premier Jean-Pierre Raffarin declared that the "anti-secession law" that the Chinese National People's Congress had adopted a month earlier was "compatible with France's 'one-China' policy" and recognized that the "one country, two systems" formula was the most appropriate for solving the Taiwan issue – ironically at a time when Beijing was showing signs of moving away from Deng Xiaoping's formula. These statements were in direct contradiction to the common policy of the EU on these issues.

More than the "comprehensive partnership" between France and China established by Chirac and Jiang Zemin in May 1997, elevated to a "strategic comprehensive partnership" by Chirac and Hu Jintao in January 2004, it has been the special interest of Paris in promoting a multipolar world in which both France and China would play a more active role that explains these statements.

Trade considerations certainly cannot be totally ignored: Paris is desperately trying to increase its exports to China. But balancing the dominant role played by the United States in the post-Cold War, 9/11 and Iraq War environment has clearly become a priority for Paris. Its attempt and true hope in 2003 to convince its EU partners to lift the arms embargo imposed on China after Tiananmen is a good illustration of this objective (see below). Although the foreign policy implemented by Chirac since George W. Bush's re-election has been aimed at improving France's relations with Washington, Paris's attitude towards Taipei has changed little.

Germany's pro-unification stance

West Germany and then the unified German government after 1990 have had a tendency to apply to the China–Taiwan rift the same approach they developed to pre-unification Germany. This has led a number of German analysts to establish a distinction between the Chinese nation and the two separate Chinese states that constitute this nation and to encourage both Beijing and Taipei to apply this formula – a formula that, as in the Korean case, would not define inter-Chinese relations as international relations, but allows for two internationally recognized governments to peacefully co-exist. Moreover, this view has recently been picked up by Ma Ying-jeou and many "pan-Blue" politicians on Taiwan.[22] And although the German government will not dare implement such an approach as long as the PRC opposes it, there has been an understandable interest in seeing Beijing and Taipei move towards a similar agreement prior to reunification.

The downside of this approach, for Taiwan at least, is that most German politicians are strongly in favour of China's reunification once the conditions are ripe (and the PRC democratizes), and the German authorities have also sometimes given credit to the idea that Taiwan's only option in the future would be to accept a unification solution very similar to Deng Xiaoping's "one country two systems" formula. For instance, when visiting China in December 2003, Chancellor Schroeder not only reasserted that his country would continue not to sell any "sensitive materials" (weapons) to Taiwan, but also compared the division of China to that of Germany before 1990, as if Taiwan had much in common with the now-defunct German Democratic Republic (GDR).[23]

Trade and business considerations also explain such statements. However, as a nation that was also once divided, Germany is instinctively "pro-unification."

China is more demanding

China's more active and demanding EU policy has also had an impact on European governments. In October 2003, the Chinese government published an unprecedented document (*China's EU Policy*) on its relations with the EU, in which it asked the Europeans to fulfil a long list of conditions before they could be considered deserving of a "strategic partnership" with China.[24] Among these conditions, the document states that "it is important" that the EU does not let Taiwanese political personalities participate in any EU activities whatever, does not have any official contacts with Taiwan or sell weapons or dual technologies to the island-state. For the first time, Beijing included in a policy document regarding one region of the world demands that it had made many times to every country (but generally on a bilateral basis).

On the whole, EU countries have abided by these "rules." And China's growing pressure and power have convinced most EU governments that the cost of any quasi-official relations with Taiwan will be too high, in particular at a time when Taiwan cannot offer so much.

Most EU states – such as France, Germany and even to some extent the United Kingdom – have therefore been proactive in preventing Taiwanese leaders from visiting the EU. Thus in the autumn of 2000, although the British government granted a visa to former President Lee Teng-hui, so that he could attend his daughter's graduation in England, it made sure that Lee would not engage in any public activities. And in November 2001, although Wu Shu-jen, Chen Shui-bian's wife, was able to receive the Freedom Prize in Strasbourg (France) in the name of her husband, Chen himself was not able to set foot on European soil, even in transit.[25]

Similarly, the EU and its major member states have been very shy about helping Taiwan join more international organizations. On Taiwan's campaign to enter the World Health Organization (WHO) as an observer, the EU has not taken the side of the US and Japan, but has instead stuck to a very legalistic position, according to which Taiwan, since it is not a state, can only join the WHO as a non-governmental organization (NGO).

Finally, regarding the preservation of the status quo across the Taiwan Strait, although the EU has adopted a policy that is very similar to the one developed by the US and the George W. Bush administration, it does not intend to bear any strategic responsibility regarding the situation in the Strait, and tends to be more critical of initiatives emanating from Taiwan than those coming from China. For instance, led by France, in 2003 most EU member-states initially refused to establish any linkage between the lifting of the arms embargo imposed upon China after Tiananmen and the military tension in the Taiwan Strait, concentrating their discussion on the (lack of) improvement in the human rights situation in this country. And it was more US pressure than the adoption by China of an Anti-Secession Law in March 2005 that sabotaged the EU's intention to abolish this embargo: the latter decision was a convenient excuse to abandon this plan. Moreover, contrary to Washington, the European Commission expressed its concern after Chen Shui-bian decided to abolish the National Unification Council in February 2006, a body that was established before the beginning of democratization (1990) and that was no longer active. Nor do European governments display the same vigilance about the ever-increasing deployments of Chinese missiles targeted at Taiwan, a development that was used by Chen to justify his decision.

The European debate on the status and future of Taiwan and its impact on policy

However, this EU Taiwan policy, based on a negative principle – not inviting any trouble with China whatsoever – is far from consensual. It is difficult to perceive differences within the EU Commission that do not reflect those that exist among EU member-states. In other words, the European Commission's view is the lowest common denominator shared by all member states, and in particular the EU Council of Ministers. The EU cannot go beyond this common policy

However, as far as China and Taiwan are concerned, there are well-known differences between the views of the European Commission and those of the EU Parliament. The latter has regularly adopted resolutions both expressing its concern about China's military build-up across the Strait and its threat to use force, as well as supporting an enhancement of Taiwan's international status. For instance, in 2001 it voted in favour of granting a visa to Chen Shui-bian when he had been barred from entering the EU to receive the prize mentioned above, and in 2002 it passed a resolution asking the EU Commission to support Taiwan's entry into the WHO and the Asia–Europe Meeting (ASEM). That same year, the EU Parliament demanded that China dismantle the increasing number of missiles (around 800 in 2006) it had targeted against Taiwan and recommended to the Commission that it work on opening a dialogue between Beijing and Taipei based on mechanisms designed to prevent regional conflict.

Resolutions adopted by the EU Parliament are generally not taken seriously by the EU Commission or the governments of its member-states, as they are not binding. But at the same time, the accumulation of similar resolutions cannot be totally ignored, because they reflect large segments of European public opinion. Interestingly, both China and Taiwan pay much more attention, and are sometimes even over-sensitive, to these statements because they both feel that they affect the image each country is trying to promote in the EU and may eventually have an impact on policy.

The weakness of the Taiwan lobby in Europe

Lobbying activities conducted by Taiwan in Europe have not been particularly successful. Two main reasons explain this weakness. On the one hand, in contrast to the United States, there has never been a large Taiwanese *émigré* community in Europe around which organizations like the FAPA (Formosan Association for Public Affairs), could be mobilized, and around which pro-independence Taiwanese activists could defend the island's cause (in particular its quest for recognized statehood). On the other hand, since the mid-1990s at least, EU–China economic and political relations have become too important both for its key member-states, which, it should be reminded, are just mid-level powers, and the Union as such to really be decisively influenced by the various facets of Taiwan's lobbying activities.

These lobbying activities are actually concentrated in Taiwan's quasi-diplomatic missions across the continent. Not very present in Europe, Taiwan's business community is not taking an active part in this lobbying effort. This situation may have slightly changed in the last few years after it realized the international importance of EU standards in various branches of industry (e.g. electronics), but it is too early to perceive an organized and regular Taiwanese business lobby in Europe. Sometimes, these activities are complemented by visits made by some Taiwanese politicians (as members of the Legislative Yuan) willing to push the island's agenda on one particular issue (such as the WHO in the last few years). Nevertheless, these trips have not generally yielded any fruit for Taiwan.

In the lobbying developed by Taiwan, the EU Commission has been identified as an important target. The Taipei government therefore has always posted in Brussels a high-ranking diplomat (former Vice-Minister of Foreign Affairs Kao Ying-mao since July 2006) who is empowered to coordinate the activities of the various representative offices operating in the Union. At the EU member-state level, these offices regularly invite local politicians to Taiwan or finance conferences or events concerning Taiwan in the host country, with the financial support of the Taiwan government and, in particular, the Ministry of Foreign Affairs (MOFA)-managed Taiwan Foundation for Democracy, or the Chiang Ching-kuo Foundation. Taiwan's democracy has been indeed since the mid-1990s, and more intensely since 2000, one of the key arguments put forward by Taipei to mobilize support, in Europe in particular, for its various causes.

On the whole, both EU politicians' visits to Taiwan and conferences organized with Taipei's support have been rather useful to Taiwan. The Chiang Ching-kuo Foundation has, for instance, financed the creation of university chairs in Taiwan studies (e.g. at the School of Oriental and African Studies of the University of London) and more academic research has been undertaken in Europe on Taiwan (illustrated by the establishment in 2004 of the European Association for Taiwanese Studies or EATS). On the whole, a better awareness of Taiwan's reality has emerged in Europe. However, how much this better awareness can be translated into changes in the EU's Taiwan policy remains to be seen. Only marginal improvements have been taking place, in particular at the EU level and in member-states already well disposed towards Taiwan.

Various factors, which have much to do with Taiwan itself and its divisions, also explain the frequent failure of these lobbying efforts. In most EU countries, Taipei's representative offices have been too poorly staffed and badly organized to carry out efficient lobbying campaigns. Since Chen Shui-bian's election, Taiwan's representatives, still dominated by pro-Kuomintang MOFA diplomats, have implemented the priorities of their new government in a very bureaucratic way and without any great conviction. For instance, they unenthusiastically organize cultural events aimed at demonstrating that the Taiwanese are not Chinese, artificially emphasizing aboriginal history and culture (see discussion above).

Taiwan's diplomatic missions also focus on reaching out to their potential friends in Europe – in other words easy rather than hard targets. They concentrate on the EU Parliament and the Taiwan friendship groups in national parliaments, which they finance with free visits to Taiwan. But this lobbying is far from fruitful, as parliaments do not usually have much say in foreign policy matters (not in France or even in Germany). Though the Taipei authorities have tried to readjust their lobbying strategy, on the ground not much has changed (for the reasons indicated above).

Since 2005 and the historic visit to China by then KMT Chairman Lien Chan, the EU has been aware of the deep division within the Taiwanese political spectrum. The new understanding between Beijing and the Taiwanese opposition parties has instilled some optimism in Europe about cross-Strait relations post-2008. In the EU today, great expectations arise from the possible election of Ma Ying-jeou as president in 2008, and there is little support remaining, including among Taiwan-leaning politicians, for the administration of Chen Shui-bian.

This new situation of course plays to China's advantage, as it makes it easier for China to manipulate European governments and public opinion about the Taiwan issue and reunification and develop its own lobbying activities which share several common features with Taiwan's (free trips to Beijing). Having said that, China continues to project a more negative image in Europe for reasons unrelated to Taiwan – its booming trade surplus that benefits from a lack of social and environmental protection regulations, its bad human rights record and its growing social unrest triggered by deepening social inequalities. China's military modernization and assertiveness toward Taiwan sometimes influence Europe's perception of China, but clearly this perception has been mainly determined in the last few years by China's economic aggressiveness, its thirst for energy resources and its potential social instability.

This new image tends to weaken the discourse that China pursues concerning unification. After all, Europe, more than any other part of the world, has witnessed a dramatic redrawing of its political map since the end of the Cold War. In 2006, a new nation, Montenegro, was created after it voted democratically for independence. The future of Kosovo is still pending but most observers already agree that it will be hard to avoid independence. Influenced by this environment, Europeans, their governments and the EU cannot agree to a solution to the Taiwan issue that: (1) would be based on the use or threat of force; and (2) is not approved by the majority of Taiwanese society.

Although, for diplomatic reasons, neither the EU nor the United States can really apply a Wilsonian approach to the Taiwan case, both of them agree on these two conditions. Yet, in Europe, probably more so than in America, and in particular in New Europe, there is a political mindset that seems more ready to contemplate democratic Taiwan's de jure independence, in particular as long as China remains authoritarian. Recognizing this, the China and Taiwan policies of the EU will remain dominated by Old Europe and based on an informal agreement among its major powers – Britain, France and Germany – an agreement that will largely continue to take into consideration China's objectives and interests.

Conclusion

In EU–China relations, Taiwan is proving more of an irritant than leverage. And it can be concluded that this irritant has been somewhat better managed in the last few years, both because of the diminishing importance of Taiwan as an economic and political partner and the relative stability across the Taiwan Strait, despite the election of Chen Shui-bian and the clumsy initiatives of both Taipei and Beijing.

The growing political and military tension in the Taiwan Strait following the missile crisis of 1995–6 and the election in Taiwan in 2000 of Chen Shui-bian, an independence-leaning president, have indeed become a subject of concern in

European chancelleries. Nevertheless, with no security responsibility in the Asia-Pacific region, but a primary focus on enhancing China's reforms and its integration into the international community, Brussels and most European capitals have adopted a soft policy towards Beijing on Taiwan – based more on a strict interpretation of the "one-China policy" than on the universality of the principle of the non-use of force. Though differences regarding Taiwan or regarding Beijing's attitude towards Taipei have appeared among EU member states or between EU institutions (e.g. the Commission and the Parliament), Europe's policy has generally been based on the hope that economic and human integration across the Taiwan Strait will gradually solve or marginalize the "Taiwan issue" over time. This has unfortunately led Europe to disregard the impact of nationalism and nation-building processes (both in China and in Taiwan) to a degree, the military build-up and power politics in a part of the world that is religiously attached to a very classical (Westphalian) or "holistic" approach to sovereignty, and one that is very different from the very model of international governance that the EU is trying hard to construct. This European penchant also explains the saga of the non-lifting in 2005 of the EU arms embargo imposed on China after Tiananmen and, more generally, the inability of the EU so far to use Taiwan as leverage over China rather than passively enduring it as an irritant.

Can this situation be changed? If the EU wants to become a major player in international affairs, and especially in Asia, it must take into more serious account all of the factors and passions that determine disputes and tensions. The case of the Taiwan Strait epitomizes to some extent what the EU, because of its own post-modern construction and despite the Balkans crisis, has tended to overlook in international affairs and should again seek to reintegrate into its foreign and security policy.

The EU has vivid experiences of both the disasters that nationalism and war can provoke and the benefits that common political values (democracy and human rights), supranational institutions and economic integration can provide. It is, in other words, equipped with an incomparable toolbox that, if it decided to be more balanced and active on the Taiwan issue, could help both sides narrow their differences, open a political dialogue without preconditions, and build up peace before agreeing upon a final solution, embarking on a unification process that will otherwise remain unacceptable to most Taiwanese for a long time to come (in particular as long as China remains ruled by a one-party system).

Notes

1   In this chapter, China refers to the People's Republic of China while Taiwan refers to the Republic of China.
2   Oskar Weggel, "Die Bundesrepublik und die Volksrepublik China. Die lange Weg zur Normalisierung", in R. Machetzki (ed.), *Deutsch-Chinesiche Beziehungen. Ein Handbuch* (Hamburg: Institute für Asienkunde, 1982), pp. 123–4.
3   François Joyaux, "Le nouveau triangle Paris-Pékin-Taipei", *Politique internationale*, No. 612 (Autumn 1993), p. 50. Harish Kapur, *Distant Neighbours. China and Europe* (London and New York: Pinter Publishers, 1990), pp. 65–8.

4 However, the recognition of the one-China policy was implicit from the very beginning. See, for example, Gunter Schubert, "German Taiwanese Relations Since 1949: A Critical Assessment," in Jean-Pierre Cabestan and Werner Meissner (eds.), "The Role of France and Germany in Sino-European Relations", *East-West Dialogue*, Vol. VI, No. 2 (June 2002), pp. 296–7.

5 Kapur, *Distant Neighbours*, op. cit., pp. 119–20.

6 It was not until 1992 that China's overall foreign trade exceeded that of Taiwan.

7 On the French case, cf. Jean-Pierre Cabestan, "France's Taiwan Policy: A Case of Shopkeeper Diplomacy," in *East-West Dialogue*, op. cit., pp. 267–8; on the German case, see Schubert, in *East-West Dialogue*, op. cit., p. 300.

8 In particular after the US and China agreed in 1982 on a third *communiqué* agreeing to the gradual diminution of US arms sales to Taiwan, provided a peaceful environment was maintained in the Taiwan Strait.

9 Jean-Pierre Cabestan, "France's Taiwan Policy: A Case of Shopkeeper Diplomacy," in *East-West Dialogue*, op. cit., pp. 276–9.

10 Schubert, *East-West Dialogue*, op. cit., pp. 299–300.

11 Personal interviews with Polish and Czech diplomats, 2004.

12 See http://ec.europa.eu/comm/external_relations/taiwan/intro/index.htm. Also see EU External Relations Commissioner Chris Patten's interview by "European Voice," 23 January 2003, http://ec.europa.eu/comm/external_relations/news/patten/ev230103.htm.

13 For instance, in September 1997, the German Economics Minister (and Vice-Chancellor) Gunter Rexrodt visited Taiwan in order to thank Taipei for having initially selected a Franco–Anglo–German consortium to build its high-speed railway. In June 1998, French Junior Minister of Foreign Trade Jacques Dondoux paid a similar visit to Taiwan.

14 Data comes mainly from *EU–Taiwan Trade and Investment Factfile 2006*, European Economic and Trade Office, May 2006 (draft), www.deltwn.ec.europa.eu.

15 There are about 10,000 Europeans living in Taiwan today.

16 *2005 Education in the Republic of China* (Taiwan), p. 53; ROC Ministry of Education website: www.moe.gov.tw In 2005, 11,600 EU visas were issued to Taiwanese students, meaning that over 20,000 Taiwanese students are now studying in Europe, 80 per cent of them in the UK, *EU–Taiwan Trade and Investment Factfile 2006*, op. cit.

17 See www.moe.gov.tw, op. cit.

18 *EU–Taiwan Trade and Investment Factfile 2006*, op. cit.

19 Françoise Mengin, "France's China Policy: From the Myth of a Privileged Relationship to a Normalisation Syndrome," in *East-West Dialogue*, op. cit., pp. 99–125.

20 Reached in late December 1993, this agreement was made public on 12 January 1994. See China, Ministry of Foreign Affairs website at: www.fmprc.gov.cn/chn/wjb/zzjg/xos/gjlb/1842/1843/t23831.htm [28 July 2005]; also see Cabestan, "France's Taiwan Policy: A Shopkeeper Diplomacy," op. cit., pp. 264–91.

21 Chirac described Chen's *revised* (under US pressure following the criticism expressed by President Bush on 9 December 2003) referendum initiative on how to address China's missile threat and open peace negotiations with Beijing as "irresponsible," "aggressive," and "dangerous for everybody."

22 Interview with Ma Ying-jeou, May 2006.

23 Since the normalization of ties with the PRC, Germany has strictly prohibited any export of military technology to Taiwan. See, for example, A. Mertes, "Die deutsch-chinesichen Beziehungen. Zur China-Politik der Regierung Kohl," in *Europa-Archiv* (1983), No. 21, p. 654.

24 See http://dk.chineseembassy.org/eng/zt/PolicyPaper/default.htm.

25 In May 2006, en route to Latin America, Chen Shui-bian's plane clandestinely stopped over in Amsterdam for refuelling, but Chen Shiu-bian himself did not leave the aircraft. The Dutch government was quite unhappy about this *fait accompli* transit.

Part IV
China's approaches to Europe

6 European studies in China

Dai Bingran

"European studies" is a somewhat vague term in China, in the sense that "Europe" could mean different things in different contexts and to different people. For the purpose of this chapter, "European studies" denotes the branch of studies related to the development of the European Union and the accompanying process of integration. With this definition in mind, the chapter will provide some reflections on the development of European studies in China, and then offer an assessment of the current state of the field.

Historical review

European studies are a relatively new scholarly field in China. Four periods might be discerned in its development.

The 1950s and early 1960s

The first period ranged from the 1950s up to the early 1960s, when few openly-published academic studies appeared and orthodox ideological concepts derived from the Soviet Union prevailed in people's thinking about Europe (as in all fields). Immediately after the founding of the People's Republic of China (PRC), China was denied diplomatic recognition and economic ties with most Western countries.[1] Only the Scandinavian countries recognized the PRC. China reacted against this rejection with more or less the same attitude.

Foreign newspapers, journals, books and radio programmes from the West were not accessible to the general public, and almost all information and news reports on Europe that appeared in the Chinese mass media were politically critical. Europe and the EC were little perceived by ordinary people, and to the extent that they had an image of Europe it was far from positive. The standard characterization of the EC during the period was as "the economic arm" of American imperialism in Europe, alongside NATO as its "military arm."

Little public perception did not, however, mean no European studies at all. Closed-circulation and classified studies were done within the Communist Party, government and intelligence organs, but scholars had no access to them. Two important research institutes active in European studies today – the Chinese

Institute of International Studies (CIIS) in Beijing and the Shanghai Institute for International Studies in Shanghai (SIIS) – were both set up during the period (respectively in 1956 and 1960), and began to pioneer research on the "capitalist world." At first, this research benefited only the government, but in the early 1960s it began to circulate among university scholars for the first time.

The early 1960s to early 1970s

The second period of development ran from the early 1960s to early 1970s, when the start of European studies was attempted. The ideological and political clashes between China and the Soviet Union during the early 1960s brought about some re-examination of China's foreign policy in general and towards Europe in particular. A breakthrough came when France, under General Charles de Gaulle, moved to recognize China diplomatically in 1964. It was about that time that a decision at the very top in Beijing was made to start international studies in certain Chinese universities in Beijing and Shanghai. This marked the start of the academic – as distinct from "governmental" – studies of Europe. Beijing University was instructed to concentrate on studies of the developing world, Renmin (People's) University in Beijing was to focus on the "socialist world," while Fudan University in Shaghai was tapped to explore the "capitalist world." Today, Fudan often proudly refers to the fact that it was by direct instruction from Premier Zhou Enlai that an Institute of World Economy (then named the Institute of the Developed Capitalist Economies) was set up in 1964 with the research focus on Western European economies. This development was unfortunately soon interrupted by the breakout of the "Four Clean-ups" Campaign (*Si Qing Yundong*) and then the "Cultural Revolution." Further development had to wait for another ten years.

The early 1970s to late 1990s

The third period began in the early 1970s and extended into the late 1990s, when European studies in China began to be organized nationally and set on a firm basis. The dramatic breakthrough in Sino-American relations and China's return to the United Nations brought it back to the world scene. The sole fact that it subsequently (after Nixon's visit) established or upgraded diplomatic relations with so many countries in so short a period, brought about a boom in international studies in China, which was then gradually recovering from the disastrous Cultural Revolution. In the sphere of European studies, the year 1973 marked an important new beginning, when a group of researchers at Fudan University collectively wrote a book titled *The Western European Common Market*.[2] This was probably the first academic work on the EC produced in China. From the current point of view, the book is only elementary and introductory, but an important feature was that it included Europe in the "intermediate zone" between the two superpowers, reflecting the formulation of Mao Zedong's doctrine of "Three Worlds," which was to be formally announced in 1974.

The establishment of the official relationship between the EC and China in 1975 gave European studies some further impetus. Academics engaged in international studies took it upon themselves to meet the people's curiosity and interests in a new type of regional organization in Europe. In October 1978, the academics active in the field gathered in Shanghai for a national convention, and they founded the Chinese Society for Western European Economic Studies. Economists, political scientists and historians made up its backbone.

The second push came when China embarked upon its path of reform and opening-up under Deng Xiaoping at the end of the 1970s. Looking at the publications on Europe and the EC that appeared in China at that time, observers could find the research focus had begun to shift from "what is the EC about?" to "how does the EC manage to do that?" It was a very challenging analytical task, especially as little information and data resources were then available in China. Foreign journals and books were still luxuries and of limited access. For the latest news, researchers had to depend largely on two indirect sources produced by the Xinhua News Agency: *Cankao Xiaoxi [Reference News]*, a newspaper of abstracts from the international press that had a limited circulation among the public, and *Cankao Ziliao [Reference Materials]*, a journal of Chinese translations of selected articles from the foreign press that circulated to high-level cadres. It was in their quest for first-hand information and data that China's European specialists first came into contact with the European Commission – which led to the setting-up of the first European Documentation Centre (EDC) in China, at Fudan University in 1980.

The 1980s saw the steady development of European studies in China, though not as rapid and widespread as in the fields of American and Japanese studies, and a great number of the current centres laid their foundation at that time. In terms of both the complement of institutions and number of researchers, by far the greater concentration was in Beijing, a lesser one in Shanghai, followed by Wuhan, Chengdu, Tianjin and Nanjing. Two institutional developments of the period worthy of special mention were the announced re-establishment of the China Institute of Contemporary International Relations (CICIR) in 1980 and the founding of the Institute of Western European Studies (IWES) in the Chinese Academy of Social Sciences (CASS) in 1981. 1984 saw a further step forward in the national organization of European studies in China when a national convention was convened in November for the founding of the Chinese Association for Western European Studies. Based in the IWES, it was to become the umbrella organization for more specialized associations like the Chinese Societies for EU, German, French and UK Studies.

In parallel to the institutional development, this period also saw the generation of Europe-related teaching programmes at a number of Chinese universities. European studies did not, however, stand as a discipline on its own, and was incorporated into specialities like world economy, international relations, international trade, international law, etc. A series of research projects were carried out during the period, resulting in the appearance of a number of books, which still remain as classics of European studies in China. Nearly all the research projects were given state funding, and carried out collectively, lasting usually two years and involving a lot of true teamwork – a feature which is unfortunately being lost today.

The late 1990s to the present

The late 1990s ushered in a new period of European studies in China, benchmarked by the implementation of the two EU–China programmes. First, the EU–China Higher Education Cooperation Programme (1998–2001), to which the Commission provided funding of near a million euros (ECU at that time). It was then the largest foreign aid to China's higher education, and its support for research and mobility attracted an ever-larger number of people – faculty and students alike – from more than 50 universities. Institutionally, it helped to increase the number of established European studies centres to 14 nationwide. Second, the current EU–China European Studies Centres Programme (2004–7), to which the Commission increased its investment to over a million euros, has the focus of supporting the 14 existing centres and to start two new ones, with the aim to build up some strong and sustainable teaching and research bases on European studies in China.

The current condition of European studies

After the developments of the past few decades, European studies is now firmly established in China as a full-fledged branch of international studies. It may be still not as popular as American studies, but has certainly risen very rapidly.

For the purpose of this chapter, a survey of the current Chinese literature on European studies was conducted. Internet searches were made of three categories of documentation: books published, postgraduate theses defended, and articles published in journals. The results show that between 1994 and 2005, a total of 1850 articles appeared in some 600 journals, 285 MA, PhD and postdoctoral theses were submitted and defended, and 307 books were published.[3] Table 6.1 gives their disciplinary distributions:

Continued focus on economic and political studies

These data reveal several trends. The figures show that economic and political studies still lead in current European studies in China, making up nearly 70 per cent of the existing literature. This is understandable. European studies in China started with economic studies. But aside from the traditional interests, there are new stimuli. The new impetus comes partly from China's search for a social-economic model suitable for its future development. Though a general consensus

Table 6.1 Disciplinary distributions of Chinese literature on European studies (1994–2005)

	General	Political	Economic	Law	Social	History	Others	Total
Books	46	58	91	59	12	16	25	307
Theses	10	70	117	47	15	11	15	285
Papers	90	484	875	184	68	18	131	1850
Total	146	612	1083	290	95	45	171	2442
Percent	6.0	25.1	44.3	11.9	3.9	1.8	7.0	100

has been reached that there is no ready model to follow, and China has to go on its own way, many seem still inclined to take the European model as a better reference, because the European ideal of balancing between economic development and social equity goes better with the concept of "Socialism with Chinese Characteristics." So there has been a lot of attention paid in China to the European model – its concepts, approaches and limitations.

Increasing efforts have been paid to studying the EU's policy mechanisms, in a quest to find some references for solving some of China's current difficulties in this sphere. EU policy mechanisms under frequent study include the Common Agricultural Policy (CAP),[4] regional policy,[5] merger policy,[6] etc. – but the most studied subject of late is financial integration. Of the twenty-odd books on European monetary integration, the euro and related topics that appeared during the period, there are a few displaying serious research, for example: Ding Yifan (1999),[7] Chen Yawen (2001),[8] Yang Weiguo (2002),[9] all of which look quite deeply into the mechanism of the euro and EMU. Studies on financial market integration touch upon the money market,[10] securities market[11] and insurance market,[12] reflecting current domestic interests and the focus on reform.

Interest in economic studies is further strengthened by the fact that China–EU economic relations saw a tremendous growth during and since the 1990s, and this has prompted studies to assess contemporary events, to suggest ways for their further development, and also to address the actual and potential difficulties. So, in addition to studies which examine China–EU economic relations (for example Yang Fengmin,[13] Qiu Yuanlun and Wang He[14]) in general, quite a number deal with specific bilateral trade issues. A very popular topic is anti-dumping, which is studied both from legal and economic perspectives.[15]

Political studies also reflect a traditional interest. During the Cold War era, Europe was regarded first as a force to be united in the "Three Worlds" doctrine, then as a balancing force against Soviet hegemony. This interest continued after the Cold War ended, as Europe is now looked upon as a potential pole in the future multipolar world order which China favours. The general disappointment expressed in Chinese studies of the CFSP reflects this attitude.[16] In addition to the understandable interest in China–Europe relations, governance at different levels is also increasingly becoming a focus, motivated, perhaps stimulated, by the domestic challenges and reforms in China. Huan Qingzhi[17] and Wu Zhicheng[18] have pioneered this area.

Mention should also be made here of the recent appearance of a few comprehensive works on European integration, among which, Zhou Jianping's *The Political Economy of European Integration*[19] is perhaps the most comprehensive in its coverage – the life-long study of a veteran Chinese Europe expert. Zhang Haibin's *An Institutional Study on European Integration*,[20] on the other hand, is a newcomer's foray into the EU's complicated institutional landscape and innovations. Li Shi'an and Liu Liyun's *History of European Integration*[21] tries to give historical description of the process, while Chen Lemin and Zhou Hong's *The Expansionist History of European Civilization*[22] delves deeply into the cultural origins and dynamics that shaped the Europe of today. It is particularly gratifying to see that several books have tackled the theoretical aspects of European integration, of which Chen Yugang's *State and Superstate: A Comparative Study of European Integration Theories*[23] is widely acclaimed.

Rising interest in law and social studies

Looking at the yearly figures of the European studies surveyed, we find a rising interest in studies of European law and society.

A growing trend for legal studies is apparent in recent years. While there appeared some substantial studies covering the general issues like EU law and legal order,[24] internal market law,[25] competition law,[26] banking law,[27] tax law,[28] environment law[29] and administrative law,[30] quite a large proportion of them take up legal issues related to China–EU trade. A noticeable example is the anti-dumping issue, which accounted for 41 out of the total of 184 articles published on European law during the period.

Studies of European society are also on the rise. This has something to do with the domestic concerns over social reform in China. Both the employment and unemployment issue and the social welfare and security issue are now very much of concern to the Chinese government and public. Similarly, the demands to address pressing infrastructure and energy problems have extended European studies in China into spheres not closely studied before – such as environment, R&D, energy, and public transportation.

Historical studies, however, still lag some way behind. This might be due to the traditional concept of historians in China that, as a post-war phenomenon, European integration should be the object of contemporary studies rather than historical studies.

Table 6.2 Yearly disciplinary distributions of published articles on European studies (1994–2005)

	General	Economics	Politics	Law	History	Society	Other	Total
1994	6	29	21	6	3	1	3	69
1995	5	33	18	1	1	3	9	70
1996	8	45	17	6	0	1	2	79
1997	11	57	20	4	2	2	6	102
1998	3	109	18	13	1	7	6	157
1999	7	135	40	19	2	7	10	220
2000	2	47	35	6	3	5	4	102
2001	11	76	61	25	0	12	16	201
2002	10	84	44	19	1	5	23	186
2003	10	67	48	29	1	9	12	176
2004	9	111	85	32	4	6	25	272
2005	6	83	78	24	0	10	15	216
Total	88	876	485	184	18	68	131	1850
%	4.8	47.4	26.2	9.9	1.0	3.7	7.0	100.0

Europe's growing popularity

European studies is much more popular now than, say, ten years ago. This is, first of all, due to the growing infiltration of the mass media into public life, and, secondly, due to the popularity of China–Europe relations. Nowadays in China, every time you open a newspaper or turn on the TV, you are sure to find some news from Europe. And it is almost certain, whenever something occurs between China and Europe, Europe specialists can expect to get calls from newspapers or television correspondents, asking for comments or interviews.

Our survey shows that some 598 Chinese journals have been engaged in publishing European studies. If each of the journals has a readership of 2,000 on average, it would mean that there would be at least some 1,200,000 people in China knowing something academically about the EU. Of the 1,850 articles published in Chinese journals, the survey counted some 1,283 authors.[31] It is surprising to find that so many people have become involved in European studies and are making efforts to write something, even though many of them were just occasional (as their names appeared just once). There is, however, a sad side to the story – that most of the "professionals" are not very productive: few, including those "old dogs" in the field, contributed more than one article per year.

Strengthened institutional build-up

Chinese institutions engaged in European studies fall into two categories: non-university research institutes and university research centres and institutes. The past decade or so has witnessed some marked improvement and development in both categories.

The first category includes the Institute of European Studies of the China Institute of Contemporary International Relations (CICIR); Institute of European Studies (IES) of the Chinese Academy of Social Sciences (CASS); European research section of the China Institute of International Studies (CIIS); Chinese Academy of International Trade and Economic Cooperation (Department of European Studies); Shanghai Institute for International Studies (SIIS); Institute of World Economy of Shanghai Academy of Social Sciences (SASS); and the Institute of World Economy at the Jiangsu Academy of Social Sciences. These institutions are either affiliated to some government ministries or belong to the academies of social sciences, and therefore are closer to policy-making centrally or locally.

The second category includes the European studies centres in Chinese universities, notably Renmin University, Peking University, and Tsinghua University in Beijing, Fudan University in Shanghai, Nankai University in Tianjin, Jilin University in Changchun, Shandong University in Jinan, Wuhan University in Wuhan, Sichuan University in Chengdu, and Guangdong University of Foreign Studies in Guangzhou. The EU–China Higher Education Cooperation Programme (1998–2001) made a big push to establish each of these centres.

To these should be added a list of centres from other universities, such as East China University of Science and Technology, Shanghai International Studies

University, Tongji University and Jiaotong University in Shanghai, Nanjing University, Zhejiang University in Hangzhou, China Foreign Affairs University, China University of Political Science and Law in Beijing, Jiangxi University of Finance and Economics in Nanchang, Yunnan University in Kunming, Hebei University in Baoding and Xian Jiaotong University. These universities also benefited from the activities of the Programme, and made efforts to establish themselves.

Among these institutes and centres, however, there exist big gaps both in research capability and in institutional development. Out of the total, some twenty could be ranked as well established,[32] in the sense that they have formed within their institutional frameworks a core of strongly motivated people, have developed regular teaching or research programmes, have the financial means to sustain themselves, and have gained a certain degree of recognition both inside and outside of their host institutions. If these twenty or so established centres and institutes can all achieve a certain degree of sustainability, European studies in China will see continuous development. This was the logic when the current EU–China European Studies Centres Programme (2004–7) was first designed.

A changed environment

The physical conditions for European studies have also improved greatly in China. When European studies got started in the 1970s, the most difficult thing was to obtain data and information resources, and in the 1980s scholars all felt hard-pressed to finance research projects, especially when it came to publication of the results. Things changed in the late 1990s. For many centres and institutes the biggest challenge and constraint is shortage of trained research staff. There is also fierce competition to get funding from international, national, ministerial and local research funds. Here the quality of human resources becomes decisive: you have to do better to become better off. To get and keep bright and promising young people is not easy. People are now quite free to choose their career, and the allure of the private sector is strong. So, when it is possible that a top MA graduate from Fudan University is able to get a higher paid job than a full professor, he or she needs a very, very strong mind and heart to resist the temptation and to choose to spend some twenty hard years to climb to a professorship.

Another dilemma is that good research needs good teamwork, but this tradition is getting lost in the new environment where salary, promotion and recognition depend more on individual excellence.

Improved quality

To attempt an assessment of the quality of European studies in China, we might have to first ask the question "why should European studies exist in China?" First, a big country with increasingly global interests like China has to know the real situation in Europe. This serves the purpose of helping policy-making both domestically and internationally. European studies in China have made great progress towards fulfilling both purposes.

In the first instance, there have been a series of basic introductory works published, which have provided Chinese readers with all the essentials concerning the EU and European integration. There have also been a series of annual reports published: the *Europe Yearbook* published by the Institute of European Studies of CASS since 1997, which reports on Europe's yearly developments, while featuring one or two themes every year; and the *EU Economic Development Report* published by the Centre for European Studies at Fudan University since 2004, which reports on the EU's annual economic developments in general and in different sectors. Among the well-established journals,[33] there are two that stand out: *European Studies* (*Ouzhou Yanjiu*), a bi-monthly edited by the IES since 1983, is the most important one in the field; *European Integration Studies* is a bi-monthly edited jointly by the Chinese Society for EU Studies (CSEUS) and the Centre for European Studies of Fudan University (it remains an "internal" journal not for open circulation or subscription) published since 1977.

At the current stage, European studies in China are capable of closely following events taking place in Europe and forming independent judgments on these new developments. Chinese scholars are also now capable of articulating their views quite confidently in international conferences without feeling amateurish any longer. It is true that European studies in China could not compete with those in Europe, especially in the depth of the studies, but a transition from the "macro" level to the "micro" level is taking place in matters that closely concern China.

To serve domestic needs has always been what the individuals engaged in European Studies are asked for and are committed to. So while Chinese scholars are doing European studies they have always kept one eye on domestic developments in China – and hence, to some extent, select research topics of potential use domestically. So the learning is now more purposeful and selective. The past two surges in European studies – around the Internal Market in the late 1980s and around the euro in the late 1990s – were oriented towards finding out the possible impact on China. At the moment, European studies in China focus on issues like trade, intellectual property, social security and welfare, CFSP and enlargement. They, too, are all closely linked to either domestic reform or Chinese foreign policy.

Ever conscious of its mission of serving Chinese reforms, it is still difficult to make an assessment of the actual impact of European studies on China's decision-making and foreign policy towards Europe and the EU. The influences are there, to be sure, but they are mostly indirect. First of all, almost all important Chinese government policy-making organs have their own think tanks of some sort,[34] some of which could range up to a staff of several hundred and carry the name of an academy or institute, and some of which are small, having just one or two persons in the role of adviser or consultant. Researchers there form policy suggestions, based either on their own research or on data and analyses they gathered from others' studies. For example, in shaping foreign policy, the Foreign Ministry not only has support from its own research institute (CIIS), but also from the embassies stationed abroad, many of which have established their own research units. Thus endowed, policy-making organs have little need to delegate or commission external studies. Some research institutes do often write and submit *Nei Can* [internal reference] reports to government bodies, but there is no telling whether their suggestions are actually accepted. Except for the few very privileged, an ordinary academic could only guess if he has influenced policy, but could hardly prove it.

Things are beginning to change, however. In formulating China's *EU Policy Paper* of 13 October 2003,[36] the Foreign Ministry held several consultation meetings with European specialists in Beijing. And on the occasion of EU enlargement, the Department of European Affairs of the Foreign Ministry organized a special seminar with the participation of specialists from Beijing and Shanghai. Research institutions affiliated with or linked to policy-making organs are now quite active in organizing and participating conferences of all sorts. But in spite of these changes, the impact of European studies on China's policy-making, and on business decisions, will be largely indirect. Its main impact remains on the shaping of public opinion through its teaching programmes and through its increased publicity.

Private consulting to business is still virgin soil to European studies in China. There are constraints both on the demand and supply sides. The big firms either have their own research capabilities, or could afford to contract consultants from professional agencies, preferably from the well-established foreign consulting companies. There have been cases of large companies commissioning some external researches,[35] but these are rare. Small and medium-sized firms might be the market, but at present most of them neither have the habit, nor have the means, to look for business consulting from research institutions. On the supply side, the current knowledge structure, research facilities and institutional capabilities of the existing institutions of European studies are far from being adequate to provide such service.

Conclusion

After some thirty years, we should feel happy about the development of European studies in China. There now is a stable cadre of researchers and scholars devoted to European studies, combining old and young, the field is much better organized, tolerably equipped, and financially supported. This should be able to ensure a fair degree of sustainability for the field, and there is no reason to be pessimistic for the future, as demand is pretty strong at the moment and will probably be getting stronger in years to come, and the demand will generate the supply.

It is true that the field is not yet able to meet the mounting demand both in quantity and quality, but it has done what it could. There is, however, still the question of defining the mission of European studies. Understandably, there should be specialists to solve questions like how Chinese shoe exports to Europe could avoid EU's anti-dumping sanction – but the fundamental mission of European studies in China lies in basic studies.

From that comes the third question of how European studies in China can serve the country's basic interests more effectively. The point here is to mobilize sufficient resources into some fundamental studies of vital importance. European scholars in China have pushed that on three occasions: the first time in the late 1980s when the Internal Market project went into full swing; the second time in the late 1990s when the euro was being introduced; and the third time now that enlargement has become a reality. Because of their scale and multi-disciplinary nature, studies like these could hardly be tackled by a single institution, and need national cooperation. Here, improved national organization would mean better quality and economy of scale.

Finally, while efforts have been made to introduce new theoretical approaches into Chinese European studies, greater attention to methodological analyses of such approaches are still too sorely needed. We hope our young European scholars will one day form a Chinese approach or even a "Chinese school of European studies."

Notes

1 During the 1950s, of the six original member states of the EC, only the Netherlands had diplomatic relations with China at the level of *chargé d'affaires*.
2 Institute of Capitalist Economies, *Xi-Ou Gongtong Shichang* [Western European Common Market] (Shanghai: Shanghai Renmin Chubanshe, 1973).
3 The file is in Chinese only. Anyone interested, please refer to the CES (Fudan) webpage at http://www.cesfd.org.cn, where a revised version will be posted.
4 Zhao Changwen, Nigel Swain: *Oumeng Gongtong Nongyezhengce Yanjiu* [Studies on EU's Common Agricultural Policy] (Beijing: City Press, 2002).
5 Li Tiande: *Oumeng Quyuezhengce jiqi Xiaoying Yanjiu* [Studies on EU's Regional Policy and Its Effects] (Chengdu: Sichuan University Press, 2003).
6 Yin Xingmin: *Oumeng Qiyehebingzhengce Yanjiu* [Studies on EU's Enterprise Merger Policy] (Shanghai: Fudan Univerity Press, 2003).
7 Ding Yifan: *Ouyuan Shidai* [The Euro Era] (Beijing: Chinese Economic Publishing House, 1999).
8 Chen Yawen, Lin Donghai: *Ouyuan Xulun* [On the Euro Continued] (Beijing: Financial Press of China, 2001).
9 Yang Weiguo: *Ouyuan Shengcheng Lilun* [Euro's Formation Theory] (Beijing: Chinese Social Science Press, 2002).
10 Zhang Jikang: *Huobishichang Jingji* [Money Market Economics] (Shanghai: Fudan University Press, 2004).
11 Qi Zhaozhou: *Oumeng Zhengjuanshichang Yitihua* [EU's Securities Market Integration] (Wuhan: Wuhan University Press, 2002).
12 Liu Wei: *Oumeng Baoxianshichang Yitihua Yanjiu* [Studies on EU's Insurance Market Integration] (Bejing: Finance Press, 2004).
13 Yang Fengmin: *Oumeng Zhongguo Jingmao Zhengce* [EU's Economic and Trade Policy Towards China] (Shanghai: ECUST Press, 2000).
14 Qiu Yuanlun, Wang He: *Oumeng Changqi Duihua Zhengce yu Zhongguo Jingmaoguanxi* [EU's Long-term China Policy and China–EU Economic and Trade Relations] (Beijing: Social Sciences Press, 2000).
15 Deng Dexiong: *Oumeng Fanqingxiao de Falu yu Shijian* [EU's Anti-Dumping: Law and Practice] (Beijing: Social Sciences Press, 2004).

16 Chen Zhimin, Gustaaf Geeraerts: *Ouzhou Lianmeng Duiwaizhengce Yitihua: Bukeneng de Shimin?* [Foreign Policy Integration in the European Union: A Mission Impossible?] (Bejing: Shishi Publication House, 2003).

17 Huan Qingzhi: *Duozhongzhili Shijiao xia de Ouzhoulianmeng Zhengzhi* [EU Politics in the Perspectives of Multi-Level Governance] (Jinan: Shandong University Press, 2002).

18 Wu Zhicheng: *Zhili Chuangxin: Ouzhou Zhili de Lishi, Lilun yu Shijian* [Governance Innovation: The History, Theory and Practice of European Governance] (Tianjin: Tianjin People's Publication House, 2003).

19 Zhou Jianping: *Ouzhouyitihua Zhengzhijingxue* [The Political Economy of European Integration] (Shanghai: Fudan University Press, 2002).

20 Zhang Haibin: *Ouzhou Yitihua Zhidu Yanji* [An Institutional Study on European Integration] (Shanghai: SASS Press, 2005).

21 Li Shi'an, Liu Liyun: *Ouzhouyitihua Lishi* [History of European Integration] (Shijiazhuang: Hebei People's Publication House, 2003).

22 Chen Lemin, Zhou Hong: *Ouzhou Wenmin Kuodazhangshi* [The Expansion History of European Civilization] (Beijing: Orient Press, 1999).

23 Chen Yugang: *Guojia yu Chaoguojia* [State and Superstate: A Comparative Study of European Integration Theories] (Shanghai: Shanghai People's Publication House, 2001).

24 A notable example is: Shao Jingchun: *Ouzhoulianmeng de Falu yu Zhidu* [EU's Law and Legal System] (Beijing: People's Court Press, 1999).

25 Mi Jian: *Ouzhou Danyishichang Falu Zhidu* [The Legal System of the European Single Market] (Beijing: Chinese Encyclopedia Press, 1994).

26 Ruan Fangmin: *Oumeng Jingzheng Fa* [EU's Competition Law] (Beijing: Law Press, 2000).

27 Li Renzhen (ed.): *Oumeng Yinhangfa Yanjiu* [Studies on EU Banking Law] (Wuhan: Wuhan University Press, 2002).

28 Zhu Hongren: *Oumeng Suifa Daolun* [Introduction to EU Tax Law] (Beijing: Taxation Press, 2004).

29 Cai Shouqiu: *Oumeng Huanjingfa Yanjiu* [Studies on EU Environment Law] (Wuhan: Wuhan University Press, 2002).

30 Zhu Shuzheng: *Oumeng Jingjixingzhengfa Tonglun* [General Introduction to EU Economic Administrative Law] (Shanghai: Orient Press, 2000).

31 Only the first author is counted if there are more than one, and collective authors are not included either.

32 A list of them with a brief profile of each is to be found in the Appendix of this chapter.

33 See the list of selected journals of European studies.

34 See David Shambaugh, "China's International Relations Think Tanks: Evolving Structure and Process," *The China Quarterly*, No. 171 (2002).

35 The CES of Fudan University had got one from the local branch of the Coca-Cola company and another from a local automobile company.

36 It is the first policy document the Chinese Foreign Ministry ever issued towards a region or a country. For the text, see: http://www.fmprc.gov.cn/eng/wjb/zzjg/xos/dqzzywt/27708.htm.

37 There are a number of provincial academies of social sciences, but they belong to the provinces, and are not in subordinate relations with CASS; none of them can compete with CASS in scale.

Appendix 1
Major Chinese institutions engaged in European studies

I. Research institutes

China Institute of Contemporary International Relations (CICIR), Institute of European Studies

The CICIR was officially established in 1980, and is the largest research institute in China specializing in international studies. In 2003, it was reorganized into a research academy, consisting of seven research institutes, three research offices and ten research centres, engaging a research staff of more than 380, including some 150 senior research fellows (equivalent to university professors), and endowed with research, teaching and publication capabilities. It has a full-scale research institute – the Institute of European Studies – specializing in European studies. It publishes a bi-monthly journal *Contemporary International Relations*, which is one of the most important Chinese journals for European studies and international studies more generally.

Address:
A-2, Wanshousi
Haidian District
Beijing 100081
Tel: (86-10-) 6841 8640
Fax: (86-10-) 6841 8641
Webpage: http://www.cicir.ac.cn

Chinese Academy of Social Sciences (CASS), Institute of European Studies (IES)

Founded in 1980, CASS is the largest Chinese conglomeration of research institutes of social sciences in China.[37] Among its 35 research institutes, there is the Institute of European Studies. The Institute's importance comes not only because it is the most comprehensive in its coverage of Europe, but also because it hosts the national academic association – the Chinese Association for European Studies – and is, therefore, the institutional epicentre of the field. Its former Directors, such as Xu Dashen, Li Zong, Chen Lemin and Qiu Yuanlun, all contributed to the development of European studies in China. Its bi-monthly journal, *European Studies*, is also the most important one in this field.

Address:
5, Jianguomennei Dajie
Beijing 100732
Tel: (86-10-) 8519 5740
Fax: (86-10-) 6512 5818
Email: ies@cass.org.cn
Webpage: http://ies.cass.cn/

China Institute of International Studies (CIIS)

The CIIS was established in 1956, and is one the first to begin international studies in China. The Institute has a research office on European studies with research fellows experienced in diplomatic careers. Affiliated with the Foreign Ministry, the Institute is closer to foreign policy-making than most other institutes. The bi-monthly *International Studies* edited by the Institute is also among the leading Chinese journals, which publishes quite a number of papers on European studies each year.

Address:
China Institute of International Studies
No.3, Toutiao
Taijichang
Beijing 100005
Webpage: http://www.ciis.org.cn

Chinese Academy of International Trade and Economic Cooperation (CAITEC)

The Chinese Academy of International Trade and Economic Cooperation is affiliated with the Ministry of Commerce. Originating from a research institute on international trade set up in 1984, it reorganized twice in 1997 and 2002 into the present Academy. The Academy includes a Department of European Studies, which specializes in trade issues and economic relations with EU and other Western European countries and most of its research fellows have had the experience of working in the commercial section of the Chinese embassies in Europe. Its monthly *International Trade* is the most prestigious Chinese journal on international trade, and often contains studies on China–Europe trade issues.

Address:
Chinese Academy of International Trade and Economic Cooperation
28, Donghou Xiang
Andingmenwai
Beijing 100710
Tel: (86-10-) 6421 6661-1120
Fax: (86-10-) 6421 2175
Webpage: http://www.caitec.org.cn

Shanghai Institute for International Studies (SIIS)

Founded in 1960, SIIS could be regarded as the equivalent of the CIIS in Beijing. It is located in Shanghai, but has traditionally been very close to the Foreign Ministry, and has an important national and international reputation for its wide range of international studies, including European studies. In its yearbook *Survey of International Affairs*, one can find features on important international events of the year. It also edits and publishes *World Outlook* twice a month, which is good for informative reading. It also publishes an informal journal *International Review* in English three times a year with articles from its research fellows.

Address:
Shanghai Institute for International Studies
No.1, Lane 845, Julu Road
Shanghai 200040
Tel: (86-21-) 5403 1148
Fax: (86-21-) 5403 0272
Webpage: http://www.siis.org.cn/

Shanghai Academy of Social Sciences (SASS), Institute of World Economy

Founded in 1958, SASS is the oldest academy of its kind in China. With 17 research institutes grouped under it, it is second only to CASS in scale. Founded in 1978, the Institute specializes in world economic studies, and ranks very high in stature. The Institute hosts a Centre for European Studies, which was founded in the late 1990s by Prof. Wu Yikang, one of the pioneers of European studies in China, and the current Chairman of the Chinese Society for EU Studies (CSEUS). The Institute edits a bi-monthly, *World Economic Studies*, where a lot of articles on European studies are published.

Address:
622-7, Huaihai Zhonglu
Shanghai 200020
Tel: (86-21-) 53063814
Fax: (86-21-) 5306 3814
Webpage: http://www.sass.org.cn/sjyjs/index.jsp

Jiangsu Academy of Social Sciences, Institute of World Economy

The history of the Institute can be traced back to 1980, and started European studies rather early. Prof. Cheng Jiming, its former Director, is a veteran of European studies in China. The bi-monthly it edits, *Forum of World Economics and Politics*, is an important journal, where you can often find studies on European subjects.

Address:
12, Huju Beilu
Nanjing 210013
Tel: (86-25-) 8339 1504
Fax: (86-25-) 8371 9177
Webpage: http://www.jsass.com.cn/suo/shi1.htm

II. University centres

Renmin University of China (RUC) Centre for European Studies (CESRUC)

RUC is the Chinese university specializing in the social sciences. The Centre originated in 1994 as an "EC Information and Research Centre," and was reorganized into a university Centre in 1996. Built on RUC's strong studies on international politics and relations, the Centre saw rapid development in recent years, and in 2000 became the Ministry of Education's key research base of European studies. Prof. Song Xinning holds a Jen Monnet Chair in European Studies, and the Centre got the title of Jean Monnet European Studies Centre of Excellence in 2005.

Address:
59, Zhongguancun Dajie
Haidian
Beijing 100872
Tel: (86-10-) 6251 2824
Fax: (86-10-) 6251 1232
Email: cesruc@cesruc.org
Webpage: http://www.cesruc.org/

Peking University (PKU), Centre for European Studies (CES)

PKU has not had a long research background on Europe, so the Centre is relatively new. Founded in 1996 in preparation for the implementation of the EU–China Higher Education Cooperation Programme (1998–2001), it rose rapidly in recent years to become one of the leading European studies centres in China. The Centre is strong in law, political science and history studies.

Address:
5407, Law Building
Peking University
Beijing 100871
Tel: (86-10-) 6275 5367
Fax: (86-10-) 6275 5367
Email: eucenter@pku.edu.cn
Webpage: http://www.pku.edu.cn/academic/euc/

Jilin University, European Studies Centre

Jilin University is the largest university in China and Asia. On European studies, the Centre started with law studies, but has of late launched into economic studies as well, based on the strong economic specialization of the School of Economics.

Address:

2699, Qianjin Dajie
Changchun 130012
Tel: (86-431-) 516 6142
Fax: (86-431-) 516 8396
Email: duli18@mail.jlu.edu.cn
Webpage: http://www.jlu.edu.cn/

Nankai University, Centre for European Studies

Nankai University started its European studies in 1975 with a research project on the Common Agricultural Policy (CAP), and has been active since, especially in economic studies. The Centre was formally launched in 1997 to adopt an interdisciplinary structure, incorporating economic, political, social and history studies.
Address:
94, Weijin Road
Tianjin 300071
Tel: (86-22-) 2350 9676
Fax: (86-22-) 2350 9676
Email: eu_center@nankai.edu.cn
Website: http://www.nankai.edu.cn/-N

Shandong University, Centre for European Studies

Shandong University has had a quite long history, and is very famous for its studies on literature, history and philosophy. The Centre was formally started in 1996 in preparation for the implementation of the EU–China Higher Education Cooperation Programme. Led by a veteran political scientist, Prof. Hu Jin, the Centre upholds its tradition for political studies, and has also launched into law, social and economic studies as well.
Address:
27, Shanda Nanlu
Jinan 250100
Tel: (86-531-) 836 4984
Fax: (86-531-) 837 0407
Email: iessdu@sdu.edu.cn
Website: http://www.sdu.edu.cn/

Fudan University, Centre for European Studies

Fudan is the earliest Chinese university to start European studies, which published the first Chinese book on the EC (*Western European Common Market*) in 1973. The Centre was formally launched in 1993 on the basis of an EC research office in existence since 1978. Used to focus on economic studies, the Centre became multi-disciplinary through the reorganization in 1996, balanced between economic, political, social and law studies. On the basis of a Jean Monnet Chair in Economics (2001), it became the Jean Monnet European Studies Centre of Excellence in 2004. It has been hosting the Chinese Society for EU Studies (CSEUS) – the Chinese academic association specializing in European integration studies – since its founding in 1984. Its regular publications include the bi-monthly internal journal *European Integration Studies*, started in 1977, and the yearbook *EU Economic Development Reports*, started in 2005.

Address:
220, Handan Road
Shanghai 200433
Tel: (86-21-) 6564 2668
Fax: (86-21-) 6564 6456
Email: ces@fudan.edu.cn
Website: http://www.cesfd.org.cn

East China Normal University, Centre for European Studies

The Centre was founded in 1997 based on the Centre for Asian European Studies. The Centre is multidisciplinary, but more focused on the studies of political science and international relations, big power relations in particular. Its current Director, Prof. Feng Shaolei, is one of the leading experts on Russian studies.

Address:
3663, Zhongshan Beilu
Shanghai 200062
Tel: (86-21-) 6223 2110
Fax: (86-21-) 6223 2113
Email: saias@126.com
Website: http://www.ecnu.edu.cn/Addr

Wuhan University, European Studies Centre

Wuhan University was also among the earliest to start European studies. The Centre was formally founded in 1996, and excels both in economic and law studies. Its former Director, Prof. Zeng Lingliang, holds a Jean Monnet Chair in law, and its current Director, Prof. Zhou Maorong, is an expert in the EU economy. *Law Review*, edited by the University's Law School, has a column on EU law.

Address:
Wuhan University
Wuchang
Wuhan 430027
Tel: (86-27-) 6875 4377
Fax: (86-27-) 6875 4745
Email: wucentre@whu.edu.cn
Website: http://www.whu.edu.cn/

Sichuan University, Centre for European Studies

Sichuan University began European studies in the 1980s when a European Documentation Centre (EDC) was established in 1985. The Centre was launched in 1996, and it now incorporates economic, cultural and historical studies.

Address:
29, Wangjiang Lu
Chengdu 610064
Tel: (86-28-) 8541 1806
Fax: (86-28-) 8541 2400
E-mail: escentre@scu.edu.cn
Website: http://www.escscu.org/

Guangdong University of Foreign Studies (GDUFS), Centre for European Studies

The Centre was founded in 1997, and has now five research offices for studies on the EU's economy and trade, law and foreign relations, culture, management and education.

Address:
No.2, North Baiyan Ave.
Guangzhou 510420
Tel: (86-20-) 3620 7055
Fax: (86-20-) 3620 7367
Email: jszhu@mail.gdufs.edu.cn
Website: http://www.gdufs.edu.cn

China University of Political Sciences and Law (CUPL), Research Centre of European Law

The Centre was created in 2002 to focus on teaching and research on European law.

Address:
25, West Tucheng Road
Haidian
Beijing 100088
Tel: (86 -10-) 6227 9614
Fax: (86 -10-) 6227 9614
Email: rcel2005@126.com
Website: http://www.rcel.cupl.edu.cn

III. National and regional associations

Chinese Association for European Studies (CAES)

CAES was founded in 1984, but its origin can be traced back to the Chinese Society for Western European Economic Studies founded in Shanghai in 1979. CAES is the national umbrella association for European studies in China, consisting of several Research Committees – called "Societies" – for national and regional studies, such as the Chinese Societies for EU, German, French and UK Studies. In 2006, it was reorganized by setting up four new Research Committees: Chinese Societies for European Integration History Studies, for EU Law Studies, for European Economic Studies, and for European Political Studies. CAES stays with the Institute of European Studies, and with its Director as President. The Secretary General takes charge of its daily management.

Address:
5, Jianguomennei Dajie
Beijing 100732
Tel: (86-10-) 8519 5740
Fax: (86-10-) 6512 5818
Email: ies@cass.org.cn
Webpage: http://ies.cass.cn/

Chinese Society for EU Studies (CSEUS)

Founded in 1984, CSEUS is a research committee of the CAES, specializing in EU and European integration studies. CSEUS is housed at Fudan University. It organizes a symposium every two years since 1986, edits and publishes a journal *European Integration Studies*, and organizes other activities, including support to research projects. It is a member of the world-wide EU studies association, the ECSA-World, and the Asia-Pacific regional ECSA, the EUSA-Asia Pacific.

Address:
Centre for European Studies
Fudan University
220, Handan Road
Shanghai 200433
Tel: (86-21-) 6564 2668
Fax: (86-21-) 6564 6456
Email: brdai@fudan.edu.cn
Website: http://www.cseus.org

Shanghai Institute for European Studies (SIES)

SIES is a local association for European studies in the Shanghai region. It was founded in 1998 on the initiative of European scholars in the region. Its members come from universities, research institutes and other public and private bodies. It organizes seminars, conferences, researches and other activities, and edits an electronic newsletter, *European Observer*.

Address:
125-3, Caoxi Beilu
Shanghai 200233
Tel/Fax: (86-21-) 6428 6409
Email: siessh@online.sh.cn

Appendix 2
Leading Chinese journals of European studies

Contemporary international relations
Bi-monthly
1981
China Institutes of Contemporary International Relations

European Integration Studies
Bi-monthly (internal)
1977
Centre for European Studies, Fudan University

European Studies
Bi-monthly
1983
Institute of European Studies, CASS

Forum of World Economics and Politics
Bi-monthly
Institute of World Economy, JASS

International Studies
Bi-monthly
1959
China Institute of International Studies

International Trade
Monthly
Chinese Academy of International Trade and Economic Cooperation

Law Review
Bi-monthly
1980
School of Law, Wuhan University

Outlook Weekly
Weekly
1981
Xinhua News Agency

World Affairs
Bi-weekly since 1934
World Affairs Press

World Economic Forum
Bi-monthly
1957
School of Economics, Fudan University

World Economic Studies
Bi-monthly
1979
Institute of World Economy, SASS

World Economy
Monthly
1978
Institute of World Economy, CASS

World Economy and Politics
Monthly
1979
Institute of World Economy, CASS

World Outlook
Bi-weekly
1987
Shanghai Institute for International Studies

7 China eyes Europe in the world

Real convergence or cognitive dissonance?

David Shambaugh

Much, if not all, Western scholarship on China–Europe relations examines the relationship from the European perspective. Drawing on the various policy "Communications" issued by the European Commission, Western analysts have been able to assess the EU's strategy for assisting in China's reforms and domestic development, dealing with a rising China, integrating the People's Republic into international institutions, and engaging China on a wide range of functional issues in pursuit of cooperative global governance. The website of the European Union's Delegation in China is also filled with data about EU programmes in China and diplomatic interactions between the two sides.[1] Individual European member state governments also publish a good deal of data on their bilateral relationships, and various European think tanks occasionally issue reports assessing the state of and issues in the relationship. However, a close reading of all of these documents, data, and studies reveals, inevitably, a strong Eurocentric bias. Very little, if anything, is written about *China's* strategy for dealing with Europe, understanding of European integration, estimate of the EU's role in world affairs, assessment of bilateral and multilateral relations with the EU and its member states, perspectives on Europe's strategies for dealing with Beijing, Chinese perceptions of Europe, and so on.[2]

To date, European Sinologists have failed to tap into Chinese publications and conduct interviews with China's "Europe Watchers" and officials responsible for European affairs, in order to illuminate the other side of the perceptual dyad. While many Chinese analysts write on these subjects, little of this material has been translated (in China or in Europe) into European languages. There is, in fact, a good case to make for establishing a systematic translation project – either within the EU or jointly between a European and Chinese institution.[3] While the websites of China's Mission to the European Union,[4] and China's Foreign Ministry,[5] include English updates of events and official policy statements in the China–EU relationship (and bilateral relations with member states), these are not analytical assessments per se. The chapters by Chinese contributors to this volume help to illuminate the Chinese perspective for Western readers, but much more needs to be done to explore the Chinese side of the relationship.

This chapter offers one (albeit American) assessment of the internal Chinese discourse on Europe and its role in world affairs. It focuses on analyses by China's

Europe Watchers working in research institutes and universities, and by some officials. It draws upon Chinese publications since 2001, although primarily during 2003–6. The analysis is divided into three main sections: China's perceptions of Europe's role in world affairs and the EU as an international actor; Chinese perceptions of China–Europe relations; and China's perceptions of the EU–US–China "triangle" and other geopolitical groupings. It then concludes with some general observations on what these analyses reveal about Chinese understanding of European affairs.

Europe's role in the world

Chinese views (official and individual) of Europe's role in the world do not exist independently. Rather, they are largely derivative from broader Chinese understandings of, and preferences for, the global system and order. That is, Chinese officials and international affairs commentators hold certain, rather uniform, views of the macro trends in the world *and* certain preferences for the evolution of the international order. As a result, their analyses of Europe's roles and actions are somewhat derivative from these broader beliefs and they thus frequently have a *cognitively dissonant* character. Cognitive dissonance, is, in essence, the natural proclivity to selectively look for confirmation of one's pre-existing beliefs and to reject evidence that contradicts these beliefs.

Many studies of the role of perceptions and misperceptions in international relations have confirmed this propensity first discovered by Leon Festinger.[6] In the case of Chinese–American mutual perceptions, beginning with Harold Isaacs' classic study in 1958,[7] numerous subsequent studies have also identified a "love–hate" dualism in mutual Sino-American images – which reflects the cognitive dissonance in both cultures.

In the case of Chinese perceptions of Europe's role in world affairs, the evidence presented in this chapter suggests that no such dualism exists, yet one *does* see cognitive dissonance at work. Many Chinese observations about Europe's role in the world derive from broader Chinese hopes for developing an international order based on non-hegemony, dispersion of power and regional multipolarity, political equanimity, cultural diversity, and economic interdependence.

There is also a remarkable homogeneity, uniformity, and conformity in Chinese perceptions of Europe and Sino-European relations. While a spectrum of views are evident on these and other issues, the respective ends of the spectrum are not very broad and the differences of viewpoint are more nuanced than distinctive. In surveying Chinese writings about Europe for this study, I looked for identifiable schools of opinion – but none were readily apparent (unlike among China's America Watchers[8]).

There also remains a strong propensity (which Michael Yahuda's chapter reminds us is long-standing) to view Europe as a unitary actor in the international arena. While some authors note the difficulties of forging consensus within the expanded EU system, others note the differences between "new" and "old" Europe following eastward expansion, and yet others note the differences between the Franco-German partnership vis-à-vis other member states – but, overall, there is still a strong propensity to view the EU as a single unitary entity acting with common purpose on the international stage. As the Chinese Foreign Ministry *EU Policy Paper* succinctly put it in 2003: "The European Union is a major force in the world … The EU is now a strong and the most integrated community in the world … the European integration process is irreversible and the EU will play an increasingly important role in both regional and international affairs."[9] To be sure, Americans often have the same proclivity to see Europe as a unitary actor, but in the American case the mistake is to take British views or the policies of the "Big Three" (UK, France, Germany) as representative of all of Europe. Chinese, unlike Americans, put much more stock in the "EU" (i.e. Brussels) as an actor – although this frequently results in neglecting the interplay and influence of member states. Indeed, with respect to China, it has been Brussels (in the form of the European Commission and Council) that has forged a common strategy and set of policies toward Beijing;[10] but Chinese commentators tend to see the EU's leadership as extending into all realms of international relations. As Song Xinning's chapter illustrates, there has been strong Chinese interest in the EU and the process of European integration,[11] but there is surprisingly little written on China's bilateral relations with individual European states.

Many Chinese commentators see Europe as symbolizing the "trends of the times" and many features of international relations today, and they see a coincidence of Chinese and European perspectives and positions. In brief, China pursues policies to promote:[12]

- multipolarity;
- sovereignty and non-interference in internal affairs;
- economic globalization;
- global governance and global institutions (with the UN at the centre);
- democratization of international relations;
- diversification of cultures, values, social systems, and political systems;
- peace, stability, and sustainable development;
- establishing a new international political and economic order;
- establishing a rational international financial and trade system;
- the Five Principles of Peaceful Coexistence (FPPC);
- a "New Security Concept" based on the FPPC.

China's Europe Watchers invariably look for – and find – overlap between these Chinese policy priorities and those of the EU.

Multipolarism, multilateralism, and globalization

In terms of multipolarity, Chinese analysts note both quantitative and qualitative indicators. For example, in the 2006 annual survey of comprehensive international power (CIP) conducted by the Institute of World Economics and Politics of the Chinese Academy of Social Sciences, Chinese analysts rank the UK 2nd, France

4th, and Germany 5th internationally (the United States ranked 1st, Russia 3rd, and China 6th) in terms of comprehensive national power (*zonghe guoli* or CNP). Although they oddly do not rank the EU collectively, if they had it is likely to have scored first in the CNP rankings. These rankings include nine separate indicators of power, which collectively comprise a CNP ranking: technological power; individual power capital (*renli ziben*); capital power (*ziben li*); information power (*xinxi li*); natural resources; military power; GDP; foreign policy power (*waijiao li*); and government dynamism (*zhengfu tiaokong li*).[13]

Qualitatively, Chinese analysts judge the EU to be acting with greater independence on the world stage across a range of issues, and in their judgment: independence (from the United States) = multipolarity. Chinese analysts are in common agreement that it is an explicit European priority to become an "independent pole in world affairs" and that it is becoming one. Wang Weiguang of the PLA's China Institute for International Strategic Studies (CIISS) claims that, "Aiming to become an independent pole in a future multipolar world, the EU has launched a vigorous omni-directional diplomatic drive."[14] In a comprehensive assessment of China's Europe policy, the China Institute of Contemporary International Relations (CICIR) claimed that, "Most [EU] member states cherish the hope of their club evolving into an independent 'pole' in the world ... [and] the EU is taking shape as an ever stronger unique political force in international life."[15] Cai Fangbai, China's former ambassador to France, argues that, "In external relations, the EU endorses global multipolarization and advocates multilateralism in responding to challenges that the world faces. The goal of the EU is to become the dominant force in Europe and sit as equals at the same table with the United States."[16] Some Chinese scholars explicitly equate Europe's role as an emerging pole as a means to "countering hegemony."[17]

Chinese analysts also recognize that the EU is a strong advocate and practitioner of multilateralism.[18] Some see this European priority as having grown out of Europe's "post-modern" foreign policy orientation,[19] and the neo-liberal school of international relations. In one analyst's view, Europe's acceptance of neo-liberalism is based on its acceptance of interdependence as the central feature of international relations, which, in turns, mandates a policy of regional integration and international cooperation – all in stark contrast to the "realist" perspective on international relations, which emphasizes state sovereignty and balance of power.[20] Contemporary globalization has intensified interdependence, making the EU recognize the need for intra-regional, inter-regional, and international institutions and "effective multilateralism," in the view of Qiu Yuanlun, a noted CASS Europe Institute researcher.[21] The neo-liberal worldview leads Europeans, Qiu argues, to also adopt different strategies in security policy: "Europeans look to economic cooperation, civil society, and conflict-resolution multilateral organizations instead of military intervention; the EU thus believes that mutual dependence is the best means to assure mutual security."[22]

Many other Chinese analysts have looked to the EU's Common Foreign and Security Policy (CFSP) as further evidence of neo-liberalism and a growing coherence in European foreign policy, although some have noted the difficulties of actually coordinating and compromising among so many states.[23] In fact, Fudan University Europe specialist Chen Zhimin co-authored a whole book describing in considerable detail the EU foreign policy process and the various structural and systemic impediments to formulating and implementing a coherent CFSP.[24] But Feng Zhongping, Director of the Europe Institute of the China Institute of Contemporary International Relations (CICIR) and one of China's leading Europe specialists, observed that in the wake of the defeated constitutional referendum in 2005 the EU's pursuit of political coherence on the world stage and implementation of CFSP has actually become a *higher priority* for the EU.[25] Although the referendum was defeated in France and the Netherlands, Feng notes that this is one feature of the proposed European Constitution that has endured the ratification setbacks in France and Holland.[26] In a separate analysis, Feng actually questions whether the EU qualifies as a "pole," noting: "In China, many people think that the EU is a 'pole' in the world, but in the US or in Europe itself, many people do not agree with this view."[27] Feng criticizes many Chinese for having overly generalized ideas of what constitutes a "pole," noting that the EU lacks the "hard power" normally associated with the term – but he tries to make the case that the EU's "soft power" and its global economic clout should warrant use of the concept, even if the EU is an "incomplete or unbalanced pole."[28]

Many Chinese commentators also focus on the cooperative aspects of CFSP,[29] and find considerable congruence with China's Five Principles of Peaceful Coexistence. Mei Zhaorong, a former ambassador to Germany and ex-president of the Chinese People's Institute of Foreign Affairs (CPIFA), asserts that, "Both sides stand for the establishment of a just and rational new international political and economic order, advocate multilateralism and democratization of international relations, oppose unilateralism and militarism, are committed to resolving international disputes through diplomatic and political means, and hope to strengthen the authority of the UN."[30] Other analysts believe than China and the EU have common ground in furthering economic globalization but countering political globalization (i.e. US political and cultural hegemony).[31] While sharing commonalities in countering political globalization, some Chinese Europe Watchers argue that the Chinese economy is, in many ways, more open that Europe's and that European protectionism (particularly in countries like France, Spain, and Italy) restricts its international competitiveness.[32]

Other European priorities

How do Chinese analysts view other EU global priorities? Some argue that the EU's priorities are almost entirely close to home. One CASS Europe Institute analyst ranks EU priorities: "The EU's No. 1 priority is still Europe itself – the development and strengthening of the EU, followed by a focus on Central/Eastern Europe and Russia. Subsequently, the EU is concerned about its neighbours in the Balkans and Mediterranean. After these, the EU looks at Asia (including China, Latin America, and America."[33] Other analysts believe that the EU has more diversified interests and priorities. Wang Weigang of CIISS argues that diplomatically the EU has three priorities: trying to bring about a better balance among the big powers, becoming an active participant in the settlement of regional hot-spot issues (like the North Korean and Iranian nuclear issues), and strengthening ties with the developing world.[34] Feng Zhongping of CICIR believes there are four priorities in its "omni-directional foreign policy": consolidating control over the ten new member states (post-2005 enlargement); stabilizing the Balkans; expanding ties with the Middle East and North Africa; and managing relations with the United States, Russia, China, India, and other Asian countries.[35]

Eastern enlargement

Eastern enlargement of the EU in 2004 attracted substantial attention from China's Europe Watchers. In May 2004 the Chinese Association of European Studies convened a conference of over forty Europe experts in Nanjing (several contributors to this volume participated). They discussed the various motivations for, and consequences of, enlargement (*kuoda*). A variety of viewpoints were expressed.[36] Some argued that the expansion made for more efficient allocation of economic resources and common European prosperity, while others noted the relative underdevelopment of the Central European economies – predicting that they would be perennial drags on West European economies. Others argued that the "strong states" (Germany and France in particular) would go out of their way to assist the "weak states." Some argued that eastward expansion provided a model worthy of study in other regions, including East Asia. Some argued that expansion married together two different, but competitive, rationales: the West European states sought to enhance their security, while the Central European states only viewed EU membership as a means to economic growth. Others disagreed with this perspective, arguing that Central European states also had a strong security motivation for joining the EU (and NATO), given their long experience with Soviet (and previously German) domination. Other participants saw enlargement through the prism of a "political vacuum" that had been left in Central Europe since the collapse of communist party-states there and in the former Soviet Union. Apparently none of the participants voiced the view that enlargement fitted into a broader Euro–American geopolitical competition in Central Europe and Eurasia.

This became a prevalent argument in subsequent analyses. Ding Yuanhong, China's former ambassador to the EU, argued in a prominent article that there was an "intense scramble for [strategic] influence [between the EU and United States] in the Central and East European countries … The 'two eastward expansions' are only one aspect of the sharpening contradictions between the US and Europe in competing for leadership over European affairs after the end of the Cold War."[37] Ambassador Ding also put forward an argument echoed by many Chinese analysts (and we shall examine it at greater length below) that the United States was trying to slow and arrest the expansion of the EU because Washington thought it better able to control these states bilaterally and via NATO.[38] Ambassador Ding assessed that, "After the Bush administration took office, the US more explicitly regarded the EU as a competitive rival to its hegemonic status. This is diametrically opposed to the strategic policy of the EU, with France and Germany at the core, to shake off the US shackle and become an 'equal partner' of the US through its internal and external expansion ... The US has now unveiled its scheme of 'divide and rule' towards the EU."[39] Ambassador Ding is not alone in this geopolitical viewpoint, as it is echoed by many other of China's Europe Watchers and strategic analysts.

Another lengthy assessment by CICIR examined the implications of eastern enlargement for China's interests.[40] The report took a balanced view of all the multiple motivations and implications of enlargement noted above, but it also focused on specific policy options for China. It argued that after a sour period of relations in the 1990s, when a number of former communist countries in Eastern Europe were critical of China because of the Tibet, Taiwan, and human rights issues, that new possibilities were opening for expansion of ties and that China needed to be *proactive* in strengthening the relationships. The report noted that this would not be easy because, economically, trade levels were still extremely modest, there were not a lot of economic complementarities between China and these countries, they lacked capital to invest in China, they lacked understanding of the China market, and they blocked visas for Chinese businessmen to visit Central Europe. Politically, it noted that many of these post-communist government still viewed the CCP and Chinese government with suspicion, criticized China's human rights record, and some (particularly the Czech Republic) still harboured certain sympathies for Taiwan and Tibet. But, it argued, China should proactively try to overcome these barriers and "educate" these societies via a combination of high-level visits, exchanges between political parties and the CCP, youth organizations, parliamentary exchanges, and youth exchanges.

China–Europe relations

Chinese views of Sino-European relations can be considered in several distinct areas: overall assessments of the relationship; analyses of the "strategic partnership" with the EU as a whole; and problem areas in the relationship.

Overall ties seen to be excellent

Since the early 1990s, Chinese analyses of the relationship are overwhelmingly positive. The 30th anniversary (in 2005) of the establishment of formal diplomatic relations between the People's Republic of China and the EU (then European Economic Community) occasioned even more effusive appraisals of the state of relations.[41] "Currently, Sino-EU relations are in the best period in history," proclaimed two analysts.[42] This anniversary coincided with the 40th anniversary of the establishment of Sino-French diplomatic relations, which also occasioned some laudatory articles.[43]

These articles discussed the twists and turns in relations over the previous decades, but were unanimous in their positive appraisal of present ties. Specific credit for improving ties was paid to the EU's Asia and China strategies, as elaborated in the policy papers of the European Commission in 1994, 1995, 1996, 1998,

2001, 2003, and 2006. The strategic decision to engage China comprehensively was the result, in the view of former Ambassador Mei Zhaorong, of the EU's recognition of the bankruptcy of the previous policies of "peaceful evolution" and "pressure tactics" – which had been practised in the wake of 1989: "The leadership of the West European countries found that, instead of collapsing under pressure, China enjoyed rapid economic growth, internal stability, enhanced national cohesion, and elevated international status. Facing the hard reality, the West European countries, proceeding from their own interests, had to readjust their China policy and resume normal relations with China step by step."[44]

Many of the commemorative articles discussed the depth and breadth of relations – detailing the annual summits, high-level visits, dialogue and consultations mechanisms, trade and investment figures, science and technology exchanges, cultural and educational exchanges, and so on. All were optimistic about the potential for future development of ties. In addition to the alleged commonalities on questions of multipolarism and multilateralism (discussed above), Chinese analysts listed a number of factors that distinguish Sino-European relations from China's relations with, for example, the United States or Japan. As Ambassador Mei put it:

> China and Europe do not have direct conflicts of interests in terms of geopolitics and strategic objectives, so neither side constitutes a threat to the other. After the return of Hong Kong and Macao to the motherland through peaceful negotiation, there no longer exist any disputes left over by history between China and Europe. All EU member states adhere to the 'One China' policy. They have few worries and suspicions about China's growing strength and consider China's development as an opportunity for Europe. China views the EU's expansion and deepening with an attitude and respect, considering the EU as a positive factor for world peace and stability.

Vice Foreign Minister Zhang Yesui, who has responsibility of European Affairs, argued the same thing (virtually word-for-word) in the pages of the CCP journal *Qiushi* (*Seeking Truth*).[45]

Other Europe Watchers believe that Sino-European relations are flourishing because of certain mutual interests and complementarities in the relationship. For example, Zhou Hong, Director of the Institute of European Studies at the Chinese Academy of Social Sciences (and co-editor of this volume), sees a number of complementarities that have driven the two sides together:[46]

- China's and the EU's economic reforms and similar mixed (socialist market) economies;
- China's and the EU's economic opportunities;
- China's Open Door policy and the EU's policies of enlargement and integration;
- a desire to learn about each other, as manifested in cultural and educational exchanges;

- mutual beliefs about social equality;
- China's FFPC and the EU's CFSP;
- a desire to promote "cooperation and development" and foster permanent world peace;
- mutual efforts to resolve troublesome global 'hot spots';
- mutual efforts to promote multipolarism;
- mutual support for building an international order based on international law and institutions, particularly the United Nations;
- deepening bilateral ties.

Many analysts were quite optimistic about the continued development of ties, particularly the development of the so-called "strategic partnership."

The strategic partnership

In 2003 the PRC and EU proclaimed a "comprehensive strategic partnership" (*zonghe zhanlue huoban guanxi*). China's Europe Watchers see this proclamation as the expression of the coincident world views of the two sides noted above, as well as the manifestation of the EU's strategic re-examination of China in the mid-1990s.[47] It also fits in well with the series of strategic partnerships China has forged with more than twenty other nations.

China's Europe Watchers identify different bases for the strategic partnership. Some see it as an outgrowth of the fact that in Europe there are no advocates of either the "China Threat Theory" (*Zhongguo weixie lun*) or the "China Collapse Theory" (*Zhongguo bengkui lun*).[48] One analyst tallied up five component parts of the China–EU relationship – economic, strategic, political, extensiveness, and Europe's "supportive and forgiving" nature – and judged that the designation was warranted simply because of its comprehensive nature.[49] Zhou Hong of CASS more soberly pointed to the "symmetries and asymmetries" between the two sides, arguing that in terms of "economic society, political systems, and historical cultures" the two sides were much more different than similar (asymmetrical), but that the two sides' "mutual understandings" and tangible cooperation on global and bilateral issues (symmetries) justified the term despite the differences between the two sides.[50] Some Europe Watchers in the People's Liberation Army argue that the term "strategic partnership" is appropriate because of the growing cooperation between the EU and China in counterterrorism, fighting organized crime, and illegal immigration; high-level defence consultations; working-level military exchanges; joint naval exercises and ship visits; and controlling regional "hot spots".[51] Other civilian analysts argue that because the relationship is global in nature, the two sides have a basis of common interests, and both are dedicated to building a "more balanced and pluralistic New World Order," the moniker is appropriate.[52] One aspect of the global nature of the relationship is in the economic sphere, where one analyst argued that the two sides were critical to upholding the global economic institutional order.[53] Communist Party international relations theorist Zheng Bijian, not surprisingly, sees the partnership as supportive of China's road to "peaceful development."[54]

Thus there exist a variety of rationales articulated among Chinese analysts to justify the "comprehensive strategic partnership." Many Chinese analysts are optimistic about the prospects for the partnership.

Problem areas

While China's Europe Watchers are generally positive and optimistic in their assessments of the relationship, some do discuss problem areas and are critical of Europe. These areas are all aspects in which the EU is either critical of China or holds back something that China seeks. In not a single instance do Chinese commentators blame the Chinese side for any difficulties. Chinese analysts distinguish between problem issues in relations and areas in which there is room for improvement.

The first problem area discussed is European criticisms of China's human and religious rights record. While recognizing that EU member states stopped condemning China in the UN Human Rights Commission 1998, ending "human rights diplomacy" (*renquan waijiao*), they are still sensitive to criticism by individual governments, NGOs, the media, and parliaments. Some Europe Watchers see these concerns as part of a long-standing European desire to "Westernize China" (*Xi Hua*), and transform it into a bourgeois republic via "peaceful evolution."[55] Some Europe Watchers claim that European criticisms derive from the fact that, "Europeans have a historically formed sense of superiority, an attribute of the [concept of] European centralism."[56] Other analysts, however, explore the origins of European criticisms of human rights in terms of differing value systems, political systems, history and culture, and conclude that because of the differences that the two sides should "agree to disagree."[57]

Another Chinese complaint is the fact that Europe has, to date, refused to extend "Market Economy Status" (MES) to China, which would have the effect of radically reducing anti-dumping penalties on Chinese exporters. As Zhang Zuqian's chapter in this volume illustrates, Chinese complaints centre around the discrimination China feels because the EU has granted such status to Russia, arguably a less marketized economy than China, and the fact that other countries and regional groupings (such as ASEAN and MERCURSOR) have granted MES to China. Some analysts, however, have done detailed studies of what China needs to do to qualify for MES.[58]

A third problem area for China is the continuing arms embargo. This too China finds discriminatory, given that it lumps China together with Myanmar, Sudan, and Zimbabwe (all states against which the EU maintains a similar embargo). Many articles complain that it is a vestige of the "Cold War mentality" and the political pressure that the United States has put on the EU to maintain the embargo. Some Europe Watchers have demonstrated a very nuanced sense of the dynamics inside the European Union and between the EU and United States concerning the lifting of the embargo, the adoption of a strengthened "Code of Conduct," the issue of dual-use technology transfer regulations, and other complex aspects of the embargo issue.[59] Other analysts, like Huo Zhengde of the China Institute of International Studies, think that the arms embargo issue is a real litmus test for the EU on four key levels: "The final results of lifting the arms sales ban will test (a) the quality of the China–EU strategic partnership; (b) the EU's independence of the United States; (c) the EU's stance on a potential crisis across the Taiwan Strait; and (d) on the US strategic position and roles in the Asia-Pacific region."[60] At the end of the day, Huo predicts that the EU will adopt a "dual policy" of lifting the arms embargo but simultaneously tightening control of weapons exports to China, "thus replacing the 'tangible' discrimination by an 'intangible' one."[61] Removing the arms ban will open the door to real strategic cooperation, Huo opines, but he also concludes that, "In the foreseeable future, it is impossible that the EU will export its most advanced weapons and technologies to China without restraint. China still has a long way to go to become a country that can import the EU's military products 'normally'."[62]

While never criticizing China for any policy mistakes or behaviour in the relationship, some Chinese Europe Watchers do offer suggestions for steps that China could take, or take in tandem with the EU, to improve relations. In 2001, analysts at the China Institute of Contemporary International Relations called for China to develop a "long-term Europe strategy," rather than relying on ad hoc, disconnected, and reactive policies.[63] The CICIR team called on the Chinese Government to publish its own EU strategy paper, to parallel those published by the EU. Indeed, this recommendation materialized in the Foreign Ministry's 2003 publication *China's EU Policy Paper.*[64] The CICIR team went further to suggest seven specific areas for joint initiatives:[65]

- In the economic area, China should: pay greater attention to small and medium-sized European companies; focus more on service trades such as finance, banking, and accounting; improve the climate for European investment in skill-intensive industries; enlarge exports of agricultural products; and anticipate the impact of eastern enlargement on China's economic interests.
- In the political arena, China should more broadly engage the EU on issues of global governance, UN reform, multilateralism and "democratization of international relations."
- Both sides should increase communication and cooperation in Eurasian affairs – particularly by combating illegal immigration, transnational crime, drug trafficking, and money laundering – and involve Russia in such activities where appropriate.
- China should make a "positive response" to the 60 "action points" contained in the EU's 2001 China policy paper, and task government departments to follow through on each.
- Both sides should jointly defend cultural diversity in the world, and exchange more bilateral cultural delegations to improve mutual understanding of European and Chinese culture.

- Both sides should maintain a "positive dialogue policy" with respect to human rights.
- Both sides should improve non-governmental exchanges – particularly media, sports, and research institute exchanges.

Such openly-published policy recommendations are unusual in China. But they are constructive and welcome, and, in retrospect, seem to have been listened to and actioned by the government. In 2003, on the eve of enlargement, CICIR published a similar set of recommendations concerning China's relations with Central and Eastern European states (noted above).[66] It is a remarkably detailed, well researched, and frank assessment of the situation in these states – including the fact that, owing to their experiences with communism and the Soviet Union, they are not innately well-disposed towards China. The CICIR report reads like a Chinese equivalent of a US National Intelligence Estimate (NIE). Indeed, as CICIR is China's main civilian intelligence analysis agency, the published report is likely a sanitized version of an internal report to the government. The report concludes with a number of recommendations for expanding economic ties, recognizing that there are relatively limited opportunities for trade and investment. Politically, it recommends an acceleration of high-level visits; the establishment of a dialogue forum along the lines of the China–ASEAN and China–Africa forums; parliamentary and party-to-party exchanges. In the cultural sphere, it suggests stepping up media, university, and research institute exchanges. However, the report notes the influence that Taiwan has established in a number of the Balkan and East European states, and that China should be wary of such contacts. The report acknowledges the differences in the area of human rights and Tibet, with the substantial East European sympathy for both causes, but suggests that these differences can be "overcome through dialogue." Finally, it notes the problem of Chinese immigration into these countries and it acknowledges that China's lax exit formalities have contributed to the outflow of criminal elements and workers who have flooded into the region.[67]

CICIR has also published a fascinating volume on *European Think Tanks and Their Research on China*.[68] This publication parallels similar volumes CICIR has published in recent years on American and Russian China specialists. It systematically catalogues all of the main (and many minor) research institutes, universities, foundations, and individual specialists who work on Chinese affairs and Europe–China relations. It reveals a remarkable grasp of the China field in Europe – far better, I would submit, than Europeans have of European studies in China. Not only does the volume include institutional profiles and individual professional biographies, but also comprehensive lists of publications, websites, financial supporters, linkages to foreign organizations, and so on. There is also extensive analysis of the substantive views expressed by Europe's China Watchers and the ways that such institutions and individuals influence European China policy. All in all, this volume (like its US and Russia counterparts) represents a remarkable open source intelligence collection effort.

Other Europe Watchers have also offered suggestions for improving ties. Professor Dai Bingran, Director of the Institute of European Studies at Fudan University (and contributor to this volume), argues that China needs to improve its image in Europe, develop people-to-people diplomacy, and accelerate "forward looking research."[69] Others, such as China's former ambassador to France, suggest that Beijing still has a lot to learn about how Brussels functions and that multi-level exchanges with all institutions of the European Union are needed, particularly vis-à-vis the European Parliament.[70]

The Sino-European-American triangle

A final area of substantial interest and research among China's Europeanists concerns relations among the EU, China, and the United States. Chinese analysts of international affairs have long been drawn to geopolitical analysis, usually involving triangles, and around 2002 they began to write about the emergence of a new Sino-European-American triangle.

The overall basis for the emergence of such a "triangle," according to Chinese analysts, is twofold: (1) tensions in the transatlantic relationship between the US and Europe; (2) the rapid development of China–Europe relations. Chinese analysts suggest that each has its own independent causes, but the consequence is that a greater symmetry in relations has developed and, as such, an interdependent triangle has formed. In the words of (retired) PLA Deputy Chief of General Staff Xiong Guangkai, "Personally, I think that China, the United States, and Europe are the most influential power centres of the world now. Their interactions will play an important role in international relations and the world's strategic architecture …. Generally speaking, the trilateral relations between China, the United States, and Europe are not balanced, but they are interactive."[71]

We have already examined in this chapter Chinese analyses of the Sino-European leg of this triangle, but what do China's Europe Watchers think the causes of transatlantic frictions have been and what are their consequences for the triangle? According to Chinese analysts, there have been five principal sources that have contributed to US–European tensions.

The first cause is said to have been the end of the Soviet Union and Cold War. According to China's former ambassador to the EU, "… the basis of the US–Europe alliance is nonexistent with the Soviet disintegration, dramatic changes in Eastern Europe, and the declining power of Russia."[72] Other analysts echoed the (mistaken) view that the transatlantic relationship and NATO alliance was a feature, and now a relic, of the Cold War. Such analysis totally fails to take account of the historical, cultural, ethnic, and political foundation of transatlantic relations. It also fails to take account of broader mutual security interests shared in common by the US and Europe.

A second cause was the consequences of 9/11. While Chinese analysts recognized the sympathy expressed by Europeans for Americans in the aftermath of the tragic events of that day, they are quick to point out that Europeans began to part ways with the way that the Bush administration defined the "war on terror" thereafter. The iteration of the "axis of evil" by President Bush in his 2002 State of the Union address was said to be the beginning of the end of transatlantic solidarity.[73]

Third, the invasion and occupation of Iraq. One did not have to be a Europe or America expert to see the frictions that emerged in the run-up to and aftermath of the US-led invasion of Iraq, but Chinese analysts were quick to study and understand the implications of the fissures caused by the decision to invade. They studiously assessed those countries that stood with and against the United States, recognizing the depth of the fracture within the EU and across the Atlantic. Some, however, argued that the disagreements ran so deep as to possibly permanently fracture the EU as an institution, NATO, and the transatlantic relationship.[74] Such predictions not only failed to materialize, but also were wrong in the basis for their judgment. Again, they failed to take account of the depth of historical, cultural, and political ties within Europe and with the United States. Another example of cognitive dissonance. While such analyses overstated the likely outcome of the rift, they correctly tapped into the depth of resentment in Europe towards the United States and its actions.[75]

One reason that Chinese analysts were perhaps too quick to jump to this conclusion is because of the fourth reason cited for transatlantic differences, i.e. the supposed long-standing European desire to be "independent" of the United States. Countless Europe Watchers make this assertion. This conclusion may again reflect poor judgment on the part of Chinese analysts – no doubt reflecting their own national desire for independence from power politics, domination, and hegemony. This is a classic example of cognitive dissonance, where Chinese analysts project on to Europeans their own desires for sovereignty and world order. To be sure, there are Europeans and even European governments who seek greater autonomy from the US, but not to the degree posited by many Chinese analysts.

Chinese analysts were particularly quick to point to the EU desire to create a separate 60,000-man rapid reaction military force, a 5,000-man police force, and a separate command structure outside NATO, as evidence of such European desires for independence. The European goal, some of these analyses posit, is ultimate and complete disintegration of NATO, "because of the necessity for Europe to gradually make its own independent security policy and build up its own defense capabilities so as to throw off piecemeal the American strings and obtain the leading right over European security affairs."[76] Another analyst argues that "NATO has been an unequal and unstandardized alliance since its formation ... The US wants burden sharing, while Europe wants power sharing. In practice, Europe is working towards its own independent defense."[77] This observer, a Europe Watcher at Shanghai's East China Normal University, also emphasizes the tensions over defence technology sharing between the US and its EU allies. Other analysts from a Chinese military think tank, the Center for International Strategic Studies, also point to the transatlantic tensions that have arisen over the eastern enlargement of NATO or the generally pro-American orientation of the Central European countries.[78]

The fifth reason Chinese analysts cite for transatlantic tensions is more epistemological, having to do with the respective *Weltanschauung* (worldview) of the two sides. In a fascinating analysis, contributors to the *2003–4 Europe Yearbook* (a biannual assessment compiled by the CASS Europe Institute) contrasted the "European Model" vs. the "American Model."[79] This comparison contrasts differences in the economic, political, strategic, and social "cultures" of Europe and the United States, and is extremely insightful. Available space unfortunately does not permit extensive quotations from this analysis, but the authors see Europeans as:

- more rational and less ideological, moralistic, or religious;
- more cultured and less shallow;
- more complex and less simplistic;
- more respectful of diversity and better integrated ethnically;
- more tolerant and less intrusive in other nations' affairs;
- more conscious of the collective society rather than individual freedoms;
- more socially tolerant;
- more diverse in media content;
- more multilateral and opposed to unilateralism in diplomacy;
- more accustomed to negotiation and peaceful resolution of differences;
- more accustomed to international law and institutions.

These and other insightful contrasts were offered by the CASS analysts. De Tocqueville could hardly have said it better. These cultural differences lay at the root of the transatlantic political differences, according to the CASS team.

Such differing worldviews also account for differences in their respective China policies, according to some analysts. The European approach to China is not only based on cooperation but is premised on helping China succeed in its internal reforms, while the United States is more confrontational, distrustful, and worried about the growth in China's external power and influence.[80]

The future of the triangle

If these are the principal sources of division between the EU and United States, in the eyes of China's Europe Watchers, how do they see the future evolution of the transatlantic relationship and the China–Europe–US triangle?

First, most Chinese analysts believe that transatlantic tensions will persist, for the reasons cited above. Some argue that there may be temporary and tactical ameliorations, but that the underlying dynamics will remain unchanged.[81] The main source of tension will continue to be: "The US policy of fostering divisions among European countries and restricting the role of Europe in international affairs ... while Europe, on the other hand, is not content with its position as subordinate to the US."[82] The US attempt to build links to the new Central European members and use them to "divide and rule" (the EU) is also judged to continue.[83] Disputes over defence and NATO are also predicted to deepen. Thus the fundamental tension is said to be between American (attempted) control and European (sought) independence.

Meanwhile, the China–Europe relationship is judged by most analysts to have developed its own strengths and independence. This is said to be another source of concern to Washington, which several analysts believe the United States will try to restrict.[84] Some Chinese observers, however, are not so sure about Europe and its intentions towards China. Huo Zhengde of the China Institute of International Studies, the Foreign Ministry's think tank, believes that Europe still exhibits hostile intent towards China:

> It has not yet given up its attempt to 'Westernize' and 'disintegrate' China. The documents on its China policy issued over the years all show that in the name of supporting China's reform and opening up and 'transforming China into an open society based on respect for democracy and the rule of law,' the EU promotes China to accept Western ideology … In the China–EU relationship, conflicts in ideology and values still remain. We should always bear in mind its attempt to 'Westernize' and 'disintegrate' China, and work out our counter-measures.[85]

Zheng also views the filing of 100+ anti-dumping cases against China, as well as MES and the arms embargo, as further evidence of the EU's hostile intent towards China.

Despite Huo's pessimism, his view is not shared by other analysts (at least in print), and the vast majority of China's Europe Watchers remain very optimistic about the future of the Sino-European leg of the triangle – even if they are more pessimistic in their assessments of US–Europe relations.

Conclusion

This chapter has examined a broad range of writings by China's Europe Watchers and some Chinese government officials in an effort to explore the domestic discourse in China about Europe's role in the world. Zhu Liqun's chapter complements this one nicely by examining Chinese students' and scholars' perceptions of Europe, while Song Xinning's and Ruan Zongze's chapters are themselves examples of such perceptions. Together, they offer an up-to-date sample of one segment of Chinese views of Europe and the EU. Several conclusions and observations emerge from the analysis in this chapter.

First and foremost, China's Europe Watchers are quite well informed about European affairs and the CFSP of the EU. Europe's China specialists also know a great deal about Chinese affairs (as Kjeld Erik Brødsgaard's chapter indicates), but the breadth and depth of Chinese research and understanding of Europe is truly impressive – perhaps even greater than vice versa. This is even more true when one considers (and Dai Bingran's chapter illustrates) that European studies in China only began 25 years ago and developed in earnest over the past decade. The input of the European Union Delegation to China, with funding from the European

Commission, has been instrumental in developing European studies in China during this period. As is evident throughout the field of international relations and area studies in China today, analysis of European affairs is straightforward, detailed, non-ideological, informed, and based on primary European sources. To the extent that such analyses reflect the quality of advice being given by the Europe specialists to the Chinese government (and it does), one can assume that China's Europe policy is well informed.

Second, a substantial majority of the analyses we have examined are very optimistic about the current state and future development of Sino-European relations. While some disputes persist (MES, arms embargo, human rights, dumping), and one should not dismiss them as unimportant, there do not appear to be any overwhelmingly negative issues clouding the development of relations – either subjectively or objectively. China clearly places much hope in its relationship with Europe – bilaterally, multilaterally, and in terms of building a better global order.

Third, while positive in their assessments, it is also evident that there is a fair amount of wishful thinking and cognitive dissonance in Chinese assessments of Europe's role in world affairs. That is, the Chinese government and international affairs research community are clear in their own mind about the kind of world order they seek to build, and Chinese analysts are quick to identify other nations and groups of states that share some or all of China's priorities, but in so doing they often are too quick to identify apparent areas of overlapping perspectives, overstate the similarities, and understate or ignore the differences. Classic cognitive dissonance.

To be sure, there are many areas of intersection between European and Chinese viewpoints and policies – but they are far from identical. In fact, it is likely that many Europeans would not fully agree with the Chinese assessments of their world views and policy preferences. It is also questionable the degree to which China buys into the European vision for world order – particularly the commitment to multilateralism and humanitarianism. Given China's centuries-old realist perspective on interstate affairs, one should not read into China's vigorous endorsement of European multilateralism a similarly firm commitment on Beijing's part.

Despite some differences, we have seen that China views Europe's role in the world very positively, and that is for the good. Such underlying perceptions will help to sustain the continued development of actual relations.

Notes

1 http://www.delchn.cec.eu.int/.
2 The only such study I could find is by Jing Men, "Chinese Perceptions of the European Union: A Review of Leading Chinese Journals," *European Law Journal*, Vol. 12, No. 6 (November 2006), pp. 788–806.
3 This could, for example, be undertaken by the European Delegation to China, by the European China Academic Network (ECAN), or by the Chinese European Studies Association.
4 http://www.chinamission.be/eng/.
5 http://www.fmprc.gov.cn/eng/gjhdq/3265/.

6 The "father" of the theory of cognitive dissonance was Leon Festinger. See his classic study *Theory of Cognitive Dissonance* (Stanford: Stanford University Press, 1957).

7 Harold Issacs, *Scratches on Our Minds* (New York: John Day & Co., 1958).

8 For a review of this literature, see David Shambaugh, *Beautiful Imperialist: China Perceives America, 1972–90* (Princeton: Princeton University Press, 1991), chapter 1.

9 *China's EU Policy Paper*, October 2003, available at: http://www.chinamission.be/eng/sbgx/zogx/CHINA%20&%20EU/t72188.htm.

10 I get the sense in discussions with many European colleagues that they are not entirely comfortable with the speed and scope of the formation of EU policy towards China in recent years. That is, there exists much greater scepticism about China among China specialists, in national parliaments, in the media, and among publics – and many believe that the European Commission and Council have moved forward too rapidly, too extensively, and too naively in fashioning its China policy.

11 Perhaps the best study of EU integration is Zhang Haibing, *Ouzhou Yitihua Zhidu Yanjiu* (Shanghai: Shanghai Shehui Kexueyuan chubanshe, 2005).

12 These are reflected in a variety of official speeches and documents. The website of China's Foreign Ministry carries a number of them. See, for example, "China Position on Establishing a New International Political and Economic Order," at: http://www.fmprc.gov.cn/eng/wjdt/wjzc/t24883.htm; "China's Views on the Current International Situation," at: http://www.fmprc.gov.cn/eng/wjdt/wjzc/t24882.htm; and "China's Views of Multipolarization," at: http://www.fmprc.gov.cn/eng/wjdt/wjzc/t24880.htm.

13 Li Shenming et al. (eds.), *2006 nian: Quanqiu Zhengzhi yu Anquan Baogao* [2006 Global Political and Security Report] (Beijing: Shehui kexue chubanshe, 2006); also available at: http://www.iwep.org.cn/.

14 Wang Weiguang, "EU Forges Ahead in its Process of Integration with Twists and Turns," *International Strategic Studies*, No. 2 (2004), p. 78.

15 Zhongguo Xiandai Guoji Guanxi Yanjiusuo Ou Meng Ketizu, "Zhongguo dui Ou Meng Zhengce Yanjiu Baogao" [Research Report on China's Policy Toward the European Union], *Xiandai Guoji Guanxi*, No. 8 (2001), p. 4.

16 Cai Fangbai, "A New Milestone in the History of European Integration," *Foreign Affairs Journal*, No. 76 (June 2005), p. 34.

17 Xue Jundu and Zhou Zhuyao (eds.), *Mianxiang 21 Shiji de Zhong-Ou Guanxi* [Directions of Sino-Europe Relations in the Twenty-first Century] (Beijing: Zhongguo shehui kexue chubanshe, 2000), chapter 4.

18 See, for example, the papers presented by Song Xinning, Liu Fei, and Zhang Linhong at the international conference "The International Politics of EU–China Relations," sponsored by the Chinese Academy of Social Sciences and the British Academy, London, April 20–1, 2006.

19 See Shi Jiayou, "'Houxiandi' Ouzhou ji dui Zhongguo de Yiyi [The Significance for China of 'Post-Modern Europe'"], *Ouzhou Yanjiu*, No. 1 (2005), pp. 1–16.

20 See Sun Xiaoqing, "Ouzhou Diquzhuyi yu 'Xin Sanjiao'" [European Regionalism and the "New Triangle"], *Xiandai Guoji Guanxi*, No. 12 (2002), pp. 14–19.

21 Qiu Yuanlun, "Dangqian Ou-Mei dui Hua Zhengce de Lilun Poxi Jiji dui Zhonguo de Heyi" [Analysis of Theories in Current European–American Policies Toward China and Their Implications], *Shijie Jingji yu Zhengzhi*, No. 9 (2001), pp. 4–8.

22 Ibid., p. 6.

23 See Liu Wenxiu and Huang Zifang, "Ou Meng Gongtong Waijiao yu Anquan Zhengce Zhi de Yinsu Pouxi" [Analysis of the Implications of the EU's Common Foreign and Security Policy], *Guoji Wenti Yanjiu*, No. 1 (2005), pp. 46–50, 27.

24 See Chen Zhimin and Gustaaf Geeraerts, *Ouzhou Lianmeng Duiwai Zhengce Yitihua: Bu Kenneg de Shiming?* [Foreign Policy Integration in the European Union: A Mission Impossible?] (Beijing: Shishi chubanshe, 2003).

25 Feng Zhongping, "Dangqian Ou Meng Xingshi, Yingxiang ji Duiwai Zhanlue" [The Recent EU Situation, Implications, and its External Strategy], in *Zhongguo Zhanlue Guancha*, Vol. 2 (Feb. 2006), p. 63.

26 Feng and his CICIR colleagues were quick to make this point in the immediate aftermath of the "constitutional crisis" of the summer of 2005. See Feng Zhongping et al, "Ou Meng 'Xianfa Weiji': Yuanyin ji Yingxiang" [Causes and Implications of the European Union's "Constitutional Crisis"] *Xiandai Guoji Guanxi*, No. 7 (2005), pp. 42–51.

27 Feng Zhongping, "Issues Related to the EU's Foreign Policy," *Contemporary International Relations*, Vol. 16, No. 4 (April 2006), p. 24.

28 Ibid., p. 26.

29 See Peng Yuan and Li Wei, "Hezuoxing Shijie Moxie: Ou Meng de Quanqiu Zhili Yingxiang" [The Cooperative Global Order: The Global Impact of European Plans], *Shijie Jingji yu Zhengzhi*, No. 11 (2003), pp. 74–9.

30 Mei Zhaorong, "Sino-European Relations in Retrospect and Prospect," *Foreign Affairs Journal*, No. 79 (March 2006), p. 23.

31 See Jiang Dong'er, "Quanqiuhua yu Ou Meng de Hezuo Anquan" [Globalization and European Cooperative Security], *Shijie Jingji yu Zhengzhi*, No. 1 (2002), pp. 47–51; and Zheng Qingzhi, "Quanqiuhua Beijing xia de Zhong-Ou 'Quanmian Hezuo Huoban Guanxi'" [Globalization's Impact on the Sino-European 'Comprehensive Strategic Partnership'] *Shandong Daxue Xuebao*, No. 4 (2002), pp. 114–20.

32 See Qiu Yuanlun, "Ouzhou Qiantu Xiyu Lianhe yu Gaige" [Future Prospects Concerning European Unity and Reform], *Ouzhou Yanjiu*, No. 5 (2003), pp. 65–80.

33 Qiu Yuanlun, cf. 19, p. 7.

34 Wang Weiguang, "EU Forges Ahead in its Process of Integration with Twist and Turns," op. cit.

35 Feng Zhongping, cf. 21, pp. 63–4.

36 Zu Qiang and Qiu Zhi, "Kuodahou Ou Meng de Neibu Fazhan Dongli yu Waibu Huanjing: Ou Meng Dongkuo Xuexu Yantaohui Zongshu" [Europe's Internal Development Directions and External Environment After Expansion: Summary of the Discussion Conference on the EU's Eastern Expansion], *Ouzhou Yanjiu*, No. 3 (2004), pp. 152–3.

37 Ding Yuanhong, "European Expansion After the EU and NATO Eastward Expansions: Three Major Challenges Confronting European Integration," *Foreign Affairs Journal*, No. 73 (2004), pp. 56–7.

38 Ibid., p. 61.

39 Ibid., p. 62.

40 See China Institute of Contemporary International Relations Central and Eastern Europe Special Group, "Zhongguo dui Dong Ou Guojia Zhengce Yanjiu Baogao" [Report on China's Policies Toward Central and Eastern European Countries], *Xiandai Guoji Guanxi*, No. 11 (2003), pp. 1–10.

41 See, for example, Mei Zhaorong, "Sino-European Relations in Retrospect and Prospect," *Foreign Affairs Journal*, No. 79 (March 2006), pp. 17–27; Zhang Linchu and Zhuang Yixiang, "The Review and Prospect of Sino-European Relations," *International Strategic Studies*, No. 2 (2005), pp. 23–31; Dai Bingran, "Zouxiang Chengxu Jiankang Wending de Zhong-Ou Guanxi" [Moving Towards a Mature, Healthy and Stable China–Europe Relationship], *Ouzhou Yanjiu*, No. 2 (2005), pp. 73–82.

42 Zhang and Zhuang, ibid., p. 25.

43 Peng Meiwei, "Huigu yu Zhanwang – Jinian Zhong-Fa Jianjiao 40 nian Guoji Xueshu Yantaohui" [Retrospect and Prospect – International Conference Remembering the 40th Anniversary of the Establishment of Sino-French Diplomatic Relations], *Ouzhou Yanjiu*, No. 1 (2004), pp. 152–4.

44 Ibid., p. 18.

45 Zhang Yesui, "Jiwang Kailai, Wedong Zhong-Ou Quanmian Zhanlue Huoban Guanxi Jinyibu Fazhan: Jinian Zhongguo yu Ou Men Jianjiao Sanshi Zhounian" [Carry Forward and Develop Further Steps of the Important Cause of the Sino-European Comprehensive

Strategic Partnership – Remembering the 30th Anniversary of the Establishment of Diplomatic Relations Between China and the EU], *Qiushi*, No. 9 (2005), pp. 58–60.

46 Zhou Hong, "Wulun Fazhan Zhong-Ou Hezhuo Huoban Guanxi de Zhanlue Yiyi" [Discussion About the Strategic Implications of Developing the China–Europe Partnership], *Zhongguo Zhanlue Guancha*, Vol. 2 (2006), pp. 7–13.

47 For the latter view, see Liu Wenxiu, "Zhongguo-Ou Meng 'Quanmian Huoban Guanxi' de Neihan yu Dingwei" [The Connotation and Orientation of the China–EU "Comprehensive Partnership], *Shandong Daxue Xuebao*, No. 2 (2002), pp. 68–73.

48 Huo Zhengde, "Lun Zhong-Ou Zhanlue Guanxi" [On Sino-European Strategic Relations], *Guoji Wenti Yanjiu*, No. 2 (2005), p. 1.

49 Wang Xiang, "Zhong-Ou Huoban Guanxi de Jidong yu Qianjing" [Retrospect and Prospect for the Sino-European Partnership], *Zhongguo Waijiao*, No. 12 (2003), pp. 35–8.

50 Zhou Hong, "Lun Zhong-Ou Huoban Guanxi zhong de Buduichenxing yu Duichenxing" [Concerning Symmetries and Asymmetries of the Sino-European Partnership], *Ouzhou Yanjiu*, No. 2 (2004), pp. 1–15.

51 Zhang Linchu and Zhuang Yixiang, "The Review and Prospects of Sino–EU Relations," *International Strategic Studies*, No. 2 (2005), p. 28.

52 Ruan Zongze, "Zhong-Ou Quanmian Zhanlue Huoban Guanxi: Cong Gouxiang dao Shixian" [The Sino-European Comprehensive Strategic Partnership: From Concept to Practice], *Waijiao Xueyuan Xuebao*, Vol. 81, No. 4 (2005), pp. 68–73.

53 Tian Dewen, "Yi Hezuo Chudai Duikang" [On Substituting Cooperation for Confrontation], *Guoji Maoyi*, No. 9 (2003), pp. 4–8.

54 Zheng Bijian, "Zhongguo Heping Jueqi Fazhan Daolu yu Zhong-Ou Guanxi" [China's Road of Peaceful Development and Sino-European Relations], *Zhongguo Zhanlue Guancha*, No. 2 (2006), pp. 3–7.

55 Mei Zhaorong, "Sino-European Relations in Retrospect and Prospect," op. cit., p. 24.

56 Ibid.

57 See Song Lizi and Zhang Xiaoding, "Zhong-Ou Renquanguan de Kaitong Jichi dui Zhong-Ou Guanxi de Yinxiang" [Sino-European Perspectives on Human Rights and Their Influence on Sino-European Relations], *Guoja Xingzheng Xueyuan Xuebao*, No. 4 (2002), pp. 87–90.

58 See, for example, Dong Li, "Ou Meng dui Hua fan Qingxiao 'Fei Shichang Jingji' Wenti Tanxi" [Exploring the EU's Anti-Dumping 'Non-Market Economy' Issue], *Ouzhou Yanjiu*, No. 3 (2003), pp. 131–47.

59 See Hou Hongyu, "Ou Meng dui Hua Junshou Jinling de 'Pojie' yu 'Fanjie'" ["Opposing" and "Breaking" the EU's Arms Sales Prohibition Against China], *Dangdai Shijie*, No. 2 (2002), pp. 20–2.

60 Huo Zhengde, "Lun Zhong-Ou Zhanlue Guanxi" [On the China–EU Strategic Relationship], *Guoji Wenti Yanjiu*, No. 2 (2005), p. 3.

61 Ibid.

62 Ibid., p. 4.

63 The EU Research Group of CICIR, "Report on China's EU Policy," *Contemporary International Relations*, Vol. 11, No. 8 (July 2001), p. 22.

64 Op. cit.

65 Europe Research Group of CICIR, "Report on China's EU Policy," op. cit., pp. 22–5.

66 CICIR Central/East Europe Research Group, "Research Report on China's Policy Toward Central/East European Countries," *Contemporary International Relations*, Vol. 13, No. 12 (December 2003). This was originally published in *Xiandai Guoji Guanxi*, No. 11 (2003).

67 Ibid., pp. 24–8.

68 CICIR, *Ouzhou Sixiangku jichi dui Hua Yanjiu* (Beijing: Shishi chubanshe, 2004).

69 Dai Bingran, "Moving Towards a Mature, Healthy, and Improving China–Europe Relationship," op. cit., pp. 80–1.

70 Cai Fangbai, "A New Milestone in the History of European Integration," op. cit., p. 38.

71 "General Xiong Guangkai's Address to the Opening Ceremony of the International Symposium on Sino–U.S.–European Relations in the New Century: Opportunities and Challenges," *Collection of Papers of the International Symposium on Sino–U.S.–European Relations in the New Century*, China Institute of International Strategic Studies and Hotung Institute of International Relations, November 18–20, 2003, Beijing.
72 Ding Yuanhong, "The European Situation in Flux," op. cit., p. 30.
73 See Shen Guoliang, "New Changes in Euro–U.S. Relations After 9/11," *International Strategic Studies*, No. 3 (2002), pp. 46–7.
74 See, for example, Discussion Group, "Yilake Weiji jichi Yingxiang" [The Iraq Crisis and its Impact], *Xiandai Guoji Guanxi*, No. 3 (2003), pp. 41–50.
75 Ibid., pp. 48–50 in particular.
76 Ma Shugui, "A Tentative Analysis of the Development of EU Independent Defense," *International Strategic Studies*, No. 3 (2002), p. 55.
77 Liu Jun, "Quanli, Weixie yu Daxiyang Tongmeng de Songlai" [Power, Threat and the Future of the Transatlantic Alliance], *Ouzhou Yanjiu*, No. 4 (2004), p. 15.
78 See Tian Di and Liu Jianyyu, "How the Strategic Architecture in the Former Soviet and East European Region is Swayed by NATO's Eastward Expansion," *International Strategic Studies*, No. 3 (2004), pp. 53–7.
79 CASS Institute of European Studies and European Studies Association of China (eds.), *Ouzhou Fazhan Baogao 2003–4* (Beijing: Shehui kexueyuan chubanshe, 2005), pp. 3–34.
80 See Hong Yousheng, "Ou Meng yu Meiguo dui Hua Zhanlue Bijiao" [A Comparison of the EU's and US Strategies Toward China], *Xiandai Guoji Guanxi*, No. 8 (2005), pp. 1–6. I agree with Professor Hong on this point. See my "The New Strategic Triangle: American and European Reactions to China's Rise," *The Washington Quarterly* (Summer 2005); and "European and American Approaches to China: Different Beds, Same Dreams?" *China Perspectives* (May–June 2002).
81 See, for example, Hu Qianhong, "Viewing the Trend of U.S.–European Relations from President Bush's European Visit," *International Strategic Studies*, No. 2 (2005), pp. 47–55.
82 Ibid., p. 51.
83 Ibid., p. 54.
84 See, for example, Huo Zhengde, "Lun Zhong-Ou Zhanlue Guanxi," op. cit.
85 Op. cit., pp. 4–5.

8 Chinese perceptions of the EU and the China–Europe relationship

Zhu Liqun

The year 2005 marked the 30th anniversary of the establishment of diplomatic relations between China and the European Union. On this occasion, a research team from the Centre for European Studies at China Foreign Affairs University was formed to conduct an evaluation on the China–EU relationship as an academic contribution to the anniversary celebration.[1] The team conducted a series of surveys and investigations, aimed at gaining insight into Chinese perceptions of the European Union and the Sino-European relationship. Assuming that university students and professional scholars are two groups relatively more conscious of this topic and more influential in Chinese society, we undertook research into those two target groups. To understand Chinese scholars' perceptions of Europe, we undertook a literature review and textual analysis. To understand students' perceptions, we undertook survey research via questionnaires. After collecting the results of the survey and textual analysis, we tried to draw some preliminary conclusions of Chinese students' and scholars' perception of the EU and Sino-European relations.

To explore the perception of Chinese scholars and university students, our survey and analysis focused on whether or not, in Chinese eyes, the EU is an independent power or pole in the international system. With this in mind, our exploration was centred around three questions. First, what is the EU's role in the world? What kind of actor is the EU and what impact has the power of the EU exerted on China and EU–US relations? Second, how do Chinese look at the China–EU relationship? What perspectives do Chinese adopt when they look at the EU? Is the development of the China–EU relationship seen by Chinese as an instrument targeting a third party – or has it been developed from mutual internal adaptation and internal changes? Third, what are the challenges facing this relationship in the future?

Perceptions of Chinese scholars

In order to understand Chinese scholars' perception of the European Union (EU), we chose to analyse some relevant articles published in the top ten Chinese journals in international studies from 1995 to 2005.[2] We focused on these ten years between 1995 and 2005, because at the beginning of the 1990s Europeans were busy with the reconstruction of the European Union, "leaving China out of its core agenda."[3] Relations between China and the EU at that time were not as dynamic as those between China and the United States. During that period, both sides placed each other on a secondary level in their foreign policies.[4] The China–EU relationship developed new dynamics beginning in the mid-1990s, since, in the view of one leading Chinese scholar, the EU first realized "China's unprecedented development had shown its potential to be a great power in the world's political, military and economic affairs. It is neither proper nor possible [for the EU] to isolate China."[5] *A Long Term Policy for China–Europe Relations*, issued by the European Commission in 1995, marked the beginning of a new phase of the relationship. It is, therefore, from that point that our review begins.

Is the EU an independent power in the international system?

Distribution of power, or the pattern of power, is often discussed in Chinese academia. Chinese studies of international relations are firmly grounded in the realist tradition. The concept of power, and the relative distribution of it, is taken by many Chinese analysts as a starting point in foreign policy analysis and as one of the most important external factors affecting foreign policy-making. After the end of the Cold War, many Chinese scholars believed that the international system was going to be structured by "one superpower with multiple powers" (*yichao duoqiang*), which would eventually lead to a multipolar world. That is to say, the international order would be based on several great powers.

Therefore, when exploring European issues, Chinese observers first look to see whether the EU can be regarded as an independent power or pole in the international system, and whether the EU has the capacities to play a role independent from the United States. Independence from the US has become a variable to judge the role of EU in the world simply because Chinese analysts believe Europe had no independent foreign policy at all for a long period of time during the Cold War, as a result of being close allies of the United States and former Soviet Union. The issue is also linked with two relevant questions. First, what is distinctive about the EU's role in the world? Second, what *kind* of power is the EU, especially compared with the United States?

With regard to the question of whether the EU can hold an important position and play a big role on the international stage, there is no consensus among Chinese scholars. Some seem quite optimistic about the strength of the EU, while some believe the power of the EU is limited to the economic domain.

Many Chinese scholars like to believe that the EU has already become an independent power or pole in the international system. As David Shambaugh's preceding chapter in this volume illustrates, there is a lot of wishful thinking going on in Chinese scholarly circles and a strong tendency to project Chinese wishes for global order on to what they perceive to be European "realities." With the continually deepening process of integration across the continent, the position of the EU has witnessed a radical change. Some believe the EU has achieved a breakthrough in its integration process, and has "enhanced its consciousness of independence and being a world power."[6] Others argue that "Western Europe is fully qualified to be a pole thanks to its developed economy, advanced technology and great political influence."[7]

Not only is the EU believed to be a world power in the eyes of some Chinese scholars, but it is also further seen as a power which has developed into one of the top three global powers, that can balance the other two – the United States and Japan."[8] Some scholars take the EU as a reference point to judge the power of the US, believing that "The estimation on the status and change of the United States in international economy and politics not only relies on American development and evolution, but also on the vicissitudes of other powers. In recent and future years, the first power that can challenge the United States seems to be the EU, which is determined by the EU's position in international economy and politics."[9]

The importance of the EU derived from its integration is also believed to further contribute to world multipolarization, which is a trend of future development of the international structure. One scholar observes, "European integration is marching in step with multipolarization of the world. The EU claims democratization, pluralization and multilateralism, which indicates an intention of multipolarization. Well-grounded on the internal and external integration during the recent half century, the EU as a whole, with its accumulating power, has begun to play a particular and important role on the international stage through the implementation of its strategic ideas and participations, which enhances multipolarization."[10]

The contrasting view holds that the influence of the EU is limited to the economic domain, as it is "essentially an economic union,"[11] which cannot be considered as a comprehensive power matching the United States and the other big powers. Some argue that the EU is not a pole yet, if estimated in accordance with many criteria – such as comprehensive power, its willingness to be a big power, its foreign strategy, diplomatic capability and international influence, recognition by the other actors and its self-characterization as a post-modern political entity.[12] These scholars look at the EU mainly from the framework of realism and believe that only hard power matters. Thus, for them, the EU is only an "economic giant," but a dwarf in political and military affairs – at most, a limp giant. Therefore it can only exert inconspicuous influence on major international issues. Nor, in the view of these scholars, has it ever achieved its intention to cast off American dominance through the process of integration.[13]

To some Chinese scholars, the EU's role is limited not because its power is confined within the economic realm, but because it is flawed by institutional defects and differences in interests and policies among its member states. As an international actor, the EU is still struggling with the aim of seeking an independent and unique voice in international affairs. Yet, to many Chinese observers, the EU seems to have no substantial and consistent strategy and foreign policy, even though it has been trying hard to build the so-called Common Foreign and Security Policy (CFSP) for years.[14]

The limited power of the EU, for the time being, does not mean a gloomy view about its future role, since Chinese are optimists and like to believe "the road is tortuous, but the future is bright." When they look forward to the EU's future position in the world, most Chinese scholars seem to adopt a quite optimistic view. They believe that European integration is an irreversible process. Europe may meet more difficulties and challenges ahead, and "it is impossible to promote itself from an ordinary power to the strongest and further to that of a world level in one action."[15] Although "the road to a 'Grand Europe' is deemed to be long, which requires time and patience, to meet obstacles, resistance and restrictions,"[16] eventually, "the EU's influence over world affairs will be more prominent with the pace of the European integration,"[17] and "the EU will become a crucial pole in future multipolar world," observe a number of Chinese scholars.[18] In Chinese eyes, the deepening of EU integration will increase the EU's economic and political power, which will result in a stronger inclination towards independence in international affairs, with Europe becoming an "effective power to check US hegemonic temptation in the future."[19] "The plan of 'Grand Europe' will transform the EU from being a regional power to a global one, which might confront the US goal of maintaining itself as the world's sole superpower."[20]

The EU model: civilian and normative power

Since 2001, more and more articles on the EU have been devoted to exploring the "European model."[21] It seems there is a constructivist turn in China's academia in general. Particularly in EU studies circles, the dominant paradigm is gradually shifting from the realist perspective of power politics to liberal and constructivist approaches, which pay more attention to the EU model as a civilian power and normative power.

Two reasons might explain this new orientation. First, the general international environment has been seen by Chinese observers as becoming more stable following the heated internal debates stimulated by the bombing incident of the Chinese embassy in Belgrade in 1999, which harmed Sino-American relations and exacerbated the Chinese view of a dangerous international environment and brought about the prevailing realist approach in China's international studies, including European studies. Second, the accession of China to the World Trade Organization (WTO) in 2001 provided a great impetus for China to be more deeply involved in the international system and paved the way for China to gain confidence with rapid economic and trade growth. China's identity is changing and the Chinese government is increasingly concerned about being a responsible international actor.

These internal changes triggered great enthusiasm among Chinese scholars towards a constructive approach when they looked at the EU, and thus facilitated Chinese Europe Watchers to eagerly learn from the European experiences of integration and governance. So the "European model" has drawn more attention among most Chinese Europe Watchers since then. Although there exist doubts on questions like whether there is a well-formed and clear definition of the "European model,"[22] most Chinese scholars tend to discuss European political, economic, social and cultural characteristics within a framework of the "European model."

They believe that "the European model is not fixed or invariable. Integration is seen as just a process of the formation of such model."[23] "European ideas" have helped the EU establish itself not only as a "civilian power," but also as a special "normative power," and the EU is trying hard to set worldwide criteria with its own norms.[24] So for many Chinese, to understand EU–US, China–EU, and China–US–EU relations should begin from the primary understanding of the "European model." To understand that model, the "American model" is always taken as a reference point, since "the way the EU deals with international affairs is very much different from that of the US."[25] As to the content of the European model, scholars lay more stress on its security community building and its multilateralism. These are viewed as distinctive features by Chinese observers.

One of the most contrasting features of the EU model is in the security field, in which the EU seeks security through regional security community building with an emphasis more on "common security" rather than "absolute security." In Chinese scholars' views, with experiences from two devastating world wars, Europeans believe from the bottom of their heart that invulnerability is just an illusion. In addition, Eastern and Southern Europe are two of the most unstable areas in the world. The European sense of vulnerability and interdependence leads them to adopt and promote ideas and policies of "common security," whereas Americans believe that by relying on the protection of the two oceans they can prevent threats and guarantee their absolute security through high-tech means such as Missile Defense Systems. Although this confidence was made to waver by the 9/11 event, the US strategy of "preemptive attack" indicates that the US will never abandon its pursuit of absolute security.[26]

As for the subject of security, Europe places more emphasis on regional security than on national security, and on realizing national security via protecting regional security. As for the object of security, after the Cold War, Europeans' sense of enmity from outside has decreased thanks to its experience of integration and building of a common security community. As for the measures to maintain security, Europe pays much attention to economic and political means (including the enlargement of the EU).[27] As for dealing with international crises, Europeans turn more to internal and external cooperation, economic and cultural exchanges, building of civil society, adoption of *rapprochement*, and establishment of multilateral institutions to decrease conflicts.[28] So European security community building is not expedient, as it realizes that only through integration can the European states break away from the vicious circle of "action–reaction–reaction."[29]

In most Chinese eyes, the EU is also the world's prime example in promoting multilateralism in international society. Since the end of the Cold War, Europe has attached importance to international institutions and organizations (i.e. United Nations), emphasized the need to respect international laws and multilateral agreements, and promoted international and regional cooperation.[30] The EU sticks to the principles of the rule of law, good governance, dialogue and coordination, persuasion and cooperation.[31] It becomes one of the most important advocates, guardians and executors of multilateralism and liberal institutionalism.

Some Chinese scholars like to take EU–China human rights dialogue as an example, believing that Europeans promote human rights in the world more by way of dialogue and the multilateral approach. In many Chinese eyes, the European concept of human rights, built through hundreds of years of development and improvement, has evolved from individual liberty and civil rights to broader social, cultural and collective rights – whereas the US only emphasizes individual liberty and civil rights, regardless of the right to social and economic equality.[32] And compared with the US, the European stand on human rights is not so tough and provocative. They limit their actions to the framework of enhancing dialogue and enunciating standpoints, and coping with the divergences on political system and ideology with other states in a way that is neither confrontational nor loud.

The impact of the EU model on the Atlantic relationship

Not only has more attention been paid by Chinese Europe specialists to the EU model in recent years, but its impact on international relations is also discussed. Most Chinese scholars believe "the EU's pursuit has established a solid foundation for this influence on international affairs."[33] In the post-Cold War era, the EU's foreign policy, stressing institutional power – in contrast to the American practice of unilateralism – increases its popularity among developing countries.[34] Chinese experts also believe the wisdom of "European ideas" in international affairs, and the successful experience of the European model can be used as a reference for China's own foreign policy and can promote Sino-European cooperation.[35]

Meanwhile, Chinese scholars attribute the essential cause of unstable development of the transatlantic relationship to ideational divergences between Europe and the United States. Some even predict that there will be a "clash" between European multilateralism and American unilateralism. In the words of one scholar, "The sticking point of US–EU contradictions are the differences in their perceptions of world order and global governance, in their adherence to 'uni' (unilateralism and unipolarity) or 'multi' (multilateralism and multipolarity), and in their characterization of international 'hegemony' or 'democracy.'"[36] These analysts hope that the European way of dealing with international affairs can curb the temptation of American unilateralism and hegemonism and help to modify American foreign policy.[37]

However, not all Chinese scholars are convinced that the EU model has fundamentally changed transatlantic relations, especially the essence of the US–EU relationship. Some point out that the EU–US frictions and divergences should not be exaggerated and the two parties always "bond to each other while reserving divergences." Although the EU has been developing its own military force with a long-term goal of establishing an independent defence system, it will not change its alliance with the US, and the framework of NATO will continue to play a dominant role in their security relationship. It is basically because both are market economy democracies with homogeneous values, which makes the EU a more independent competitor but not a challenger against the United States."[38] Indeed the EU has become more independent after the end of the Cold War, which makes the Atlantic strategic bond looser and more incoherent, thus creating more frictions across the Atlantic. Especially in recent years after 9/11, aggressive US foreign policy is seen as having broadened and deepened their differences. However, based on their similar social systems and ideology, and the new environment of anti-terrorism, transatlantic countries will keep their alliance stable in the long run and give priority to cooperation and coordination.[39] So for some Chinese scholars, the EU–US relationship is just like that between a "quarrelsome couple," but "contending without breaking up."[40]

From the review of these Chinese publications, it can be concluded that there is no consensus on the impact of the EU model on international affairs, especially on EU–US relations, even though most Chinese scholars believe the EU has already developed a unique model of the world, and it is a result of many years of effort towards integration.

Sino-European relations: a long-term strategic partnership?

All Chinese scholars gave high appraisals of current Sino-European relations, acknowledging the China–EU relationship has formed an "all-round, broadened-areas, and multi-dimensional cooperative framework, growing from economic cooperation to strategic interdependence."[41] It has achieved compelling progress with 30 years of development, especially when compared with the ups-and-downs in Sino-American and Sino-Japanese relations. Some further noted that "the comprehensive strategic partnership is not expedient, but a correct choice based upon the prudent considerations of both sides."[42]

When explaining the reasons why the China–EU relationship is on a good track and why Chinese scholars seem to take an optimistic view of the relationship, the explanation is quite diversified, with changes of focus over time.

Two approaches to the foundation of Sino-European relations

Most scholars hold that the China–EU relationship possesses a unique condition which is lacking in China–US and China–Japan relations, which helps to establish a comparatively equal bilateral relationship, regardless of political and emotional disputes. This is because, as the scholars believe, after China's resumption of Hong Kong and Macau, there are no historical disputes and geopolitical conflicts between the two parties. Both sides possess the strength of will and recognise the need to maintain world and regional peace, without the intention to establish an international or regional hegemony in their respective regions.[43] This congenital condition is well discussed by almost every Chinese analyst when touching upon Sino-European relations. But when they review other factors, two different approaches seem to be involved.

Some scholars like to believe the dynamics of improving China–EU relations derive from the strategic consideration of targeting a third party and from a need to build a multipolar world. This was really the case during the 1990s when the idea of multipolarity was prevalent in China and when Sino-American relations had deteriorated after the bombing of the Chinese Embassy in 1999. For many Chinese scholars, a multipolar world is attractive both to China and to Europe. They hold the view that China and Europe share many identical views on the "construction of the international order."[44] Both happen to be "fellow travellers" on the road to multipolarity. Most scholars find that the goals of China's modernization and of European integration are both consistent with the developmental trend of multipolarization. Both have strongly sensed that their future strategic status will be largely based on their relations with the outside world, especially on their attitudes towards the international order.

The collaborative Sino-European promotion of world peace and stability is the paramount correspondent point of their strategies, and will endow their cooperation with essential meaning.[45] Specifically, with respect to the UN and international law, "both sides hold compatible propositions and make efforts to maintain the authority of the UN."[46] Some argue that "They strongly hold that international contention – whether shown as conflicts between states, nations, races, cultures or religions – stem primarily from historical and social differences, which should be solved peacefully via dialogues and negotiations within the framework of international laws and institutions."[47] It is because of those identical views that a solid basis for the relationship has been built.

However, this view is obviously not shared by all. One noticeable phenomenon is that more and more scholars began to take an inward-looking perspective, raising the criticism that analysis from the angle of anti-American hegemony "lacks historical profundity." They see that the increasing common interests of both sides are mainly caused by their respective internal changes after the end of the Cold War, not by strategic consideration of targeting the United States.[48] Opines one, "The Chinese reform and opening up is, to some extent, a process of self-adjustment, through learning from the outside world and drawing on the experiences of human progresses."[49] Another observes, "To change itself has become one of the main sources for China's growth and the principal way to exert its influence over the world."[50]

China understands the EU from the perspective of its own development, hoping to use their experiences for reference. It has been learned that China should "interpret the particular history and reality of the European development, from which we can draw useful lessons to deepen Sino-European relations and promote our own development. Many factors, including the history of the European integration, its new progress, and its future development trend, are of great benefit for us to correctly interpret Europe, and to build the Sino-European strategic partnership. Moreover, those factors will also be of importance for China to deal with new challenges."[51]

Chinese are sincerely keen to understand the European experience that has accumulated in the process of integration. For instance, they admire how the EU keeps an appropriate balance between unity and diversity, power centralization and power sharing, production and distribution of social wealth, and between traditions and modernity.[52] One scholar observes that "Europe is still in the integration process, giving priority to the spirit of compromise. Thus, democracy and negotiation trump coercion and force. France and Germany were brought together through economic cooperation to political rapprochement and unification; and gradually enlarged this model to European unity."[53] The European way, advocating tolerance, diversity and sustainable development, to some extent, shows the direction of human advancement.[54] This is the way that China should learn for its pursuit of peaceful development and regional prosperity and stability.[55]

For Chinese scholars, the China–EU comprehensive strategic partnership is based on the interests of both sides. Some see it as "open and constructive, not making an alliance against a third party. Such a partnership is not only compatible with their interests, but also beneficial to world peace, stability and development. The deepening of the China–EU relationship is a strategic transition of international power, which will promote international democracy among states. It will help to establish a new international order, strengthen the UN's functions, advance the ASEM (Asia–Europe meeting) process, and exert profound strategic influence on sustainable development worldwide."[56]

Challenges facing China–EU relations

Generally speaking, for many Chinese Europe watchers, there is still a long way to go to realize the professed Sino-European "comprehensive strategic partnership." Due to the different phases of development they are exercising, different internal and external challenges they are facing, and different prescriptions to global governance and international affairs they are offering, it is not easy for China and European countries to solve many problems and obstacles facing them. While providing complementary measures to each other's approach, the asymmetry between them has constituted structural and functional problems, which will become the main source of China–EU divergences.[57]

Analysing the possible differences between China and Europe, Chinese scholars often discuss several in particular. First of all, there is an asymmetry in security goals and orientation. Although China's security goal is gradually transitioning to one of comprehensive security, its core is still political and military security. Yet the goal for EU members has surpassed traditional security, transferring to the non-traditional realm emphasizing human and social security. Its favoured measures include some elements with which China does not agree, e.g. "humanitarian intervention."[58]

Second, the complexity of the EU policy-making process may lead its China policy into a vicious circle of "discussion without decision." The particular interests and internal conflicts of EU members may constrain the implementation of China–EU foreign and security cooperation, as the Common Foreign and Security Policy of the EU is not mature enough and their interests conflict and diverge (e.g. UK vs France and Germany, small and medium-sized powers vs great powers, "New Europe" vs "Old Europe"). Thus the CFSP makes unsteady progress because of its "dual structure" and complicated internal decision-making and operational process.[59]

Third, some believe that "the Sino-EU relationship has not surpassed the difficulties caused by different ideologies and values."[60] Although the EU pays more attention to global strategy and economic interests than ideology in its China policy, scholars still hold that the EU has not abandoned its scheme to "Westernize China" (*Xihua*). These Chinese scholars argue that Europe encourages China to fully accept Western ideology and "to completely integrate into the international community."[61]

Fourth, the American reaction is becoming an important factor affecting the relationship. The China–EU relationship is becoming more mature, from a derivative relationship that once was subject to US–Soviet relations, to an independent one.[62] Although this independent relationship is developing fast, it still lacks stability. "The United States is the leading external influence on the relationship between China and Europe, keeping them from developing a completely independent relationship and expanding their mutual foreign and security cooperation," observes one scholar,[63] while another argues that, "It [the US] is both stimulation and constriction, making the most important external parameter to have impact on the Sino-EU relationship."[64] Furthermore, the United States is an ally of many EU members, its power has exerted great influence over the EU's policy on China and its leadership in the trilateral relationship. Says one Chinese expert: "Although the Sino-European foreign and security cooperation does not aim at any third party, it is still hard for the US to accept and recognize it, because of its psychological effects on Americans and its influence over international affairs."[65]

In addition, the US is always a priority on both the Chinese and European policy agenda. In a world where comprehensive power decide a nation's international influence, China and the EU must develop their interrelations as well as consolidate their relations with the United States. Yet the latter is much more important than the former, both in the two parties' strategy and in practice. As one Chinese scholar summarizes: "The effects of America are complex, variable, and dual; yet, it is an external parameter, which is not a direct influence strong enough to completely arrest Sino-EU cooperation."[66]

It is a common view among Chinese scholars that problems like human rights, ideology and Tibet will still affect the China–EU relationship for a period of time to come, and that the problems of the arms embargo and China's Market Economy Status are out of tune with the proclaimed "comprehensive strategic partnership." However, these problems will not be solved in one stroke, especially when the arms embargo has become such a touchstone in China–EU and China–US relations. Observes one expert: "The proposal to lift the arms ban compels the EU to make a hard decision between the maintenance of EU–US alliance and the strengthening of China–EU strategic cooperation. In other words, to lift the ban requires the EU to find a balancing point between two policies – to adapt to Chinese development or to give consideration to its ally, the United States. The final result of the issue will test the quality of the Sino-European strategic relationship, the degree of the EU's independence and its stand in the potential Taiwan

Strait Crisis."[67] If these problems are not solved properly, neither China–EU nor EU–US relations will see a healthier and more stable development.

Chinese students' perceptions of Europe

University students were also selected as our target group to illustrate a different sector of Chinese society's perceptions of Europe and the EU. The prime consideration for the choice proceeded from the assumption that the Chinese general public had less concern and knowledge about the EU and played little role in China's European policy.[68] Young people receiving higher education in China are those who are most capable of receiving information and assuming potential leadership. After graduation, they will join the Chinese elite and play important roles in the society. Though public opinion is becoming more conspicuous in China, and begins to exert an impact on policy-making, the professional scholars and university students are the groups most influential in China's current politics and foreign policy-making. It is hoped that from this survey of university students, readers can learn more of their opinions about the EU, and the differences between perceptions of the scholars and the students.

Since university students are studying different majors with no focus exclusively on European affairs, a questionnaire was therefore administered to explore their views. The 600 questionnaires were distributed on campuses and random samples were taken in six universities: namely, Tsinghua University, Beijing University, Renmin University, Beijing Normal University, Beijing Institute of Technology and Beijing University of Posts and Telecommunications. Each university received 100 random samples. Of the 600 samples, 550 valid replies were returned. Among the valid samples, there were 308 males, accounting for 56 per cent of the total, and 242 females, accounting for 44 per cent of the total. Table 8.1 shows the distribution of the samples' educational background, different regions they come from, curricular majors, and gender. After collecting

Table 8.1 Survey Sample Characteristics

Background	Category	Valid sample	Percentage (%)
Gender	Male	308	56.00
	Female	242	44.00
Major	Science	221	40.18
	Arts	303	55.09
	Other major	26	4.73
Region	East China	85	15.45
	South China	65	11.82
	North China	219	39.82
	Central China	68	12.36
	West China	64	11.64
	North-east China	49	8.91

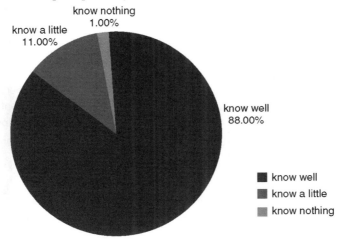

Figure 8.1 Do you know the EU?

the questionnaires, *Epidata* was used for data input to ensure the quality of statistics. The statistical analysis of the data was conducted with SPSS 11.5.

According to the survey, the findings of the respondents' knowledge about the EU and China–EU relations can be presented as follows.

Students have basic, but not accurate, knowledge. For university students, we designed several elementary questions in the first part of the questionnaire. As a result, we find that 88 per cent of the participants think that they know the EU well, 11 per cent of them know a little, while only 1 per cent of them know nothing.

On some detailed questions about the EU, the result is quite different from general findings expressed in Figure 8.1. With some questions – for example how many member states are in the EU, which member state is currently holding the EU chair, when China's first official document on the EU was issued, and which member state is China's biggest trading partner – it was found that not many of the respondents got the right answers. As Figure 8.2 illustrates, it can be seen that most of the participants do not have a very thorough knowledge of the EU, even though almost all of them have a basic conceptualization of what the EU is.

Students are in favour of the EU's role in the world. University students in China also have a positive view of the EU's global role. The findings below from Figures 8.3 to 8.7 reveal that most respondents believe that EU is powerful enough to play an important role in the world. Even though the majority of the participants think of the EU as an economic power, a large number of them still treat the EU as a comprehensive power in the world, and more than half of the students hold that hard power and soft power are equally important. They believe that the European integration has increased its significance and influence all over the world.

When asked whether the EU is already one "pole" of power in today's world, 52 per cent of the participants answered "yes."

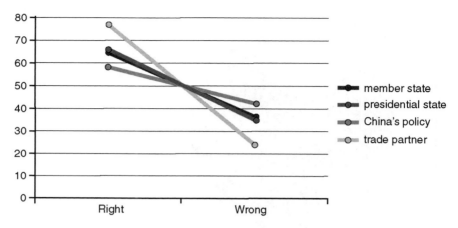

Figure 8.2 Degree of accuracy of students' answers to detailed questions

When asked in which field(s) the EU is most powerful, the participants answered differently. The majority think that the EU is only an economic power, but 34 pe rcent of them believe that the EU is a "comprehensive power" (see Figure 8.4).

When asked "which is more important, hard power or soft power?" 52.18 per cent of them regarded both elements as equally important (see Figure 8.5).

When asked "what is the EU's advantage in international affairs?" 66 per cent of the participants answered "European integration," 12 per cent answered "democracy and rule of law," and 13 per cent answered the EU "development model" (of social

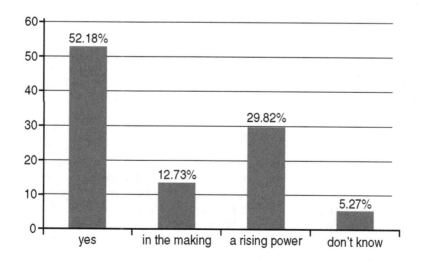

Figure 8.3 Do you think the EU is one "pole" of power in today's world?

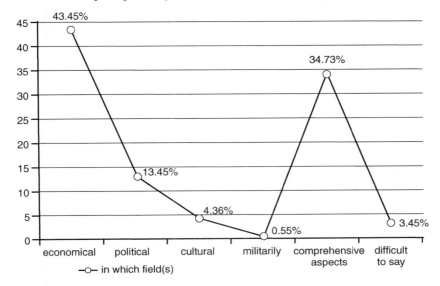

Figure 8.4 In which field(s) is the EU most powerful

and economic fields). It seems that most of the participants think the European integration process increases the EU's power (see Figure 8.6).

When asked "which is the better model to follow when dealing with international affairs, European or American?" almost half of the respondents chose the European model, while 22 per cent chose both (see Figure 8.7).

Students' doubts about the future EU absence of conflict. Although many participants appreciated the European model, it seemed that they are not sure whether Europe would be able to avoid conflicts in the future. 42.5 per cent of

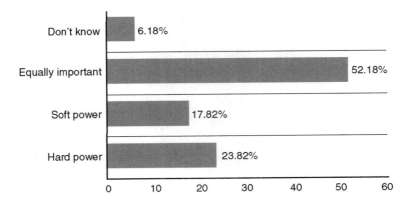

Figure 8.5 Which is more important, EU hard power or soft power?

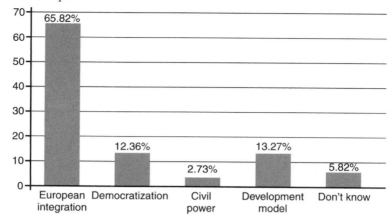

Figure 8.6 What is the EU's advantage in international affairs?

them are not sure whether power politics have already been eliminated in Europe through the integration process. More than 25 per cent of them thought definitely not yet. Such a large percentage of them gave a negative answer (see Figure 8.8).

Considering that 32 per cent of student respondents believe that the EU emphasis on multilateralism is a result of its shortage of military capability, the doubt on whether Europe has, through its integration, solved the conflicts resulting from power politics is noticeably still present. As for the question of whether or not there is a "fundamental difference between the EU and the US with regard to the current and future international order," 32 per cent thought the EU and the US hold different views, but 53.27 per cent of them did not consider the difference to be

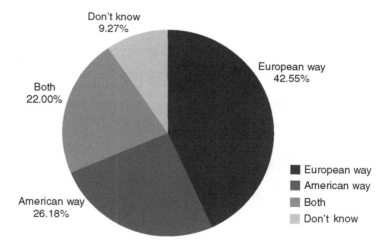

Figure 8.7 Which is the better model to follow when dealing with international affairs, European or American?

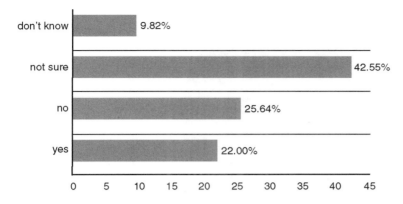

Figure 8.8 Do you think Europe has overcome power politics?

crucial. It seems that Chinese students stress less the difference between Europe and the United States than Chinese scholars do (see Figures 8.9 and 8.10).

Students' views of the importance of the EU to China. As for the importance of the EU in China's foreign policy, 62 per cent and 31 per cent of respondents believe it is very important and fairly important respectively. These two groups comprise 93.46 per cent of all participants (see Figure 8.11).

When asked whether the importance of the Sino-European relationship was increasing or decreasing, 67 per cent of the participants thought it was on the rise, which indicates most of them believe that the relationship is improving (see Figure 8.12).

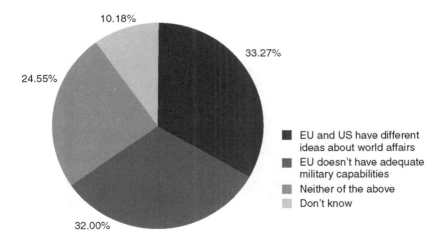

Figure 8.9 Reasons why the EU emphasizes the role of multilateralism in international affairs?

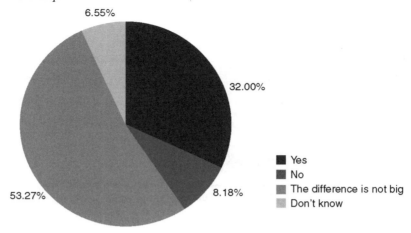

Figure 8.10 Is there any difference between the EU and US on the concept of world order?

When responding to the question of "which side is more active in developing the bilateral relations?" 39.45 per cent of the participants think that both China and EU are equally active in improving the bilateral relations, while 38 per cent think that China is more active (see Figure 8.13)

In answering the question "to what extent is the Sino-European relationship affected by the US?" 42 per cent of those surveyed held the opinion that the US is "extremely influential." Students who chose "very influential" and "generally influential" account for 20 per cent and 28.5 per cent respectively (see Figure 8.14).

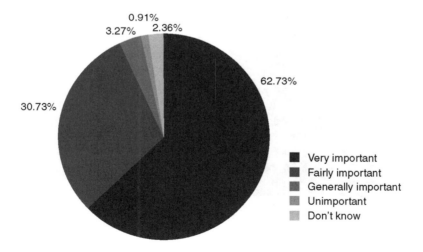

Figure 8.11 Is Europe important in China's foreign strategy?

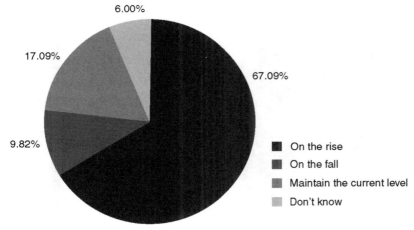

Figure 8.12 Is the importance of Sino-European relations increasing or decreasing in recent years?

When asked why the EU has not yet abolished its arms embargo on China, 50 per cent of the respondents believed that two reasons were most relevant: one is the US objection, and the other is that the EU had not enough trust in China in security affairs. Only 8 per cent think that the EU does not trust China, which is far less than the 28 per cent who think the objection of the US is the main reason.

As for the reasons why the EU has not yet recognized China as a market economy, 47 per cent chose that the EU considers China's economy to be still far from being a market economy, and that China and the EU have different social systems. The second-ranking choice is the impact of trade disputes between China and the EU, accounting for 16 per cent (Figure 8.16).

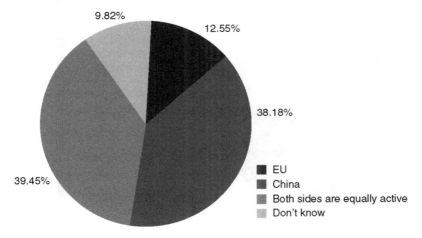

Figure 8.13 Which side is more active in bilateral relations between China and the EU?

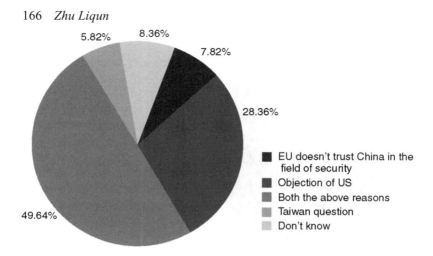

Figure 8.14 Reasons why the EU has not yet abolished the arms embargo against China

On the question as to how to evaluate the human rights dialogue between China and the EU, there is a striking contrast between the 67.82 per cent students choosing positive perspectives and the 8.36 per cent choosing a negative perspective (Figure 8.17).

When asked about the common strategic interests in developing a China–EU relationship, 56.91 per cent of the participants choose "promoting the development of multi-polarization and containing unilateralism." Another 26 per cent think that the common strategic interests between China and the EU lie in promoting democracy, rule of law and a harmonious world order. It is obvious that most participants

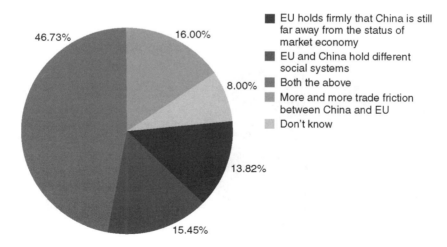

Figure 8.15 Reasons why the EU has not yet recognized China as a market economy

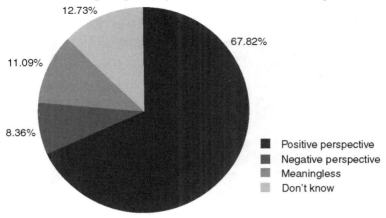

Figure 8.16 How do you view the human rights dialogue between China and the EU?

have a clear, preferential view about the common interests between China and the EU (Figure 8.18).

Lastly, in responding about how to evaluate China–EU relations in the past 30 years, 36.55 per cent of the participants choose "fairly satisfied" and 37.64 per cent feel "generally satisfied." In contrast, respondents who chose either "satisfied" or "not satisfied" are fewer than 10 per cent. It is evident that most students have a positive view of the development of China–EU relations in the past 30 years. The figures also reflect that young students expect further development and improvement of bilateral relations (see Figure 8.19).

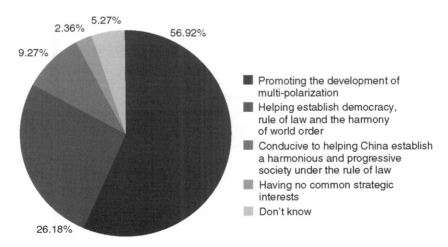

Figure 8.17 What are the common strategic interests in developing bilateral relationships between China and the EU?

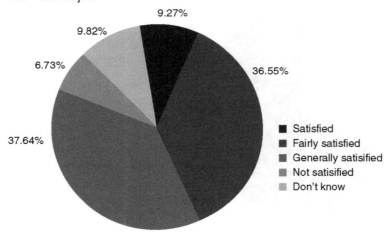

Figure 8.18 How to evaluate the past 30 years' Sino-EU relations?

Several preliminary conclusions can be drawn from the analysis of the results of the questionnaire:

1   University students in China know about the EU and think highly of its position in the international system, acknowledging that the EU's power and advantages come from its economic achievements and integration process.
2   Though most students do not think that European integration has eliminated conflicts and wars resulting from power politics, they appreciate and acknowledge the European development model rather than the US model, including European ideas about the international order.
3   Most students take a positive attitude towards the current status of the Sino-European relationship. They believe that the Sino-European relationship enjoys a prioritized position in China's foreign relations.

Further development of this bilateral relationship is of strategic significance, which is especially beneficial to promoting democratization and institutionalization of international relations and containing unilateralism. Most students took a positive approach to understanding the EU's China policy – such as the human rights dialogue between the EU and China, market economy status and the arms embargo issue – from which no hostile or confrontational feeling exists among the university students, which indicates a new generation of Chinese with a more cooperative and open approach when they look at world affairs. This will become a significant help for maintaining a long-term stable and healthy relationship between the EU and China.

Conclusion

Based upon our analysis of the student survey and the textual analysis of scholars' writings, generally speaking, there is a high consistency among the scholars and the university students in understanding the EU and the China–EU relationship – even though the scholars are more informed about the details of European affairs since most of them are specialists on international and European affairs, whose understanding is more profound than that of the non-specialized students. Both scholars and students take a positive, straightforward and non-ideological approach to looking at the EU and China–EU relations. This is quite similar to what David Shambaugh has found in his research in the preceding chapter.

Two other notable points merit mention. The first is that both scholars and students believe that the EU is becoming more powerful and playing a more important role in the world because of its integration process, even though some scholars still have some doubts about the EU's independent role in the world. As a driving force to promote the institutionalization and democratization of international relations, the EU is regarded as a constructive and normative power in international society and a power significantly helpful to international peace and stability. They give high praise to the EU model, believing it can be transferred or applied to East Asian community building. In some Chinese eyes, even though the power of the EU is limited to the economic field, its model of development and its level of integration give it a unique position in the world. They believe the European ideal is more creative and the European model more attractive, representing the aspirational direction of human social advancement.

But it has to be pointed out that the Chinese analysis of the EU's power and its role is more qualitative and inferential than quantitative and empirical. Most of the qualitative analyses use diversified or equivocal expressions, especially with regard to the estimation of EU power. The concept of "pole," or phrases like "strategic power," "central power," or "important power with great effects and influence in Europe and in the world," are often used casually in analysing the EU from a power (realist) point of view, without any quantitative measures. This problem might be closely linked with the broader and longer perspective that Chinese often take while analysing the international environment. They incline to define the EU from a long-term evolutionary perspective and the trend of transformation of the international power structure. Consequently, the views about the EU and its role in the world are always general and sometimes inaccurate (David Shambaugh's chapter refers to this as a sort of Chinese cognitive dissonance). To some extent, the positive perception of the EU and China–EU relations contains a sort of wishful thinking. This can be proved by the evidence that, on the one hand, Chinese scholars exaggerate the importance of the EU as a whole, while on the other hand they simultaneously criticize the CFSP of the EU as unable to even achieve its minimum goal of speaking with one voice on the international stage. This kind of contradiction, however, is also the result of Chinese dialectical habits of thinking and analysis, left over from the residual Marxist-Leninist-Maoist ideology. The negative side of this dialectical analysis is precisely the lack of precision and accuracy in analysis.

The second point is that both the scholars and the students are likely to take the United States as an intervening factor when they look at the EU and China–EU relations, but there is a subtle change, especially in recent years, as Chinese are gradually becoming more inward-driven and not third-party-driven when they approach the EU. While either the EU's power or the EU model are judged by Chinese as important, the United States is always an important silent factor lurking in the background. This is particularly the case during the ten years our research covers. A new and dynamic trend, however, looming in recent years, is that the influence of the US factor is declining (except in some special areas such as the arms embargo issue), due to the changes of internal and external environments both in China and in Europe.

Especially from the Chinese side, scholars are more keen to look at Europe within its internal dynamics, since the 28 years of reform and opening-up (*gaige kaifang*) have strengthened the linkages between the Chinese and international markets, thus leading to a profound change in China's understanding of globalization, international society and self-identity. China has not only profoundly realized the convergence between international interests and its own, but also gradually has constructed its own identity as a responsible member in the international community. It reflects a fundamental change of Chinese attitude towards international affairs, where Chinese increasingly ask what they can do for the world rather than what the world can do to them. This fundamental change profoundly transformed Chinese perceptions of the international system, including the perception of the EU and China–EU relations.

In the foreseeable future, the US will still be a persistent factor that will influence mutual understandings between China and the EU, but it will not be able to exert a dominant impact on the EU and Europe–China relations. Chinese scholars will tend to look at the EU from China's own needs, to pay more attention to "European experiences" and to explore how China will develop itself by learning from Europe. To understand Europe from the perspective of China's own advancement will be more conspicuous in the future.

Notes

1 The research team was headed by Prof. Zhu Liqun, Director of the Centre for European Studies at China Foreign Affairs University. The team consists of Dr Sun Junhua and other four PhD candidates – Hui Gengtian, Lin Minwang, Zhu Jiejin, Zhong Shujia – and one MA student, Lu Wei. The co-authors are particularly grateful to David Shambaugh, Zhou Hong and Song Xinning for their advice on this chapter.
2 The ten journals include: *European Studies* (sponsored by the Institute of European Studies, Chinese Academy of Social Sciences, CASS), *World Economics and Politics* (sponsored by the Institute of World Economics and Politics, CASS), *Contemporary International Relations* (sponsored by China Institute of Contemporary International Relations, CICIR), *International Studies* (sponsored by China Institute of International Studies), *The Contemporary World* (sponsored by International Department, Central Committee of CPC), *Peace and Development* (sponsored by Institute of Peace and

Development Studies), *International Review* (sponsored by Shanghai Institute of International Studies), *International Forum* (sponsored by Beijing Foreign Studies University), *International Politics Quarterly* (sponsored by Beijing University), *Foreign Affairs Review* (sponsored by China Foreign Affairs University).

3 Richard Louis Edmonds, "China and Europe since 1978: An Introduction", in Richard Louis Edmonds (ed.), *China and Europe since 1978: A European Perspective* (Cambridge: Cambridge University Press, 2002), pp. 1–2.

4 Wu Baiyi, "Guannian Zhuanbian yu Neisheng Dongli – Houlengzhan Shiqi Zhong-Ou Guanxi Benyuan Chutan" [Changed Perceptions vis-à-vis Pragmatic Incentives: An Analysis of Root Causes of the Sino–EU Relations] in *Ouzhou Yanjiu* [European Studies], No. 1 (2006), p. 30.

5 Qiu Yuanlun, "Zhong-Ou Guanxi Xianzhuang yu Weilai" [The Current Status and Future of Sino–EU Relations] in *Shijie Jingji yu Zhengzhi* [World Economics and Politics], No. 10 (2004), p. 8; Franco Algieri, *EU Economic Relations with China: An Institutional Perspective*, ibid, pp.78–9.; and Wu Baiyi, op. cit., p. 30.

6 He Lan, "'9 · 11' Shijianhou de Zhong-Ou Guanxi Jiqi Fazhan Qianjing" [The Sino-European Relationship and Its Prospect after the 9/11 Event] in *Guoji Guancha* [International Observation], No. 1 (2005), p. 48.

7 Pole (in Chinese, *Lji*) is often used by many Chinese scholars to describe a power centre which attracts others to follow. It is mainly defined from the perspective of hard power. Su Huimin, "Xi'ou Zai Duojihua Shijie zhong Xunzhao Ziwo" [Western Europe Pursuit of its Independence in a Multipolarizing World] in *Heping yu Fazhan* [Peace and Development], No. 2 (1999), p. 45.

8 Zhou Jun, "Oumeng de Da Ouzhou zhi Lu" [The Grand-European Road for European Union] in *Shijie Jingji yu Zhengzhi* [World Economics and Politics], No. 9 (2001), p. 10.

9 Qiu Yuanlun, "Cong yu Oumeng de Bijiao zhong Kan Meiguo" [A Study on the United States through its Comparison with the European Union] in *Xiandai Guoji Guanxi* [Contemporary International Relations], No. 3 (2004), p. 22.

10 Wang Yi, "Ouzhou de Yitihua yu Duojihua" [The Integration and Multipolarization in Europe] in *Guoji Wenti Yanjiu* [Journal of International Studies], No. 6 (2002), pp. 39, 43.

11 Chen Zhiqiang, "Xin Guoji Zhixu Goujianzhong de Oumeng" [The European Union in the Construction of a New International Order] in *Nankai Daxue Xuebao* [Journal of Nankai University], No. 2 (2000).

12 See Zhang Maoming, "Shixi Oumeng zai Shijie Geju zhong de Weizhi" [An Analysis on EU's Position in the International System] in *Shijie Jingji yu Zhengzhi* [World Economics and Politics], No. 4 (2002).

13 Chen Zhiqiang, op. cit.

14 Zhang Maoming, op. cit., pp. 62–3.

15 Zhang Zuqian, "Ouzhou Sanjiao Geju de Xingcheng, Xianzhuang he Fazhan Qushi" [The European Tripolar System: Formation, Current Status, and Developing Trend] in *Shijie Jingji yu Zhengzhi* [World Economics and Politics], No. 2 (2000). Also see Zhang Maoming, op. cit., p. 61.

16 Zhou Jun, op. cit., p. 12.

17 Chen Chaogao (ed.), *Ouzhou Yitihua yu Shijie* [European Integration and the World] (Beijing: Shishi Chubanshe [Current Affairs Press], 1999), p. 178; Zhang Maoming, op. cit., p. 61.

18 Jiang Jianqing, op. cit., p. 14.

19 Su Huimin, "Huzun Gongjin Yingjie Xinshiji – Tan Zhongguo Oumeng Guanxi" [To See the New Century with Mutual Respect and Common Progress – On Sino-European Relations] in *Guoji Wenti Yanjiu* [Journal of International Studies], No. 4 (1998), p. 13.

20 Tong Tianqi, "Oumeng de Duiwai Zhanlue" [EU's Foreign Strategy] in *Guoji Wenti Yanjiu* [Journal of International Studies], No. 2 (2001), p. 36.

21 The EU model is defined by Chinese scholars from both internal and external aspects. From the internal side, Europe pays more attention to a balanced development of

economy and society. From the external side, Europe is an actor advocating multilateralism, institutionalism and security community building – all of which are believed good for international society and human advancement.

22 Zhang Jun, "Cong Ya-Ou Huiyi Jincheng Kan Fazhan Guoji Guanxi de 'Ouzhou Moshi'," [A 'European Model' of International Relations from the Perspective of the Asia–Europe Meeting] in *Ouzhou Yanjiu* [Chinese Journal of European Studies], No. 1 (2006), p. 4.

23 Chen Zhirui, "'Ouzhou Moshi yu Ou-Mei Guanxi' Yantaohui Zongshu" [A Summary of the Seminar "European Model and European–American Relations"] in *Ouzhou Yanjiu* [Chinese Journal of European Studies], No. 4 (2003).

24 Liu Xige, "Qianxi Zhongguo tong Oumeng de Waijiao yu Anquan Hezuo" [An Analysis on Sino–EU Foreign and Security Cooperation] in *Guoji Wenti Yanjiu* [Journal of International Studies], No. 6 (2003), p. 27.

25 Zhang Jun, op. cit., p. 3.

26 Qiu Yuanlun, "Cong Wuda Guanjianci Rushou Liaojie Ouzhou Waijiao" [Understanding European Diplomacy from Five Key Words] in *Xiandai Guoji Guanxi* [Contemporary International Relations], No. 3 (2002), p. 23.

27 Chen Zhirui, op. cit.

28 Qiu Yuanlun, op. cit., p. 23–4.

29 Su Huimin, "Huzun Gongjin Yingjie Xinshiji – Tan Zhongguo Oumeng Guanxi" [To See the New Century with Mutual Respect and Common Progress – On Chinese–European Relations] in *Guoji Wenti Yanjiu* [Journal of International Studies], No. 4 (1998), p. 13.

30 Liu Xige, op. cit., p. 27.

31 Qiu Yuanlun, op. cit., p. 24.

32 Chen Zhirui, op. cit.

33 Wu Baiyi, op. cit., p. 29.

34 He Lan, op. cit., p. 48.

35 Liu Xige, op. cit., p. 27.

36 Wang Yi, op. cit., p. 43.

37 Chen Zhirui, op. cit.

38 Zhang Maoming, op. cit., p. 65.

39 Liu Xige, op. cit., p. 30.

40 Wang Yi, op. cit., p. 43.

41 Shi Jiayou, "'Houxiandai' Ouzhou Jiqi dui Zhongguo de Yiyi" [A "Post-Modern" Europe and Its Significance to China] [Chinese Journal of European Studies], No. 1 (2005).

42 Sun Yanhong, "Zhongguo-Oumeng Guanxi de Fazhan yu Weilai – 'Jinian Zhong-Ou Jianjiao 30 Zhounian' Xueshu Yantaohui Zongshu" [The Development and Future of the Sino–EU relations – A Summary of the Seminar "the 30th Anniversary of the Establishment of Sino-European Relations"] in *Ouzhou Yanjiu* [Chinese Journal of European Studies], No. 3 (2005), pp. 154–5.

43 Dai Bingran, Ibid.

44 Shi Jiayou, op. cit., p. 15.

45 Liu Xige, op. cit., p. 28; Xu Kaiyi, op. cit.

46 Wu Baiyi, op. cit., p. 29.

47 Dai Bingran, op. cit., pp. 74–5.

48 Wu Baiyi, op. cit.

49 Liu Xige, op. cit., p. 27.

50 Zhang Baijia, "Gaibian Ziji, Yingxiang Shijie" [Change Ourselves, Influence the World] in *Huanqiu Shibao* [Global Times], 18 February 2002.

51 Shi Jiayou, op. cit.

52 Zhai Dongsheng, "Nansha Zhong-Ou Wenhua Luntan: Ouzhou Daigei Women de Qishi" [The Sino-European Forum on Culture in Nansha: The Inspiration Brought by Europe] in *Ouzhou Yanjiu* [Chinese Journal of European Studies], No. 6 (2005), p. 151.

53 Wu Baiyi, op. cit., p. 24.

54 Huo Zhengde, "Lun Zhong-Ou Zhanlue Guanxi" [On Sino-European Strategic Relations] in *Guoji Wenti Yanjiu* [Journal of International Studies], No. 2 (2005), p. 1.
55 Shi Jiayou, Ibid.
56 Liu Jiansheng, "Zhong-Ou Guanxi: Cong 'Erli' Dao 'Buhuo'" [The Sino-European Relations: From "30 Years Old" to "40 Years Old"] in *Liaowang Xinwen Zhoukan* [Outlook News Week], 12 September 2005, p. 55.
57 According to Zhou Hong, the asymmetry is shown in four aspects – economy and society, political system, history and culture. Yet she also dialectically stresses that there is also symmetry within asymmetry, which nurtures opportunities for the partnership. Both need to understand each other's "way," seeking the complementarity of this asymmetry and win–win solution, and enhancing the cooperative partnership. See Zhou Hong, "Lun Zhong-Ou Guanxizhong de Buduichenxing yu Duichenxing" [On the Asymmetry and Symmetry in Sino-European Relations] in *Ouzhou Yanjiu* [Chinese Journal of European Studies], No. 2 (2004).
58 Liu Xige, op. cit., p. 28.
59 Liu Xige, ibid.
60 Huo Zhengde, op. cit., p. 5.
61 Huo Zhengde, ibid., p. 4.
62 Feng Jian, "Oumeng Dongkuo de Zhengfumian Xiaoying Fenxi" [An Analysis on the Positive and Negative Effects of Eastern Enlargement of EU] in *Ouzhou Yanjiu* [Chinese Journal of European Studies] No. 4 (2002), p. 95.
63 Liu Xige, op. cit., p. 30.
64 Huo Zhengde, op. cit., p. 3.
65 Liu Xige, op. cit., p. 30.
66 Liu Xige, ibid.
67 Wu Liming, "Oumeng Jiechu Duihua Junshou Jinling de Fenqi he Tuoxie" [The Divergences and Compromises on EU's Lifting the Arms Ban on China] in *Liaowang Xinwen Zhoukan* [Outlook News Week], 18 October 2004, p. 50.
68 The general public in China is more concerned about Japan and the United States, and this has exerted a big influence on the foreign policy towards them.

9 China's view of European integration and enlargement

Song Xinning

Chinese perceptions of European integration can be divided into different categories, i.e. the view of the Chinese government, the view of Chinese academics, and the view of the Chinese public – although there are interactions among these different groups. This chapter will mainly focus on the views of Chinese academics, and basically the understanding of the author himself.

The European Community/European Union as a political entity

Studies on European integration started in China during the 1970s. The first Chinese book was written by a group of Chinese scholars in Shanghai, entitled *The West European Common Market*.[1] At that time, Chinese studies of Europe were poorly developed (see Dai Bingran's chapter in this volume) and were viewed in the context of the "capitalist world," "state-monopoly capitalism," and "imperialism." Those few scholars who researched the nature of the European Economic Community emphasized three aspects: (1) the EEC was regarded as a political entity of the Western imperialist countries; (2) the EEC was regarded as an American ally and tool of the United States in Washington's control Western Europe and (3) the EEC was regarded as a political entity of struggle among the two superpowers, i.e. the Soviet Union and the United States. These hypotheses were rooted in the Leninist "Theory of Imperialism" (*Diguozhuyilun*) and the Maoist theory of the "Three Worlds." According to Lenin's theory of imperialism, there were three major reasons for West European countries to establish the EEC.

First, the Common Market was seen as the result of the imbalanced development of capitalist politics and economics. The power of the United States was seen as superficial and temporary although it was the most powerful capitalist country in world economics, trade and finance. Because of the economic and energy crises in the 1970s, the United States became weaker and weaker. At the same time the economic growth of France, West Germany, and Italy became more rapid, and the balance of power had changed. The perceived goal of a united Western Europe was to improve their international position and break away from the control of the United States.[2]

Second, the Common Market was seen as the result of the struggle between Western Europe and the United States. The establishment of the "Socialist Camp" led by the Soviet Union and the collapse of the colonial system in the world had reduced the imperialist spheres of influence. The struggle for market share in the developed and developing world became more acute. The aim of the six Western European countries to form the Common Market was to solidify their market control in Europe and to enlarge their spheres of influence in the world.[3]

Third, the Common Market was viewed as being based upon the development of "monopoly capitalism," especially state-monopoly capitalism (*guojia longduan zibenzhuyi*). Monopoly was the most important economic characteristic of imperialism. The six Western European countries were all typical monopoly capitalist countries. After World War II, state-monopoly capitalism in Germany, France and Italy developed very fast. The cooperation among monopoly organizations and monopoly capitalist states had its historical tradition and developed further after World War II. The European Community of Coal and Steel was the first step of international monopolization in Europe. The EEC symbolized the highest level of the cooperation between private monopoly and state monopoly in Europe.[4]

According to the "Three Worlds" theory, Western Europe was regarded as the "Second World," which was the ally of the United States and the possible united front with China for fighting against the Soviet Union. Chinese scholars recognized the role of the United States in the process of European integration. According to them, the goal of the United States was to control Western Europe through economic, political and military unification in Europe. Along with the growth of their economic capacities, West European countries realized that they had to keep the power of European integration in their own hands. The step was to form the EEC in order to be independent from the United States.[5] At the same time, Western Europe faced the military threat from the Soviet Union – thus, they had to keep the military alliance with the United States via NATO. But the military alliance would not prevent the economic and political competition between the Western Europe and the United States. The establishment of Western European Common Market indicated that Western Europe had become an important power and increasingly autonomous actor in the capitalist world against Soviet and American hegemony.[6]

After the 1990s, when European studies in China became more social science-oriented, Chinese scholars started to pay more attention to the function of the European Communities and later the European Union.

The EU as an entity of regional cooperation

The EEC/EC and EU were not established explicitly to counter-balance any other major power in world politics and economics. The main catalyst and dynamics are to maintain economic prosperity and peace among European countries through regional cooperation. The process of European integration started in the field of steel and coal in the 1950s, and then expanded to trade and agricultural policy in the 1970s, monetary cooperation in the 1970s, to a single market in the 1980s and 1990s. The latest step is to establish economic and monetary union. Differing from the economic cooperation in other parts of the world the EC/EU is a group of sovereign states within a certain institutional framework and in many fields, especially in international trade, the EC/EU acts as a single entity.

The EC/EU as a supranational institution

The function of the EC/EU in Europe and the world takes place through the institutional framework of the European Commission, the European Parliament, the European Court of Justice, etc. Many Chinese scholars pay attention to the characteristics (instead of the nature in terms of the traditional Leninist view) and the function of these European institutions. The essential element of the supranational institution is the transfer and sharing of national sovereignty. As such, the EC/EU as a supranational institution is a new framework in international relations. The three main characteristics of the EC/EU as a supranational institution include its voluntary nature, equality, transfer and sharing of national sovereignty. The core is the voluntary transfer of national sovereignty. This makes it differ from the alliance and other kinds of regional or international cooperation.[7]

European integration as a process

Integration (*yitihua*) is a new term in Chinese international studies. What integration is and how to define integration is still hotly debated in China. The Western theory of integration was introduced to China in the late 1980s and mainly from Western IR theories, such as Karl Deutsch and Robert Pfaltzgraff. In the 1990s, when Chinese scholars talked about integration, it was a very broad concept with very little concern for European integration.[8] Many scholars did comparative studies on the European Union and APEC. From the middle of the 1990s, Western Integration Theory started to be introduced to Chinese IR studies. Scholars of European studies started to pay attention to the theoretical development along with the European integration process. Entering into the twenty-first century, Political Economy and International Political Economy approaches became more and more popular in the Chinese academic world, and many Chinese scholars looked at European integration from new perspectives, especially the functionalist approach and the political economy approach.[9]

For Chinese nowadays, integration became a special concept relevant mainly to European affairs. According to some Chinese scholars, integration is defined as: "A process of different sovereign entities to become a single entity in a certain way."[10] As a process, the European integration has three major characteristics.

First, integration is a process for independent sovereign states to become a single sovereign entity (not necessarily a new sovereign state). The main actors in the process are sovereign states. So it is a new kind of inter-state or international relations. The goal of integration is the merger, combination or amalgamation of the traditional nation-state, no matter what kind of forms such as federation, confederation or others. So it is basically a political and legal process. In order to bring about the process, it is very important for the political and economic elites and politicians to play essential roles. At the same time it is impossible to develop the process without certain legal arrangements and institution-building.

Second, integration is a process of transfer and share of national sovereignty. As a process for different sovereign states to become a single sovereign or legal entity, it is inevitable to touch upon the transfer or share of national sovereignties. Because of this characteristic, integration is very different from inter-state or international cooperation.

The transfer of sovereignty is a very complicated issue. There are essentially two kinds of sovereignty transfer. First, there is the automatic or self-restriction of national sovereignty. A good example is to join international organizations, such as the WTO, which have binding legal effects on sovereign states. In this case the state does not lose sovereignty. It has the right to withdraw or not to restrict its own sovereignty by many meanings. Second, there is the transfer of sovereignty to some other supranational institutions. In this case, the nation-state transfers some of its sovereign power to some other institution. Once transferred, it is not easy to get it back. But to transfer sovereignty does not necessarily mean to forfeit sovereignty. It is mainly dependent on to whom sovereignty is transferred. If one state transfers its sovereignty to another state, it is a zero-sum loss. But in the integration process, member states transfer part of their sovereignty to certain supranational institutions in which they also take the part of the decision-maker. In this case the transfer of national sovereignty is also a sharing of sovereignty with others. For smaller countries, it even means an enlargement of sovereignty.

Third, integration is a process of comprehensive political, economic and social interaction at different levels. First, it is a political-economic interaction at the European level, i.e. the communalization of European politics and economics, such as European institutions. At the same time, it is a political-economic interaction among member states, the member states and EU institutions or supranational institutions. Second, from the global aspect, the development of European integration and its impact on the EU as a global player, the EU role in the global political economy is also a political-economic interaction. Economically, the EU has the same economic power as the United States. But politically, the EU is much less powerful than the United States. The EU is a kind of soft power or civilian power. Whether this is good for world development or not is very much debatable.

There is no simple or pure economic and political integration in the process. Economic integration includes political integration, and political integration promotes economic integration. In the process of integration, politics and economics always go together. The political process needs the economic foundation, and the economic process needs the political and legal institutions as the guarantee.[11]

European integration as a model

European studies in China have become more and more popular since the mid-1990s. One of the reasons for it was EU-funded programmes in Chinese universities, think tanks and research academies. From 1997 to 2001, the European Commission and Chinese government implemented the first EU–China Higher Education Cooperation Programme with 9.76 million ECU funding from the EU. The programme supported 14 centres for European studies in China and more than 500 Chinese scholars in the field of European studies. From 2005 to 2007, the EU–China European Studies Centres Programme with 11 million euros supports 20 centres for European studies in China. Another reason for the interest among Chinese in doing European studies is the relevance of European experiences to China's domestic and international development. In other words, the interest of Chinese is in looking at European integration as a potential model, possibly applicable to China–Taiwan relations and/or as a possible model for Asian integration. The relevance of the European model can be divided into several aspects.

The European model of political development

Since the end of the Cultural Revolution in the late 1970s, China has faced the problem of the political legitimacy of the rule of the Communist Party of China (CPC). In the first 40 years of the People's Republic of China, the basis of the legitimacy of the CPC was neither public participation nor social or economic welfare, but the charisma of the personal leadership such as Mao Zedong and Deng Xiaoping, the ideology of communism plus nationalism and the centralized political system. After the beginning of domestic reform and opening up to the outside world, the ideology of communism has lost its base. Nationalism is also a challenge to the current leadership. Along with the market economy system, decentralization has become the common demand from local levels. None of the political leaders in China has a position as strong as Mao or Deng. Although the Chinese Communist Party leadership are facing a number of big challenges, most Chinese still believe that no other political forces can or should replace its ruling position. This is because it was the Communist Party of China that started the process of reform and open-up policy and has provided a better living standard to the Chinese people.

Along with the economic reform, political reform became a crucial issue in China. Many Chinese believe that political reform in China should start with the reform of the Communist Party. After Deng Xiaoping's "Socialism with Chinese Characteristics," Jiang Zemin put forward the so-called "Three Represents," and Hu Jintao has the slogans of "Promoting the Ruling Capacity of the Communist Party" and the "Harmonious Society." Before putting forward those strategies, the Chinese government supported various research projects on the European social democratic parties. For many Chinese scholars, the role and function of European social democratic parties are a good example for the CPC to improve its position in Chinese society.[12]

The European model of social and economic development

Along with the market economy reform in China, China has rapid economic growth, as well as social problems such as regional imbalances, enlarged gap between rich and poor, public health, floating population from rural areas to major cities, etc. China faces big problems of social instability which could pose a challenge to the ruling position of the Communist regime.

As a result of these domestic social problems, Chinese scholars started to study the European model of social welfare in the 1980s. At first they were primarily interested in the so-called "Nordic model."[13] Since the late 1990s, when European studies became one of the hot topics in international studies, many Chinese scholars have paid special attention to the European welfare state, social welfare and social security systems, and the EU regional policy. From 1998–2001, the EU–China Higher Education Cooperation Programme provided funding for 143 collaborative research projects, including 27 projects related to the EU social policy (social security system, welfare state, public health, ageing, employment policy, environmental policy, etc.), about 19 per cent of the total. Among the 440 Chinese visiting scholars supported by the Programme, 117 of them (26.6 per cent) did research projects related to European social policies.[14] There are also hundreds of articles published in Chinese journals on these topics.

For Chinese scholars, if China establishes a social security system to solve the social problems in the transitional period, the state will still play an essential role. The European social security model is thus more relevant to China than the American model – although both of them have their own problems.[15]

The European model as a new approach to regional cooperation in world affairs

European integration is the most successful example of regional cooperation in the world. European integration is also a special European phenomenon due to the level of economic development, political culture, and historical tradition in Europe. But there is still something that has universal value. First, the approach of European integration that starts from functional cooperation and then expands to other fields is a good way to promote regional cooperation. Second, institutionalization and legalization are a basis to promote regional cooperation from low political fields to high politics. Otherwise, it is very difficult for member states to transfer national sovereignty. It is also one of the reasons why APEC and East Asian regional cooperation are not very successful.

In world affairs, although most European countries are in a close alliance with the United States, they are demonstrating much more independence in international affairs. During the Cold War era, according to Mao's Theory of the Three Worlds, Chinese analysts regarded the EC as one of the important counterbalances to the United States. China regarded the EC as an informal alliance against the contending hegemony of the two superpowers and a potential pole in a possible multipolar world. After the end of the Cold War, many Chinese believed that the contradictions among Western countries (United States, Western Europe and Japan) would become more intensified and the international structure would more likely become a multipolar one. In the late 1990s and early 2000s, more Chinese scholars came to realize that the Western countries were still in the same family and economic globalization meant *tighter* interdependence among them. The basic tendency of the international structure would not be mulitpolarity, but non-polarity![16] Under this circumstance, the role of the EU would not be an independent pole, but a soft power in the world political economy.

What global role would the EU play as a soft power? First, the EU plays an important role in the world economy because of its economic capabilities. Second, the EU has the potential capacity to play a more important role in world politics, although it has not had a real "Common Foreign and Security Policy" (CFSP). Third, the EU plays a more and more important role in international institutions such as the United Nations and WTO.[17] Fourth, as an ally of the United States, the EU plays a different role mainly due to its differing diplomatic style from the United States.[18] The EU prefers the multilateralist approach to solving international problems through negotiations and dialogues. It also provides development aid to many developing countries. The EU concept of "Effective Multilateralism" has been well received among Chinese scholars as well as the Chinese government. The role of the EU and the multilateralist way of dealing with international affairs provide good examples for global governance in the contemporary world and for the future.

The European model as an example of "peaceful rise"

China's "peaceful rise" is a hotly debated topic in China, although the Chinese government has officially abandoned the term in favour of "peaceful development." Yet there remain different ideas about China's "peaceful rise" in China. One of the ideas is "China's Peaceful Rise and the Experience of Europe." According to some Chinese scholars, China's peaceful rise is not a historical exception. After World War II, Europe, the European Community, and later the European Union developed as an important world power through a process of peaceful rise. What China can learn from the European experience includes three aspects.

First, it is to establish good relationships with the countries in Europe through the regional integration process. Because of European integration, the European countries work together in all fields such as economics, politics and military affairs. The integrated Europe extended from six countries to the current twenty-seven, with the prospect of even more in the future. The gradually integrated European continent has become the most peaceful and stable region in the world. This process of integration may hold promise for the future evolution of the East Asian Community (EAC).

Second, as Europe has integrated and risen in global influence it has been careful to maintain a good relationship with the major power (the United States) through political and military alliance. Europe and the United States share common political values and social and economic systems. Because of the shared experiences of World War II and the Cold War with the Soviet Union, Western Europe and the United States forged a strong transatlantic bond, as well as political and military alliance. Although there were different national interests between Europe and the United States, Western European countries enjoyed the leadership and took the free ride on American hegemony. Because of the Euro–US alliance and economic interdependence, the rise of Europe did not challenge the United States. They even shared leadership in world politics and economics with the United States. This is the so-called "Western Collective Hegemony."[19] During the Iraq War since 2002, some EU member states had divergent views with the United States. Many Chinese scholars regarded the EU–US alliance as being in a troubled period. Some even predicted that the foundation of transatlantic relations had been fundamentally changed, while other Chinese scholars argued that the EU was still in line with the United States. The only difference between the United States and the EU was over how to deal with the Iraq issue – not the basic goal of regime change in Iraq.[20]

Third, the EU is to play a more active role in the world community through cooperation with the international institutions and the developing countries. The EC/EU was not only a free rider on US hegemony, but China was also a free rider on the international institutions jointly founded by the United States and the Western European countries in the 1950s and 1960s. After the 1970s, the EC/EU came to play a more and more important role in institutions through cooperation with the United States and in international institutions. So the role of the EC/EU in the world community is complementary instead of a challenge to US hegemony and the contemporary international system or international order. This has benefited China.

As China's involvement in international institutions grows, the EU's "Effective Multilateralism" may serve as a model for China's increased responsibilities for global governance. For China, the multilateralist approach of the EU is more welcomed by the international community than the unilateralist role of the United States. The reason for this includes three major elements: (a) the EU provides more development aid to the developing world than any other developed countries. Good examples are the Lome Convention and various European cooperation programmes with the developing countries; (b) the European countries are more active in promoting South–North dialogues and cooperation; (c) the EU always plays a role in the world community via "soft power."

For Chinese scholars, because the EU wisely and successfully coped with the three major relationships – the relationship with neighbouring countries, the relationship with the hegemonic power and the relationship with the international community – there is no negative argument in China on the "peaceful rise of Europe." If China would like its peaceful rise to be acceptable within the world community, China should learn from the European experience.[21]

EU enlargement as both opportunity and challenge

China did not pay much attention to the EU enlargement before 2004. When Chinese analysts looked at the first enlargement in the 1970s, they still followed the traditional thoughts of Leninism and Maoism. According to Shanghai scholars, the first enlargement of the Western European Common Market showed that "It has become a political and economic power that can counter-balance American Imperialism and Soviet Revisionism. It makes American Imperialism and Soviet Revisionism face serious challenges."[22] The further enlargement in the 1980s and 1990s did not attract the attention of Chinese scholars because most of the new members were the smaller and less developed countries in Europe. The fifth round of enlargement of the EU in 2004 was regarded as a very important event in European integration and world affairs.

EU enlargement as a successful outcome of European integration

When Chinese Europe specialists looked at the latest rounds of EU enlargement, some argued that there was a special reason for the EU member states to encourage the process: to integrate Central and East European countries into the Western capitalist orbit and to constrain Russia. There were also a few scholars who held the opinion that one of the goals of EU enlargement was to compete with the United States. But most Chinese scholars in European studies emphasized that enlargement was an inevitable outcome of European integration (although some argued that the process of enlargement was too fast and too ambitious). For the Central and Eastern European countries, the application process had gone on for more than a decade. During the process, domestic political and economic transition was quite successful due to the support of the EU and the EU member states. For them, joining the EU had many benefits. But the main attraction is the successful process of European integration. It provided economic prosperity, political stability and security to all EU members and to Europe as a whole. Of course, there is the problem of keeping a balance between enlargement and deepening the integration.[23]

EU enlargement as both opportunity and challenge to EU–China relations

The main concern for China concerning EU enlargement is the impact of the enlargement on EU–China relations. For most Chinese specialists, EU enlargement provides more opportunities than challenges.

Political and economic opportunities from EU enlargement

Politically, EU enlargement means the increase of economic and political capabilities of the European Union. Chinese always stress that a strong EU is good for world peace, stability and development. Because the EU–China relationship has improved smoothly since the mid-1990s, and both sides agreed to establish a "comprehensive strategic partnership" in 2003, an enlarged and stronger EU is also good for the further development of EU–China relations, as well as China's position in the world community.

Economically, the EU enlargement means the enlargement of the EU market. The European Union has become more and more important for China's domestic economic development and external economic relations. The EU became the number one trading partner for China, and China became the number two trading partner of the EU in 2004. The EU enlargement will provide more opportunities for EU–China economic cooperation.

Political and economic challenges from EU enlargement

Although the EU enlargement provides more opportunities than challenges, the negative impacts still cannot be ignored. Politically, the EU enlargement will simultaneously increase the capabilities and, at the same time, it will decrease the efficiency of the EU as a singular actor in world politics. Europe's different voices during the Iraq War is a good example. Many Chinese discussed the intra-European and transatlantic disputes between the so-called "Old Europe" and "New Europe" at that time.[24] Enlargement may also have a negative impact on EU–China political relations because many new EU member states were former Communist countries. After the collapse of the Soviet Union and East European Communist Party-states, there remains a strong ideological prejudice in some of these new member states towards China, because it is still governed by the Communist Party of China. Good examples are the attitude of Poland and the Czech Republic on the arms embargo issue towards China, as well as their stance on the Tibet issue and criticisms of China's human rights record.[25]

Economically, EU enlargement brings three major concerns for China. Firstly, there will likely be increasing economic competition with the new EU member states. The new members have the same comparative advantages as China in many tertiary industries. Their level of economic development and labour costs are very similar to China's. As part of the European single market, the new Central and Eastern European members will be strong economic competitors of China in the European market. Another field of competition will be foreign direct investment (FDI). Because of the economic gap, the EU needs to provide bigger funding through investment to support the economic development of the new members. It will affect the FDI flow from Europe to China. Then there is the anti-dumping issue. Before joining the EU, the 10 new members had quite flexible anti-dumping policies towards China. But after joining the EU, these new members follow the tough EU regulations on anti-dumping. Until the EU grants China Market Economy Status (MES), the anti-dumping issues will be problematic. Third, agricultural products may cause problems. Due to the EU Common Agriculture Policy, the EU has a fixed tariff quota to Chinese agricultural products. If the EU does not increase the quota, it will affect China's agricultural exports to the new member states. But the Chinese economic ties with the new member states are still marginal. In 2003, the trade between China and the 10 new members was near $8.2 billion, about 1 per cent of China's foreign trade. The potential problems between China and the 10 new members will be short-term and it affects only 0.5 per cent of Chinese exports to Europe. In the long-term, enlargement provides more market opportunities for China.[26]

Conclusion

Big changes have taken place in China's view of European integration and enlargement since the middle of the 1990s. It essentially changed from an ideological approach to a more scientific, pragmatic and objective one. Three major reasons affected the changes.

The first was the introduction of scientific research approaches to China, basically from the Western world. European studies is not just part of international studies and comparative politics – it is a multidisciplinary field, incorporating political science, economics, sociology, law, history, etc. With more new approaches in the field, Chinese scholars have started to look at European integration and enlargement from more scientific and academic perspectives.

Second, the positive development of EU–China relations has made a definite impact. Since 1995 when the European Commission first put forward the China policy "Communication," EU–China relations have developed rapidly and smoothly. EU–China relations are regarded by many Chinese international relations specialists as the best bilateral relationship in all of China's foreign relations. The development of EU–China relations stimulates not only the interests of Chinese scholars in European studies, but also financial and human resources in the field.

Third, China's domestic political, economic and social development has affected the field of study. Since 1978 when China started the reform and opening-up process, great political, economic and social changes have taken place in China. As a transition period China makes great progress in economic growth, and China also faces extremely serious political and social challenges.

However, China's view of European integration and enlargement remains diverse. This chapter has sought to illustrate the range of opinions in China, from the perspective of the author. Yet, despite the range of views evident, it is certain that Chinese scholars have paid close attention to the twin processes of European enlargement and integration.

Notes

1 Editorial Group, *Western European Common Market* (Shanghai: Shanghai Renmin Chubanshe, 1973).
2 Ibid., pp.7–9.
3 Ibid., pp.9–12.
4 Ibid., pp.12–16.
5 Ibid., pp.4–6.
6 Ibid., pp.1–2.

7 Song Xinning, "Political Economy Approaches to European Integration Studies," *International Perspective*, No. 5, 2005.

8 See Wang: Yizhou, *Western International Politics: History and Theories* (Shanghai: Shanghai Renmin Chubanshe, 1998); Ni Shixiong, *Contemporary Western International Relations Theories* (Shanghai: Fudan University Press, 2001).

9 Hu Jin (ed.), *Theories and Practice of European Integration in the Early Years* (Jinan: Shandong Renmin Chubanshe, 2000); Hu Jin (ed.), *Theories and Practice of Contemporary European Integration* (Jinan: Shandong Renmin Chubanshe, 2002); Song Xinning, "Political Economy Approaches to European Integration Studies," op. cit.

10 Song Xinning, ibid.

11 Ibid.

12 See Song Xinning, "The Impact of Domestic Politics on Chinese Foreign Policy", in Weixing Chen and Yang Zhong, (eds.), *Leadership in a Changing China*, (New York: Palgrave Macmillan, 2005), pp.147–68. After the "Three Represents" were announced by Jiang Zemin, some people in China argued that the strategy was to change the CPC into a European-style social democratic party.

13 See Huang Fanzhang, *Sweden: The Practice and Theory of Welfare State* (Shanghai: Shanghai Renmin Chubanshe, 1987); Huang Anmiao and Zhang Xiaojin, *Analysis of the Swedish Model* (Harbin: Heilongjiang Renmin Chubanshe, 1989); Zhang Xiaojin and Li Tianqing, *From Functional Socialism to Funding Socialism: Theory and Practice of Swedish Social Democratic Party* (Harbin: Heilongjiang Renmin Chubanshe, 1989); Zhang Yunling (ed.), *The Nordic Social Welfare System and Reform of China's Social Security System* (Beijing: China Social Sciences Press, 1993). Zhang Ping, *Sweden: A Good Example of Social Welfare Economy* (Wuhan: Wuhan Daxue Chubanshe, 1994).

14 EU–China Higher Education Cooperation Programme: *Programme Report (1997–2001)*, Beijing, PMO, 2002.

15 See Qiu Yuanlun and Luo Hongbo (eds.), *Comparative Studies on Employment Policy in the EU and China* (Beijing: China Economics Press, 1998); Du Peng, *The European Aging Issue and Policies* (Beijing: China Population Press, 2000); Zhang Jianhua, *European Integration and the EU Economic and Social Policy* (Beijing: Shangwu Yinshuguan, 2001); Zhang Keyun, *Regional Economic Policy: Theoretical Basis and the Practice of the EU* (Beijing: China Light Industry Press, 2001); Tian Dewen, *European Social Policy and European Integration* (Beijing: Social Sciences Document Press, 2005); Zhou Hong, *Whither the Welfare State?* (Beijing: China Social Sciences Press, 2006).

16 Song Xinning and Chen Yue, *Introduction to International Politics* (Beijing: Renmin University Press, 2000), p. 90.

17 Zhang Maoming, *The European Union: Studies on the Capacity of International Action* (Beijing: Dangdai Shijie Chubanshe, 2003).

18 Song Xinning, "EU–US Relations from the Perspective of Iraqi War," *Teaching and Research*, No. 4, 2003.

19 Song Xinning, "Rethinking of the Theory of Hegemonic Stability," *China Book Review* (Hong Kong), September 1998.

20 Song Xinning, "EU–US Relations from the Perspective of Iraqi War," op. cit.

21 Song Xinning, "China's Peaceful Rise and the European Experiences", *Teaching and Research*, No. 4, 2004.

22 Editorial Group, *Western European Common Market*, op. cit., p. 187.

23 A database of Chinese language journals (www.cnki.net) identifies about 600 articles discussing EU enlargement issues from 2000 and 2006. The most representative articles include Wu Yikang, "The EU Enlargement and Institutional Reform," *Contemporary International Relations*, No. 3, 2002; Wu Xian, "Divergence and Integration: Dynamics, Measures and Background of the EU Enlargement", *World Affairs*, No. 7, 2003; Fang Lei, "Analysis of the Effects of the EU Enlargement," *China Journal of European Studies*, No. 4, 2003; Dai Qiu, "The EU after Enlargement: Opportunity and

Challenges", *German Studies*, No. 2, 2004; Mei Zhaorong, "Historical Enlargement of the EU and Its Impacts", *Journal of International Studies*, No. 5, 2004; Qiu Zhi, "The Dynamic Base of the EU Enlargement", *Forum of World Economics and Politics*, No. 4, 2004; Feng Shaolei, "The EU Enlargement and Great Power Game", *Russian Studies*, No. 2, 2004; Ding Yuanhong, "EU Enlargement and European Integration," *Peace and Development*, No. 2, 2004; Dai Bingran, "Political Implications of EU Enlargement," *International Perspective*, No. 2, 2004; Pan Qichang, "Opportunities and Risks of the EU Enlargement," *Contemporary World*, No. 5, 2004. The latest book published in China is by Zhang Shujing, *Economic Integration after EU Enlargement* (Beijing: Peking University Press, 2006).

24 Zhao Huaipu, "The US New Europe Strategy," *China Journal of European Studies*, No. 4, 2004.

25 There is no official publication on this issue but lots of inside discussion.

26 Wang Hongtao, "The EU Enlargement and Its Impacts on EU–China Economic and Trade Relations", *Situation of World Economy*, No. 1, 2005; Zhang Shujing, "The Effects of Enlargement on the EU Trade," *International Economic Cooperation*, No. 11, 2005; Zhang Xiying, "Impact of EU Enlargement on China: Policy Considerations," *Economic Forum*, No. 24, 2004; Zhang Shujing, *Economic Integration after EU Enlargement* (Beijing: Peking University Press, 2006).

Part V
China–Europe commercial relations

10 Europe's commercial relations with China

*Robert Ash**

Europe's commercial relations with China operate at two levels, which do not wholly overlap but are not mutually exclusive. One is the bilateral level of trade and investment relations between China and individual countries of Europe.[1] The other is the collective level of such relations between China and the collective organization of the European Union, of which an increasing number of European countries have become members.[2] Both levels of relations are embraced in this chapter, although for reasons of space it is impossible to treat individual European countries' commercial relations with China in as much detail as I would have wished.

What follows is a preliminary exploration of some of Europe–China foreign trade and investment developments, as viewed through the prisms of EU–China economic relations, and the bilateral commercial relationships between some single European countries and China. The structure of the chapter is as follows. First, I provide an overview of the evolution of a collective European economic strategy towards China, captured in the increasingly close trade and investment relations that have emerged between Brussels and Beijing. There follows a brief comment on the general importance of FDI inflows and outflows to and from China, as well as a note on the same in respect to the EU and Europe. The third section is a quantitative analysis of trade and FDI flows between Europe and China, viewed mainly, but not solely, from EU and non-EU perspectives. In an attempt to capture an essential element of European commercial relations with China, the fourth section touches on the European corporate experience in China, including consideration of some of the barriers that continue to impede the development of closer EU–China commercial relations. Finally, I offer some concluding observations on the future.

The evolution of the EU's economic strategy towards China

Nicola Casarini has described the evolution of EU–China relations between their inception in 1975[3] and the publication twenty years later of the EU's programmatic statement of its long-term strategy towards China[4] as a shift from a "secondary relationship" towards a "partnership."[5] The remarkable expansion of EU–China economic relations during this period is captured in the finding that alongside the emergence of the EU as an engine of global economic growth, the EU has become China's single largest trading partner, while China has become the EU's second-largest.[6] Between 1978 and 2005 EU–China trade increased more than sixtyfold to reach €210 billion.[7]

Excellent accounts of the development of Sino-European relations are available elsewhere,[8] and it would be redundant to cover the same ground in detail here. Instead, the chronology on the page opposite summarizes the main events that have shaped such developments, with particular reference to the evolution of EU–China economic relations. Concealed within this skeletal outline of events are important shifts in attitudes and policies by both sides. For example, while the Cold War persisted and Sino-Soviet political rapprochement remained unfulfilled, China's view of the EU in the 1970s and into the 1980s was shaped by its desire that Western European countries should be a "bulwark against 'Soviet hegemonism'."[9] By the second half of the 1980s, changes in the international realpolitik had, however, compelled the Chinese government to revise its view. The collapse of the former Soviet Union and the accompanying process of democratic transition throughout Central and Eastern Europe signalled the end of the bipolar international system – and with this the supposed inevitability of global nuclear conflict – and the emergence, in Chinese parlance, of a new "multipolar" world. On-going integration within Europe underlined the force of this argument. From the late 1980s, Chinese leaders, such as Deng Xiaoping, Hu Yaobang (CCP Secretary-General) and Premier Zhao Ziyang, increasingly urged a united Europe to assume new global responsibilities. As Zhao Ziyang put it during a visit to the Netherlands in May 1997:

> The unification of Europe, its growth and strength, the strengthening of the cooperation between China and Western Europe, and the rapprochement between Eastern and Western Europe will play an important role for the maintenance of global peace.[10]

It was against this background and in the expectation of a new international role for Europe that China sought to strengthen its relations with the European Union. Not least, China began to view closer economic ties with EU Member States as a means of reducing its technological dependence on the United States and Japan.

Realization of China's aspirations vis-à-vis Europe was critically dependent on the EU's willingness to show reciprocity in the formulation and implementation of its own policies towards China. Measured by the growth of EU–China trade, the European response was significant. Chinese Customs Statistics show that between 1975 and 1984, the value of bilateral merchandise trade increased by 10.5 per cent p.a., but that during the next five years (1985–9), the corresponding figure was 31.9 per cent p.a.[11] The momentum of accelerated trade growth was seriously disrupted by the political upheavals in Beijing of spring and summer 1989. Following the "Tiananmen Massacre," the European Commission, as well as European countries

Chronology of China–EU economic relations

1978	EC–China Agreement on Trade. Establishment of EC–China Joint Committee
1979	Visit to China by Roy Jenkins (President of European Commission). First meeting of EC–China Joint Committee in Beijing.
1983	Initiation of first EC–China Scientific Cooperation Programme.
1984	Initiation of first EC–China cooperation project in business management training and rural development.
1985	EC–China Agreement on Trade and Economic Cooperation. Visit to China by Jaques Delors (President of European Commission).
1986	EC–China WTO accession negotiations begin.
1987	EC co-financing of NGO development activities in China for first time.
1988	Opening of EC Delegation in Beijing.
1989	China–EC relations frozen, following 4 June "Tiananmen Massacre". Sanctions imposed on China by EU.
1992	Resumption of EC–China bilateral relations. Beginning of environmental dialogue.
1993	EU provides aid to UN World Food Program's projects in China for first time.
1994	European Investment Bank establishes first project in China.
1995	EUI adopts strategy paper ("A Long-Term Policy for China–Europe Relations"). European Community Humanitarian Office (ECHO) gives humanitarian aid to China for first time.
1998	EU adopts policy paper ("Building a Comprehensive Partnership with China"). Agreement on Scientific and Technological Cooperation signed in Brussels (takes force in 2000).
2000	EU and China reach bilateral agreement on China's accession to WTO.
2001	EU adopts paper ("EU Strategy Towards China: Implementation of 1998 Communication and Future Steps for a More Effective EU Policy").
2002	EU approves "Country Strategy Paper, 2002–6." EU, World Bank and Chinese government host Dalian Environment Conference. EU–China Maritime Agreement signed.
2003	Chinese government releases its first-ever "EU Policy Paper." EU publishes policy paper ("A Maturing Partnership: Shared Interests and Challenges in EU–China Relations"). Visit to China by EU Trade Commissioner (Pascal Lamy) to strengthen EU–China trade relations and cooperation in Doha Development Agenda. EU and China take part in ASEM Economic Ministers Meeting (Dalian). EU and China sign Agreement on GALILEO (the Civil Global Navigation Satellite System). Initiation of dialogue on industrial policy. Initial dialogue on intellectual property.
2004	EU and China sign "Approved Destination Status" (ADS) agreement on tourism. EU and China sign joint statement on EU–China Science and Technology cooperation, renewing previous (1998) agreement. EU and China sign Customs Cooperation Agreement. EU and China sign Agreement on Peaceful Nuclear Research. EU becomes biggest trading partner of China, with China as EU's second-biggest trading partner.
2005	EU and China sign Textile Agreement. EU and China sign Joint Declaration on Climate Change. Memorandum of Understanding on China–EU Dialogue on Energy and Transport Strategies signed.
2006	EU adopts paper ("China: Closer Partners, Growing Responsibilities"). EU issues policy paper ("EU–China Trade and Investment: Competition and Partnership").

Sources: EC Chronology of EU–China Relations (available at European Commission website at http://www.delchn.cec.eu.int/en/eu_and_china/Milestones.htm); and EU Chamber of Commerce in China, "Chronology of EU China Relations," *EuroBiz*, Sept. 2004 (available at http://www.sinomedia.net/eurobiz/v200409/special0409.html).

operating at an individual level, imposed punitive economic sanctions, including freezing all government loans. As a result, between 1989 and 1991, trade between the EU and China was halved (from US$23.5 billion to $11.6 billion). However, this interruption was temporary,[12] and following swift recovery, renewed growth was re-established. Broadly speaking, this has continued to the present day.

The expansion of EU–China economic relations after 1984 was striking. But it would be misleading to suggest that such growth reflected a clearly formulated view by the European Commission of how commercial ties should evolve. Indeed, the early 1990s were characterized by growing tension between China and two leading EU Member States – the UK and France[13] – and it was left to Germany to formulate a more positive and pragmatic "China policy model."[14] It was, in fact, not until 1995, with the publication of its programmatic document (*A Long-Term Policy for China–Europe Relations*), that the EU for the first time articulated a coherent strategy towards China.[15] The document was unequivocal in its belief that relations with China were bound henceforth to be "a cornerstone in Europe's external relations, both with Asia and globally."[16]

At the heart of this vision were two core convictions, to which the EU has since consistently subscribed. The first was that a coherent strategy towards China was essential to "the credibility of [the EU's] emerging common foreign and security policy."[17] The second was the recognition that China's economic upsurge since the early 1980s had critical implications both for Europe's future growth and for European firms' profitability and competitiveness. Arguing from the premise that the momentum of reform and opening-up in China was irreversible, the Commission concluded that European industry had no choice but to involve itself in what was likely to become the most dynamic market in the world[18] – "involvement" here being interpreted as an explicitly two-way process that would embrace efforts by the EU to facilitate China's economic, legal and political reforms, and support its integration into the global economy (including the World Trade Organization [WTO]), while also furthering European economic interests through expanded trade and investment. In short, constructive engagement was henceforth to be the EU's guiding principle in its relations with China.

The 1995 policy document marked a watershed in the EU's relations with China. From it has flowed subsequent developments not only in terms of economic ties, but also of political and security relations. In terms of the EU's economic strategy towards China, there is a logical consistency that links the content of the 1995 document with the policy thrusts of subsequent important statements – most notably, those of 1998,[19] 2001[20] and 2003.[21] Brussels' advocacy of closer EU–China relations elicited an enthusiastic response in China, where the most public official expression of the desire for closer relations was the publication in 2003 of a "White Paper" on China's EU policy.[22] This document was unequivocal in its support for the further development of economic and commercial ties between China and the EU, and put forward the strategic goal that the EU should become "China's largest trading and investment partner."[23]

The release of policy statements by China and the EU coincided with a significant strengthening of the institutional framework in which the two sides have sought to achieve closer economic relations. In particular, the process of sectoral dialogue has intensified greatly in recent years. These are viewed by both sides as a means of exchanging information and consolidating policy coordination, as well as giving an impetus to new initiatives.[24] Sectoral dialogues now embrace a very wide range of activities,[25] and in a real sense they define the infrastructure of governance for EU–China economic and commercial relations (see Francis Algieri's chapter in this volume). It is noteworthy that many of them are broadly based and offer the prospect of facilitating further reform in a number of sensitive areas of the Chinese economy, including state-owned enterprise and the financial sector. Such outcomes promise to benefit both sides, albeit in different degrees and for different reasons. In particular, sectoral dialogue that encourages regulatory reforms and promotes a convergence of views and policies between China and the EU in economic (e.g. industrial, financial or monetary) and social (labour and employment) spheres may help strengthen China's commitment to abide by accepted international norms and regulations, and so embed it more firmly in the global community.

If sectoral dialogue can help promote China's closer integration into the international community, the process of enlargement of the European Union may assist in fulfilling a parallel economic and political transformational goal on behalf of the ten countries of Central and Eastern Europe which joined EU-15 in 2004.[26] The dynamic of EU enlargement has important implications for future economic and commercial relations between China and Europe. From the Chinese perspective, enlargement offers new opportunities associated with the steady increase in the size of the single European market. It is, however, still too early to speculate about the extent to which such market opportunities will be translated into reality.[27]

The most recent EC "Communication" on EU–China relations was published in October 2006.[28] In some respects, their message is an endorsement of that contained in previous communications; in others, however, they strike a new, more critical note.[29] Thus, alongside the familiar rehearsal of the mutual gains from closer commercial ties,[30] both documents give considerable attention to obstacles to market access inherent in China's continued use of tariff and non-tariff barriers to trade, its discriminatory treatment of European operators – especially in regard to government contracts – and restrictions on investment in both secondary and tertiary sectors. The growing concern of the Commission is unequivocally expressed in both communications:

in Europe there is a growing perception that China's as yet incomplete implementation of WTO obligations and new barriers to market access are preventing a genuinely reciprocal trading relationship.[31]

EU companies often find themselves competing on unfair terms in China. The absence of conditions of fair market competition and inadequate legal protection pose serious problems. China's policies on the environment, social standards, currency valuation and natural resources can distort trade.[32]

The explicit inference of such perceptions is that the EU will in future bring greater pressure to bear on the Chinese government in an effort to achieve more openness and fairness by China in its economic and commercial relations with the EU.[33]

The growing importance to China of FDI inflows and outflows[34]

One of the main factors that have contributed to high levels of GDP growth in China since the 1980s is the *volte-face* displayed by the government in Beijing towards the role of Multinational Enterprises (MNEs) and foreign direct investment (FDI) as vehicles for promoting modernization and development. During the Mao Era, MNEs were viewed as a means of capitalist exploitation of poor countries and were debarred from conducting business in China. By contrast, the economic reforms initiated by Deng Xiaoping emphasized the positive role of inward flows of capital – especially FDI – as an important catalyst of development.

The upshot of this fundamental change in the Chinese government's economic mindset has been a steady expansion in FDI inflows on a scale unprecedented not only in China itself, but also in any other country in modern economic history.[35] Both short-term and long-term interests have encouraged foreign investors in industrialized countries, as well as in some Newly Industrializing Economies (NIEs), to establish themselves in a market of seemingly limitless potential. The scramble for concessions on the Chinese mainland that characterized the activities of western imperialist nations in the nineteenth century – later, Japan too – was mirrored at the turn of the twentieth century by a scramble among enterprises throughout the world to establish production facilities on Chinese soil, often, but by no means exclusively, in cooperation with indigenous firms. Many of these activities have been directed towards export processing, although foreign firms have increasingly sought a Chinese presence in order to seek a share in the Chinese market. Low land rents and cheap labour, the establishment of Special Economic Zones (SEZs) and other essentially locational advantages have been among the instrumental incentives offered to foreign investors.

The main source of Chinese FDI inflows has been the extended Chinese diaspora – especially in Hong Kong, Taiwan and Singapore. By contrast, although the rate of expansion of FDI from Japan, the United States and European countries has been quite rapid, as a share of total inflows their contributions have remained fairly modest. Table 10.1 below provides a summary overview of national and regional origins of FDI inflows into China for 2005, as published by the Chinese Ministry of Commerce. The Asian dominance of such inflows is the most striking feature and is not in doubt, even though the figures are subject to a significant margin of error.[36]

Table 10.1 The regional origins of FDI inflows to China, 2005

	FDI, 2005 (US$ '000)
Total	**60,324.6**
Asia	**35,718.9**
Hong Kong, China	17,948.8
Japan	6,529.8
Singapore	2,204.3
Republic of Korea	5,168.3
Taiwan, China	2,151.7
Africa	**1,070.9**
Europe	**5,643.1**
EU-15	5,193.8
EU-25	5,255.0
Non-EU Europe	388.1
Latin America	**11,293.3**
Cayman Islands	1,947.5
Virgin Islands	9,021.7
North America	**3,730.0**
United States	3,061.2
Oceanic and Pacific Islands	**1,999.0**
Samoa	1,351.9
Others	**869.4**

Source: National Bureau of Statistics (NBS), *Zhongguo tongji nianjian* [*TJNJ*] (China Statistical Yearbook), 2006 (Beijing: tongji chubanshe, 2006), p. 754.

The estimates reveal that in 2005, the European share of utilized FDI inflows to China was 9.4 per cent – 8.7 per cent from EU-25 Member States. Even allowing for round-tripping FDI, it is likely that Hong Kong remains the single most important source of FDI, although the inclusion of Taiwanese capital routed to China through Central America has almost certainly propelled Taiwan into second place ahead of Japan, South Korea and Singapore. The share of the United States in total FDI inflows was a mere 5.1 per cent in 2005.

As the following figure indicates, since the mid-1990s Hong Kong's share in FDI inflows has declined quite consistently and sharply. At the end of the 1990s, Europe and the USA vied with Taiwan as the second-largest source of FDI to China.[37] But thereafter, the increasing relative importance of Taiwan and South Korea contrasted with a decline in the European and North American shares – the latter falling to its lowest point for more than a decade.

That the cheapness of Chinese land and labour has attracted European investors to relocate their activities in China is undeniable. The case in favour of Western European firms undertaking FDI in China merely on grounds of lower factor costs is, however, weaker than that of other MDCs by virtue of such firms' access to cheap land and labour in Central and Eastern Europe (CEE).[38] In the two countries to have most recently acceded to the EU – Bulgaria and Romania – wage costs are said to be comparable with those of both China and India.[39] In the wake of foreign trade liberalization and regulatory reforms in former CEE socialist countries

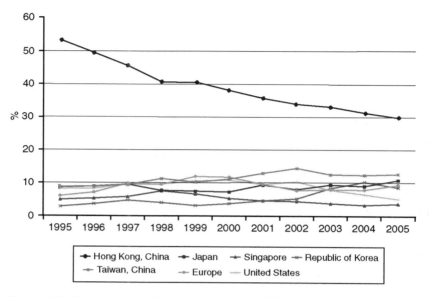

Figure 10.1 Changing national and regional shares of China's inward FDI, 1995–2005

during the early 1990s, there was a surge in FDI inflows from the European Union – a process that has been strengthened by a second phase of intra-European investment.[40] Meanwhile, in its 2005 *World Investment Report*, UNCTAD highlighted the "major transportation and logistical advantages" to established European MNEs resulting from the 2004 eastward expansion of the EU, adding that these "could potentially become a magnet for efficiency-seeking investment."[41] The economic consequences of EU enlargement no doubt help explain Europe's declining share in Chinese FDI inflows in recent years.[42] By the same token, it is likely that European MNEs have been most strongly motivated to invest in China in order to seek access to Chinese markets.[43] Interestingly too, just as Chinese TNC investors in Europe have sought to use buy-outs in order to secure overseas market access, so too OECD MNEs have also recently begun to engage in cross-border mergers and acquisitions (M&As) for the same purpose.[44]

An aspect of China's emergence as a global economic power that has only recently begun to attract serious attention among analysts is the increasing role of Chinese companies as overseas investors. The scale of Chinese outward investment is already sizeable and in 2005 China was the seventeenth-largest overseas investor in the world.[45] According to UNCTAD, the cumulative stock of outward Chinese FDI grew, on average, by 20 per cent p.a. between 1990 and 2000 to reach US$27,768 million; by 2005, the corresponding figure had reached US$46,311 million.[46] Although such figures imply almost a halving in the rate of annual growth after 2000, they conceal an extraordinary surge in Chinese FDI in 2005 from US$1,805 to US$11,306 million – a rise of more than 500 per cent in a single year.[47] The spectacular rise is likely to have reflected a decision to use some of China's enormous foreign exchange reserves to acquire foreign assets (especially oil). The drivers of such investment are Chinese MNEs, some of whose overseas holdings are sizeable. In 2003, for example, just two Chinese government-affiliated companies – SINOPEC and the China State Construction Engineering Corporation – employed almost 40,000 people overseas, with foreign sales of US$ 9 billion.[48] A more recent initiative was the takeover by Lenovo (China) of IBM's personal computer division. In short, complementing its role as the single most important destination for inward FDI among developing countries, China has also come to assume a leading role among such countries as a source of global *outward* investment.[49]

That Chinese foreign investment will continue to expand rapidly is not in doubt. UNCTAD has forecast that China, alongside India and South Korea, will account for an increasing share of Asian outward FDI, including large-scale M&As. Globally, the internationalization of Chinese MNEs will also continue, not least through investment in non-Asian countries: in energy and natural resources (Africa and Latin America), steel (Brazil), and property and real estate (Russian Federation).[50] A survey sponsored by Roland Berger Strategy Consultants and published in 2003 revealed that 90 per cent of China's top 50 companies had already invested overseas or had made plans to do so in the near future.[51]

Chinese companies' overseas investment plans embrace developed, as well as less developed, countries. Von Keller and Zhou's study reveals that 45 per cent of China's top 50 firms placed a high priority on investment in developed country markets, while only 38 per cent of them prioritized their less developed counterparts. Concealed in these statistics is an interesting finding to the effect that North America is viewed by Chinese investors as an increasingly more attractive investment destination than Western Europe.[52] This seems to reflect their perception of North America as a more unified market entity, compared with more fragmented market conditions in Europe, characterized by differing linguistic and legal traditions, and business customs.[53]

In developed countries, CNOOC's unsuccessful bid (2005) for Unocal Corp. and Lenovo's earlier successful purchase of IBM's personal computer operations, making it the world's third-largest PC manufacturer, attracted huge media attention. These are by no means the only examples of a growing trend towards the internationalization of Chinese enterprises through their activities in MDCs. In 2002, for example, China's TCL Multimedia acquired Schneider Electronics AG for some €8.2 million, while in 2004, TCL joined with France's Thomson Co to form TTE – the world's largest television manufacturers.[54] TCL also took a majority stake with the French telecommunications company, Alcatel, in a new mobile handset joint venture (TAMP), with an anticipated manufacturing capacity of 20 million sets a year.[55] Such activities are evidence of a more aggressive stance by Chinese enterprises, designed to improve their global corporate image through the acquisition of established foreign brand names. However, whether this strategy self-evidently reflects Chinese firms' growing international strength is questionable. As James Kynge has observed, in contrast to Japanese firms' efforts to internationalize themselves in the 1980s on the basis of their already considerable "corporate clout", achieved through the development of their own brand images,

Chinese enterprises have sought to extend their international image by "selling products [e.g. those produced by Thomson and Schneider] under European brand names rather than substitute them with [their] own."[56] Chinese brands that have secured a significant degree of global penetration are relative rarities.[57] Nor, for the time being, have Chinese firms matched the global trend whereby TNCs have come to play a major part in global research and development (R&D). Indeed, it is a salutary reminder of China's still nascent role in this respect that although two Chinese companies – PetroChina and Sinopec – were listed among the top 20 firms in developing countries in terms of R&D spending in 2003, their *global* rankings were a lowly 219th and 337th.[58]

The standard neo-classical assumption that profit maximization is the sole motivation of firms' economic behaviour has long been discredited. It is, however, an acceptable generalization that a firm that ignores profitability cannot succeed. Chinese firms are no exception to this rule, and the trend towards Chinese TNCs' internationalization is closely connected with their search for higher profits. There is, for example, evidence that narrowing domestic profit margins have encouraged Chinese firms to seek more profitable markets overseas.[59] Paralleling the experience of TNCs from other countries, the overseas operations of Chinese firms seem often to have generated higher profits than their domestic activities.[60] The case of China State Construction Engineering Corporation (CSCEC), cited in UNCTAD's 2006 *World Investment Report*, provides telling evidence in this regard: although its foreign operations embodied less than a half of its total assets and accounted for less than a quarter of its total sales, they nevertheless generated more than 80 per cent of CSCEC's profits.[61] Such findings should, however, not be interpreted as indicating that foreign asset acquisitions have been a cast-iron guarantee of improved profitability for Chinese TNCs. Rather, the evidence suggests that potential benefits of internationalization are most likely to be forthcoming where the acquisition of foreign assets takes place without the need for significant integration between existing domestic operations and new overseas ventures.[62]

Consideration of the factors that lead Chinese firms to invest overseas throws useful light on China's European investment engagement. In general, FDI outflows from China have sought to fulfil one or more of six main goals.[63] They are: to secure resources; to access markets; to obtain know-how; to enhance efficiency; to secure strategic assets; and to achieve diversification. Surveys indicate that resource-seeking investment in European countries has had a low priority among Chinese investors.[64] To the extent that higher efficiency reflects lower costs, efficiency-seeking outward FDI by Chinese firms also has limited relevance to their activities in Europe, since EU producers cannot match China's domestic land and labour costs. The three most important motivations to invest in Europe are to secure new markets, to access modern know-how and technology, and to extend brand imaging. Chinese companies have increasingly looked overseas to extend their markets for products, such as textiles and electronics, which are in excess supply domestically. In addition, companies whose initial success owes most to their role as Original Equipment Manufacturers (OEMs) for foreign brand names recognize the potential to market and sell these products themselves overseas –

especially in the EU and USA.[65] At times, FDI has also enabled Chinese firms to overcome EU trade barriers and secure permanent market access through the direct establishment of foreign affiliates in European countries.[66]

Knowledge acquisition is an essential condition of economic development, and for Chinese firms the acquisition of advanced managerial and organizational know-how, as well as the most up-to-date technologies, commands a high premium in their efforts to improve competitiveness and realize the benefits of catch-up vis-à-vis developed countries. Flows of FDI into China have been an important means of securing access to such "goods". However, reluctance by MDC and MNE investors to make available the most advanced technologies has impeded realization of the full benefits of this process. Hence the attraction of *outward* FDI by Chinese firms in order to overcome such constraints. In particular, the acquisition of or mergers with foreign firms[67] can be a useful way of facilitating technology access. It is also no coincidence that Chinese firms are beginning to establish Research and Development (R&D) centres overseas: as of 2005, for example, 11 such centres had been established by Chinese TNCs (including Huawei and Haier) in EU member states.[68]

Know-how and technology are not the only "strategic assets" that Chinese investors in Europe seek. An increasingly important goal, to which reference has already been made, is the acquisition of international brand names. TCL's purchase of Schneider Electronics (2002) and its subsequent (2003) establishment of a joint venture with the ailing French television company Thomson Electronics are prime European-based examples of Chinese investors' strategy in this regard. In addition to acquiring valuable brand names, activities such as those of TCL in Germany and France offer benefits of improved strategic positioning within foreign – in this case, European – economies.[69] Diversifying into new markets also helps Chinese TNCs reduce risks, such as those associated with unfavourable domestic economic conditions (for example, market saturation and excess supply). More ready access to capital and foreign currency is another advantage to TNCs operating abroad that has, at least until recently,[70] been denied to Chinese firms operating only in China.

Notwithstanding its rapid growth in recent years China's outward investment remains modest when compared with inward FDI. For example, UNCTAD data show that the cumulative stock of inward FDI during 1981–2004 was more than six times greater than that of cumulative outward FDI (see Figure 10.2).

The sharp decline in China's outward FDI growth during 2001–4 reflected a general slowing in FDI activity throughout the global economy. For China, the situation was exacerbated in 2003 by the impact of SARS, which caused delays in the implementation or postponement of outward investment activities. With the health threat brought under control and with global FDI recovery under way, outward FDI flows from China showed a marked increase in 2005. This more assertive and buoyant upward trend is likely to persist in the coming years.

If purely economic considerations have dominated the rationale of FDI decision-making between individual European countries and China, broader strategic and political issues have helped shape the European Commission's investment and

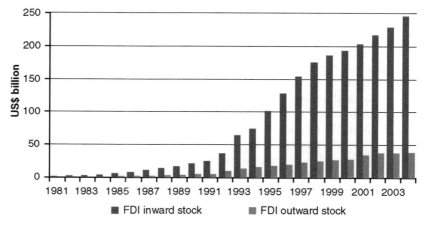

Figure 10.2 Comparison of Chinese inward and outward FDI stock, 1981–2004

economic policy vis-à-vis China. In Brussels, as in Washington, it is axiomatic that the development of closer commercial and economic ties contains the wherewithal to influence not only the Chinese government's policies towards economic reform and liberalization, but also its stance on important political and legal issues (including human rights).

Trade and investment relations between the EU and China: a quantitative analysis

Merchandise trade

Detailed annual estimates of Chinese exports to, and imports from, the EU and other comparator regions and countries between 1980 and 2005 are shown in Appendix A (see Tables 10.A1 and 10.A2). From these I have derived the following summary table (Table 10.2), which shows the increasing profile of the European Union as a trading partner vis-à-vis China since the 1980s:.

In interpreting these figures, it is important to keep in mind ongoing changes in the geographical scope of the EU. EU enlargement has brought benefits to China in terms of increased market size,[71] harmonization of product standards and marketing regulations, and increased scope for the free movement of goods on entry to any one of the 25 EU Member States. However, there are also disadvantages associated with enlargement, such as increased price competitiveness resulting from the incorporation of low-cost CEE industries within the EU framework, and the extension to CEE countries of EU anti-dumping regulations.

The estimates in Table 10.2 highlight the accelerated trade growth between China and the EU, the most rapid expansion having taken place in the wake of China's WTO accession. In particular, Chinese exports to EU countries grew more rapidly during

Table 10.2 The changing relative importance of the EU as a destination for Chinese exports and source of Chinese imports

	World	Asia	Industrial countries	European Union	Hong Kong	Japan	United States
Average rate of export growth (% p.a.)							
1980–89	12.63	17.00	9.92	8.50	19.67	8.49	18.17
1990–99	13.93	9.18	19.31	19.07	5.35	14.46	25.27
2000–05	25.52	25.27	24.29	28.43	22.47	17.23	25.40
Share of China's average annual global exports (%)							
1980–89	100.00	41.66	39.68	11.92	31.91	18.64	7.84
1990–99	100.00	40.23	50.33	13.94	26.23	17.13	17.18
2000–05	100.00	35.20	54.43	17.72	17.12	13.36	21.16
Average rate of import growth (% p.a.)							
1980–89	13.12	28.99	9.21	13.30	41.01	8.23	8.32
1990–99	10.85	13.58	10.56	9.62	−5.81	12.35	9.50
2000–05	25.91	26.84	19.41	19.08	10.03	19.93	16.59
Share of China's average annual global imports (%)							
1980–89	100.00	20.59	63.76	17.50	15.53	25.12	13.87
1990–99	100.00	36.46	52.00	15.16	9.63	20.23	11.70
2000–05	100.00	37.50	42.41	12.70	2.70	16.96	8.48

Source: Appendix A, Tables A1 and A2.

2000–5 than to any other comparator region. The outcome of these trends is captured most dramatically in two findings. The first is that in 2003 the EU overtook the United States to become China's second-most important trading partner. The second is that in 2004 it overtook Japan to become its single most important partner. Another major watershed concealed in Table 10.2 is the value of the EU's bilateral trade vis-à-vis China having consistently exceeded that of PRC–Hong Kong trade since 2005.

The accelerated expansion of Chinese exports to the EU was not, however, reciprocated in the growth of European exports to China. These contrary trends suggest that the balance of trade was turning against the European Union – a finding that is confirmed in Table 10.3.

During the 1980s, China suffered a rising bilateral deficit in its trade with the EU.[72] But having peaked in 1989, it subsequently contracted, and since 1996 has been transformed into a steadily increasing surplus. Indeed, during 2001–5 it rose by almost 800 per cent to more than US$70 billion. This constituted the EU's largest bilateral trade deficit.[73] From Beijing's perspective, the growing imbalance reflected structural issues associated with export-orientated activities by Taiwanese, Japanese and South Korean firms operating in China. But through Brussels' eyes, the deficit is more a reflection of the effects of the Chinese government's deliberate use of restrictive and discriminatory practices which have

Table 10.3 The balance of EU–China merchandise trade

	Chinese exports to EU (US$ m.)	Chinese imports from EU (US$ m.)	Balance of trade (US$ m.)
1980	2,686.0	3,346.0	−659.4
1981	2,821.1	3,238.7	−417.6
1982	2,493.3	3,238.7	37.5
1983	2,801.6	3,792.0	−990.4
1984	2,503.9	3,916.8	−1,412.9
1985	2,742.7	7,053.8	−4,311.1
1986	4,747.1	9,240.7	−4,493.6
1987	4,726.0	8,624.6	−3,898.6
1988	5,502.4	9,429.9	−3,927.5
1989	5,598.6	10,297.5	−4,498.9
1990	6,412.4	9,513.4	−3,101.0
1991	7,273.2	9,423.1	−2,149.9
1992	8,225.2	10,985.6	−2,760.4
1993	12,729.9	16,069.6	−3,339.7
1994	16,256.5	18,920.5	−2,664.0
1995	20,213.4	21,579.5	−1,366.1
1996	20,959.7	20,134.1	825.6
1997	25,223.5	19,308.7	5,914.8
1998	29,788.7	20,848.4	8,940.3
2000	40,783.0	30,730.8	10,052.2
2001	44,299.9	36,343.9	7,956.0
2002	52,487.0	32,439.6	13,047.4
2003	78,472.8	54,477.2	23,995.0
2004	107,265.0	70,131.2	37,133.8
2005	143,851.0	73,559.4	70,291.6

Source: Appendix A, Tables A1 and A2.

impeded access to China's markets. The deficit has been the source of strained relations between China and the EU, prompting calls for revaluation of China's currency and protectionist demands from the business sector – especially those engaged in textile and footwear production in southern European countries. Pressure on Beijing to address such issues will no doubt intensify.[74] Meanwhile, there is also considerable unease about the further expansion of European exports of high-technology products, of which EU Member States are already the largest supplier to China.[75]

The figures in Table 10.2 leave no room for doubt as to the increasingly important role that the EU has come to play in China's global trade. What they do *not* show is the extent to which closer ties with China have affected the EU's global trading profile. Table 10.4 seeks to address this issue.

The figures are revealing. On the one hand, they confirm the sharp rise in China's importance as a trading partner of the EU – perhaps here caught most strikingly in China's increasing share in the EU's trade (exports and imports) with Asia. On the other hand, they remind us that the rapid growth of EU–China trade notwithstanding, China's contribution to the EU's global trade remains quite

Table 10.4 The changing relative importance of China as a destination for EU exports and a source of EU imports

	Developing countries	Asia	China	Industrialised countries	Hong Kong	United States
Share of EU's average annual global exports (%)						
1980–89	21.47	3.98	0.59	76.95	0.52	7.76
1990–99	20.81	5.56	0.81	77.93	0.87	7.21
2000–05	22.53	5.41	1.40	76.62	0.70	8.41
Share of EU's average annual global imports (%)						
1980–89	23.18	23.18	0.55	76.30	0.70	7.61
1990–99	20.86	20.86	1.69	78.18	0.71	7.64
2000–05	26.71	26.71	3.76	72.55	0.61	6.37

Source: Appendix A, Tables A3 and A4.

marginal, accounting for under 4 per cent of all imports, and less than 1.5 per cent of its global exports (2000–5). There is, however, a major qualification to this finding. The IMF statistics from which the figures in Table 10.3 have been calculated include intra-EU trade. If, instead, the EU's own statistical usage is adopted, a different finding emerges. This is highlighted in Table 10.5.

Both sources confirm the increasing importance of China as a trade partner of the EU since 2001. China's profile looms larger, however, in the calculations based on EUROSTAT coverage, reminding us of the significance of intra-EU trade.

It will be useful to conclude this account of EU–China trade by considering its functional distribution. The following table provides a snapshot of the breakdown, by product category, of EU exports to, and imports from, China in 2005 (see Table 10.6).

Table 10.5 China's trade position vis-à-vis the EU

	Following IMF usage		Following EUROSTAT	
	China's share of total EU exports	China's share of total EU imports	China's share of total EU exports	China's share of total EU imports
2001	0.98	2.58	3.42	8.30
2002	1.28	2.84	3.87	9.51
2003	1.49	3.77	4.69	11.21
2004	1.61	4.25	5.00	12.35
2005	1.62	4.92	4.88	13.45

Source: IMF data (in US$) from Appendix A, Tables A3 and A4;
EUROSTAT data (in euro) from European Commission, *DG Trade Statistics*, 16 May 2006;
see also EU, *External and Intra-European Trade: Monthly Statistics* (Brussels, EC, 2005).

Table 10.6 Functional distribution of EU–China trade, 2005

EU exports to China			EU imports from China		
Products (by SITC category)	Euro m.	As %	Products (by SITC category)	Euro m.	As %
Machinery and transport equipment	30,971	59.9	Machinery and transport equipment	73,144	46.3
Manufactured goods classified by material	6,137	11.9	Misc. manufactured articles	53,948	34.1
Chemical and related products	5,025	9.7	Manufactured goods classified by material	17,393	11.0
Misc. manufactured articles	3,220	6.2	Chemical and related products	4,965	3.1
Crude materials (inedible), except fuels	3,101	6.0	Crude materials (inedible), except fuels	2,279	1.4
Food and live animals	590	1.1	Food and live animals	2,074	1.3
Commodities and transactions	572	1.1	Mineral fuels, lubricants and related materials	750	0.5
Beverages and tobacco	198	0.4	Commodities and transactions	377	0.2
Mineral fuels, lubricants and related materials	63	0.1	Beverages and tobacco	68	–
Animal and vegetable oils, fats and waxes	20	–	Animal and vegetable oils, fats and waxes	34	–
Total	**51,746**	**100.0**	**Total**	**158,040**	**100.0**

Source: EUROSTAT (*Comext, Statistical regime 4*). Data exclude intra-EU trade.

Concealed in these figures is the finding that China ranks first as a source of imports of iron and steel, and office and telecommunications imports to the EU; fourth as a source of agricultural products, and iron and steel; and fifth as a source of chemicals, transport equipment, and textiles and clothing. The European Union ranks first as a supplier of non-agricultural raw materials to China; second as a source of power and non-electrical machinery, and iron and steel; fourth as a source of transport equipment imports; and fifth as a supplier of office and telecommunications equipment. Of the EU's €106,294 million trade deficit vis-à-vis China in 2005, trade in office and telecommunications equipment accounted for 42 per cent; its deficit on the textiles and clothing account (€20,973 million) accounted for a further 20 per cent.[76] Estimates of Chinese imports and exports from and to individual European countries are given in Appendix B (Tables 10.B1 and 10.B2).

From these I have extracted data for the most important EU Member States and non-EU countries, from which Figures 10.3 and 10.4 have been constructed.

Germany is easily China's single most important trading partner, followed by France, Italy and the United Kingdom (but notice also the sharp rise in the importance of the Netherlands as an export destination). For the time being, outside EU Member States, Russia alone comes close to these countries, the recent increase in its trade with China having been especially noticeable.[77]

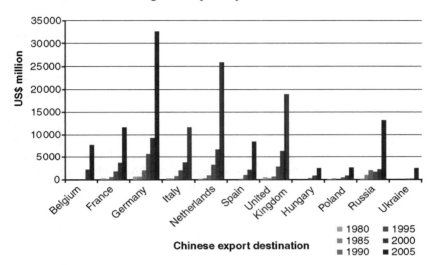

Figure 10.3 Leading European destinations for Chinese exports

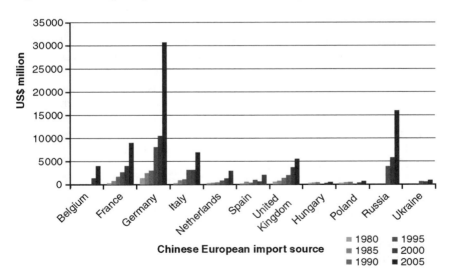

Figure 10.4 Leading sources of Chinese imports from Europe

Foreign direct investment

European FDI in China has its origins in the opening of Chinese coastal cities, as required by the terms of the Treaty of Shimonoseki (1894), following China's defeat by Japan. Between the mid-1890s and 1936, more than 200 "foreign affiliates" and joint ventures were set up in China by Western European firms.[78] During this period, UK companies held a dominant position among European countries, accounting for about 83 per cent of cumulative European investment in China.[79] From the time of the First World War, Japanese investment activities in China expanded rapidly, especially in Manchuria and parts of northern China, and Japan eventually replaced the UK as the dominant investment force in China.[80] Major European firms active in China before the Second World War included AEG, Bayer, Fiat, General Accident (now Aviva), GEC (now Marconi), Philips, Siemens and Unilever, all of which have returned to China, where they once more have a significant presence.

Klenner has argued that the creation of the four Special Economic Zones in Guangdong and Fujian in 1980 held little attraction for most potential European investors, who required an advanced urban industrial and trade infrastructural framework for their activities.[81] Accordingly, except for resource-seeking investment, European companies' FDI and production activities have been overwhelmingly based in eastern China – especially core cities, such as Beijing, Tianjin, Shanghai and Guangzhou – where firms have benefited from cheap land and labour, a highly-developed infrastructure (notably, good transport and communications facilities) and growing access to an increasingly prosperous domestic market.[82]

In the immediate wake of the implementation of China's open door policy, the involvement of European petroleum companies (for example, BP and Elf – the latter, since 2000, incorporated into TotalFinaElf) in joint oil exploration projects in the South China Sea lent a high profile to European FDI activities in China. The establishment, in the first half of the 1980s, of several large-scale manufacturing subsidiaries of European MNEs strengthened this profile.[83] Unlike investment in China originating in Japan, South Korea and the Chinese diaspora in Asia, EU countries' FDI has been more strongly orientated towards high-tech, knowledge-intensive and therefore higher-value-added activities (see also below). Although the functional distribution of European subsidiaries in China has been dominated by manufacturing,[84] the impact of China's accession to the WTO has more recently been reflected in growing involvement by European companies in retail trade and services.[85]

The figures in Table 10.7 show FDI inflows (contractual and utilized) from the EU to China between 1986 and 2004:.

Although the average estimates show that EU FDI flows to China, both in contractual and utilized terms, have steadily risen, a glance at the table shows that annual fluctuations in both have also been quite marked. The impact of the "Tiananmen Massacre" of 1989 apart, the EU seems to have lagged behind other countries (regions) in the wake of Deng Xiaoping's "southern tour" [*nanxun*] in 1991, and again following China's WTO accession in 2000. From a comparative

Table 10.7 EU FDI in China, 1986–2004

	Projects		Contractual FDI		Utilized FDI	
	Number	As % of national total	Value (US$ m.)	As % of national total	Value (US$ m.)	As % of national total
1986	32	2.14	351.94	10.57	178.53	7.96
1987	40	1.79	422.93	11.40	52.71	2.28
1988	87	1.46	285.31	5.39	157.27	4.92
1989	78	1.35	332.89	5.94	187.61	5.53
Average 1986–89	–	–	348.27	7.77	144.03	5.17
1990	82	1.13	224.22	3.40	147.35	4.23
1991	163	1.26	759.39	6.34	245.62	5.63
1992	763	1.56	963.60	1.66	242.97	2.21
1993	1,726	2.07	3,181.76	2.86	671.24	2.44
1994	1,464	3.08	5,629.58	6.81	1,537.69	4.55
Average 1990–94	–	–	2,151.71	3.97	568.97	3.55
1995	1,582	4.27	7,419.77	8.13	2,131.31	5.68
1996	1,167	4.75	6,759.22	9.22	2,737.06	6.56
1997	1,040	4.95	4,228.82	8.29	4,171.15	9.22
1998	1,002	5.06	5,939.38	11.40	3,978.69	8.75
1999	894	5.28	4,095.66	9.94	4,479.06	11.11
Average 1995–99	–	–	5,688.57	9.21	3,499.45	8.32
2000	1,130	5.06	8,855.16	14.20	4,479.46	11.00
2001	1,214	4.64	5,152.84	7.45	4,182.70	8.92
2002	1,486	4.35	4,506.93	5.45	3,709.82	7.03
2003	2,074	5.05	5,854.32	5.09	3,930.31	7.35
2004	2,423	5.55	8,361.89	5.45	4,328.61	7.14
2005	–	–	–	–	5,193.78	8.74
Average 2000–05	–	–	6,546.23 (2000–04)	6.78	4,304.11	8.20

Source: Chinese Ministry of Commerce (MOFCOM), Foreign Investment Administration website, available at www.fdi.gov.cn/common/info.jsp?id= ABC00000000000027429. 2005 utilized FDI from *TJNJ*, 2006, op.cit.

perspective, the EU's 8.7 per cent share of total Chinese utilized FDI receipts in 2005 may be compared with that of Hong Kong (29.8 per cent),[86] Taiwan (12.6 per cent),[87] South Korea (8.6 per cent), Japan (10.8 per cent) and the United States (5.1 per cent).[88] It would, however, be wrong to read too much into the low shares of China's national FDI coming from Europe and the USA. As Barysch observes, whereas investors from Hong Kong, Taiwan, South Korea and Japan have tended to relocate production activities in China to take advantage of cheap land and labour, with an emphasis on re-processing for re-export, their European and

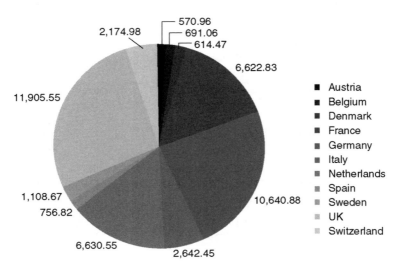

Figure 10.5 Major European sources of FDI in China, 1995–2005

American counterparts have engaged in higher value-added, high-tech projects, which have had a "catalytic impact" on China's development.[89] European and US investment has also focused to a greater extent on meeting domestic market demand within China, not least among the growing urban middle class.[90] Other major EU MNCs with a significant presence in China include Alcatel, BASF, Carrefour, Ericsson, Hoechst, Janssen, Nokia, Philips, Pharmaceutica, Siemens and Volkswagen. European companies are also playing a leading role in the construction of a number of multi-billion ethylene projects that are at the heart of petrochemical development in China.

From estimates of utilized FDI from individual European countries shown in Appendix C (Table 10.C1), Figure 10.5 highlights the contributions of the leading players during 1995–2005.

The estimates in Table 10.7 show that between the first and second halves of the 1990s, EU FDI to China grew, on average, by almost 44 per cent p.a., but subsequently sharply decelerated (the corresponding figure for 1995/99–2000–5 was 3.8 per cent p.a.). Even so, in 2005 FDI inflows to China from EU Member States were two and a half times greater than a decade earlier. But as a share of total outward FDI from the EU, China's receipts remain quite insignificant – partly, once again, because of the competing attractions of investment within the EU itself. It is a telling indication of the impact of enlargement that during 2001–3, 7.1 per cent of all EU FDI went to new Member States, compared to a mere 1.6 per cent to China.[91]

The European corporate sector in China – perceptions and reality

One of the most interesting expressions of a European corporate view of China is contained in a recent survey of business leaders' perceptions of the commercial opportunities and challenges associated with China's recent economic growth.[92] As Table 10.8 indicates, Western European companies share the optimism of other regions in terms of their perception of China as a business opportunity now and in the foreseeable future.[93] This bullish attitude was reflected in the expectation that China's contribution to Western European companies' global sales would more than double (from 5 to 12 per cent) between 2006 and 2009. More bearish concerns are reflected in the belief that by 2009 Chinese companies will control 7 per cent of the home market – slightly higher than in North America, but significantly less than in the Asia Pacific.

In terms of their readiness to tap China's commercial potential, Western European firms emerged less favourably than their counterparts in North America and the Asia Pacific (Table 10.9).

One interpretation of these responses is that European firms' involvement in China is more strongly oriented towards the past than to the future. Although a higher proportion of Western European companies had been fully operational in China for ten years or more than that of North American and Asia-Pacific firms, significantly fewer of them than in other regions had devised a China business strategy and many fewer expected to become fully operational there within the foreseeable future (3–5 years).

The Hay Group survey also provides interesting insights into perceptions of individual European countries' capacities to succeed in doing business in China.[94]

Table 10.8 Global business leaders' views of China as a commercial opportunity

	Total	Western Europe	Asia Pacific	North America
Do you view China as a business opportunity rather than a business threat?	Yes: 83%	Yes: 85%	Yes: 90%	Yes: 84%
Do you regard China as the greatest opportunity facing your business?	Yes: 49%	Yes: 44%	Yes: 63%	Yes: 43%
What share of the home market do you expect to be controlled by China in 2009?	8%	7%	11%	6%
(a) Share of global sales revenue from China (2006, actual)	6%	5%	9%	6%
(b) Share of global sales revenue from China (2009, expected)	14%	12%	16%	15%

Source: Hay Group, *Waking up to China*, op. cit., pp. 12, 13 and 21.

Table 10.9 Readiness to do business with China (%)

	Total	Western Europe	Asia Pacific	North America
We have been fully operational in China for over 10 years	14	17	12	15
We have been fully operational in China for 1–3 years	10	11	15	7
We have formulated a business plan and will establish operations within 1–3 years	14	11	17	10
We do not have a strategy for investing and doing business in China	24	30	15	25
We have been fully operational in China for more than 3 years	9	7	10	12
We have skeleton operations in China	14	15	20	7
We have formulated a business plan and will establish operations in China within 3–5 years	8	4	10	10
Other	7	6	2	14

Source: Hay Group, *Waking up to China*, op. cit., pp. 25–6.

On the one hand, Western Europe contains two of the top six countries regarded as most likely to be successful: the UK (ranked second) and Germany (sixth). On the other hand, two other European countries – Italy (ranked bottom) and France (the fifth-worst placed) – stand alongside Brazil, India and Indonesia as the least likely to succeed in China.

Perceptions aside, an interesting aspect of the activities of European investors in China is that the scale of their FDI involvement has not always been matched by the financial returns accruing from it.[95] The failure to generate more substantial profits no doubt reflects the existence of many barriers – economic, technical, legal and cultural – facing businessmen (especially those from outside Asia) operating in China. It also highlights European investors' determination to establish a foothold in China in anticipation of continuing economic growth and rises in income that will spawn increasing longer-term market opportunities for them. From such perspectives, it is of some interest that in the late 1990s a survey of EU companies with FDI operations in China revealed that half of them had failed to realize profit and cost-reduction expectations.[96] But in contrast to this apparently disappointing financial performance, almost 70 per cent of companies claimed to have fulfilled or over-fulfilled their *strategic* targets, and around 90 per cent of them expressed satisfaction with the market share they had achieved in China.[97] The long-term orientation of European investors' involvement in China emerges clearly from these findings.[98]

There is evidence that this orientation has started to pay dividends, and the profitability of EU firms in China has begun to increase. A poll undertaken by the EU Chamber of Commerce in China (EUCCC) found that the share of respondent European companies operating in China expecting to generate profits rose sharply between 2005 and 2006 from 61 per cent to 83 per cent. By contrast, the proportion of firms suffering losses fell from 23 to just 7 per cent, while 71 per cent of loss-making enterprises expected to have become profitable within three years.[99] The survey noted that 92 per cent of survey respondents had "a very positive market outlook" vis-à-vis China. It also confirmed that European companies were less interested in China as a manufacturing base than as a market – the "production of goods in China for China" had become the main factor motivating such companies to establish operations on the mainland.[100] Meanwhile, market penetration, as well as the search for low-cost labour, was encouraging firms to diversify their operations within China, as a result of which the proportion of EUCCC members based in Shanghai, Beijing and Guangzhou had fallen from 71 per cent (2004) to 57 per cent (2005). Recent years have also seen smaller-scale European companies entering China in the hope of emulating the success of their larger-scale counterparts.

EU MNCs are now well established in all of China's major economic sectors.[101] In some, they have had a presence for many years. For example, the origins of Volkswagen's involvement in China lie in a Joint Venture (JV) agreement signed between Volkswagen AG and Shanghai Automotive Industry Corporation in 1984 that led to the establishment of Shanghai Volkswagen. A second JV agreement with First Automobile Works resulted in the creation of FAW-Volkswagen. Such initiatives were the basis of the German company's subsequent economic success in China, captured in its achieving a maximum market share of almost 55 per cent at the end of the 1990s. This success has, however, not been maintained. In the face of competition from US and Asian companies, as well as of increasing domestic car production, its market share fell to 17 per cent in 2005, when Volkswagen China recorded an unprecedented operating loss of €119 million, forcing it to cut its annual production target for 2008 from 1.6 million to 900,000 units.[102] The downturn in VW's fortunes led to radical restructuring, which at the time of writing appears to have succeeded in halting and reversing the financial decline. Thanks to cost reductions and the introduction of new models (including the Polo Jinqing and Jinqu compact cars), in the first nine months of 2006 VW China's sales rose by 29 per cent, leading to predictions that the company would achieve annual profits of €74 million.[103]

Mobile telephones have been one of China's most buoyant markets in recent years.[104] Finland's Nokia Oyj is one of three European mobile telephone producers (the others are Sweden's Ericsson and Germany's Siemens[105]) with a major presence in China. Nokia has been selling mobile phones in China since 1990, and by 2005 its market share sales had reached 22 per cent (cf. 17 per cent in 2002).[106] Recent years have seen the maintenance of a strong momentum of sales growth for all Nokia products, but especially its mobile telephones. During January–September 2006 sales of cell phones – some 36.6 million of them – were already more than 11 per cent greater than in the whole of the previous year.[107] To date, Nokia's cumulative investment in China is well in excess of US$4.5 billion. The most recent evidence of the company's continuing strong commitment to China is the construction of a new national headquarters in Beijing.[108]

In recent years, the rapid expansion of China's retail sector – increasing, on average, by around 15 per cent p.a. since the mid-1980s – has mirrored its remarkable growth record. As a result, China has become an increasingly favoured destination for foreign retail companies, especially since December 2004, when, in accordance with the terms of China's WTO accession, previous restrictions on overseas retailers were lifted. The French MNC, Carrefour, has played a leading role in meeting changes in consumer demand associated with rising incomes. Carrefour opened its first supermarket in China in 1995 – a year later than US Wal-Mart – since when it has become the largest foreign retail company operating on the mainland (in 2006 it had 79 stores in 32 Chinese cities,[109] compared with the 50 stores in 30 cities managed by Wal-Mart). In terms of sales revenue, Carrefour is well ahead of Wal-Mart, earning US$2.2 billion from its Chinese operations in 2005 – over 80 per cent more than its American rival's sales revenue.[110] China is now the French retail company's fifth-largest national market in the world.[111]

The experiences of Carrefour, Nokia and – despite the difficulties it experienced in 2004–5 – Volkswagen are examples of major successes achieved by European companies operating in China. In providing these vignettes, I do not intend to suggest that these are in any way representative of the experience of European firms.[112] What is, however, probably common to all companies that have sought to operate in China is the difficulties that they have had to overcome in order to pursue their activities there. It is to these that I now briefly turn.

China's accession to the WTO was premised on the expectation that previous artificial barriers to conducting fair and equitable economic and commercial relations would gradually be removed in the interests of establishing a "level playing field" for its trading and investment partners. In fairness, it must be acknowledged that significant progress in this direction has been made since China joined the WTO in 2001 – most notably, through tariff reductions. But there is a strong consensus within the European Commission and among companies based in EU Member States that the maintenance of non-tariff barriers and other restrictions have continued to prevent what the EC's latest EU–China policy paper describes as a "genuinely reciprocal trading relationship between Europe and China."[113]

The Hay Group survey, to which reference has already been made, also highlights business leaders' perceptions of some of the obstacles to doing business in China.[114] Of these, the most serious *economic* barrier was the lack of adequate protection of intellectual property rights, with more than half of respondents expressing an expectation that IPR infringements would have a damaging effect on their business operations within the next five years. Respondents considered cultural and linguistic differences to be the most serious *organizational* barrier to engaging commercially with China. Meanwhile, other criticisms have been levelled against the Chinese government for the lack of regulatory transparency and a tendency to implement new laws within an unreasonably short period of their promulgation, to the detriment of foreign companies' ability to comply with their provisions.

The development of EU–China trade and investment relations is a dynamic process that is constantly evolving. For all the difficulties that continue to impede that process, there is a feeling that in recent years European companies have gained a leading edge over the United States and Japan in their efforts to reap the benefits of the increasing globalization of the Chinese economy.[115] It remains to be seen whether more populist views within EU Member States – most notably, in France – that see globalization as more of a threat than an opportunity will undermine the European advantage. More likely, the most important factor shaping future EU–China commercial relations will be the extent to which the European Commission and EU-based companies succeed in persuading their governmental and entrepreneurial counterparts in China to fulfil their WTO obligations, liberalize trade, improve IPR protection and enhance the terms of competition.

Concluding comments

Since 1995 successive policy documents issued by the European Commission attest to the growing importance of China as a trading and investment partner. This process mirrors similar developments that have affected other countries and regions of the world, but in one sense it has also eclipsed those developments, the EU having become for the time being China's largest trading partner, accounting for 19 per cent of its external trade.[116] Data and other evidence presented in this chapter further attest to the importance, both to China and the EU, of European companies' investment in China.

The most recent (October 2006) official EC Communication on EU–China economic and commercial relations marks something of a watershed in terms of the policy discourse in which the Commission has been engaged since the publication of its 1995 programmatic document. It goes much further than its predecessors in its condemnation of China's continued IPR violations and maintenance of market barriers, and in its warning that failure by the Chinese government to address such problems could seriously undermine the future development of trade.

The EC's 2006 document is also at pains to stress the need to resolve outstanding economic and trade problems between the two sides through dialogue, rather than resorting to a more confrontational approach – let alone using retaliatory measures that might serve only to harm the economic interests of both sides. In favour of this measured approach, a framework for negotiation-through-dialogue already exists in the form of the various sectoral dialogues that are already under way between the two sides.[117] At the same time, the EC is also explicit in its determination, in the event of failure to reach a negotiated settlement of outstanding issues, to use more formal legal channels to effect dispute resolution.[118]

In the end, however, the most powerful instrument available to the Commission in seeking to exert leverage over China probably lies in its ability to withhold coveted Market Economy Status (MES).[119] For the time being, the EC's view remains that China does not meet the conditions necessary for MES to be granted to China – a decision that is clearly a source of annoyance, as well as concern, to the Chinese government. When those conditions will be met, it is impossible to say, not least because their fulfilment is likely to depend on progress not only in the

area of economic reform, but also on improvements in social and political development.[120] As usual, politics may well, in the end, be the critical factor shaping future
EU–China economic relations.

Notes

* I am grateful to my research student, Jan Knörich, for making available to me a rich collection of research materials on Chinese outward FDI, and for generously sharing with me his
thoughts on Chinese investment in Europe. My thanks too to Chris Hughes (LSE) for
drawing my attention to a PhD thesis written by one of his research students, Nicola
Casarini (*A Critical Analysis of European Union Foreign Policy towards China, 1995–
2005*), on which I have drawn in the second section of this chapter. Finally, I am indebted to
the very helpful and collegial comments of participants in the preliminary conference on
"China and Europe", held in Berlin in the summer of 2006. To acknowledge, in particular,
the substantive and editorial assistance given by David Shambaugh is not to detract from the
contributions of other colleagues in Berlin towards helping me clarify my thoughts. Any
opaqueness that remains is entirely my own fault.

1 An entire paper could be written on what constitutes, or ought to constitute, "Europe."
   Suffice to say that the comprehensive statistics presented in this paper include Green-
   land, Iceland, Turkey, Belarus, Ukraine and Moldova; but they exclude Israel, Armenia,
   Azerbaijan and Georgia. One or two tiny European countries (e.g. Andorra, the Vatican)
   have been omitted because of the negligible – sometimes zero – significance of their
   commercial relations with China.
2 The main distinction drawn in this paper is between EU-15 (Austria, Belgium, Denmark,
   Finland, France, Germany, Greece, Ireland [Irish Republic], Italy, Luxembourg, Netherlands, Portugal, Spain, Sweden and the United Kingdom) and EU-25 (EU-15 plus
   Cyprus, Czech Republic, Estonia, Hungary, Latvia, Lithuania, Malta, Poland, Slovakia
   and Slovenia). Currently, there are five candidate countries seeking EU membership.
   They are Bulgaria, Croatia, Former Yugoslav Republic of Macedonia, Romania and
   Turkey.
3 Before 1975, economic relations between China and Europe were conducted exclusively on a bilateral country-to-country basis.
4 European Commission, *A Long-Term Policy for China–Europe Relations* (Brussels:
   European Commission, 2005. Ref. COM(1995) 279/ final).
5 Nicola Casarini, *A Critical Analysis of European Union Foreign Policy towards China,
   1995–2005* (unpublished University of London PhD thesis, 2006).
6 Pierre Defraigne, "From a partnership focused solely on trade to a broader, but still
   trade-based, China–EU strategic partnership," P. Defraigne (ed.), *The EU, China and
   the Quest for a Multilateral World* (Paris: Institut Français des Relations Internationales
   (IFRI) and Beijing: China Institute of International Studies, 2006), p. 34.
7 European Commission website (http://ec.europa.eu/trade/issues/bilateral/countries/
   china/index_en.htm), accessed on 11 October 2006.
8 E.g., see Kay Möller, "Diplomatic relations and mutual strategic perceptions: China and
   the European Union" and Franco Algieri, "EU Economic relations with China: an institutional perspective", both in Richard Louis Edmonds (ed.), *China and Europe: A European Perspective* (Cambridge: Cambridge University Press, 2002), pp. 10–32 and 64–
   77; Katinka Barysch (with Charles Grant and Mark Leonard), *Embracing the Dragon:
   The EU's Partnership with China* (London: Centre for European Reform, 2005); and
   Nicola Casarini, *A Critical Analysis of European Union Foreign Policy towards China,
   1995–2005*, op. cit., ch.2.
9 Möller, "Diplomatic relations and mutual strategic perceptions," op. cit., p. 13.

10 Quoted in Casarini, *A Critical Analysis of European Union Foreign Policy towards China, 1995–2005*, op. cit., p. 41.

11 National Bureau of Statistics (NBS), *Zhongguo tongji nianjian, 2005*, hereafter *TJNJ*, various issues.

12 Recovery after the resumption of economic relations in 1992 was swift, and by 1993 two-way trade had reached a new high of US$26.05 billion.

13 Sino-British relations were bedevilled by problems associated with the retrocession to China of sovereignty over Hong Kong; French arms sales to Taiwan meanwhile caused a serious deterioration in relations between Paris and Beijing.

14 As a result, by the mid-1990s Germany was well ahead of both France and the UK as China's most important European trading partner. For further consideration of the German "China policy model," see Christoph Nesshöver, "Bonn et Paris face à Pékin (1989–97): vers une stratégie commune?", *Politique Etrangère*, 1999, No.1, pp. 91–106."

15 For full text of the 1995 document, see ec.europa.eu/comm/external_relations/china/com95_279en.pdf. Note that an EU 1994 document – *Towards a New Asia Strategy* – is an important part of the policy context in which the 1995 China strategy paper was formulated.

16 EC, *A Long-Term Policy*, op. cit., p. 3.

17 Katinka Barysch, *Embracing the Dragon*, op. cit., p. 7.

18 EC, *A Long-Term Policy*, op. cit., p. 4. Tellingly, the document added (p. 5) that "[a]n active role for EU business in China, *where US and Japanese competition is already fierce*, is essential" (emphasis mine) – an indication of the EU's intention to use its economic relations with China in order to improve its competitiveness vis-à-vis the two other major global economic powers.

19 *Building a Comprehensive Partnership with China*, which called *inter alia* for a strengthening of the EU–China political dialogue, further EU support for China's transition to "an open society based upon the rule of law and the respect for human rights," more assistance in facilitating China's integration into the global economy and trading system, and enhancement of the EU's profile in China. The full text of the document can be found at http://ec.europa.eu/comm/external_relations/china/com_98/com98_c.htm.

20 *EU Strategy Towards China: Implementation of 1998 Communication and Future Steps for a More Effective EU Policy* (available at http://ec.europa.eu/comm/external_rela-tions/china/com01_265.pdf).

21 *A Maturing Partnership – Shared Interests and Challenges in EU–China Relations* (for full text, see http://ec.europa.eu/comm/external_relations/china/com_03_533/com_533_en.pdf), which highlighted China's "more constructive and proactive" foreign policy, praised its role as an "increasingly energetic player in world affairs" and noted the "new maturity" of the EU–China relationship.

22 Information Office of the State Council of the PRC, *EU Policy Paper* (issued on 13 Oct. 2003). The full text of the document is available at http://www.fmprc.gov.cn/eng/zxxx/t27708.htm (the website of the Chinese Ministry of Foreign Affairs).

23 Ibid.

24 An overview of on-going sectoral dialogues between China and the EU is available at the EU's website (see http://ec.europa.eu/comm/external_relations/china/intro/sect.htm).

25 These include competition policy, consumer product safety, customs cooperation, education and culture, employment and social affairs, energy (including nuclear energy), environment, space cooperation, the European Galileo programme, informa-tion society, intellectual property rights, macroeconomic and financial sector reforms, maritime transport, regulatory and industrial policy, sanitary and phytosanitary issues affecting food safety, science and technology, textile policy, and trade policy. Future areas of dialogue are expected to cover agriculture, civil aviation, general transport and the pursuit of balanced development (ibid.).

26 The same can be said of Romania and Bulgaria, which will join the EU in 2007 – and of others, such as Croatia, Macedonia and Turkey, which may join in the future.

27 Some argue that increased trade within an expanding EU will be detrimental to the economic interests of China, e.g., the application of a dynamic computable general equilibrium (CGE) model led Hiro Lee and Dominique van der Mensbrugghe to conclude that in the wake of enlargement from EU-15 to EU-25 – and subsequently, following the accession of Bulgaria, Croatia, Romania and Turkey, to EU-29 – China would suffer serious economic and welfare consequences as a result of declining exports of apparel and leather goods to Europe. See their "EU enlargement and its impacts on East Asia", *Journal of Asian Economics*, No.14 (2004), pp. 843–60.

28 *China: Closer Partners, Growing Responsibilities* (issued on 24 October 2006 and available in full at http://ec.europa.eu/comm/external_relations/china/docs/06-10-24_final_com.pdf). An accompanying policy paper – *EU–China Trade and Investment: Competition and Partnership* – was published simultaneously (see http://trade.ec.europa.eu/doclib/docs/2006/october/tradoc_130791.pdf).

29 See Tobias Buck and Richard McGregor, "EU takes tough line with China on Trade", *Financial Times*, 24 October 2006).

30 The Commission's trade policy paper notes the favourable impact for both EU firms (in terms of enhanced competitiveness) and consumers (in terms of the prices of manufactured goods) of access to cheap inputs available in China (*EU–China Trade and Investment: Competition and Partnership*, op. cit., pp. 5–6).

31 EC, *EU–China: Closer Partners, Growing Responsibilities*, op. cit., p. 7.

32 EC, *EU–China Trade and Investment*, op. cit., p. 9.

33 See especially *EU–China Trade and Investment*, op. cit., Section 3 ("The EU'S Response and Priorities for Action," which notes the EC's decision to undertake "a comprehensive review of market openness in China and China's implementation of its WTO commitments" p. 11.

34 There is no universally accepted definition of FDI, and differences in reporting and in measurement conventions are the source of major difficulties in compiling and interpreting FDI statistics. The problem is captured in the finding that the difference between estimated FDI flows to China in 2004 based on host country (i.e. Chinese) sources and investing country sources was of the order of 13 per cent (UNCTAD, *World Investment Report, 2005*, op. cit., p. 36). The existence of illegal capital outflows also bedevils interpretation of Chinese FDI data – a problem whose origins lie mainly in corrupt and illegal practices, such as the formulation of false invoices, asset swaps and the well-attested phenomenon of "round-tripping" (whereby capital leaves China only to re-enter the country in the guise of foreign capital in order to secure beneficial fiscal or other treatment). Despite such uncertainties, UNCTAD data are likely to give a give a reasonably accurate picture of Chinese FDI outflows, not least because most illicit outflows of capital from China (e.g., "round-tripping") are not strongly related to FDI outflows (see Eunsuk Hong and Laixiang Sun, "Go overseas via direct investment: internationalization strategies of Chinese corporations in a comparative prism," *China Quarterly*, No. 187 (September 2006), pp. 610–34; on accounting problems, see David Wall, "Outflows of Capital from China," Organisation for Economic Cooperation and Development [OECD], Working Paper No. 123 (Paris: OECD, 1997).

35 According to authoritative evidence, 87 per cent of transnational corporations (TBCs) ranked China as the most attractive investment destination in the world. In second place equal were India and the United States (each receiving 51 per cent of TNC responses) (United Nations Conference on Trade and Development [UNCTAD], *UNCTAD World Investment Report* [*WIR*], *2005: Transnational Corporations and the Internationalisation of R&D* [New York and Geneva: United Nations, 2005], Box I.3, p. 34).

36 On the one hand, the degree of Asian dominance shown in Table 10.1 is exaggerated by the phenomenon of the "round-tripping" FDI – the practice whereby Chinese capital is transferred to Hong Kong, but is subsequently re-routed back to China as the basis of

some of its FDI inflows. It is widely believed that as much as 20–30 per cent of such capital transfers return to China as round-tripping FDI, and one recent study suggests that the figure could be as high as 50 per cent (Geng Xiao, "People's Republic of China's round-tripping FDI: scale, causes and implications" [ADB Institute Discussion Paper No. 7, July 2004]). On the other hand, the degree of Asian dominance is under-stated by the widespread use of the Cayman and Virgin Islands as covers for Taiwanese investment in China (a very high proportion of the US$11.3 billion of FDI shown to have originated in Latin America is in fact capital re-routed from Taiwan to the mainland).

37 In 1999, their shares of total FDI inflows were 14 per cent (Taiwan), 11.9 per cent (Europe) and 10.5 per cent (USA). Note that Taiwan's contribution to FDI is under-stated, being based on the conservative assumption that 50 per cent of FDI inflows recorded as having originated in the Cayman and Virgin Islands in fact constitute Taiwanese capital.

38 In addition, just as shared historical, linguistic and cultural traditions have encouraged and facilitated the disproportionate contribution of FDI in China from the overseas Chinese diaspora, so similar factors have also worked in favour of investment ties between "rich" and "poor" Europe.

39 UNCTAD, *World Investment Report, 2005*, op. cit., p. 79. Bulgaria and Romania were formally admitted to the EU on 1 January 2007. See also Fabrice Mazerolle, "Trade and FDI between EU and China: data trends and policies", (available at http://secwww.gdufs.edu.cn/site/newscenter/printpage.asp?ArticleID=1014, June 2006), who provides charts showing the median gross annual wage for skilled and unskilled workers in China and other countries (regions). (See figure overleaf.)

40 Thus, "the most competitive economies in Central Europe are now host to well-capitalized subsidiaries of MNEs that are increasingly used as bridgeheads for direct investment in other countries of the CEE region" (OECD, *International Investment Perspectives*, 2005 Edition (Paris: OECD, p. 33).

41 UNCTAD, *World Investment Report, 2005*, op. cit., p. 79.

42 Even so, in 2004 China (including Hong Kong) was the principal destination for EU FDI taking place outside the EU (see EC, *European Union Foreign Direct Investment Yearbook*, 2006 [Luxembourg: European Communities, 2006], p. 24).

43 This was also the broad conclusion reached by Daniel Van Den Bulcke, Haiyan Zhang and Maria do Cée Esteves in their *European Union Direct Investment in China: Characteristics, Challenges and Perspectives* (London and New York: Routledge, 2003).

44 Cf. the takeover of Harbin Breweries by Anheuser-Busch in 2005 (*International Investment Perspectives*, op. cit., p. 25).

45 United Nations, *UNCTAD WIR, 2006: FDI from Developing and Transition Economies: Implications for Development* (New York and Geneva: United Nations, 2006), Box II.7, p. 55. The UNCTAD Report also contains a useful summary of China's "going-global strategy" (Box VI.4, p. 210).

46 *UNCTAD WIR, 2006*, op. cit., p. 305, Annex Table B.2.

47 *UNCTAD WIR, 2006*, op. cit., p. 301, Annex Table B.1.

48 UNCTAD, "Country fact sheet" (www.unctad.org/fdistatistics, accessed June 2006). In 2003, three Chinese banks – Industrial and Commercial Bank of China, Bank of China, and China Construction Bank – were ranked in the world's top 50 largest financial TNCs: together, they had 623 foreign affiliates – 543 of these run by the Bank of China – employing 55,090 staff (ibid.).

49 Ping Deng, "Foreign investment by multinationals from emerging countries: the case of China," *Journal of Leadership and Organisational Studies*, September 2003, p. 113. See also Michael Vatikiotis, "Outward bound," *Far Eastern Economic Review* (*FEER*), 5 February 2004.

50 *WIR, 2005*, pp. 62 and 74.

(a) Unskilled workers

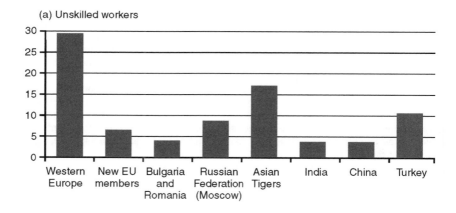

(b) Skilled workers

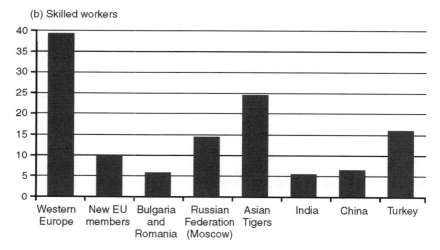

Source: UNCTAD. based on Mercer Human Resource Consulting. "2005 international geographic salary differential report". www.mercerhr.com

51 Eugen von Keller and Wei Zhou, *From Middle Kingdom to Global Market: Expansion Strategies and Success Factors for China's Emerging Multinationals* (Roland Berger Strategy Consultants, Shanghai, 2003).

52 Thus, 23 per cent of surveyed Chinese companies regarded investment in North America as a high priority in the immediate term, compared with only 15 per cent in the European market. However, while Chinese firms displayed a declining interest in western European markets, they showed an increasing interest in CIS markets (ibid.).

53 Europe's heterogeneity can, however, work to its advantage: Ernst and Young's *European Attractiveness Survey* for 2006 reveals that "at a global level, the European zone is placed first among the principal world zones in terms of its attractiveness, benefiting from the combination of Western Europe's maturity (68 per cent of respondents cite Western Europe as one of their three preferred zones, up five points on 2005) and Central and Eastern Europe's dynamism (52 per cent of responses for Central and Eastern

Europe)." The report adds that "Europe's image in the eyes of investors is improving: 47 per cent consider that its attractiveness has improved over the course of the last year. 2006 shows Europe returning to its level of popularity of 2004, following a fall in 2005" (the Survey can be accessed at www.ey.com/global/content.nsf/International/ Press_Release_-_European_Attractiveness_Survey_2006).

54 TTE's assets were valued at €430 million and its annual capacity was estimated to be 20 million colour TV sets (Accenture, *China and the European Union: Business Issues and Opportunities* (Accenture Policy and Corporate Affairs, 2005), p. 2). See also *People's Daily Online*, 11 October 2004; and Vatikiotis, *FEER*, 5 February 2004, op. cit., Li Dongsheng, Chairman and CEO of TCL – and *Fortune*'s "Asian Businessman of the Year" in 2003 – was unequivocal in his statement that "our goal is to become a Chinese Sony or Samsung" (*The Economist*, 8 January 2005).

55 TAMP thereby became the largest mobile producer in China, and the 7th largest in the world (*China and the European Union: Business Issues and Opportunities*, op. cit., p. 2).

56 James Kynge, *China Shakes the World: The Rise of a Hungry Nation* (London: Weidenfeld and Nicolson, 2006), p. 162.

57 An example is Galanz, which by 2002 had captured 40 per cent of the European market in microwave ovens under its own name (Ming Zeng and Peter J. Williamson, "The hidden dragons," *Harvard Business Review*, Vol. 81, No.10 (October 2003).

58 *WIR, 2005*, op. cit., p. 120. R&D spending by PetroChina in 2003 was US$265 million, compared with US$6,841 million by Ford Motor (the top-ranked firm). *WIR, 2006* observes that two major Chinese electronics firms – Haier and Huawei – "are illustrative of the trend of R&D units being located mainly in developed countries" (op. cit., p. 185; see also Box VI.4, p. 210).

59 In an interview with Kynge, Li Dongsheng stated that against the background of thin profit margins associated with domestic over-supply, "the only answer was to build a bulwark in offshore markets where decent margins could be collected to reinforce the home front" (*China Shakes the World*, op. cit., p. 163). Haier's purchase of an Italian refrigerator company in Padova is an example of a Chinese firm's attempt to increase profit margins by securing new markets overseas.

60 This is the finding of Yang Yao and Yin He, "Chinese outward investing firms: a study for FIAS [Foreign Investment Advisory Service]/IFC [International Finance Corporation]/MIGA [Multilateral Investment Guarantee Agency]" (Beijing: China Centre for Economic Research, Beijing University, 2005, cited in *WIR, 2006*).

61 *WIR, 2006*, op. cit., p. 174, Box V.3.

62 *WIR, 2006*, op. cit., pp. 174–5.

63 See Ping Deng, "Outward investment by Chinese MNCs: motivations and implications" (*Business Horizons*, Vol. 47, No. 3 (May–June 2004), pp. 8–16.

64 See Uwe Reinert and Stephan Altrichter, *China Goes West – Eine Chance für die deutsche Wirtschaft* (München, Düsseldorf and Zürich: Bain and Company Germany, 2005), which presents the results of a survey of 50 Chinese companies that had already invested in Europe. Russia's ability to supply China with large-scale energy exports is the most obvious exception to the general statement about resource-seeking FDI made in the text. Some estimates indicate that oil and gas purchases from Russia could provide China with up to 20 per cent of its energy imports by 2011, although competition from Central Asian countries and a perception that Russia is not wholly reliable as a secure source of energy (cf. difficulties surrounding the planned building of the Eastern Siberian to the Pacific Ocean [ESPO] crude oil pipeline) counsel caution in projecting the scale of Sino-Russian energy trade and cooperation. Currently, China is Russia's second-largest trading partner after the EU. See "Gas diplomacy," *China Economic Review*, Vol. 16, No. 6 (June 2006), pp. 21–3. To what extent Ukraine might become a supplier of *grain* to China remains for the time being in the realm of speculation.

65 Thus, Keller and Zhou: "in light of European Union trade barriers, a Shandong textile company's 15 per cent stake in a Spanish textile firm has a substantial marketing

benefit" (op. cit., p. 11). It is instructive that Haier Inc. was set up in 1984 as an OEM refrigerator manufacturer; in 2000, it established Haier Europe which now operates in 13 European countries and has purchased Padova (Keller and Zhou, op. cit., p. 10; see also fn. 13).

66 "[G]rowing trade surpluses with ... European countries have led to the need to circumvent tariff and non-tariff barriers to exports which are increasingly crucial, as China's own domestic markets ... are glutted with consumer durables ..." (Robert Taylor, "Globalisation strategies of Chinese companies: current developments and future prospects," *Asian Business and Management*, 2002, No.1, p. 213). In the same article, see also Taylor's interesting comments on the potential benefits of investment in Anatolia by Chinese textile, food processing and farm equipment manufacturers in advance of Turkey's expected membership of the EU.

67 E.g., the purchase of MG Rover by Nanjing Automotive, or of ThyssenKrup by Shagang.

68 UNCTAD, *World Investment Report, 2005*, op. cit., p. 150.

69 TCL also has a presence in Poland.

70 In 2006 some categories of Chinese investor have benefited from new rules, through the Qualified Domestic Institutional Investor (QDII) scheme, allowing them to use foreign currency reserves to invest in overseas financial assets.

71 EU-25 comprises a consumer market of around 500 million people.

72 Eurostat data, expressed in ECU/Euro, show that in 2005 the EU's bilateral deficit vis-à-vis China exceeded its combined deficit with Russia, Japan, South Korea and Taiwan. The same source reveals that in 2005, the deficit with China (ECU/euro 106.29 billion) was marginally greater than its entire Extra-EU-25 deficit (ECU/euro 106.09 billion.).

73 Notice that EU-15 has generated an increasing trade surplus with China in *services*, in which there exists significant room for further growth. See Accenture, *China and the European Union: Business Issues and Opportunities* (Accenture Policy and Corporate Affairs, 2005), p. 2.

74 In its bilateral negotiations with China on WTO accession, the EU pressed for specific tariff concessions, as well as seeking to secure even better terms than the US in areas such as telecommunications and insurance, in which the EU had particular interests.

75 The EC's 2004 European Competitiveness Report notes that "China's industrial policy has selectively attracted FDI in technology intensive industries in order to benefit from foreign technology and organizational 'know how'" (EC, IP/04/1400, 25 November 2004).

76 EUROSTAT (*Comext, Statistical regime 4*), *DG Trade Statistics*, op. cit. The rising bilateral trade deficit is likely to become an increasingly sensitive issue, although it has not yet elicited the same degree of concern as the parallel problem has in the United States.

77 Outside the EU, Turkey has emerged as an increasingly important destination for Chinese exports. In terms of shipments to China, Switzerland ranks second to Russia outside the EU.

78 Daniel Van Den Bulcke et al, *European Union Direct Investment in China*, op. cit., p. 51. This study is a rich source of information on EU–China trade and investment relations, from which I have greatly benefited in writing this section.

79 During 1885–1936 the UK established 155 enterprises in China, with associated investment of US$1,200 m. Next in importance were Germany (23 enterprises and investment of $82 million), Belgium (5 enterprises, US$12 million), France (1S, 18 enterprises, $12 million.) and Italy (5 enterprises, US$6 million). Ibid. A detailed analysis of British investment in China before the Second World War is available in David Swan, *British Industrial Investment in Mainland China, 1895–1940* (University of London PhD thesis, 2006).

80 In turn, between 1945 and 1949, the USA replaced Japan as the dominant foreign investor in China.

81 Wolfgang Klenner, "China and the EU: Trade, Capital Flows, Strategic Issues." I am grateful to Prof. Klenner for making this paper available to me. Data cited by Daniel Van

Den Bulcke et al (*European Union Direct Investment in China*, op. cit., p. 70, Table 4.12) show that during 1979–96 only 5.4 per cent of EU subsidiaries were located in SEZs – a figure that would have been a good deal lower, had it not been for a significant SEZ presence by Austrian and Danish firms.

82 Except for the UK, European company affiliates in China before the Second World War tended to be concentrated in particular regions (French in Guangdong and Shanghai, German in Shandong). The British presence was much less regionally focused. See Daniel Van Den Bulcke et al., *European Union Direct Investment in China*, op. cit., p. 51.

83 The most significant of these were the establishment, in 1983 of subsidiaries by Alcatel-Bell and Pilkington, respectively worth US$39.5 m. and $29.9 m. (Daniel Van Den Bulcke et al., *European Union Direct Investment in China*, op. cit., p. 54).

84 Over 86 per cent of EU subsidiaries listed in the (as it was then) Ministry of Foreign Trade and Economic Cooperation (MOFTEC) database of foreign-invested enterprises, 1979–96, were engaged in manufacturing (Daniel Van Den Bulcke et al., *European Union Direct Investment in China*, op. cit., pp. 61–2).

85 By the end of 2006, most restrictions on foreign investment in banking and finance had been lifted. Existing barriers to investment in telecommunications and service industries are expected to be removed during 2007 and 2008.

86 But note that various factors – notably, re-routing capital that originates in China back to the mainland (the phenomenon of "round-tripping") – have led to the exaggeration of FDI flows from Hong Kong.

87 This figure includes half of FDI reported as originating in the Cayman and Virgin Islands.

88 *Zhongguo tongji nianjian, 2006*, op. cit., pp.

89 Barysch, *Embracing the Dragon*, op. cit., p. 38. Low wages and land prices are probably a greater attraction to smaller-scale European investors, although it is noteworthy that such investors have also enjoyed access to such advantages much closer to home in Eastern Europe, where additionally the business environment has had many similarities with that of EU-15 Member States.

90 "China's emerging middle classes love French designer handbags … German cars … and Italian pizzas" (ibid.). The competitiveness of some British, Dutch, French, German and Swedish firms has enabled them to achieve a high domestic market penetration rate in China. Major European designer brands, such as Giorgio Armani, Jean-Paul Gaultier, Nina Ricci, Karl Lagerfield and Louis Vuitton, all have a presence in Shanghai (some in other cities too). Cartier recently opened a flagship store in Shanghai and, as of 2005, planned to open another seven elsewhere in China (Accenture, *China and the EU*, op. cit., p. 3).

91 European Commission, *Communication to the Commission: The EU Economy: 2005 Review – Summary and Main Conclusions* (Brussels, EC: 22 November 2005, COM(2005)XXX), p. 4.

92 Hay Group, *Waking up to China – Are You Ready? The Impact of China on Global Business* (London, Hay Group: 2006). The survey of global business leaders – almost a third of participants were CEOs, Presidents or Managing Directors; most of the remainder were Board-Level Executives – was conducted in 2006 for Hay Group by the Economist Intelligence Unit. 19 industries were represented, ranging from medium-scale firms to large-scale MNCs. 43 per cent of participants belonged to firms whose headquarters were in Western Europe. I am indebted to David Shambaugh for alerting me to the existence of this survey. See also *Financial Times*, 14 July 2006.

93 The findings in Table 10.8 may be compared with those of the 2006 European Business Confidence survey, which indicated that 92 per cent of respondents were optimistic about the general business outlook in China (see the remarks of Giorgio Magistrelli, then Secretary-General of the European Union Chamber of Commerce in China, on 12 September 2006 in http://www.ek.fi/businessforums/eu_china/en/liitteet/esitys_Magistrelli. pdf).

94 Hay Group, *Waking up to China*, op. cit., p. 16.

95 But not only European.

96 Daniel Van Den Bulcke et al, *European Union Direct Investment in China*, op. cit., p. 103. Only 15 per cent of companies claimed to have exceeded their expectations.

97 Ibid.

98 Thus, "... European MNEs [have been] clearly oriented towards the domestic Chinese market. The potential growth of its market size [has] also encouraged European firms to establish a strategic presence in China" (Daniel Van Den Bulcke et al, *European Union Direct Investment in China*, op. cit., p. 104).

99 EUCCC, *Position Paper, 2006–7*, cited in *EuroBiz* (Journal of the EU Chamber of Commerce in China), Nov. 2006.

100 Ibid.

101 Useful sectoral overviews with a strong EU–China trade and investment orientation are available from EC websites, as follows: http://trade.ec.europa.eu/doclib/docs/2006/july/tradoc_129427.pdf (machinery); http://trade.ec.europa.eu/doclib/docs/2006/july/tradoc_129428.pdf (pharmaceuticals); http://trade.ec.europa.eu/doclib/docs/2006/july/tradoc_129431.pdf (telecommunication services); http://trade.ec.europa.eu/doclib/docs/2006/july/tradoc_129430.pdf (sustainable technologies); and http://trade.ec.europa.eu/doclib/docs/2006/july/tradoc_129429.pdf (retail trade).

102 *Financial Times*, 18 October 2005.

103 Bloomberg News, 11 September 2006; *China Daily*, 20 November 2006.

104 China was expected to have almost 450 million mobile phone users by the end of 2006.

105 Siemens has a long history of involvement in China, having set up its first permanent office in Shanghai in 1904.

106 *Taipei Times*, 25 February 2005.

107 *Taipei Times*, 2 December 2006.

108 The new HQ is scheduled to open in the Beijing Economic-Technological Development Area late in 2007. According to Nokia's Chairman and CEO (Jorma Ollila), it will be a new hub for Nokia's activities in China, Hong Kong, Macau and Taiwan, and will house the company's R&D centres and its mobile phone manufacturing base (quoted in *China Daily*, 24 May 2006).

109 From Urumqi in the northwest to Harbin in the northeast, and from Kunming in the southwest to Shenzhen in the southeast. In addition to its hypermarkets, Carrefour also operates "Champion" supermarkets and "Dia" convenience stores. In 2006 Carrefour launched an on-line shopping service for its customers.

110 http://www.zhonghuarising.com/2006/08/carrefour_vs_walmart_in_china.html: "Carrefour vs. Wal-Mart in China."

111 For an interesting insight into Carrefour's China strategy see the interview with Jean-Luc Chéreau (President of Carrefour China) in Peter N. Child, "Lessons from a global retailer: an interview with the president of Carrefour China" in *The McKinsey Quarterly*, Special Edition 2006, "Serving the New Chinese Consumer."

112 As Barysch observes, "For every company that has made money, there are many more that have failed to turn a profit. Some have given up in frustration. But the majority struggle on under the motto 'you cannot afford not to be in China'." (*Embracing the Dragon*, op. cit., pp. 38–9).

113 EC, *EU–China Trade and Investment*, op. cit., p. 8; and see above, p. 9. Nor, it should be added, have tariffs uniformly been reduced to expected levels ("China has maintained a number of tariff peaks in some industries of particular importance for the EU such as textiles and clothing, leather and fur, ceramics, steel and vehicles"; ibid.). The Chinese response to such criticisms would doubtless include allegations against Brussels of its unfair treatment in imposing anti-dumping duties on imports of clothes and shoes from China.

114 Hay Group, *Waking up to China*, op. cit., p. 11.

115 See Simon Kennedy, "Europe surpasses U.S., Japan in gains from trade," Bloomberg.com (available at http://bloomberg.com/apps/news?pid=20601109&sid=azozwpvbIYas&refer=home).

116 EC, *China: Closer Partners, Growing Responsibilities*, op. cit., p. 6.
117 See above pp. 7–8.
118 Thus, "where trade irritants arise between China and the EU, the EU will always seek to resolve them through dialogue and negotiation. However, where this fails, the Commission will use the WTO dispute settlement system to resolve trade issues with China and to ensure compliance with multilaterally agreed rules and obligations" (EC, *EU–China Trade and Investment*, op. cit., p. 13).
119 Alongside the EU's refusal to lift its arms embargo against China, its refusal to grant it MES status is the most contentious source of disagreement between the two sides. For further consideration of both issues, viewed from a Chinese perspective, see the chapter by Zhang Zuqian in this volume.
120 In this respect, cf. the following remark made by the EU Trade Commissioner, Peter Mandelson, during a visit to China in February 2005: "The technical aspects [on which the granting of MES status to China will be decided] are vital, but … attitudes towards granting market economy status will be influenced by a broader perception of how China is developing, in its political, social and economic behaviour, both at home and abroad" (quoted in Barysch, *Embracing the Dragon*, op. cit., p. 43).

Appendix A1

Trends in EU–China's merchandise trade

Table 10.A1 Exports from China to the EU and other comparable regions and countries

	World	Asia	Industrial countries	European Union	Hong Kong	Japan	United States
	Exports from China to following partner countries and regions (US$-billion)						
1980	18,139.2	6,533.0	8,117.5	2,686.6	4,353.2	4,032.2	982.6
1981	21,476.2	7,432.4	9,455.8	2,821.1	5,262.7	4,746.6	1,505.1
1982	21,865.5	7,224.5	9,397.3	2,493.3	5,180.6	4,806.4	1,764.7
1983	22,096.1	7,657.3	9,346.8	2,801.6	5,796.7	4,517.0	1,713.0
1984	24,824.9	9,348.8	10,427.2	2,503.9	6,586.1	5,155.0	2,312.5
1985	27,331.0	10,708.2	11,430.0	2,742.7	7,148.1	6,091.4	2,336.2
1986	31,369.6	12,606.9	12,606.9	4,747.1	9,776.3	5,078.6	2,632.7
1987	39,465.3	17,227.7	14,589.1	4,726.0	13,764.2	6,391.8	3,030.4
1988	47,663.6	22,375.6	17,470.0	5,502.4	18,239.2	8,046.4	3,398.7
1989	52,914.4	26,844.6	19,023.1	5,598.6	21,915.9	8,394.7	4,413.6
1990	62,760.1	33,603.3	21,975.6	6,412.4	27,162.6	9,210.4	5,313.9
1991	71,996.9	41,069.4	25,011.3	7,273.2	32,137.6	10,251.8	6,198.0
1992	85,621.0	47,114.3	30,007.8	8,225.2	37,511.3	11,699.3	8,598.3
1993	91,695.9	33,785.0	47,818.6	12,729.9	22,067.5	15,782.3	16,976.5
1994	120,869.0	48,675.2	61,918.9	16,256.5	32,365.4	21,489.8	21,421.4
1995	148,959.0	59,673.3	76,500.6	20,213.4	36,003.5	28,466.4	24,473.9
1996	151,168.0	56,492.2	81,823.9	20,959.7	32,904.0	30,888.3	26,730.6
1997	182,920.0	72,466.4	93,821.7	25,223.5	43,798.4	31,819.8	32,743.9
1998	183,746.0	63,391.1	101,588.0	29,788.7	38,782.2	29,718.1	38,000.6
1999	194,936.0	64,622.9	111,151.0	32,058.3	36,890.6	32,399.1	42,003.1
2000	249,208.0	82,860.1	140,301.0	40,783.0	44,519.8	41,654.0	52,161.7
2001	266,709.0	87,691.4	148,948.0	44,299.9	46,502.5	45,078.2	54,395.1
2002	325,744.0	110,696.0	177,455.0	52,487.0	58,483.3	48,483.0	70,063.8
2003	438,365.0	198,613.0	238,773.0	78,472.8	76,288.6	59,422.6	92,633.2
2004	593,360.0	198,341.0	319,274.0	107,265.0	100,878.0	73,514.3	125,155.0
2005	762,338.0	249,713.0	409,847.0	143,851.0	124,505.0	84,097.2	163,348.0

Source: International Monetary Fund (IMF), *Direction of Trade Statistics*, available at http://esds.mcc.ac.uk/WDS_DOTS/TableViewer/tableView.aspx?ReportId=26497.

Table 10.A2 Imports to China from the EU and other comparable regions and countries

	Imports to China from following partner countries and regions (US$-billion)						
	World	*Asia*	*Industrial countries*	*European Union*	*Hong Kong*	*Japan*	*United States*
1980	19,505.0	1,704.4	14,370.7	3,346.0	568.9	5,168.9	3,830.2
1981	21,630.5	2,366.0	16,105.2	3,238.7	1,236.3	6,183.0	4,682.4
1982	18,920.4	2,542.0	13,039.2	2,455.8	1,314.2	3,901.7	4,304.6
1983	21,312.6	2,711.8	14,524.7	3,792.0	1,709.8	5,495.2	2,753.0
1984	25,953.4	4,142.6	17,967.1	3,916.8	2,830.2	8,056.9	3,837.1
1985	42,480.2	7,097.6	29,901.9	7,053.8	4,762.1	15,178.4	5,198.7
1986	43,275.4	8,199.9	28,919.9	9,240.7	5,572.0	12,463.2	4,718.2
1987	43,222.7	10,919.5	26,499.5	8,624.6	8,437.0	10,087.2	4,835.6
1988	55,352.2	15,708.1	30,571.4	9,429.9	12,004.7	11,062.1	6,633.0
1989	59,141.4	16,850.2	31,767.4	10,297.5	12,540.4	10,533.9	7,863.6
1990	53,809.7	20,582.4	26,940.1	9,513.4	14,565.0	7,655.9	6,591.0
1991	63,876.8	26,628.5	31,392.5	9,423.1	17,543.3	10,031.7	8,010.3
1992	81,871.5	34,074.8	38,018.6	10,985.6	20,538.7	13,685.6	8,902.7
1993	103,628.0	35,961.0	54,395.7	16,069.6	10,501.1	23,302.5	10,632.8
1994	115,706.0	38,931.4	64,644.8	18,920.5	9,487.8	26,318.9	13,976.7
1995	132,164.0	44,572.6	73,227.9	21,579.5	8,599.0	29,007.3	16,123.2
1996	138,949.0	48,831.7	72,807.2	20,134.1	7,839.0	29,190.2	16,178.9
1997	142,163.0	52,508.4	71,338.4	19,308.7	6,997.3	28,989.6	16,289.8
1998	140,385.0	52,700.5	72,482.5	20,848.4	6,666.7	28,306.8	16,977.3
1999	165,718.0	60,219.7	86,649.5	25,800.7	6,892.4	33,768.2	19,488.7
2000	225,175.0	82,726.3	105,770.0	30,730.8	9,431.3	41,520.3	22,376.1
2001	243,567.0	86,190.2	117,323.0	36,343.9	9,423.5	42,810.3	26,221.0
2002	295,440.0	112,071.0	132,599.0	39,439.6	10,787.9	53,489.0	27,251.4
2003	412,836.0	156,574.0	177,436.0	54,477.2	11,119.1	274,150.8	33,938.9
2004	561,422.0	211,212.0	232,782.0	70,131.2	11,800.4	94,372.1	44,772.6
2005	660,218.0	250,808.0	251,242.0	73,559.4	12,232.0	100,468.0	48,944.5

Source: International Monetary Fund (IMF), *Direction of Trade Statistics*, available at http://esds.mcc.ac.uk/WDS_DOTS/TableViewer /tableView.aspx?ReportId=26497.

Table 10.A3 EU exports to China and other comparable countries and regions

	World	Asia	Developing countries	China	Industrial countries	Hong Kong	United States
	\multicolumn{7}{l}{*Exports from EU to following partner countries and regions (US$ billion)*}
1980	777,863.0	24,422.4	195,742.0	2,890.4	566,931.0	3,148.6	41,460.0
1981	716,164.0	24,389.6	196,995.0	2,455.9	504,488.0	3,093.5	45,601.1
1982	689,121.0	24,928.4	181,770.0	2,389.7	495,613.0	3,173.7	46,110.6
1983	673,019.0	24,961.0	169,152.0	2,906.6	493,068.0	2,960.6	49,831.4
1984	690,712.0	26,206.7	161,861.0	3,395.0	517,190.0	3,304.7	63,274.1
1985	729,636.0	30,342.6	160,789.0	6,321.9	557,028.0	3,675.0	71,026.0
1986	891,777.0	36,917.7	173,977.0	7,532.1	703,524.0	4,530.5	80,508.3
1987	1,068,840.0	44,730.5	192,053.0	7,481.1	862,067.0	5,858.6	90,383.1
1988	1,188,600.0	52,122.0	209,629.0	7,829.5	963,045.0	7,287.6	92,516.5
1989	1,263,930.0	57,207.1	223,377.0	7,787.6	1,023,310.0	7,794.9	93,844.4
1990	1,513,780.0	67,011.7	266,414.0	7,647.3	1,231,810.0	8,888.1	105,202.0
1991	1,513,760.0	69,637.3	271,248.0	7,776.3	1,230,010.0	9,699.4	95,606.4
1992	1,601,620.0	79,066.1	293,786.0	9,697.6	1,296,330.0	12,051.0	103,322.0
1993	1,492,650.0	92,416.3	322,536.0	14,898.5	1,143,410.0	13,950.3	107,506.0
1994	1,716,390.0	109,799.0	361,681.0	16,448.3	1,321,430.0	16,851.1	124,308.0
1995	2,097,520.0	138,162.0	455,920.0	19,429.0	1,609,730.0	21,011.9	137,202.0
1996	2,161,670.0	144,110.0	490,276.0	18,761.8	1,639,230.0	22,386.3	146,944.0
1997	2,191,000.0	142,863.0	510,856.0	18,878.6	1,648,420.0	23,215.1	161,213.0
1998	2,262,760.0	111,892.0	491,368.0	19,386.3	1,744,700.0	19,333.6	180,235.0
1999	2,327,430.0	113,270.0	465,231.0	20,924.8	1,846,080.0	16,823.7	198,893.0
2000	2,409,220.0	127,401.0	501,437.0	23,522.8	1,892,280.0	19,032.1	218,837.0
2001	2,435,780.0	128,914.0	521,775.0	27,765.8	1,891,840.0	19,537.7	220,153.0
2002	2,595,570.0	137,974.0	567,796.0	33,199.8	2,003,760.0	19,365.5	232,078.0
2003	3,108,210.0	165,856.0	691,459.0	46,329.3	2,393,510.0	20,663.7	257,543.0
2004	3,715,190.0	205,309.0	858,832.0	59,796.5	2,823,770.0	23,874.4	293,221.0
2005	3,984,460.0	223,550.0	970,332.0	64,362.9	2,976,450.0	25,614.9	313,551.0

Source: International Monetary Fund (IMF), *Direction of Trade Statistics*, available at http://esds.mcc.ac.uk/WDS_DOTS/TableViewer/tableView.aspx?ReportId=26497.

Table 10.A4 EU imports from China and other comparable countries and regions

	EU imports from following partner countries and regions (US$ billion)						
	World	*Asia*	*Developing countries*	*China*	*Industrial countries*	*Hong Kong*	*United States*
1980	876,471.0	31,452.4	256,196.0	3,152.6	613,026.0	5,767.6	71,707.2
1981	777,263.0	27,469.1	230,586.0	2,984.3	540,839.0	5,048.8	65,898.5
1982	737,166.0	26,266.9	206,997.0	2,815.6	524,490.0	4,622.3	60,678.0
1983	707,145.0	25,941.0	186,423.0	2,836.7	514,586.0	4,803.9	55,715.0
1984	715,234.0	27,923.2	187,182.0	2,989.1	521,659.0	4,749.3	56,515.8
1985	747,482.0	28,039.7	185,203.0	3,439.8	555,172.0	4,388.8	57,304.5
1986	877,475.0	37,305.8	174,203.0	5,080.3	694,620.0	6,411.9	61,591.0
1987	1,072,290.0	51,891.0	202,142.0	6,980.0	895,105.0	8,082.9	72,265.3
1988	1,208,980.0	63,749.7	221,078.0	8,799.9	975,294.0	9,571.0	86,187.7
1989	1,299,400.0	68,518.8	240,363.0	10,341.9	1,046,460.0	9,520.3	98,687.3
1990	1,561,110.0	82,613.4	288,563.0	13,526.1	1,263,470.0	10,618.6	113,902.0
1991	1,609,300.0	97,767.8	304,542.0	18,294.3	1,297,970.0	11,461.9	121,110.0
1992	1,673,890.0	107,239.0	306,089.0	21,267.4	1,360,760.0	11,822.1	120,083.0
1993	1,461,830.0	108,453.0	306,235.0	24,245.3	1,136,600.0	11,024.0	112,597.0
1994	1,666,780.0	122,716.0	348,131.0	28,333.2	1,294,670.0	11,577.2	125,806.0
1995	2,015,640.0	146,921.0	421,531.0	33,375.5	1,570,300.0	13,778.0	145,996.0
1996	2,078,550.0	163,351.0	452,860.0	37,140.1	1,602,600.0	14,331.0	155,650.0
1997	2,108,870.0	174,915.0	475,376.0	42,179.6	1,606,360.0	14,882.2	170,148.0
1998	2,213,370.0	191,167.0	489,771.0	46,672.2	1,700,820.0	16,645.0	180,983.0
1999	2,303,190.0	196,603.0	506,667.7	51,622.7	1,780,950.0	17,034.8	181,179.0
2000	2,452,540.0	223,748.0	600,619.0	63,232.0	1,838,850.0	17,845.2	195,260.0
2001	2,424,000.0	216,695.0	603,785.0	68,886.7	1,793,460.0	16,049.9	182,233.0
2002	2,523,190.0	230,215.0	637,339.0	80,727.4	1,859,360.0	16,172.6	175,993.0
2003	3,058,710.0	292,750.0	802,059.0	115,308.0	2,239,940.0	17,391.8	183,466.0
2004	3,696,840.0	372,762.0	1,016,570.0	156,977.0	2,657,620.0	21,122.0	205,648.0
2005	4,018,400.0	423,068.0	1,193,510.0	197,770.0	2,796,200.0	21,809.9	214,890.0

Source: International Monetary Fund (IMF), *Direction of Trade Statistics*, available at http://
esds.mcc.ac.uk/WDS_DOTS/TableViewer/tableView.aspx?ReportId=26497.

Appendix B

Trade between China and European countries

Table 10.B1 Exports from China to European countries

	Exports from China to each European country (US$ m.)					
	1980	1985	1900	1995	2000	2005
Austria	14.70	17.20	48.56	169.63	308.79	883.50
Belgium	–	–	–	–	2,300.76	7,740.07
Belgium-Luxembourg	97.20	163.80	329.53	1,181.92	–	–
Luxembourg	–	–	–	–	53.60	2,039.57
Denmark	41.20	73.10	131.40	308.54	782.02	2,789.85
Finland	26.50	22.70	90.81	175.75	836.92	3,626.73
France	340.50	227.70	653.56	1,844.43	3,714.58	11,700.80
Germany	710.50	745.70	2,062.11	5,672.19	9,278.09	32,537.00
Greece	7.70	20.50	68.74	192.55	578.70	1,936.15
Ireland	5.00	6.70	16.53	106.64	336.28	3,184.39
Italy	351.10	294.40	872.61	2,067.49	3,802.31	11,696.60
Netherlands	196.80	327.00	942.83	3,232.66	6,687.17	25,876.10
Portugal	0	3.60	41.53	106.05	260.82	914.10
Spain	49.60	63.30	212.58	1,013.21	2,151.950	8,485.99
Sweden	86.00	60.60	140.69	396.35	828.08	2,577.31
United Kingdom	563.70	357.50	663.66	2,790.81	6,310.24	18,983.10
EU-15	**2,490.50**	**2,383.80**	**6,275.13**	**19,258.22**	**38,230.31**	**134,971.25**
Czech Republic	–	–	–	139.52	354.07	1,668.26
Cyprus	0	8.40	38.62	44.350	151.86	287.31
Estonia	–	–	–	7.22	61.79	311.67
Hungary	49.70	81.80	23.61	325.49	897.11	2,494.92
Latvia	–	–	–	1.20	26.30	281.91
Lithuania	–	–	–	1.98	29.01	361.08
Malta	5.00	2.20	3.82	14.05	76.17	301.15
Poland	141.40	266.50	71.20	471.96	860.41	2,598.34
Slovak Republic	–	–	–	31.95	40.36	309.46
Slovenia	–	–	–	17.51	55.62	265.95
EU-25	**–**	**–**	**–**	**20,313.40**	**40,783.00**	**143,851.29**
Belarus	–	–	–	10.01	41.12	81.28
Bulgaria	34.60	20.10	35.81	32.44	80.83	441.75
Croatia	–	–	–	3.20	79.96	573.71
Czechoslovakia	147.30	224.60	304.95	–		
Norway	147.00	19.50	48.22	222.69	486.61	1,322.47
Romania	513.00	282.70	188.50	156.96	192.39	1,370.52
Russia	228.30*	1,037.30*	2,047.90*	1,674.16	2,233.27	13,210.80
Switzerland	205.40	150.80	164.16	413.62	748.11	1,955.82
Turkey	0	69.70	49.03	430.65	1,077.89	4,251.78
Ukraine	–	–		73.80	136.43	2,492.21

*Data for former Soviet Union

Source: Chinese Ministry of Commerce (MOFCOM), Foreign Investment Administration website at http://www.fid. gov.cn/common/info.jsp?id=ABC000…; and NBS, *Zhongguo tongji nianjian*, various issues.

Table 10.B2 Exports to China from European countries

	Exports to China from Europe (US$ m.)					
	1980	*1985*	*1990*	*1995*	*2000*	*2005*
Austria	90.90	159.60	305.91	563.44	860.50	1,611.48
Belgium	–	–	–	–	1,386.25	4,006.24
Belgium-Luxembourg	82.60	312.60	329.73	1,203.98	–	–
Luxembourg	–	–	–	–	45.67	150.64
Denmark	52.30	106.70	140.66	318.51	550.28	1,194.57
Finland	68.90	125.90	166.16	621.67	1,926.14	2,628.43
France	314.70	717.80	1,673.67	2,648.72	3,955.24	9,026.60
Germany	1,332.90	2,447.40	2,979.95	8,034.73	10,411.30	30,668.20
Greece	15.20	65.70	49.86	20.06	48.07	86.73
Ireland	0.40	7.30	8.80	48.69	377.48	1,423.03
Italy	248.80	902.70	1,086.86	3,116.17	3,091.25	6,934.34
Netherlands	157.00	274.30	399.83	818.08	1,236.23	2,925.42
Portugal	0.00	16.20	33.88	38.64	46.95	323.94
Spain	69.90	546.40	325.41	909.18	623.00	2,083.42
Sweden	99.00	263.10	262.42	999.63	2,199.10	3,130.01
United Kingdom	540.00	753.60	1,383.40	1,971.85	3,592.64	5,511.25
EU-15	**3,072.60**	**6,699.30**	**9,146.54**	**21,313.34**	**30,350.09**	**71,704.30**
Czech Republic	–	–	–	87.95	75.77	371.62
Cyprus	0.00	0.00	1.62	2.61	0.57	2.84
Estonia	–	–	–	1.46	5.10	57.93
Hungary	83.90	109.90	112.65	30.92	80.78	366.04
Latvia	–	–	–	14.84	2.78	8.99
Lithuania	–	–	–	0.99	9.69	11.48
Malta	0.00	0.00	0.00	0.76	14.75	237.98
Poland	189.50	244.60	252.63	83.59	156.66	557.92
Slovak Republic	–	–	–	36.14	22.81	183.06
Slovenia	–	–	–	6.92	11.80	57.25
EU-25	–	–	–	**21,579.51**	**30,730.80**	**73,559.36**
Belarus	–	–	–	28.53	72.51	490.37
Bulgaria	30.40	39.10	101.43	20.23	9.14	90.49
Croatia	–	–	–	14.82	5.07	43.83
Norway	27.50	113.40	169.12	224.82	539.59	1,144.57
Romania	524.60	585.80	213.74	190.03	107.13	292.39
Russia	264.10*	1,016.50*	2,212.84*	3,798.83	5,769.48	15,886.40
Switzerland	235.20	277.00	403.97	944.54	1,466.83	3,894.47
Turkey	0.0	40.10	52.44	143.89	126.75	632.79
Ukraine	–	–	–	539.92	454.60	784.92

* Data for former Soviet Union.

Source: Chinese Ministry of Commerce (MOFCOM), Foreign Investment Administration website at http://www.fid.gov.cn/common/info.jsp?id=ABC00000000000027429; and NBS, *Zhongguo tongji nianjian*, various issues.

Appendix C

National European sources of FDI to China

Table 10.C1 Ranked utilized FDI flows from European countries to China, 2005

	Utilised FDI (US$ m.)	As share of total European FDI to China (%)
Germany	1,530.04	27.11
Netherlands	1,043.58	18.49
United Kingdom	964.75	17.10
France	615.06	10.90
Italy	322.01	5.71
Switzerland	205.88	3.65
Spain	196.90	3.49
Luxembourg	142.00	2.52
Sweden	111.45	1.97
Denmark	100.43	1.78
Russia	81.99	1.45
Austria	76.30	1.35
Romania	57.10	1.01
Belgium	53.84	0.95
Hungary	45.45	0.81
Poland	26.24	0.46
Norway	26.24	0.46
Finland	21.72	0.38
Ireland	9.73	0.17
Czech Republic	5.52	0.10
Portugal	4.13	0.07
Liechtenstein	2.86	0.05
Greece	1.84	0.03
Gibraltar	1.55	0.03
Ukraine	1.26	0.02

Note: Countries investing less than US$1 m. not included.

Source: NBS, *Zhongguo tongji nianjian, 2006*, op.cit.

11 China's commercial relations with Europe

Zhang Zuqian

Since China and the EEC, the forerunner of the EU, established diplomatic relations in 1975, great progress has been made in their bilateral commercial relations. Today commercial ties between China and the EU not only are the core elements of their relationship and central to their interests, but also serve as the driving force for development of their relationship as a whole. However, obstacles to the development of their commercial relations still remain. Many of the obstacles result from entrenched institutions on both sides, and thus are difficult to overcome. The further development of bilateral commercial relations depends, to an extent, on whether China and the EU will be able to overcome these obstacles.

The evolution and current state of China–EU commercial relations

When China established its diplomatic relations with the EEC in 1975, the volume of their bilateral trade was only $244 million in total. As both China and the EEC were under the severe threat posed by the Soviet Union, the motivations for the establishment of their diplomatic relations were largely security and strategic, rather than commercial ones.[1] Of course, both China and the EU had other considerations for setting up their diplomatic relations. China pursued an independent foreign policy after breaking away from the Soviet Union, Beijing hoped to see a Europe playing a more independent role from the two superpowers as it became more united and powerful through integration. China's foreign policy has still embodied this consideration up to the present time. At the same time, the EEC hoped to see China gradually come out of its self-imposed diplomatic isolation and move closer to the West strategically and politically.

Significant changes took place in China's political as well as commercial relations with the EEC around 1978, when China embarked on the road of economic reform and opening-up to the outside world. With the reorientation of Beijing's policy, economic growth was given the top priority and preoccupied the leadership. In order to speed up the realization of its modernization programme, China shifted its economic orientation to pursue an export-led strategy and attached greater importance to her foreign economic ties, including those with Europe. At the same time, European businessmen began to realize the great potential of the

Chinese market, as the Chinese economy, vitalized with economic reform, was growing faster and faster. Under such circumstances, China–EU trade and economic relations have expanded dramatically. Some Chinese scholars even claim that for a long time the commercial ties have been the sole concrete element of the China–EU relationship.[2]

The efforts made by both China and the EU were also conducive to the rapid development of bilateral commercial relations. For China, promoting China–EU economic relations was one of the strategic decisions made by the Chinese leaders in the initial years of economic reform. When meeting with former British Prime Minister Edward Heath in 1985, Deng Xiaoping told him that, for the previous three years, the Chinese government had been considering how to increase economic ties with Europe. Deng stressed, "It was our policy to do so."[3]

In 1978 and 1979 China and the EC respectively reached a trade agreement and an agreement on textile trade for the first time in the history of their relations. In 1980 the EC began to grant the Generalised System of Preferences (GSP) treatment to China. In 1985 China and the EC signed the trade and economic cooperation agreement, which further enhanced China–EU commercial relations.

China benefited a great deal from the preferential agreements with the EU and its member countries. According to the EU, China is the second-largest beneficiary (out of 180 nations) of the EU's GSP scheme, under which the EU grants autonomous trade preferences to imports from developing countries. It has a share of more than 11 per cent of all effective preferential imports under GSP. The EU also supported China's accession to the WTO, although the EU, taking advantage of China's anxiousness to enter the WTO, asked for far more concessions than the US did during the negotiations for the bilateral China–EU agreement on the WTO, which was finally signed in Beijing on 19 May 2000 and enabled China to enter the WTO eventually in 2001.

Thanks to the rapid growth of China's economy, active efforts from both sides, as well as accelerating globalization,[4] China–EU trade and economic relations have developed rapidly. Since 1978 China–EU trade has increased more than thirty-fold and reached €175 billion in 2004. China and the EU have also become mutually important trade partners. By 2003, bilateral trade accounted for 14.7 per cent and 5.7 per cent respectively of China's trade and the EU's external trade.[5]

Since the EU's enlargement in 2004, EU has become China's number one trading partner (ahead of the US and Japan), while China is the EU's second biggest trading partner (only after the US). In 2005–6 China–EU trade remained on the upswing. According to the statistics released by the Chinese Ministry of Commerce, China–EU trade increased by 15.3 per cent in 2005 and 21.1 per cent from January to July in 2006 respectively.[6]

Investment from the EU in China

The growth of investment from the EU and its characteristics are also impressive. When China and the EC established their diplomatic relations in 1975, European investment to China was virtually non-existent. However, in the early years of the

1980s European enterprises began to invest in China. Britain and Germany had been the two largest foreign investors in China (excluding Hong Kong as the external investor in mainland China) before American companies began to invest heavily in China around the middle of the 1990s. According to the statistics released by the Chinese Ministry of Commerce, by the end of 2005 the EU was the third-largest investor from abroad (only next to the US and Hong Kong) in China, with stocks of $62.352 billion.[7]

To date, there are more than 20,000 European-funded enterprises in China. Many world-famous European companies have set up factories or local branches in China. For instance, the Finnish telecom giant Nokia started with a five-employee China unit in 1985 and now employs 4,700 workers in China, accounting for 8 per cent of its workforce worldwide. Its sales in and outside China were $3.32 billion and $3.3 billion respectively in 2005.

Compared with the foreign direct investment (FDI) from other parts of the world, the investment from the EU has the characteristics of relatively high technology and capital-intensiveness. In terms of size for each case of FDI, the figures for contracted and realized investment from the EU countries in 2005 were respectively $4.08 million and $2.34 million on average, while the figures from the US and Japan were respectively only $2.09 million and $1.06 million and $2.02 million and $1.45 million. These figures mean that the EU's FDI in China is more capital- and technology-intensive than the FDI from the US and Japan.[8]

It is especially worth noting that the EU is the key regional provider of governmental loans to China. In one article, *Beijing Review* says that by the end of 1999, contracted governmental loans made by EU countries and their official financial organizations had totalled $16.16 billion, accounting for 44 per cent of the total loans by foreign governments and official organizations to China.[9] The importance of governmental loans made by EU countries does not only lie in the amount, but in the intent that the governments of EU countries obviously encourage their citizens and enterprise to expand their commercial ties with China.

Generally speaking, China is satisfied with the investment from Europe in terms of its quantity as well as quality. Probably because of the experience learned not only from cooperation with European partners in joint-ventures, but also with the partners from the US, Japan and South Korea, Chinese entities now more frequently express their discontent with their European partners. Chinese partners in the joint-venture with German automobile producer Volkswagen complained that the headquarters of Volkswagen earned too much money in China, but brought too little advanced technology to China. It was reported that in 2003 the total volume of its products turned out by its China-based joint-ventures accounted for only 14 per cent of its global sales, yet around 80 per cent of its annual profits were materialized from its activities in China. The prices of the automotive parts Volkswagen sold to its Chinese partners are usually 30 per cent higher than those in Germany. As nearly all the equipment and facilities, including the shelves and sweepers, at the factories of Shanghai Volkswagen were imported from Germany, this joint-venture does not play the expected role promoting the development of other industries in China.[10] European auto manufacturers protested that China would impose higher tariffs on imported car parts, while their Japanese and South Korean counterparts did not. Chinese media claimed that it was simply because of the difference in business practice between European and Japanese and South Korean automakers. After setting up joint ventures with Chinese partners, Japanese and South Korean car makers usually move their production of car parts to China, but the European companies still keep it at home and import the parts for assembly lines.[11]

Chinese investment in the EU

One of the latest developments regarding capital flows between China and the EU is that Chinese enterprises, encouraged by the "go-out" policy pursued by Chinese government, have begun to invest abroad, including in EU countries. According to the relevant statistics released by the Chinese Ministry of Commerce, by the end of 2004 Chinese non-financial institutions invested $44.8 billion in total abroad, of which $507 million was invested in EU countries, accounting for 1.13 per cent of the total Chinese investment abroad.[12] So far, the EU as a whole – with the exception of Germany and Britain – is not one of the major destinations for Chinese outbound FDI, but its share of Chinese FDI has been increasing conspicuously. In 2004 the stocks of Chinese FDI in Europe (including Russia and other countries in the former Soviet Union area) was $750 million, accounting for 1.7 per cent of the entire stock of Chinese FDI, but in 2005 Chinese FDI in Europe rose by $256 million, accounting for 6.3 per cent of the entire Chinese FDI annually.[13] By 2003, the total volume of Chinese investment in Germany was around €162 million. According to the prediction made by the German Federal Ministry of Economics, Chinese investment in Germany could rise as much as ten times by 2010.[14] In my view, the figures regarding Chinese foreign investment are absolutely not complete, because it is common knowledge in China that many individuals and enterprises do not bother themselves to register their foreign investment (for various reasons). However, one thing is certain: that with its foreign reserves rapidly increasing (now in excess of $1 trillion), China is expected to become a more important investor abroad.

It is also reported that the EU's new members in Central and Eastern Europe have become more important destinations for Chinese FDI. To date, an estimated 3,500 Chinese firms have partnered in small and medium-sized enterprises, including 50 Chinese state-owned trading corporations operating in Hungary.[15] Two factors are favourable for Chinese firms' decision to invest in the new EU members. First, as an advisory pamphlet distributed by the EU Commission's Delegation in Beijing stressed, one of the benefits of the EU's enlargement for Chinese investors is that they will enjoy the same favourable treatment throughout the enlarged EU. Second, the twelve new East European members of the EU are increasingly looking to China for investment, as their economies lag far behind the original fifteen members.

In his 2005 speech at the National Council of French Employers, Premier Wen Jiabao said that one of the important new characteristics of Sino-French economic relations was the upsurge of two-way investment in these two countries, and Wen cited the merger of China's TCL Corp television business with France's Thomson SA and Alcatel Mobile Phones Limited as good examples for the internationalization of Chinese enterprises.[16]

At the 2005 China International Fair for Investment and Trade (CIFIT) held in the port city of Xiamen in Fujian Province, some European governmental agencies for investment promotion tried very hard to woo Chinese investors. To invest in Europe helps Chinese enterprises to get advanced technology and world-famous brands as well as to expand their business quickly across Europe, many European participants said. "To invest in Italy is a shortcut for Chinese enterprises to enter Europe," said the commissioner of the Italian Trade Commission and Chief Representative in Shanghai, referring to Italy's strategic location that can give access to three large markets, namely, the EU countries, Russian region and the southern Mediterranean area.[17]

Germany, as the largest economy in the EU and China's most important commercial partner in Europe, seems to be the favourite destination in Europe for Chinese investors. According to an article in *Die Welt* on 11 November 2005, by the end of 2004 Chinese investors had purchased around 300 German firms, most of them were the small and mid-sized ones with annual sales between 1 million and 10 million euros. As most of the purchases were not registered, the actual figure was surely much bigger, *Die Welt* claimed.[18]

Small European countries such as Sweden are also attractive to Chinese investors. Reportedly, Chinese investment in Sweden has gathered momentum in the past few years, especially in technology, hotels and consumer goods. Among the Chinese firms already operating in Sweden are telecom equipment makers Huawei Technologies and ZTE Corp., Shanghai Automotive Group and the Guangsha Group, which is based in China's Zhejiang Province. Huawei and ZTE both have their R&D centres established in Stockholm and Huawei's R&D centre is also the first of its kind in Europe. The advantage of Sweden as the destination for Chinese investment lies in its technology and its geographical location as a hub of northern Europe and as a stepping stone to Europe as a whole.[19]

The EU as a source of China's imported technology

Many researchers have noticed the importance of increasingly close China–EU cooperation in science and technology. Compared with China's commercial relations with other parts of the world, China–EU commercial relations are more technology-intensive. It is the widely accepted view in Chinese academic circles and diplomatic community that Europe is the largest source of China's imported technology.

In fact, the Chinese government realized the importance and feasibility of Europe as a major resource of technology as early as the beginning of the 1980. During his talk with other Chinese leaders in July 1983, Deng Xiaoping stressed that China should take advantage of economic difficulties in West European countries to import more technology. The following is the part of Deng's speech released in his *Selected Works*:

We should open our country wider to the outside world. Now that the West European countries are beset with economic difficulties, we should lose no time in seeking their cooperation, so as to speed up our technological transformation. We should do the same with the East European countries, because some of their techniques are more advanced than ours and some of ours are needed by them. China provides a huge market, so many countries wish to develop cooperation or do business with us. We should seize this opportunity. It is a matter of strategic importance.[20]

According to the statistics released by Chinese authorities, between 1981 and 1996 around 48 per cent of all the imported technologies were introduced from the EU.[21] By October 2004 China introduced as many as 18,530 items of advanced technology and equipment worth $80 billion from the EU countries.[22]

China–EU official cooperation in science and technology has thrived for the last two decades. Both sides signed a science and technology agreement in 1998, laying a solid base for their further cooperation. By 2002, Chinese scientists participated in 82 research projects under the EU's Fifth Framework Programme in the fields of information technology, energy, materials, life science, agriculture, environment and natural resources. The total funds financing the projects taken part in by China exceeded €92 million. Since the EU opened its Sixth Framework Programme (from 2002 to 2006) at the end of 2002, Chinese scientists have joined nearly 60 projects, with a total fund of €200 million in telecommunication materials and food safety.[23]

The fruitful science and technology cooperation surely helps to promote the expansion of China–EU trade and economic relations. As Chinese Minister of Science and Technology Xu Guanhua claimed, bilateral science and technology cooperation is conducive to enhancing market development, expanding the space for their industries to develop, accelerating the industrial transformation. For instance, the successful cooperation between Datong Telecom Technology and Industry Group, one of the Chinese telecom giants, and Siemens, on third-generation mobile phone technology TD-SCDNA, will further expand China–EU commercial exchanges in the telecommunication industry.[24]

China's government highly appraises the EU as the largest resource for China's imported technology. In his speech delivered at the National Council of French Employers, Chinese Premier Wen Jiabao indicated that fruitful China–EU cooperation in the Galileo programme, biological technology, aviation and space industry embodies the highlighted strategic significance. Premier Wen called for further China–EU cooperation in the high-tech field.[25]

At the China–EU High Level Forum in May 2005, Chinese Minister of Science and Technology Xu Guanhua claimed that the EU and its members are China's extremely important strategic partner in terms of China's foreign scientific and technological cooperation. He argued that China–EU cooperation in science and technology would become the cornerstone for China–EU overall strategic partnership.[26]

Problems from China's perspective

The rapid expansion of China–EU commercial relations does not necessarily mean that both sides are satisfied with the current state of bilateral commercial relations. In fact, both China and the EU have a lot of complaints. In China, many believe that the EU handles trade and economic relations unfairly and discriminatively. In an article published in the Journal *International Trade*, the two authors from the Chinese Ministry of Commerce argue that there are ten difficult outstanding problems for China–EU trade and economic relations. They are:

- a sizeable and increasingly bigger China trade surplus;
- quick increase in EU's anti-dumping cases against Chinese exports;
- numerous EU technical trade barriers;
- more uncertainties in the post-quota era;
- increase in disputes of intellectual property protection;
- less GSP treatment for Chinese exports;
- slow increase of the EU's investment in China and limited opportunities for Chinese investment in the EU;
- relatively low level of high-tech exchanges and cooperation;
- underdeveloped cooperation of small and medium-sized enterprises and failure to launch the negotiation on compensation for China's loss caused by the EU's enlargement.[27]

Most Chinese scholars argue that the most critical outstanding problem negatively affecting China–EU commercial relations is that the EU refuses to grant full Market Economy Status (MES) to China and lift its arms embargo on China.

Market economy status

In June 2004, the EU released the assessment of China's Market Economy Status, saying that China failed four of five EU criteria for Market Economy Status, i.e., state influence on enterprises, corporate governance, property and bankruptcy law and financial sector. As the EU had already granted the full Market Economy Status to Russia and Ukraine, whose economies were even unqualified for WTO membership, few Chinese people think the EU's assessment was fair or well-grounded. Immediately after the release of the assessment report, Vice Minister of Commerce Yi Xiaozhun complained that the report was an unfair outcome. *China Daily* even retorted that no one, not even the EU countries, is a perfect market economy.[28]

The EU's unfair approach to China's request for full market economy status is not accepted even by some foreign observers. The author of an article published in the *Financial Times* argues that China's economic status is far more than an academic debating point. "Non-market economy is a relic of the Cold War that has decreasing relevance to economic reality in China today. Its main function is as a tool of economic *realpolitik* and a sop to protectionist lobbies in importing countries," the author said.[29]

Without the status of a full market economy, China is an easy target of the EU's anti-dumping measures. In his speech at a conference on anti-dumping in Beijing in 2004, Patrick Santer, Chairman of the Law Committee of the Parliament of Luxembourg, said that during the period of 2000 to September 2004 the EU Commission initiated 120 new anti-dumping measures, 24 of them involving Chinese products, placing China at the top of the list.[30]

The most important reason why the EU can easily impose an anti-dumping tax on Chinese products is that the EU can "legally" choose "a comparable analogue country" to measure whether Chinese producers export their goods at artificially low prices. In the case of Chinese shoes, the EU chose Brazil as "the comparable analogue country." Everybody knows that Brazil is absolutely not the right choice as the average income in Brazil is much higher than in the parts of China where most of the shoe factories are located. Otherwise, the investors of shoe factories would flock to Brazil rather than choose the rural areas of Guangdong Province and Wenzhou suburbs for the sites of their factories.

One of the editorials in Singapore's newspaper *The Straits Times* argues that it is ridiculous to accuse Chinese and Vietnamese shoe-makers of dumping. It can be a strategy to defeat competitors in a high capital-intensive industry such as steel manufacturing, but in the low capital-intensive industries such as shoe-making, it is a losing strategy by unreasonably low prices to drive competitors out of market. New competitors will easily emerge in the market thanks to the low entry-level for starts-ups.[31]

The EU Commissioner for Trade Peter Mandelson argues that the surge of Chinese textiles in the EU will hurt the producers in vulnerable developing countries like Bangladesh and Morocco.[32] If one takes a closer look at Chinese textile exports and their impact, they will find that Mandelson's argument is not as tenable as it seems on the surface. According to an article in the *Financial Times*, the latest figures have shown that the most significant displacement by China has been exports previously originating from Hong Kong, Macao and Taiwan – not the developing countries Mr Mandelson is kindly eager to protect.[33]

It is understandable that the EU is under pressure from some of its member countries to curb the cheap imports from China. These countries or the industrial sectors concerned have a fear that cheap Chinese imports will force their domestic production to reduce or even to shut down. This fear is reasonable only to an extent. Investment abroad is generally motivated by economies of scale and access to foreign markets. For example, only 5 per cent of all French investment abroad is associated with relocation.[34]

No matter the considerations that motivate the EU's anti-dumping measures, they have caused great loss to Chinese exports to the EU. In 1999, the EU imposed a 44.6 per cent anti-dumping tax on colour TV sets from China, which shut out nearly all Chinese colour TVs from the EU market. Seven Chinese TV makers were exempted from the EU's anti-dumping tariffs simply on condition of accepting strict quantitative ceilings and price freezing in definite periods of sales.[35]

When the EU decided to impose the anti-dumping tax on Chinese shoes, the spokesperson of the Chinese Ministry of Commerce angrily said, "The EU decision is a step backward."[36] The *China Daily* even argued, "It is not an overstatement to claim that China has become the world's largest victim of protectionism."[37]

The EU's anti-dumping measures are a double-edged sword, hurting some of the EU countries and consumers as well. During the debate whether the EU should impose anti-dumping tariffs on Chinese and Vietnamese shoes, Danish Economics Minister Bendt Bendtsen argued that the cost to European consumers of more expensive Asian shoes could be almost ten times greater than the economic benefit for European shoe producers.[38]

Therefore, it is in both sides' interests to refrain from resorting to anti-dumping measures. China–EU commercial relations will develop more smoothly if the EU grants the full market status to China as early as possible.

The arms embargo on China

This issue is largely a political one in China–EU relations, as Beijing has reiterated that to lift the arms embargo, as a symbolic move, would help to make a China–EU overall strategic relationship worthy of the name. But this claim does not necessarily mean that this issue does not have any impact on China–EU economic relations. China's EU Policy Paper also argues that the EU's ban on arms sales to China is a barrier to greater bilateral cooperation on defence industry and technology. The lifting of the arms embargo will certainly promote – at least to an extent – China–EU trade and economic cooperation related to duale technologies and products.

Although Chinese officials and diplomats frequently avow that China is not planning to purchase a large quantity of European weapons even if the EU lifts its arms embargo immediately, people are still speculating what European weapons and military technologies China might buy in Europe. For instance, Frank Umbach of DGAP in Berlin argues that Beijing is certainly interested in acquiring specific niche technologies and minor weapons systems such as radar, air-to-air missiles, sonar equipment, torpedoes and other important force multipliers to increase the fighting capabilities of both its old and new weapon systems.[39]

The author of an article published in *Wide Angle*, a Hong Kong-based monthly, predicts that the products of information technology will be the priority for China's arms imports from the EU. Without the arms embargo, China will be able to further expand its participation in joint development of military technologies and products with the EU countries.[40]

Because of pressure from Washington, differences in the EU as well as the political changes in Berlin and Paris, the EU shelved the plan to lift the arms embargo on China. It was said that the EU's work on a new "Code of Conduct" on arms exports, meant to prevent sensitive military equipment from falling into Chinese hands in a post-embargo era, had also been delayed. This change in the EU's dealing with the arms embargo is surely disappointing to Beijing. In contrast to the fact that in the previous three years Chinese officials and diplomats liked to use overly enthusiastic words for praising the EU's positive attitudes towards China, Chinese Foreign Minister Li Zhaoxing did not utter a single word about the current state of China–EU relations at the press conference following the 2006 session of the National People's Congress.

Future prospects

China–EU commercial relations will expand further in the foreseeable future as long as the growth of the Chinese economy is sustainable. By far, in spite of excessively pessimistic predictions that China would collapse soon economically and politically, it is more certain that the Chinese economy will grow rather than dwindle. Thanks to the great complementarity, there is huge potential to be tapped for the expansion of China–EU commercial relations. For example, the annual investment in China from the EU's big member countries such as Germany, France, Britain and Italy accounts for only 0.5–1.5 per cent of these countries' total annual FDI respectively.[41] France, as the fifth-largest economy in the world, falls far behind Germany in term of their trade with China. In 2004, the total volume of China–France trade was €17.009 billion, only as much as one third of China–German trade (€49.553 billion).[42] During Premier Wen Jiabao's visit to France last December, both countries set up the target of reaching €40 billion for their bilateral trade in five years.

Superficially, in Chinese academic circles, there is little controversy about the prospect for the development of China–EU commercial relations. Largely because of the favourable factors such as great untapped potential, official support from both sides' governmental departments, sustainable economic growth of the Chinese economy, as well as further development of European integration and enlargement, some Chinese scholars even optimistically predict that China–EU commercial relations will prevail over any other China's bilateral commercial relations in terms of size and importance.[43]

However, some Chinese scholars are more sober-minded when exploring the prospects for China–EU commercial relations. For instance, Professor Qiu Yuanlun, a long-time Europe hand, argues that as many of the issues frustrating China–EU relations result from the internal causes of both sides, the easing or solution of these issues will surely depend on positive actions by both sides. In this sense it will take a long time.[44]

The EU complains that its trade deficit reflects the effect of market access obstacles in China, while China claims that European protectionism is on the upswing. According to the EU's complaint, in China there are remaining problems such as barriers to imports of specific goods (price control, discriminatory registration requirements, arbitrary sanitary standards), obstacles to investment (geographical restrictions, joint venture requirements, discriminatory licensing procedures, outright closure of certain sectors to foreigners, restrictive foreign exchange regulations) and the unsatisfactory business environment (protection of intellectual property rights etc.).[45] The easing or solution of these issues will depend on the deepening of economic reform in China, which is surely a long and gradual process. For the foreseeable future, as it is very difficult to expand domestic demand in the economy, China has to continue to depend on exports for economic growth.

What China has seen in Europe are the slow economic and social reforms (e.g. the recent massive demonstration and riot over the French government's proposal for first employment contract) and their negative effects on the EU's external economic relations – both making the EU more hostile to imports from developing countries, especially from China. For instance, it is reported by the *Financial Times* that only three countries, two of them are new members, voted in favour of the Chinese and Vietnamese shoe curbs while nine countries (including the Nordic countries, Ireland and Slovenia) voted against them at the meeting in March 2006 discussing how to respond to booming Asian shoe exports.[46] Nevertheless, interim tariffs were imposed on Vietnamese and Chinese shoes.

Fewer people by far are optimistic about the prospect of economic and social reform in France and other European countries with a big burden of social security and obsolete industrial sectors. The situation in the new member states of the EU is even worse. When I visited Poland, Hungary and the Czech Republic in November 2004, I took a close look at the consumer goods at the supermarkets and department stores and found that these countries could hardly compete with imported Chinese consumer goods if they opened their doors wider.

There are several recent developments which will make China–EU trade and economic disputes more frequent and fierce than ever. Firstly, with the increasing pressure for appreciation of the Chinese currency *renminbi*, and the EU's increasingly more frequent anti-dumping measures on Chinese labour-intensive products, as well as the relevant encouraging policies adopted by Chinese government, Chinese enterprises are striving vigorously to develop and produce higher-end goods that will compete more directly with the products made in Europe and the United States.[47]

In 2005, China began to export cars to Europe in significant volume for the first time. At the beginning, most Chinese-made cars exported to Europe were the cheap mini-car Jazz and SUV (recently it was reported that Chinese automotive makers had decided to make big investments in R&D to develop better cars for export). SAIC Motor, a subsidiary of the Shanghai Automotive Industry Corporation or SAIC, is planning to invest $1.25 billion in building research and development centres, a car assembly plant and an engine factory. SAIC Motor set a target of selling 200,000 own-brand cars by 2010, with 45,000 of them shipped to overseas markets, including Europe.[48] As China is about to become the third-largest automotive maker in the world, overtaking Germany in 2006, the potential for China's automotive exports is huge. It is reasonably expected that China and the EU will have disputes about car imports very soon.

Moreover, as the Chinese government has decided to develop middle-sized passenger-airplanes, the prediction made by Peter Mandelson will materialize in the future: "China's high-tech economy is growing. We won't be trading Airbuses for T-shirts for much longer."[49] Another statement by Mandelson will also possibly come true. It is that "Yesterday textiles, today footwear, tomorrow what?

Consumer electronics? Cars? Where will it go and when will it end? We are at the beginning of the China story and not the end."[50]

However, it is also possible that China will resort to the weapons of anti-dumping and other protectionist methods to kick similar European products out of the Chinese market when China thinks it necessary to protect its infant automotive manufacturing industry and passenger-airplane manufacturing industry.

Secondly, Chinese enterprises will fight back more actively and more success-fully in their trade disputes with the EU. To many foreign observers' bewilderment, in the past Chinese enterprises were strangely inattentive to the EU's anti-dumping measures and other protectionist actions. In some cases relevant Chinese enterprises did nothing in response. Chinese enterprises' inaction for foreign trade and economic disputes largely resulted from the political and industrial institutions at home. On one hand, most Chinese enterprises, as the beginners of trade and other foreign economic activities, do not have much knowledge about how to protect their interest with international laws and regulations. On the other hand, Chinese enter-prises are not in a position to organize themselves into an interest group. All the industrial associations in China are actually under the government's direct control. The heads of these associations are usually governmental officials, who do not have much interest in the performance of the enterprises under their direction. What they are most concerned about is to strictly follow the instructions from the government so that their promotions will be ensured.

Now things are beginning to change. First, more and more Chinese enterprises have learned in their practice of trade and foreign economic relations how to protect their interest within the context of international laws and regulations. And they are hiring foreign law firms to defend their commercial cases and interests. With more relevant knowledge and experience, Chinese enterprises are going to have less tolerance for the EU's protectionist actions.

Second, in order to protect their own interests, foreign and outside investors began to teach and urge Chinese enterprises to react to the EU's protectionist moves. For instance, in the case of responding to the EU's anti-dumping move on Chinese shoes, Taiwanese investors in mainland China play a role. The president of the Association of Taiwanese businessmen in Guangdong Province initiated setting up an alliance of eight shoe factories for responding to the EU's anti-dumping on Chinese shoes. This alliance raised money and hired Chinese as well as European lawyers to defend their interest.[51]

With the expansion of the export of cars and other higher-value goods, the foreign investors will more vigorously make joint efforts with their Chinese part-ners to protect their interests. As the foreign investors in the automotive and other higher-value industries usually are the big European, American and Japanese companies (such as Volkswagen, General Motors and Honda), with more capa-bility and intellectual resources in response to the EU's protectionist moves, the EU will find it more difficult or even more self-destructive to resort to anti-dumping measures on Chinese imports.

Third, with the deepening of economic reform, the ties between enterprises and industrial associations as well as government have become closer than before. In the above-mentioned case of the Taiwanese businessmen's role, the establishment of an alliance for responding to the EU's anti-dumping measures on Chinese shoes obtained official approval from the government. Some industrial associations have realized that they can benefit financially from providing service to enterprises. Of course, sometimes such service involves corruption. Now the Chinese government also encourages enterprises to stand up to foreign countries' protectionism.

Last, but not least, with the lessening fear that the EU dares to undermine its vital interests on issues such as the Taiwan question and national security, China is less willing to make concessions to the EU's demands on the soaring trade deficit, protection of intellectual property rights, and access to the Chinese market.

Conclusion

It is common that disputes increase numerously and extensively with the expansion of trade and other economic exchanges. China–EU commercial relations are, however, somewhat different. Generally speaking, both sides are in historical transition, although different in nature. In the coming years, China, in the gradual process of economic modernization, will continue to pursue an export-led strategy for its economic development while some member countries of the EU are making their efforts to protect uncompetitive labour-intensive industries. With such a background many of the problems in their bilateral commercial relations will hardly be eased or solved unless both sides are successful in their internal transitions. Without further economic reform and a fundamental change in the sources of economic growth, both of them will help to enhance domestic demand, China's imports from Europe will not expand significantly, and the EU trade deficit will grow rapidly. For the EU, without successful reform in its member countries' economic and social institutions, China will remain "the biggest single challenge of globalization in the trade field," as Peter Mandelson put it in his Wolfsberg speech.

It is quite sure that China and the EU will be partners and competitors simultaneously. But it remains to be seen whether their overall strategic partnership will become more difficult than it is now, at least in terms of their bilateral commercial relations.

Notes

1 Wu Xian, "Zhong-Ou Huoban Guanxi Zhong de Jingji Liyi Quxiang" [The Economic Incentives in the China– EU Partnership] in Zhou Hong and Wu Baiyi (eds.), *Gongxing yu Chayi: Zhong-Ou Huoban Guangxi Pingxi* [China–EU Partnership: Possibilities and Limits] (Beijing: Zhongguo Shehui Kexue Chubanshe, 2004, pp. 25–43).
2 Qiu Yuanlun, "Dangqian Zhong-Ou Guangxi de San'ge Tedian yu Sanda Wenti" [Three Characteristics and Three Major Problems of Current China–EU Relations] in *Zhongguo Pinglun* [China Review], No. 1 (2006), pp. 47–51.
3 *Selected Works of Deng Xiaoping*, Volume III (1982–92), (Beijing: Waiwen Chubanshe, 1994), p. 125.
4 Wu Xian stresses the importance of globalization in the rapid expansion of China–EU trade and economic relations. See Wu Xian, "Zhong-Ou Huoban Guanxi Zhong de Jingji Liyi Quxiang" [The Economic Incentives in the China–EU Partnership] in Zhou Hong/

Wu Baiyi (ed.) *Gongxing yu Chayi: Zhong-Ou Huoban Guangxi Pingxi*, op. cit., pp. 25–43.

5 Li Gang and Yao Ling, "Yaosu Hubu – Zhongguo yu Oumeng Jingji Guangxi Fazhan Qianli Fenxi" [Complementarity of Elements: Analysis of Potential for Development of China–EU Economic Relations] in *Guoji Maoyi*, [International Trade], No. 9, (2004).

6 See website of Chinese Ministry of Commerce, www.mofcom.gov.cn.

7 See website of Chinese Ministry of Commerce, www.mofcom.gov.cn. The Delegation of the European Commission to China claims that by July 2004 the stocks of EU FDI in China were over €118 billion. See website of the Delegation: www.delchn.cec.eu.int.

8 Wu Yikang, "Buduan Gengxin Zouxiang Chengshu de Zhongou Guangxi – Jinian Zhong-Ou Jianjiao Sanshi Zhounian" [Continuously Renewed and Maturing China–EU Relations – For the Thirtieth Anniversary of Establishment of Diplomatic Relations Between China and the EU], in *Ouzhou Yitihua Yanjiu* [European Integration Studies], No. 2 (2005), pp. 6–12.

9 *Beijing Review*, 2 May 2002, pp. 7–9.

10 www.xinhuanet.com, 18 November 2005.

11 *Chinese Youth Daily*, 1 December 2005.

12 Department of Foreign Investment Administration, Ministry of Commerce of PRC, "2004 Niandu Zhongguo Duiwai Zhijie Touzi Tongji Gongbao" [Communiqué for the Statistics of Chinese FDI in 2004].

13 Source: Press Office of Chinese Ministry of Commerce, 16 February 2006.

14 Shanghai-based *News Morning Post*, 17 August 2006.

15 "The Eastern Conundrum," *EuroBiz*, January 2005.

16 *People's Daily Online*, 6 December 2005: http://english.people.com.cn/200512/06/eng20051206_225813.html.

17 *Beijing Review*, September 29, 2005, pp. 24–5.

18 The Chinese version of this story was published in *Cankao Xiaoxi*, one of the most popular newspapers in China.

19 *Beijing Review*, September 29, 2005, pp. 24–5.

20 *Selected Works of Deng Xiaoping*, Volume III (1982–92), (Beijing: Waiwen Chubanshe, 1994), p. 43.

21 Wu Yikang, "Buduan Gengxin Zouxiang Chengshu de Zhong-Ou Guangxi – Jinian Zhongou Jianjiao Sanshi Zhounian" [Continuously Renewed and Maturing China–EU Relations – For the Thirtieth Anniversary of Establishment of Diplomatic Relations Between China and the EU], in *Ouzhou Yitihua Yanjiu* [European Integration Studies], No. 2 (2005), pp. 6–12

22 *People's Daily*, 6 January 2005.

23 *People's Daily Online*, http://english.people.com.cn/ 14 May 2005.

24 Xu Guanhua, "Zhongguo Keji Fazhan Zhanlue ji Zhong-Ou Keji Hezuo de Qianjing" [China's Strategy for the Development of Science and Technology and Prospect for China–EU Scientific and Technological Cooperation], in *Xinhua Wenzhai* [Xinhua Abstracts], No. 23 (2005), pp. 136–9.

25 *People's Daily Online*, 6 December 2005. http://english.people.com.cn/200512/06/eng20051206_225813.html.

26 Xu Guanhua, "Zhongguo Keji Fazhan Zhanlue ji Zhong-Ou Keji Hezuo de Qianjing" [China's Strategy for the Development of Science and Technology and Prospect for China–EU Scientific and Technological Cooperation], in *Xinhua Wenzhai* [Xinhua Abstracts], No. 23 (2005), pp. 136–9.

27 Li Gang and Cui Yanxin, "Zhong-Ou Shida Daijie Nanti" [Ten Big Outstanding Problems for China and the EU], in *Guoji Maoyi* [International Trade], No. 1 (2005), pp. 10–15.

28 *China Daily*, 30 June 2004.

29 Guy De Jonquières, "China Dealt Unfair Hand in Global Game," *Financial Times*, 3 May 2006; Reprinted in *Straits Times Interactive*, 3 May 2006.

30 See www.gmw.cn/content2004-11/09/content_129067.htm.

31 "Dumping or Efficiency?" *The Straits Times Interactive*, 25 March 2006.
32 Peter Mandelson, "Competition and Partnership Can Go Hand in Hand," *International Herald Tribune*, 9 April 2005.
33 Raphael Minder in Brussels, "China Textiles to EU Jump 40 Per Cent," *Financial Times*, 27 November 2005.
34 Olivier Cattaneo, "The Yellow Peril", *YaleGlobal Online*, reprinted in *The Straits Times Interactive*, 9 October 2004.
35 *China Daily*, 30 March 2006.
36 *Idem.*
37 *China Daily*, 10 April 2006.
38 *Financial Times*, 19 February 2006.
39 Frank Umbach, "EU's Links with China Pose New Threat to Transatlantic Relations," in *European Affairs* (Spring, 2004).
40 Yu Yang, "Zhongguo Neng Cong Ouzhou Mai Shenme Wuqi?" [What Kind of Weapons will China Purchase from Europe?], in *GuangJiaojing Yuekan* [Hong Kong: Wide Angle Monthly], 16 May – 15 June 2004, pp. 52–5.
41 Zhao Jinping, "Woguo Zhongchangqi Jingji Fazhan de Waibu Huangjing" [The External Environment for China's Middle and Long Term Economic Development], in *Guoji Jingji* [International Economy], No. 2 (2005) pp. 58–62.
42 Eurostat.
43 Zhang Jianxiong, "Zhong-Ou Guangxi de Weilai" [The Future of China–EU Relations], available at: http://Cass.net.cn/file/.
44 Qiu Yuanlun, "Dangqian Zhong-Ou Guangxi de San'ge Tedian yu Sanda Wenti" [Three Characteristics and Three Major Problems of Current China–EU Relations] in *Zhongguo Pinglun* [China Review], No. 1 (2006), pp. 47–51.
45 See website of the Delegation of the European Commission to China: http://www.delchn.cec.eu.int/.
46 *Financial Times*, 16 March 2006.
47 Keith Bradsher, "China's Next Competitors: South Korea, then Europe", *International Herald Tribune*, 20 April 2006.
48 Keith Bradsher, "Carmaker in China Strikes Out on Its Own," *International Herald Tribune*, 11 April 2006.
49 Peter Mandelson, "Competition and Partnership Can Go Hand in Hand," *International Herald Tribune*, 9 April 2005.
50 *Financial Times*, 15 June 2005.
51 Xiao Hua, "Zhongguo Xieye Lianhe Qilai!" [All Shoemakers in China, Unite!], *Nanfang Zhoumo* [Southern China Weekly], 13 April 2006. *China Daily*, 3 April 2006.

Appendix A

Table 11.A EU 25 trade with China (August 2005)

	August 2005					Accumulated 2005*											2004
	Imports	% total	% change	Exports	% total	Imports	% total	% change	Exports	% total	% change	Trade total	% total	% change	Trade balance	% change	Trade total
EU 25*	14,353	100	34	4,329	100	97,488	100	23	32,613	100	2	130,101	100	17	-64,875	38	175,224
Germany	2,979	21	26	2,120	49	21,224	22	24	13,494	41	-5	34,718	27	11	-7,729	170	49,553
UK	2,269	16	25	353	8	15,030	15	20	2,474	8	11	17,504	13	19	-12,556	22	24,022
Netherlands	2,330	16	48	213	5	15,470	16	36	1,596	5	6	17,066	13	33	-13,875	41	21,164
France	1,333	9	30	375	9	8,947	9	20	4,058	12	16	13,005	10	18	-4,889	22	17,010
Italy	1,155	8	27	329	8	9,331	10	21	2,959	9	0	12,290	9	15	-6,372	33	16,272
Spain	975	7	51	107	2	6,264	6	36	970	3	20	7,234	6	34	-5,293	40	8,295
Belgium	848	6	40	201	5	5,415	6	27	1,630	5	5	7,045	5	21	-3,785	40	9,075
Sweden	336	2	35	136	3	2,006	2	27	1,251	4	-11	3,257	3	9	-756	338	4,620
Austria	228	2	101	99	2	1,435	1	38	1,103	3	42	2,538	2	39	-333	26	2,671
Hungary	328	2	15	24	1	2,352	2	12	180	1	-30	2,532	2	8	-2,172	18	3,719
Denmark	292	2	36	57	1	1,773	2	28	532	2	0	2,304	2	20	-1,241	45	2,957
Finland	207	1	65	120	3	1,166	1	44	1,003	3	-14	2,169	2	10	-163	-146	3,343
Poland	276	2	70	60	1	1,583	2	0.004	299	1	44	1,882	1	5	-1,285	-7	2,780
Ireland	150	1	56	62	1	930	1	12	551	2	37	1,481	1	20	-379	-12	1,932
Luxembourg	169	1	-15	17	0.4	1,229	1	3	88	0.3	28	1,317	1	5	-1,141	2	2,119
Greece	146	1	28	6	0.1	1,126	1	23	44	0.1	29	1,170	1	23	-1,082	23	1,478
Czech Rep.	146	1	38	21	0.5	939	1	-33	155	0.5	6	1,094	1	-29	-784	-37	2,106
Portugal	51	0.4	26	12	0.3	364	0.4	24	96	0.3	30	460	0.4	25	-268	22	560
Slovakia	24	0.2	23	6	0.1	203	0.2	-22	55	0.2	13	258	0.2	-17	-148	-30	430
Estonia	26	0.2	39	3	0.1	180	0.2	14	18	0.1	-4	198	0.2	12	-161	16	261
Lithuania	29	0.2	71	1	0.02	174	0.2	23	7	0.02	12	181	0.1	23	-168	24	246
Slovenia	20	0.1	60	3	0.1	125	0.1	-31	27	0.1	25	152	0.1	-25	-98	-39	267
Cyprus	18	0.1	35	1	0.01	126	0.1	-3	9	0.03	823	135	0.1	3	-117	-9	182
Latvia	12	0.1	148	0.4	0.01	60	0.1	23	5	0.02	-15	65	0.1	18	-55	28	81
Malta	6	0.04	67	2	0.04	36	0.04	-23	9	0.03	-17	45	0.03	-22	-27	-25	81

Source: Eurostat   Unit: million Euro

Appendix B

Table 11.B EU 25 trade with China (December 2004)

	December 2004						Accumulated 2004*											2003
	Imports	% total	% change	Exports	% total	% change	Imports	% total	% change	Exports	% total	% change	Trade change total	% total	% change	Trade balance	% change	Trade total
EU 25*	10,929	100	13	4,193	100	13	126,220	100	20	47,913	100	20	174,133	100	16	-78,307	19	146,566
Germany	2,554	23	17	1,708	41	10	28,558	23	27	20,995	44	15	49,553	28	22	-7,564	80	40,740
UK	1,880	17	20	344	8	25	20,539	16	19	3,483	7	25	24,022	14	20	-17,057	18	20,066
Netherlands	1,982	18	37	213	5	24	18,733	15	27	2,326	5	39	21,059	12	28	-16,406	26	16,415
France	1,039	10	23	679	16	96	11,645	9	21	5,364	11	14	17,009	10	19	-6,281	28	14,288
Italy	897	8	36	400	10	10	11,827	9	24	4,445	9	15	16,272	9	21	-7,382	29	13,403
Belgium	578	5	12	199	5	2	6,615	5	20	2,293	5	1	8,908	5	15	-4,322	34	7,764
Spain	582	5	22	92	2	1	7,072	6	25	1,142	2	4	8,214	5	22	-5,929	30	6,755
Sweden	217	2	12	151	4	-22	2,503	2	9	2,036	4	3	4,539	3	6	-468	43	4,263
Hungary	284	3	-12	18	0.4	37	3,398	3	17	321	1	104	3,719	2	21	-3,078	12	3,072
Finland	155	1	56	162	4	-2	1,369	1	21	1,956	4	50	3,325	2	36	586	255	2,437
Poland	169	2	-27	31	1	77	2,341	2	-9	453	1	101	2,794	2	0	-1,888	-19	2,786
Denmark (3)	–	–	–	–	–	–	1,984	2	9	707	1	11	2,691	2	10	-1,277	8	2,451
Austria	117	1	-13	92	2	3	1,436	1	-9	1,151	2	27	2,587	1	5	-285	-57	2,475
Czech Rep.	92	1	-65	17	0.4	-42	1,797	1	-26	209	0.4	-2	2,006	1	-24	-1,587	-28	2,631
Ireland	131	1	37	61	1	-22	1,277	1	16	639	1.3	10	1,915	1	14	-638	23	1,684
Luxembourg (3)	–	–	–	–	–	–	1,815	1	17	86	0	-32	1,902	1	13	-1,729	22	1,676
Greece	111	1	15	9	0.2	13	1,418	1	16	58	0.1	8	1,476	1	16	-1,360	16	1,277
Portugal	37	0.3	17	6	0.1	-59	459	0.4	23	101	0.2	-33	560	0.3	7	-357	61	521
Slovakia	26	0.2	-50	3	0.1	-48	368	0.3	-25	62	0.1	-49	430	0.2	-30	-305	-17	615
Estonia	42	0.4	75	3	0.1	-38	342	0.3	33	28	0.1	5	370	0.2	30	-313	36	284
Slovenia	11	0.1	-58	2	0.1	-10	237	0.2	-18	30	0.1	15	268	0.2	-16	-207	-22	317
Lithuania	23	0.2	-25	1	0.02	-74	221	0.2	-18	9	0.02	30	230	0.1	-17	-212	-19	276
Cyprus (3)	–	–	–	–	–	–	168	0.1	-16	2	0.003	102	170	0.1	-15	-166	-16	200
Latvia	5	0.05	17	1	0.02	-73	72	0.1	21	8.7	0.02	-41	81	0.05	9	-63	41	74
Malta (3)	–	–	–	–	–	–	26	0.02	-70	7	0.01	-12	33	0.02	-65	-19	-76	95

Source: Eurostat   Unit: million Euro

Part VI
China and Europe in a global context

12 The EU and China in the global system

Volker Stanzel *

Chinese, Europeans, and others, possess "mental maps" giving them orientation in the political and societal world around them – cognitive maps which have been imprinted upon their consciousness during the twentieth century. Now, however, we observe changes in the world so dramatic that we need to ask ourselves whether we still have the right maps in our minds or whether the ones we still use might not mislead us when we try to find our way ahead. China is a perfect example – now having an impact unimaginable only a decade ago and impacting the global system in ways we are yet to fully understand. Several new features characterize our world today.

A new international setting: the need for new "rules of the road"

First, the end of the Cold War means more than the end to a time when two super-powers threatened each other and a large part of the world's population faced instant extinction. The Cold War had also contributed to a world order with a high degree of both stability and complexity. The international institutions which set rules for international behaviour, such as the United Nations and its sub-organiza-tions, or the World Bank or the IMF, remained almost as "frozen" as the overall worldwide situation, because any major change would have threatened the balance between the two superpowers and the two major blocs. The interest of the two superpowers in having institutions guide behaviour between states lay in avoiding "chaotic" conflicts which might possibly lead to a "hot war" between the United States and the Soviet Union. This interest guaranteed that international institutions were kept intact, even in phases of limited armed conflicts such as the Vietnam War or the Soviet invasion of Afghanistan, or throughout the period of decolonization.

Our post-Cold War world is characterized by the atrophy, or the threatened breakdown of many of those institutional structures. As a result, the international order as we knew it is crumbling. Efforts to adapt the United Nations to the new situation by successive Secretary Generals of the United Nations indicate that we need a new world order, or at least new "rules of the road" if we want to avoid incalculable risks of multiple conflicts (even Jihad terrorism may be understood as the promise of a new "order" in an increasingly disoriented world). Those rules may or may not evolve naturally; but the members of the international community that have a stake in its functioning will find it in their interest to take on responsibility for how a new world order appears. The appearance of new major actors on the world stage means that defining a new global order will have to involve them. China and other Asian countries, with their newly-found economic and political strength, will have to have a greater say in how the new rules for the behaviour of states are written. When we work within, and try to reshape, the global system, Asian countries need to be more involved.

The second phenomenon is the new quality of globalization. World trade expands due to the opening of new markets. World trade also expands due to the fact that industrial production has moved from "vertically integrated production" to worldwide "horizontally integrated production." The process of producing components of products at the most distant locations until assembled and shipped as one has become possible because of the globally expanding labour market. This in turn has led to continually decreasing prices. Expanding trade also means that not only traditionally tradable goods – the hardware of globalization – are making their way around the globe. The software of globalization, i.e. formerly little tradable goods, such as knowledge and information, has become mobile as well. They have become as sellable and buyable as material goods. Thus, the competitive advantages of industrialized societies – strong in knowledge, education and creativity – increasingly shrink.

The new phase of globalization has moved far beyond trade in simple material or immaterial goods. Participatory movements, emancipation and hedonistic "world culture" phenomena are traded too and have become elements of "modernization," subverting the authority of traditional structures, world views, even religions, leading in cases of extreme destabilization to what today is known as "failing" states. Asia's new economic dynamism has contributed to this development as well as to its speed – as it has to the globalization of dangers. Natural disasters that affect a country may severely limit its economic performance and thus have a negative impact on world trade. SARS, and now avian flu, demonstrate how quickly pandemic diseases may spread due to the increase in international travel. International crime, the trade in arms, humans or drugs complement the trade in goods in a negative way. The new character of globalization means that many become richer, few become poorer, while the wish to join the globalization process becomes ever stronger. With new opportunities comes the danger of new threats and the question of who will be able to devise the appropriate "rules of the road".

Lastly, we are confronted with the phenomenon of an increasing number of global centres of gravity. Here, the rise of East-Southeast Asia is the most conspicuous. This rise would not have the impact we observe without the rise of China. However, the rise of China can only be comprehended in its full dimension if we take into consideration how its economy is interwoven with the economies of the whole crescent reaching from Japan down to Australia.[1] The new economic and political stature of China, as well as the emergence of ASEAN, the resurgence of the Japanese economy, the dynamism of the so-called "tiger economies," the growing supra-regional policy of India and its new economic growth – all these

factors have brought about a tendency towards more cohesion among Asian countries that goes beyond the economic successes.

The region does not yet speak with one voice – far from it – but like a common
thread we observe the efforts to establish new structures and organizations, and at
least the will of the region to determine its own agenda.[2] When we say the region is
a new centre of gravity in the world's economy, and is on its way to become a
centre of gravity in global politics as well, then we mean that whatever such a
"centre" does, its actions or non-actions may affect the whole world. Gravity
centres are not the "poles" that the myth of a "multipolar world" wants to see – they
are conglomerates of states of very different characteristics, not centralized entities
with a unified political will. Gravity centres are rather like the centre of spider
webs without a spider,[3] and the strings of these webs are the lines of interest that
span across the globe from the sources of natural resources to laboratories where
medicines against pandemics are developed, or where silly caricatures suddenly
have repercussions leading to the death of demonstrators far away.

A new international setting: old and new stakeholders

In dealing with the new environment of the twenty-first century brought about by
these three phenomena,[4] in drawing those new "mental maps," the influence the
centres of gravity can exert will be a major factor. Certainly the strongest (the US),
and that of a "traditional" one (Europe), but also of the most important new one –
the East Asian crescent driven forward by China's dynamism – will all push the
world in new directions. How do these centres of gravity exert influence? The most
important factor is their ability to create order within their own regions, and to have
an impact outside too – not necessarily, but possibly also globally. They might
contribute to the solution or to the aggravation of regional and global problems. For
that they need the capability and the will to use economic, diplomatic and, if necessary, military resources. Another means of influence is their so-called "soft
power," which more sustainably transcends economic impact and military power
with its attraction and integrationist strength of values and culture. It is striking
how much a point of discussion the question of China's soft power or "cultural
power" has become not only in the West, but even more so in China's think tanks
and media over only the past year.[5]

Europe and East-Southeast Asia (and in the future other "centres" as well), at the
side of the United States, have all become "stakeholders" of order in the world.[6]
For decades Japan has experienced what China and the other countries in the
region are experiencing now – what they do may have global consequences, and
"the crisis of one will be the crisis of all."[7] The Chinese government's transparency
about new health threats may prevent the spread of pandemics. Good governance
that prevents corruption domestically will also impede the spread of international
crime. Whether the value of the RMB is allowed to freely float or not, it has an
impact even on other continents. The efficient organization of the textile industry
in China may mean poverty to workers in that same industry some thousand kilo-
metres away.

China and its neighbours will have to find a new way to manoeuvre on the international stage. Here, the EU has been developing into a partner with which Asian countries approach an increasing number of common problems. ASEM (the Asia–Europe Meeting) has gradually become the most important forum for this purpose.[8] It has developed into a forum where both leaders of governments and government agencies as well as experts from administrations and civil society meet on a large range of global issues. It thus offers institutionalized opportunities for countries to learn about each other's views and approaches to questions concerning both Europeans and Asians – in ways that have not been possible in the past and which may influence opinion-building and help prepare operative decisions taking into regard each other's attitudes.

The EU and China

Since the establishment of diplomatic relations between the EU and China in 1975,[9] and despite signing a "Cooperation Agreement" in 1985, the EU was for a long time of secondary importance to China's foreign policy, and vice versa.[10] This has changed. It has changed in the economic field already, and is changing politically as well. Today, the EU is China's most important trading partner in the world, with a total trade volume of ca. €200 billion (€150 billion China to EU; €50 billion EU to China).[11] Of the EU's external trade, 10 per cent takes place with China. The example of Airbus – about to build an assembly plant in China – shows the "intensity" of technology transfer between the two sides,[12] cooperation in the Galileo satellite navigation system, or the nuclear research reactor ITER, all indicate the progress of scientific cooperation. In education, there is the successful example of the China Europe International Business School (CEIBS) in Shanghai and a China–Europe Law School in Beijing.

The EU provides technical assistance for a broad range of projects in China, including the organization of village-level elections, including the training of observers and producing education material for the voters, and it pursues a human rights dialogue. Both China and the EU today call their relationship "strategic." That is to say, if we follow the definition supplied by the EU's representative to China, Serge Abou, that the areas of cooperation cover China's "strategic needs,"[13] and that it is in Europe's interest to contribute to the success of China's reforms as China's stability and prosperity are "an indispensable factor for global balance." This becomes manifest in an annual "strategic dialogue," five regular "expert level" meetings, and twenty "sectoral dialogues" covering topics ranging from political analyses to social or environmental issues.[14]

This new quality of relations was difficult to foresee or forecast. For China, the EU – and its predecessor the European Community – was an organization difficult to understand. China tended to see mainly the irreconcilability of national interests.[15] Since 1990, the EU with its transformation and enlargement was even harder to understand. China's view of the world was an inherently traditional one: countries vying with each other for, if not supremacy, at least advantages over one another. The EU seemed to be an example of that kind of world. A handful of countries, nine at the beginning of the EU–China relationship, bound together by the need to cooperate, but led by whom? Correspondingly, China's expectations were that one or the other of the stronger European countries sooner or later would take the lead and dominate Europe (and possibly stand up to the "sole remaining super-power").[16]

While the usage of this multipolar world rhetoric continued (and continues occasionally even today),[17] with increasing depth of EU–China relations, comprehension of the EU in China increased. The progress of comprehension may have been aided by the necessity to find not only economically viable but also politically reliable partners for China's reform and opening policy. Its own region, important as it was, presented complications, China's peace-oriented policies notwithstanding. Deng Xiaoping, after China had gone to war four times during the first thirty years of the People's Republic's existence, prescribed a policy of keeping a low profile in foreign affairs and making an effort to create a "peaceful environment" for China's concentration on its economic development.[18] Despite the success of this policy, China at times even agreed to territorial compromises, in creating an "added value" of trust beyond close economic relations, thus facilitating both China's economic development and its integration into the world economy, its major gains were achieved not in the arena of that new centre of global gravity. In Asia, tensions still abound.

Firstly, for some years now, China's "neo-mercantilist" strategies to assure its supplies of natural resources have been the cause of competitive tensions in the region, and increasingly globally. The competition over energy resources exacerbates existing rivalries between China and some of its neighbours. China and Japan are in a contest over a future Russian oil pipeline in Siberia, and at the same time over a small offshore gas field in the East China Sea. Despite flourishing economic relations, the Chinese–Japanese conflict over the former Japanese Prime Minister's visits to the Yasukuni Shrine for the war dead (including fourteen "Class-A" war criminals) and other nettlesome issues brought the political relationship between Japan and China to their lowest point since the establishment of diplomatic relations in 1972. South Korea and Japan are in a phase of deteriorating bilateral relations over both territorial and moral questions. The situation in the South China Sea is calm, yet the territorial problems there are left unresolved; ethnic and religious tensions often lead to armed violence in Southeast Asia. The proliferation of regional institutions reflects the awareness of the potential of a new global gravity centre here, yet so far there is no working mechanism for solving the problems or resolving the conflicts of the region. ASEAN + 3, ASEAN + 1, the East Asian Community (EAC), the Shanghai Cooperation Organization (SCO), the ASEAN Regional Forum (ARF), or APEC do not possess sufficient coordinating powers to obligate the leaders of the East-Southeast Asian gravity centre in a way that would enable them to act in concert. Possibly the fact that the countries of the region possess very different political systems makes it even more difficult to establish institutions which would require partly giving up national sovereignty in order to gain in influence collectively.[19]

Possibly Europe, with its economic strength, became the attractive partner with which to share a "strategic" partnership and promised the many advantages that both sides enjoy today. Both Europe and China had much to offer each other in terms of economic profits. Chinese experts today understand that EU countries are on the path towards more unity in structures and policies, struggling with the need to combine integration with enlargement, and China's leaders and institutions display patience in waiting for a more cohesively acting partner.[20] China's official view of the main features of EU–China relations thus is that of a "solid political foundation and strong mutual trust"; "emerging as each other's key trading Partner with great potentials"; "enjoying wider consensus on major global and regional issues"; "having found the right way to resolve differences through dialogue."[21] Is it a surprise that 2004 became the "Year of Europe" in China?[22]

Mutual adaptation efforts

To appraise the development towards the present quality of the relationship, the question remains how Europeans saw and explained that process themselves.[23] At least some official observers in China have a clear understanding of what happened: "After about three years' contest, the leaders of Western European countries found that, instead of collapsing under pressure, China enjoyed rapid economic growth, internal stability, enhanced national cohesion and elevated international status. Facing the hard reality, the Western European countries, proceeding from their own interests, had to readjust their China policy and resume normal relations with China step by step," writes Mei Zhaorong, foreign policy advisor to China's leaders and former diplomat. Ambassador Mei continues for pages in that triumphalist tone.[24] If an influential person like Mei takes that point of view, it deserves attention and consideration.

On the European side, have economic advantages pushed aside political aspects of the EU–China relationship that had hindered mutual accommodation? The policy of reform and opening to Europeans had indeed for a long time been tied to the expectation of farther-reaching political change. The appearance of democratic movements ("Democracy Wall," Wei Jingsheng, etc.) in the early 1980s, various reform initiatives by two consecutive General Secretaries of the Communist Party of China (Hu Yaobang, Zhao Ziyang) and, lastly, the student demonstrations on Tiananmen Square had seemed to confirm that expectation. Later, the upheavals throughout the Communist world after the fall of the Berlin Wall had led to the assumption that China would experience a similar fate. In hindsight, it seems almost ironic that the spectacle of Tiananmen may have impeded an armed reaction by East German authorities, thus allowing the fall of the Berlin Wall. The spectacle of the fall of the Berlin Wall, the Iron Curtain and the Soviet Empire in due course may well have been the decisive warning signal to Chinese leaders to prevent similar developments in China. The danger of what during the days of *Ostpolitik* used to be called "change by *rapprochement*" was certainly not lost on China, where the party leader appealed in the early 1990s that it was necessary for China to build a "Great Wall of Steel" in their hearts and souls against Western "bourgeois contamination." Deng Xiaoping argued that reform and opening meant that "a few flies" might come in through the window, but that certainly political liberalization along the Western model was out of the question. The present "fourth generation" leaders in China have echoed that position with the 2006 "White Paper on Democracy," which argues that Western style democracy is not a suitable model for China.[25]

The discussion in Europe of whether or not trade might promote political change subsided after the Asia crisis of 1997–99. China's economic and societal change became fast and far-reaching and created a situation so unknown and fresh that recipes from Cold War times quickly became outdated.[26] The various strategy papers coming from the European Commission in Brussels reflect well the changing perception: emphasizing "constructive engagement" (1995) via the objective of a "comprehensive partnership" (1998) to the effort to define "shared interests and challenges" (2003)[27] until they arrive in 2005 at the following, now quite concrete, objectives of the EU's China policy:

- to engage China further, both bilaterally and on the world stage, through an upgraded political dialogue;
- to support China's transition to an open society based upon the rule of law and respect for human rights;
- to encourage the integration of China in the world economy through bringing it fully into the world trading system, and supporting the process of economic and social reform that is continuing in China;
- to raise the EU's profile in China.[28]

This adaptation of the EU's China policy to the changes occurring in the country follows the orientation of the Commission's Asia strategy papers and is part of the EU's Asia policy, which today includes all the dimensions of Europe's Common Foreign and Security Policy, with its engagement in the ASEM process, the ARF, formerly with KEDO, as well as the EU's participation in various UN Peace-keeping Operations in Asia. It is therefore more than simply the question of whether it had become imperative to use both chances of cooperation and of new economic opportunities. The EU has reacted to a development of China, which has brought about changes in its economy (so much so that industrialized countries discuss whether China is not already a full-fledged market economy) and in its society, in its role in the world to put it at the core of that new East-Southeast Asian centre of global gravity. Constructive cooperation across the board therefore has become an evident necessity for an EU that is occupied with global developments.[29]

New challenges for the relationship

Only since about 2005 has a new problem arisen for both the EU and China in their relationship. It is of an international, fundamental and very new nature. During the past few years international concerns have been increasing that

China's needs for energy and other resources will change the situation on the most important world commodity markets. In turn, concerns in China rise over whether the country has sufficient means available to secure supplies of the commodities it needs if it wants to continue its economic growth.[30] In the oil market at present, China makes efforts to control its supplies from the oil wells all the way to China's coast, signing exclusive agreements with producer countries, buying or building oil exploring and trading companies, and developing strategies to defend the oil routes or to develop land-based lines of supply. This is at variance with the strategy of the majority of oil-consuming countries who, after 1974, and within the framework of the International Energy Agency, found it most rational to leave energy supply security to the markets. China's strategy might possibly create tensions which would be detrimental to its overall objective of maintaining a "peaceful development,"[31] and might lead to conflict with the EU as well.[32]

There is a marked contrast between, on the one hand, the effort to explain China's objective of creating "win–win" situations for itself and all its partners,[33] of drawing even on the tradition of an admiral of the fifteenth century to show that China through the millennia pursued the Confucian principle to pacify through its model and to create harmony between all countries, conquering "in greatest benevolence without war" (Confucius),[34] and, on the other hand, an attitude that has become increasingly self-confident and even risk-friendly. One example of that attitude is the concerted international campaign to receive support for China's "Anti-Secession Law" of March 2005, which negatively influenced the EU's drive towards lifting the arms embargo against China.[35] Another one is Beijing's six-month-long campaign to change the dynamics of reforming the Security Council of the United Nations. Armed with the argument that UN reform must take more time for deliberation, must take into account the interests of the Third World and should be "democratic," special emissaries paid a series of visits to most countries in the world. Independent of the actual discussion in New York they made one thing plain: the proposals tabled so far would not meet Beijing's approval – a strong point in view of Beijing's veto power but carrying the risk of antagonizing not only the group of four countries (plus some yet unnamed African countries) hoping for a permanent seat on the Security Council, but also the large number of countries of the South hoping for greater influence on world affairs through a better working UN.

That risk-friendly and value-free diplomacy now seems to bring about more risks than solutions. A case in point is Iran. China is discovering that the new role which it claims also means that now it carries more of the burden of responsibility should there appear a country in the Middle East developing or possessing nuclear arms. In the case of Sudan, Zimbabwe or Venezuela, China has argued that its energy needs required good relations even with these countries because China had no alternatives. But what if the regimes supported by China later turn out to be dangers for their neighbours or their own people? With all its economic growth China has acquired a greater role in the world (which it sees as its due), and now finds itself confronted with the need to take on responsibilities of a dimension never truly imagined before, except rhetorically.[36] China has developed successfully into a country of which the world expects that it not only will abide by global rules but it will want to have a say in how these rules are being rewritten.

At the same time China finds itself tied into a web of dependencies, it discovers that its new-found strength and freedom allow room for manoeuvre but simultaneously subjugate it with all its regional neighbours to common constraints. While in the past Asian countries were able to wait for decisions of global importance to be taken by others, their new strength, their new power to influence global events, gives them the responsibility to analyse situations and to devise strategies on their own.

Here lies the problem: China has come far on its way from simply integrating into the world economy to integrating fully into the political world community. A country that depends in its development and prosperity on what is happening in the world will try to influence the making of the rules of the game. But in which way? A "world power" may well try the unilateralist option, forcing its will upon its partners. Or, it may try to create "coalitions of the willing", creating alliances that help it get its way. Lastly, it may try to make use of international organizations and institutions in order to arrive at compromises most satisfactory to a majority of the states involved.

The question here is: in view of the overall problems in East-Southeast Asia, whether China and its neighbours will discover that bilateral solutions as "traditional" nation-states are not sufficient any more to deal with the consequences of a dissolving world order and dynamically progressing globalization processes. Even traditional notions of balance of power, or of "multipolarity" of nation-states have so far not proved able to help get very far in developing the new "rules of the road" for the world. In a world of interdependence, a world of different actors needing each other to exist and develop, in such a world it proves more advantageous to represent one country's or one region's interest together with that of others. The more "multilateralist" the approach, the more partners are involved, the more efficient a solution can be.[37] International rules and norms as alternatives to the use of armed or non-armed force are the foundation of international policies in the age of interdependence. Cooperating in the global community multilaterally therefore also has become the task and responsibility of East Asian countries as they wish to develop a global policy. If it wants to pursue a sustainable policy reflecting and using its strength, China will have to bring its neighbours in its region along.[38] To come to terms with its new status as a world power and the heavy burdens of responsibilities that it acquired along the way, China and the countries of East Asia will have to join other countries in exploring ways to at least minimize the risk and to maximize the opportunities derived from the new globalization processes.

Cooperating on global governance

Multilateral cooperation in itself does not mean that there are already new "rules of the road," not mention a new world order. For that, an overarching universal framework is indispensable. The United Nations in the twenty-first century will remain the most important forum of global rule setting. There is no other organization that commands comparable global legitimacy even though it is not a legitimacy that is truly democratically based. To shape the world of the new century, however, the United Nations cannot remain as it was created in 1949. It has to reflect a world consisting of almost 200 countries. Before the UN can define "rules of the road" for the world, it therefore needs to be reformed itself. China, represented in the UN as Asia's sole P-5 country, possesses sufficient global weight to contribute to the reform of the United Nations. The danger, if we do not get an efficient, reformed UN would be that different forms of cooperation in smaller circles will evolve, disregarding the interests of a larger number of states.

A major factor in creating a stronger UN would be contributing to developing further international law. Legally bound international relations would increase accountability and transparency of the way states deal with each other. They would improve the rule of law over the use of sheer power in international relations. It is not enough to subscribe to the values of international law – the rule of international law can only be a basis for international relations if countries accord to this law precedence over national law. To give new stability to the world and to replace the crumbling structures of the Cold War age with a new world order shaping the norms of future stability, a conviction of the importance of international law will have to grow worldwide, and foremost in the countries forming the new centres of gravity. This is the most concrete part of the task facing China in the twenty-first century: strategic problem-solving multilaterally and mainly by rebuilding the United Nations. "Strategic" means that common problems have to be identified together and solutions have to be charted and implemented together. Such "strategic partnerships" are possible only if all involved work from the same basis. Anachronistic ideas of statehood or of state sovereignty will only lead to traditional national solution efforts – bound to fail – instead of transnational ones, adequate to today's global challenges.[39]

Therefore, enhancing the existing mode of cooperation between the EU and China by venturing into the core areas of global governance may help overcome the "new challenge" to the relationship consisting in the burden of new responsibilities for China and the countries of its region. The two sides might therefore examine how to systematically and strategically approach major concrete issues and areas such as the following, prioritized not in order of urgency but of long-term impact (Bates Gill's chapter in this volume also considers how many of these issues might also be open to greater China–Europe–United States cooperation):[40]

1   *Global governance*:

   •   How to reform the UN? Do we need additional global or regional institutions with the rise of new economic powers among the countries of the South?

- How to reform international law? How to establish an international rule of law (including in the area of human rights)?
- How to redefine "state sovereignty" in the age of globalization, how to promote regional and inter-regional cooperation? How to support the cooperation of regional organizations?

2   *Global economic relations*:

- How to avoid international conflicts over energy and other vital resources?
- How to solve conflicts over global trade liberalization inside and outside the WTO?
- How to assure internationally coordinated, efficient and sustainable environment policies?
- How to assure sustainable development in transforming and modernizing countries?

3   *International crisis management*:

- How to develop cooperative strategies and policies to deal with terrorism?
- How to cooperatively combat and prevent international crime (trade in humans, drugs, arms, money laundering)?
- How to deal with, and prevent, global health risks?

4   *International conflict management*:

- How to make the international non-proliferation regimes more efficient, how to deal with violators?
- How to put into place workable and efficient peacekeeping structures and forces?
- How to prevent or solve armed regional and internal conflicts?
- How to support states threatened with the "failure" of their statehood, how to eradicate its root causes, how to "manage" radical ideologies dangerous to peace?

Value partners?

For Europe, the question arising from the increasing intensity of the EU–China relationship is one of its prospects. If the EU and China in the global system have become "interest partners" in that they pursue similar interests and objectives multilaterally and in the UN system, are they then what we might call "value partners" too? Many differences persist. The question of the rule of law and of human rights in China has been defused to a degree by the evolving human rights concept in China, which is best represented by the fact that since 2004 there is a human rights clause in the Chinese constitution. Yet as long as there are arbitrary justice, torture, hard labour camps, restricted press and media freedom and limited individual, religious (Tibet, Christian churches) and social freedom, whenever there is a more conspicuous individual case it will still easily turn into a political problem between the two sides.

Then there is the question of the EU arms embargo, and the question of peaceful or non-peaceful resolution of the Taiwan question.[41] There are economic disputes, where mainly the problem of the violation of intellectual property rights outsizes anything that has happened in the past when Japan, South Korea and others began their economic take-off. The question whether the EU will grant China Market Economy Status (MES) has turned from a question of only a technical nature into one of political symbolism. The problematic nature of the question of value partnership between the EU and China becomes starkly clear when seen in comparison with Europe's relationship to the US.[42] The transatlantic relationship is based on values and thus for Europe supersedes all other relationships. Even though some Chinese think tankers speculate that economic realities will at some point force Europe to stand against the US,[43] the majority realize that, in comparison, there is an imbalance in the EU–China relationship in that the EU in most cases tends to have more understanding for American objectives and interests than for China's.[44] If efficiency and trust of the future EU–China relationship is contingent upon shared values, then, from the European point of view, that inevitably needs to be addressed at some point.[45]

These differences are not matters to be resolved easily simply by relying on common interests – it is in the cultural distance that remains even in the age of globalization where the difference between interest and value partnership lies. This distance results from different histories and different cultural developments.[46] Therefore the best that Chinese and Europeans – and others – can do today is lead an open dialogue on value questions. It is not just the "hard facts" of politics and economics that decide the quality of the EU–China relationship and the limits and the potential of cooperation in the international arena. More decisive in the long run is "cultural" exchange, an exchange on "values" in the widest sense.[47] Because values are involved, such an exchange is not easy – it is the question of how to deal with alien ways of thinking and behaving. Therefore, only if cultural exchange is dense, will societies in due time be able to understand each other and each other's values – values upon which interests are based. Mutual comprehension provides the basis for productive cooperation in both politics and economics.

If Chinese and Europeans know so much about each other today and are able to cooperate fruitfully, they owe it to a high degree to the cultural exchange between their countries during past decades and centuries. Such a cultural exchange would be less sustainable were it confined to institutionalized exchange. Due to the process of globalization our societies have an increasing number of partners worldwide. That might lead to a relative decrease in importance for existing partnerships. Governments on their own can only achieve so much. This then is the field of civil society and the day-to-day encounters in shared experiences. Only the innumerable actors that constitute a "civil society" have the combined potential to initiate an exchange of knowledge on values, philosophies, and visions that may come to constitute a robust basis upon which political and economic leaders can build. Therefore, to draw those new "mental maps" in the twenty-first century, both in China, in Asia, and in Europe, is less and less a task for politics and business. It is more than ever a task for both European and Chinese society.[48]

Outlook: the EU and China in the new international setting

A close relationship with Europe promises China economic and political benefits, and support in various ways for its policy of reform and opening. In comparison, defining China's relationship to its superpower neighbour, the United States, or achieving more cohesiveness in its own, politically and economically diverse, East Asian region, is more complicated and problematic. For Europe, in turn, to develop close relations with the fastest and largest of the newly rising economic (and increasingly political) powers of East Asia opens new and promising economic and trade opportunities, and allows cooperation with an ever more influential partner in tackling global and regional questions.

Thus, the EU–China relationship has seen marked and rapid improvements across the board. Today, Europe is China's most important trading partner in the world, China is Europe's most important trading partner in Asia, Europe supports with a number of measures China's reform policy, both cooperate in science and technology, and both lead several dialogues on major bilateral and multilateral issues.

Towards the end of the decade, however, the EU and China find themselves confronted with a new international setting characterized by an increasingly unstable international environment as well as forces of globalization that subvert existing national and international institutions and value systems. The challenge for the two centres of gravity in the world, Europe and East Asia (with China as the centrepiece), as much as for the United States, therefore consists in jointly trying to define new global "rules of the road" or, better, a new international order. The growing intensity of their cooperative relationship would seem to facilitate that task. There is, however, a new and growing obstacle which carries the potential of impeding closer EU–China cooperation on major problems. It is the increased awareness in China that a greater role in world affairs brings along a greater burden of responsibilities. Whether China will be able to shoulder that burden and play an accordingly constructive role commensurate with its new strength remains to be seen.

The EU and China therefore need to work constructively on two strategies. Dedicating themselves to a multilateralist approach in cooperating on concrete questions of global governance would be the short/medium-term one. Thus the reform of the United Nations, adapting global economic relations to the changes caused by the newly rising economic powers, cooperating in both crisis and conflict management should be on the agenda of the so-called strategic partnership between the two.[49] A more medium-long-term strategy would be a deliberate effort to overcome the value distance and the cultural gap still existing between Europe and China. The objective here would be to aim, over time, at creating a true value partnership enhancing the existing interest partnership in a similar way as is the case at present between the Atlantic allies.

Notes

* The views expressed herein are solely the author's personal views and in no way represent official positions of the German Government.

1 Fifty per cent of China's exports globally, and 60 per cent of its exports to the EU are processed goods: products that have been assembled from semi-finished goods imported mainly from other Asian countries. Also, see Bao Hong, "An Analysis of the 'China Factor'," in *International Understanding*, Vol. 1 (2006), pp. 17–22; and Thomas Heberer, *Die Rolle Chinas in der internationalen Politik* (China's Role in International Politics) (Bonn: German Development Institute, 2006), pp. 1–37. More generally, see Volker Stanzel, "Asia's Role in the World: A View from Europe," in Xuewu Gu (ed.), *Europe and Asia* (Baden-Baden: Nomos Verlagsgesellschaft, 2002); John Humphrey/ Dirk Messner, "Unstable Multipolarity? China's and India's Challenges for Global Governance" in *die briefing paper 1/2006* (German Development Institute, Bonn: 2006).

2 See, for example, Francoise Nicolas, "East Asian Economic Integration – Past Experience, Current State of Play and Future Prospects," in Willem van der Geest (ed.), *The European Union's Strategic Interests in East Asia*, Vol. II (Brussels: European Institute for Asian Studies/Nomisma, 2005); and Heribert Dieter, *Bilaterale Freihandelsabkommen im asiatisch-pazifischen Raum* (Bilateral Free Trade Agreements in the Asia-Pacific Region) (Berlin: Stiftung Wissenschaft und Politik, 2006); also Liu Jiangyong and Yan Xuetong, "Some Tentative Thoughts on Establishing an East Asian Security Community," in *Foreign Affairs Journal*, Vol. 71 (March 2004), pp. 73–88.

3 Kay Möller, however, preferred to speak of "nerve centers of international politics." See Kay Moeller, *Für eine europäische Fernostpolitik* (For a European Far East Policy) (Berlin: Stiftung Wissenschaft und Politik, 2004), p. 7.

4 David Shambaugh's analysis comes to the conclusion that there are actually four "principal trends that define the new global order: China's rise; US military supremacy and unparalleled power; the EU's increasing coherence and economic weight; the acceleration of technological and economic globalization." See David Shambaugh, "The New Strategic Triangle: U.S. and European Reactions to China's Rise," in *The Washington Quarterly* (Summer 2005), pp. 7–25.

5 A well known Chinese think-tank director, whose identity I withhold, observed in a discussion in April 2006: "It is China's responsibility to be a teacher of the world." Also as a very recent example: "Shijie pingshuo Zhongguo ruanshili" (The World Criticizes China's Soft Power), in *Global Times*, 2 June 2006, p. 1, or "Meiguo xiang Zhongguo xuexi shema?" (What Can the U.S. Learn from China?), in *Global Times*, 13 June 2006. For Western views of China's soft power potential see Joseph S. Nye, "The Rise of China's Soft Power," *The Wall Street Journal Asia*, 29 December 2005; Bates Gill and Yanzhong Huang, "Sources and Limits of China's 'Soft Power'," in *Survival* Vol. 48, No. 2 (Summer 2006), pp. 17–36; Sebastian Bersick, "Political Issues Shaping EU–China Relations," *Briefing Paper*, Europe China Academic Network, June 2006. Aptly, Michael Yahuda proposed the term "soft foreign policy" for a situation where the use of "power" is not yet required, or possible.

6 It is not any more a question of only China becoming a "responsible stakeholder" as Robert B. Zoellick in his since famous statement to the National Committee on US–China Relations on 21 September 2005 has argued (http://www.state.gov/s/d/rem/53682.htm), it is a question of the responsibility of all the major players confronted with a new and fluid international situation. For some time, the question was one of "managing" China – a concept which Robert Kagan has proved to be out of date: Robert Kagan, "The Illusion of 'Managing' China," *The Washington Post*, 15 April 2005. Compare also Frank Umbach, "Veränderungen im Verhältnis der Machtfaktoren zueinander" (Changes in

Power Factor Relationships) in *Trend*, (2003), pp. 40–4; and David Shambaugh, "European and American Approaches and Policies Toward China: Different Beds, Same Dreams?" (*Lecture at IFRI Centre Asie*, Paris, 10 January 2002).

7 Tony Blair, "Idealismus wird zur Realpolitik" (Idealism Becomes Realpolitik), in *Frankfurter Allgemeine Zeitung*, 30 May 2006, p. 10., and Blair's foreign policy speeches of 21 March 2006 (London), 27 March 2006 (Canberra) and 26 May 2006 (Washington).

8 See, for example, the excellent overview in Japan Center for International Exchange/ University of Helsinki, Network for European Studies, *ASEM in its Tenth Year: Looking Back, Looking Forward* (Tokyo/Helsinki, 2006), and Council for Asia–Europe Cooperation (ed.), *The Rationale and Common Agenda for Asia–Europe Cooperation* (Tokyo/London, 1997). Also see Frank Umbach loc cit., and Christian Hauswedell, "A German View of European-Asian Relations," Lecture in Canberra, Australia, 21 April 2004.

9 Even before the People's Republic had assumed China's seat in the UN in 1971, Beijing had proposed the establishment of diplomatic relations with the European Community. On early relations see Oskar Weggel, *Weltgeltung der VR China* (Global Role of the PR China) (Hamburg 1986), and Stefan Friedrich, "Europa und China in den neunziger Jahren" (Europe and China during the Nineties), in *Aus Politik und Zeitgeschichte*, B27/98 (1998). Most interesting is a comparison with the situation only a few decades earlier, see "Schriften des Forschungsinstituts der Deutschen Gesellschaft für Auswärtige Politik," *Die Außenpolitik Chinas* (The Foreign Policy of China) (München/Wien: Oldenbourg, 1975), pp. 281–6.

10 See Gustav Kempf (Volker Stanzel), *Chinas Außenpolitik* (China's Foreign Policy) (München/Wien: Oldenbourg, 2002), pp. 123–30; also see Oskar Weggel, "Chinas Außenpolitik am Ende des 20. Jahrhunderts: China and the EU, Apple of the Eye" (China's Foreign Policy at the End of the Twentieth Century) in *China Aktuell*, vol. 01/99 (January 1999), pp. 34–8.

11 2005 figures from Eurostat. Approximately $74 billion EU to China, $143 billion China to Europe, total $217 billion. For comparison, US–China trade: $49 billion US to China, $162 billion China to US, total $211 bn; $100 billion Japan to China, $84 billion China to Japan, for a total of $184 billion. Also see Zhang Zuqian's and Robert Ash's chapters in this volume.

12 Serge Abou, "The EU and China: Towards a Mature Partnership" (note that he speaks of *legal* technology transfer), speech in Beijing, 7 April 2006.

13 Abou, ibid. As for the Chinese point of view, no one has given a better definition than the Chinese Premier Wen Jiabao: "'Strategic' means that the cooperation should be long-term and stable, bearing on the larger picture of China–EU relations. It transcends the differences in ideology and social systems and is not subjected to the impact of individual events that occur from time to time. 'Partnership' means that the cooperation should be equal, mutually beneficial and win-win. The two sides should base themselves on mutual respect and mutual trust, endeavor to expand converging interests and seek common ground on the major issues while shelving differences on the minor ones." See Wen Jiabao, "Vigorously Promoting Comprehensive Strategic Partnership between China and the European Union," Lecture in Brussels, 6 May 2004.

14 Topics of expert level meetings: Migration; Human Rights; Asian Affairs; Nonproliferation; Conventional Arms Exports. The (irregular) sectoral dialogues concern Customs, Energy, Textile Trade, etc.

15 See Feng Zhongping, "EU's China Policy Analyzed," in *Contemporary International Relations* (hereafter: CIR) 8/4 (1998); Zhou Hong (ed.), *Da-Oumeng, Xin-Ouzhou* (Beijing: Zhongguo Shehuikexue Chubanshe, 2005; also Ding Yuanhong, "EU Enlargement and European Integration," in *Foreign Affairs Journal*, Vol. 71 (March 2004), pp. 89–93. Also see Stefan Friedrich, "China's Policy vis-à-vis the European Union. Interests, Context, and Implications for Europe," in China Aktuell (Hamburg), November 1997; and Xu Zhixian, "On the Foreign Strategy and the Trend of China Policy of the

US, Western Europe, and Japan at the Turn of the Century," in *Contemporary International Relations*, No. 8 (1998). Also see Dai Bingran's overview of European studies in China in this volume. It is to be admitted that even for Europeans it is not that easy to comprehend how the EU's foreign (and China) policy is being made, considering that it is not the European Commission but still the member states via their Common Foreign and Security Policy mechanism who are responsible.

16 See Xue Mouhong, "Die neue Weltordnung: Vier Mächte und eine Supermacht?" (The New World Order. Four Powers and One Superpower?), in: *Beijing Review*, 39/1995; Liu Sun/Li Shaopeng, Li Wenkai, and Sun Botao, *Ouruoba* (Europe) (Beijing: Zhongguo Renmin Daxue Chubanshe, 1997); Donald W. Klein, "Japan and Europe in Chinese Foreign Relations," in Samuel S. Kim (ed.), *China and the World. Chinese Foreign Policy Faces the New Millennium* (Boulder: Westview Press, 1998).

17 Dai Bingran, "The EU's Role in the Post-Cold War Period: The Road to Becoming One of the Poles in the New Multipolar World," in Xuewu Gu (ed.), *Europe and Asia*, op. cit; Shen Qiang, "Trend Towards a New Multipolar World in the Context of Multilateral Relations of States in Asian Geopolitics," in *Foreign Policy Journal*, Vol. 74 (December 2004), pp. 12–23.

18 See Ruan Zongze, "Safeguarding World Peace and Promoting Common Development – How Deng Xiaoping's Diplomatic Ideas Came into Being and their Rich Contents," in *Foreign Affairs Journal*, Vol. 73 (September 2004), pp. 1–7. On the official Chinese view of China's regional policy see also Jin Guihua, "Developments Trends of East Asian Cooperation – A Perspective from the East Asia Summit," in *Foreign Policy Journal*, Vol. 79 (March 2006), pp. 73–6. Cf. also Jochen Buchsteiner, "Asiatische Zukunftsmusik" (Future Tunes of Asia), in *Frankfurter Allgemeine Zeitung*, 17 December 2005.

19 See Manfred Mols, "Probleme und neue Herausforderungen in Ost- und Südostasien" (Problems and New Challenges in East and Southeast Asia) in *KAS/ Auslandsinformationen 5/06* (Konrad-Adenauer-Stiftung, Berlin: 2006), pp. 21–46.

20 See Dai Bingran, loc. cit.; and Department of Policy Planning, Ministry of Foreign Affairs, People's Republic of China, *China's Foreign Affairs* (Beijing: Shijie Zhishi Chubanshe, 2004), pp. 331–6.

21 Ibid., pp. 331–2.

22 *Far Eastern Economic Review*, 12 February 2004, pp. 26–9. Also, see David Shambaugh, "China and Europe: The Emerging Axis," *Current History* (September 2004), pp. 243–7; and his chapter in this volume.

23 After all, one might possibly indeed call "the history of the relations between China and Europe (...) a history of inconsistency on the part of the Beijing regime ..." See Pierre Baudin, "China und die Europäische Union: Zwiespältige Beziehungen" (China and the European Union: Ambivalent Relations), in: *KAS/ Auslandsinformationen 5/06* (Konrad-Adenauer-Stiftung, Berlin: 2006), pp. 47–71.

24 Mei Zhaorong, "Sino-European Relations in Retrospect and Prospect," *Foreign Affairs Journal*, Vol. 79 (March 2006), pp. 17–27.

25 See chapter I of Information Office of the State Council of the People's Republic of China, *Building of Political Democracy in China*, Beijing, 2005.

26 This change often carries with it political implications which are a far cry from anything happening in the Soviet Union in the past and therefore necessitate new analyses; cf., as one conspicuous example, China Society for Human Rights Studies, Inclusion of Human Rights in the Constitution, Beijing 2004.

27 The difference lies mainly in the increasingly solid substance to both the economic and the political issues to be discussed jointly, describing thus the path towards the establishment of the above-mentioned sectoral dialogues. As often, some member states had been ahead of the Commission in this development as shown by Germany's East Asia Strategy Paper of 2002 which already had tried to place national economic interests in a balanced relationship with global political and security interests. Cf. http://

www.auswaertiges-amt.de/www/de/infoservice/download/pdf/asien/ostasien.pdf (with English language version).

28 Consult the EU Commission's website: http://ec.europa.eu/comm/external_realtions/ china/intro/index.htm. Developments have thus been faster than expected. See Frank Umbach and Andreas Fulda, "Zur Zukunft der EU–China–Beziehungen im 21. Jahrhundert" (On the Future of EU China Relations in the Twenty-first Century), in *ASIEN*, Vol. 89 (October 2003), pp. 47–56.

29 See Hanns W. Maull, "Hat Europa eine Asienpolitik? Braucht es eine?" (Does Europe Have an Asia Policy? Does It Need One?), *Speech on the occasion of the 50th anniversary of the German Association for Asian Studies*, Berlin 5 April 2006; William Wallace and Young Soogil (ed.), *Asia and Europe. Global Governance as a Challenge to Cooperation*, (Tokyo/Washington, D.C.: Council for Asia–Europe Cooperation, 2004); Sebastian Bersick, op. cit.; Christian Hauswedell, op. cit.; and several contributions in Bates Gill and Gudrun Wacker (eds.), *China's Rise: Diverging U.S.–EU Perceptions and Approaches* (Berlin: Stiftung Wissenschaft und Politik, 2005). A comparison of US and EU policies towards China or an analysis of the US' China policy, however relevant, remains as much outside the limited scope of this paper as the equally important China–Japan or the China–Russia relationship. Therefore, literature on these topics is not referred to here, but see the chapters in this volume by Bates Gill, Ruan Zongze, and David Shambaugh.

30 See David Hale, "China's Insatiable Appetite," in *Asian Wall Street Journal*, 16 May 2005; Frank Umbach, *Future Chinese Energy Security Strategies: Implications for China's Foreign and Security Policy* (Berlin: DGAP paper, May 2006). See also C. Fred Bergsten, Bates Gill, Nicholas R. Lardy, and Derek Mitchell, *China: The Balance Sheet* (New York: Public Affairs, 2006); Xuewu Gu and Kristin Kupfer (eds.), *Die Energiepolitik Ostasiens* (East Asia's Energy Policy) (Frankfurt/New York: Campus Verlag, 2006); Michael T. Klare, "Fueling the Dragon: China's Strategic Energy Dilemma," *Current History*, April 2006, pp. 180–5; James Kynge, *China Shakes the World* (London: Weidenfeld & Nicolson, 2006), puts the energy question into the wider frame of resource supplies and environmental problems. Wesner/Braun show how much China's academics are aware of the conflict potential of China's energy strategy: Friederike Wesner/Anne J. Braun, "Chinas Energiediplomatie: Kooperation oder Konkurrenz in Asien?" (China's Energy Diplomacy: Cooperation or Competition in Asia?), in: *SWP-Zeitschriftenschau 5* (Stiftung Wissenschaft und Politik, Berlin: June 2006).

31 See David Shambaugh, "China Engages Asia," in *International Security*, Vol. 29, No. 3 (Winter 2004/2005); Zheng Bijian, *Peaceful Rise – China's New Road to Development* (Beijing: Central Party School Publishing House, 2005).

32 Cf. Roland Götz, *Europa und China im Wettstreit um Russlands Erdgas?* (Europe and China Competing for Russia's Natural Gas?) (Berlin: SWP-Aktuell, 2006); also Janis Vougioukas, "Notfalls mit Soldaten. China nimmt seine Interessen in Zentralasien wahr." (With Troops, if Necessary: China Takes Care of its Interests in Central Asia) in *Süddeutsche Zeitung*, München, 16 June 2006, p. 21. Basically, however, Bates Gill is, of course, correct when he observes in his chapter in this volume, "to the degree European policymakers see 'threats' emanating from China, they tend to be on either questions of 'soft security,' such as economic competition, illegal immigration, transnational crime, smuggling of drugs and contraband, environmental issues, and human rights, or on 'hard security' issues which have only an indirect impact on European security, such as Chinese proliferation. Indeed, it is clear the EU and individual European capitals see greater threats emanating from within China as a result of the country's remarkable but often messy social, economic and political transformation. Hence the strong European concern to assist Beijing smoothly and sustainably transition toward a more open and marketized socioeconomic system while avoiding destabilizing unrest and other

domestic challenges" – even if that is easily explained for one thing by the fact that the EU and China, unlike the US and China, do not share a common border.

33 The peace-orientation of China's foreign policy has been expounded various times by party General Secretary and President Hu Jintao himself; cf. his speech to the UN on 15 September 2005, "Build Toward a Harmonious World of Lasting Peace and Common Prosperity" reprinted in *Beijing Review*, No. 42, October 2005).

34 Li Rongxia, "Significance of Zheng He's Voyages" in *Beijing Review*, Vol. 48, No. 28 (July 2005).

35 See Daniel Fried as quoted by Bates Gill in his chapter in this volume.

36 See Bao Hong, loc. cit.; Volker Stanzel, "Aufstieg zur Weltmacht" (Becoming a World Power), in Volker Ullrich/Eva Berié (eds.), *Weltmacht China* (China a World Power) (Frankfurt am Main: Fischer, 2005); Baudin, op. cit.

37 This thesis certainly needs to be discussed at greater length. For the purpose of this paper it may suffice to indicate the successes of greater multilateral approaches such as in Afghanistan over other, less successful efforts. For several thorough analyses of the question of multilateralism in Asia and on the part of China. See, for example, Knut Dethlefsen and Bernt Berger (eds.), *Regional Security Architecture and Multilateralism* (Shanghai: Shanghai Institute for International Studies/Friedrich-Ebert-Stiftung, Shanghai, 2004).

38 It may be this choice expressed by Zhang Zhijun, the deputy head of the International Liaison Department of the Chinese Communist Party, when on 5 February 2006 at the Munich Conference on Security Policy he said that China's policy is based on the princi-ples of international law, that China hopes to settle traditional and non-traditional secu-rity issues through international cooperation and to jointly deal with global threats and challenges; also see Ding Gan, "Women zheyang yingxiang shijie" (This is How We Influence the World), in *Guoji shibao*, Beijing, 31 July 2006.

39 Intriguingly, in a survey undertaken in 2005 among 10,250 people in nine countries of the world, at least Germany and Chinese proved to be two peoples most convinced that a new world order will have to rely on the United Nations, cf. http://today.reuters.com/news/news   Article.aspx?type=top News&storyID=2006-06-02T074257Z_01_L02336855_RTRUKOC_=_USA-CHINA-SURVEY.   xml&page Number=1&imageid=&cap=&sz=13&WTModLoc=NewsArt-C1-Article Page1. Cf. also Heribert Dieter, *Abschied vom Multilateralismus?* (Farewell to Multilateralism?) (Berlin: Stiftung Wissenschaft und Politik, 2003).

40 See Zhou Hong, "Wulun Fazhan Zhong-Ou Hezhuo Huoban Guanxi de Zhanlue Yiyi" (Discussion About the Strategic Implications of Developing the China–Europe Partner-ship), in *Zhongguo Zhanlue Guancha* Vol. 2 (2006), pp. 7–13; Mark Leonard and Andrew Small, *EU–China: Towards a Global Partnership*, published by the Chinese Academy of Social Sciences and The Foreign Policy Center (May 2005); Also of interest: John Humphrey/Dirk Messner, "China and India as Emerging Global Gover-nance Actors: Challenges for Developing and Developed Countries," in: *IDS Bulletin Vol. 37 No. 1* (Institute of Development Studies, Bonn: January 2006), pp. 107–13.

41 The Taiwan issue and the question how the EU perceives it have been kept outside the framework of this discussion. But see, for example, Adam Ward, "The Taiwan Issue and the Role of the European Union," Remarks to Stiftung Wissenschaft und Politik/CSIS Conference, April 2005; Heberer loc. cit., 50–2; Gunter Schubert, "Becoming Engaged? The European Union and Cross-Strait Relations," in: *ASIEN*, Vol. 89 (October 2003), pp. 5–25.Also see Jean Pierre Cabestan's discussion of Taiwan as an "irritant" in EU–China relations in this volume.

42 See Ruan Zongze's chapter in this volume, and Andreas Schockenhoff, "Deutsche Außenpolitik unter der Regierung Merkel" (German Foreign Policy under the Merkel Government), Lecture at the International Department of the Central Committee of the Communist Party of China, Beijing, 19 April 2006. It might seem tempting to try to draw

up a list of "values" and then compare how far they are shared values at the present time. However, "values," as the history of philosophy, religion, or of the discussions at e.g. the former Human Rights Commission of the United Nations in Geneva has amply demonstrated, lend themselves to varying interpretations which makes agreement on the principle easier but leaves the disagreement in the substance unresolved. Would not even the fiercest adversaries agree on the fundamental "value" of "peace"? It is precisely the point of the argument in this part of this chapter that larger efforts are necessary to bridge the distance which still exists between Europe and China in the most fundamental cultural questions of which "values" are but one part.

43 As a very good example, see the arguments put forward by Wang Jian, Li Xiaoning, Qiao Liang, Wang Xiangsui, *Xin Zhanguo Shidai* (The New Warring States Era) (Beijing: Xinhua Chubanshe, 2003).

44 Sometimes, that may even be true the other way round as well.

45 Tony Blair, loc. cit., argues that globalization creates interdependence which enforces common values if common systems of managing global problems are to function.

46 If David Shambaugh diagnoses "cognitive dissonance" between Europe and China, might we speak here of "cultural dissonance"?

47 See Seán Golden, "Socio-Cultural Aspects of the Relationship between the EU and East Asia, with Particular Reference to China," in Willem van der Geest, loc. cit.; also Brunhild Staiger, "Timeline of Chinese–European Cultural Relations," in *China Aktuell*, Vol. 6/04 (June 2004), pp. 648–63.

48 See Sebastian Bersick, loc. cit. More generally, see Barthold C. Witte, "Die Mühen der Ebene" (The Pains of the Plains) *Frankfurter Allgemeine Zeitung*, 8 June 2006.

49 As well as in their relationship with the United States; see also Bates Gill's chapter in this volume.

13 The United States and the China–Europe relationship

*Bates Gill**

In recent years, American views toward the Europe–China relationship reflect both increased attention and increasing concern. This derives in part from the fact that the ties between Europe and China – countries with which the United States has deep and long-standing interests – have grown dramatically closer in recent years, and particularly during a period of some trans-Atlantic tension in the early-to mid-2000s. In addition, increased American interest in Europe–China relations also reflects greater concern in recent years over the possible lifting of the European Union (EU) arms embargo on China.

Nevertheless, Washington's policy elite remain largely unaware of the remarkable scope and nature of China–Europe ties and their implications for US political, diplomatic and economic interests for the years ahead. Preoccupied with challenges in Iraq, in Afghanistan, and with the broader global effort to counter terrorism, Washington has not focused sufficient attention – beyond a narrow fixation on the arms embargo issue – on the interesting and important developments in Europe–China relations. As a result, the reaction of US policymakers and analysts to China's burgeoning relationship with Europe tends to be negative and zero-sum, framed in terms of Europe and China teaming up to counterbalance or even constrain American action on the international stage.

For China and Europe, this situation presents both opportunities and challenges. On the one hand, there is a critical need for European and Chinese leaders to shape the debate in Washington about the positive aspects of Europe–China ties and promote a more cooperative approach to Europe–China–United States relations. On the other hand, American policymakers and analysts across the political spectrum will continue to harbour certain concerns about Europe–China relations for the foreseeable future, especially regarding signs of closer military-technical cooperation. Either way, given the importance of the United States to Europe and to China, Washington's views on Europe–China relations cannot be ignored and need to be understood and taken seriously in Europe and in China.

This chapter examines and analyses American views of Europe–China relations in three principal parts. First, the chapter presents the two key "schools" or "camps" in the United States on Europe–China relations. Second, the chapter outlines some of the mechanisms – both official and nongovernmental – which involve Americans examining Europe–China relations, with a particular focus on trans-Atlantic mechanisms. In a third and concluding section, the chapter discusses the challenges and opportunities for Europe–China–US relations in the years ahead.

Differing US views on Europe–China relations

Most of the debate in the United States on China–Europe relationship revolves around the arms embargo question. However, in addition, there are also public voices urging a more strategic, comprehensive, coherent, and well-informed response to deepening Europe–China ties.

Broad-based opposition to lifting the arms embargo

Opposition to lifting the EU arms embargo is one of the few foreign policy issues in the United States that has galvanized broad agreement, not only between the executive and legislative branches of government and within the bureaucracy itself, but even across party lines. Rightly or wrongly, American policymakers oppose lifting the arms embargo primarily due to their belief that such action would unduly and dangerously contribute to modernizing the Chinese military, and possibly threaten US security interests in the Asia-Pacific region. Others put it more bluntly: lifting the embargo means that American servicemen and women might one day face European weapons in the hands of Chinese soldiers. Others stress that lifting the embargo would "send the wrong signal" to China in light of continued serious concerns over its human rights record.

In late 2003, officials in the Pentagon and White House began to recognize the potential within the EU for lifting the embargo. During the Irish presidency of the EU in early 2004, Washington dispatched envoys to express American concerns, especially regarding the possible contribution to Chinese military modernization which might result from lifting the ban. Back in Washington, the arms embargo question became an issue of contention both within the Executive Branch, and between the White House and Congress. In mid- to late-2004, the US Senate Republican Policy Committee, at the time chaired by Senator John Kyl, began to focus considerable resources on the issue to generate opposition to lifting the ban within the Congress, and to pressure the White House, including the President.

Within the Executive Branch, two approaches emerged. One side favoured reaching an arrangement with European partners whereby the EU would lift the embargo, but also establish a new and stronger trans-Atlantic framework on arms export controls. This compromise approach was also favoured in many European capitals, including in London. The other side, on security and human rights grounds, was opposed to lifting the ban and to negotiating a new framework. With pressure mounting on Capitol Hill, including threats that lifting the embargo would result in legislation restricting arms procurement cooperation with European partners, and with lingering bad blood between the Washington and certain European capitals such as Paris and Berlin, the White House vetoed a compromise approach. During his February 2005 trip to Europe, President Bush reiterated his "deep concern" that lifting the embargo would unsettle the balance across the Taiwan Strait, and he warned European leaders about the consequences of transferring high-technology to China's military.[1]

In March and April 2005, Administration officials kept up the pressure on the EU, with Under Secretary for Political Affairs Nicholas Burns saying that the US "strongly opposes" lifting the embargo[2] and former Deputy Secretary of State Robert Zoellick warning that the decision "could come at a stiff price in terms of trans-Atlantic defense ties."[3] Under Secretary of Defense Peter Rodman told a Congressional panel that it was not just "an abstract issue of political symbolism," but one that "could directly affect the safety of American military personnel in the Asia-Pacific region."[4] Taking another tack, Secretary of State Condoleezza Rice also warned that lifting the embargo would "send the wrong signal about human rights."[5]

During this period, in March 2005, the Chinese National People's Congress passed the Anti-Secession Law, codifying the right to use force against Taiwan, which further bolstered the argument in Washington (as well as in Europe) against lifting the arms embargo. As US Assistant Secretary of State for European Affairs Daniel Fried recalled:

> We had a sharp debate with the European Union about the China arms embargo. I remember that embarrassing moment when the European Union delegation arrived in Washington to try to tell us why lifting the arms embargo was a good thing, which was the very day the Chinese National People's Congress passed the Anti-Secession Law. Well, my European Union colleagues were discomfited, to put it mildly.[6]

Opposition to lifting the embargo cut across political lines within Congress, with the US House of Representatives voting overwhelmingly 411 to 3 in support of a non-binding resolution condemning the EU decision to consider lifting the embargo.[7] Citing concerns about regional peace and stability in the region, the House threatened retaliatory measures to restrict sensitive technology transfers to European allies.[8] Senator Richard Lugar, Republican chairman of the Foreign Relations Committee and Senator Joseph Biden, ranking Democrat on the Committee, warned that the US Congress would retaliate if the arms embargo was lifted.[9] Senator Biden was joined by Republican Senator Gordon Smith in sponsoring a non-binding Senate resolution urging the EU to maintain its arms embargo on China, which passed unanimously on 17 March 2005.[10]

In addition, nongovernmental voices also joined the chorus in opposition to lifting the arms embargo: "If the EU carries out this threat [to lift the arms embargo] – and make no mistake, this would be a genuinely hostile act against the United States – the trans-Atlantic tiffs of recent years could come to seem minor, and Bush could be saying a final farewell to old allies rather than renewing strategic bonds."[11] Others saw the arms embargo issue causing a "schism at the heart of the post-Cold War relationship."[12] For a number of critics, the "breathtakingly myopic and stupid policy" was an example of European mercantilism in action, currying favour with China for preferential commercial treatment and to open up a new arms market for European weaponry.[13] The US Senate Republican Policy Committee, in starkly stating that "the PRC is a strategic competitor and threat to the U.S. and its allies," called on the Europeans to "acknowledge the danger of lifting the arms ban; stand by their democratic principles; and demonstrate their solidarity with the United States on key security issues."[14] Other commentators criticized the apparent lack of European concern for the consequences removing the arms embargo would have on the balance of power across the Taiwan Strait.[15] Going further, others accused France in particular of seeking an opportunity to "ever fulfill the Gaullist fantasy of balancing the United States on the global stage" by pursuing closer relations with China.[16]

While many of these nongovernmental opinions emerged from "conservative" or "neo-conservative" quarters, similar views were shared by others across the political spectrum. For example, David Shambaugh, a China expert based at George Washington University and one of the leading American observers of Europe–China relations, also argued against lifting the embargo. In an opinion piece issued in February 2005, he refuted the principal European arguments for lifting the embargo, and concluded: "Lifting the arms embargo on China is ill-advised. If anything, it needs to be strengthened. Both Europe and America can continue to enjoy robust relations with Beijing while maintaining their respective arms embargoes. China will just have to live with it until it comes to terms with Tiananmen and stops putting military pressure on Taiwan."[17]

Calls for a more strategic approach to Europe–China relations

For a number of years prior to the arms embargo imbroglio of early 2005, a handful of observers recognized the geopolitical shift portended by deepening Europe–China ties, foresaw the looming political problems surrounding the arms embargo issue, and urged a more strategic and well-informed US policy toward these developments, including the establishment of a trans-Atlantic dialogue on Asia and China. Most of this work was carried out by nongovernmental researchers and policy analysts; there is little public evidence that such strategic thinking was developed within the United States government, even as Europe–China relations intensified in the early 2000s.

David Shambaugh has been one of the most prolific and attuned scholars writing on China–Europe relations and his interest in and analysis of the subject dates back to the mid- to late-1980s. Drawing from his professional experience and networks on both sides of the Atlantic, his work provides in-depth comparative analysis of how Europeans and Americans differ and converge in their respective views of China, both among policymakers and among academic researchers.[18] While opposing a lifting of the EU arms embargo, he recognized the importance of taking a more strategic approach in trans-Atlantic relations regarding China, and was a very early advocate of an official US–Europe dialogue on Asia and China affairs. Shambaugh argued that "the interaction of the United States, China, and the EU will be a defining feature of the international system in the years to come." As such, policymakers and analysts must pay far greater attention to understanding this "new strategic triangle" and the governments themselves must bring joint agreement and action to bear "on the most important and overarching issue: to manage China's integration into the established global systems smoothly and peacefully."[19]

The present author also urged policymakers "first and foremost to place the arms embargo question in the larger context of China–EU relations" and "to recognize that the arms embargo question in the EU is part of an ongoing, comprehensive, and carefully constructed strategy to build a fundamentally different kind of relationship with China. This effort has two principal aims: (1) to integrate China as a responsible member of a multipolar global community and multilateral international institutions and (2) help China address its domestic sociopolitical and socioeconomic challenges at home – so-called capacity building or 'good governance.'"[20] The present author argued that under certain conditions it is possible to lift the EU arms embargo on China, stem the export of militarily-relevant technologies from Europe to China, and strengthen trans-Atlantic consultations to help shape positive outcomes in the face of China's rise and evolving Europe–China–US relations.[21] He also argued that the US government "establish a regular mechanism for strategic dialogue and consultation between the United States and Europe on Asia and China."[22] Two Europeans resident in the United States – Robin Niblett and Michael Yahuda – have also been active in promoting research and exchanges on Asia and China across the Atlantic, and likewise urged a more strategic approach and regularized dialogue on these questions.[23]

Transatlantic exchanges regarding China and Europe–China–US relations

Nongovernmental and semi-official exchanges

Nongovernmental groups such as think tanks and university-based centres have been by far the most active in promoting trans-Atlantic dialogue on Asia and China. For example, the Henry L. Stimson Center partnered with DGAP Berlin in 2001–2 to carry out transatlantic discussions on China, which resulted in a published report calling for greater and more regularized dialogue across the Atlantic between government and nongovernment specialists to address China and related issues in Asia.[24] The RAND Corporation has also carried out discussion with French partners.[25] In 2005, the Center for Strategic and International Studies (CSIS) and the Stiftung Wissenschaft und Politik (SWP) carried out two such dialogues (February 2005 and April 2005) involving nongovernment policy analysts and middle- to senior-level officials, including a US Deputy Director of National Intelligence. The report issued from those meetings identified perceptual and normative differences between Europe and the United States in their approaches toward China, and cautioned against over-expectations regarding US–EU "coordination" of China policy.[26] The most long-term and sustained of these trans-Atlantic exchanges have been the American-European Dialogue on China, organized by David Shambaugh and Francois Godement (January 2002, June 2003, May 2005, January 2007). These meetings involve mid- to senior-ranking officials from Europe and the United States, and the discussions and working papers are considered off-the-record.

These meetings have served the valuable purpose of regularly bringing interested US and European scholars, policy analysts and officials together to review shared and divergent perceptions, assessments, and policies toward China. These meetings have increasingly included US and European officials (from both member governments and from the EU), who participate in an unofficial capacity, and this has helped raise the salience and profile of more frequent and better-informed trans-Atlantic dialogue about China.

However, thus far these meetings have fallen short of fully informing the policy communities on both sides of the Atlantic. One problem is numbers: only a small handful of US and EU experts and officials focus regularly on these topics and seriously consider policy responses. Virtually all of these nongovernmental trans-Atlantic dialogues have called upon governments in the United States and Europe to institute a more formal and regularized official channel for discussions regarding Asia and China. Unfortunately, the trans-Atlantic political furore over the arms embargo issue – in spite of years of forewarnings within the nongovernmental exchanges – exposed missteps on both sides of the Atlantic, and indicated how much more work can be done to connect the unofficial and official discussions.

In November and December 2004, the US–China Economic and Security Review Commission (USCESRC) – established by Congress to monitor and report on the economic and national security dimensions of US trade and economic ties with China – conducted meetings in Europe with political leaders, policy analysts and business representatives, and concluded, in part, that "enhanced dialogue between the United States and Europe on China and broader global strategic issues was overdue" and that the "United States needs to work closely with the EU and European member states to address areas of mutual security concerns regarding China."[27] While acknowledging the "different levels of priority and focus" Europeans place on the security relationship with China compared to the United States, the report on the USCESRC noted areas of potential trans-Atlantic cooperation regarding China policy, especially on human rights, the rule of law, corporate governance and enforcing World Trade Organization (WTO) compliance.

Official trans-Atlantic exchanges and cooperation

As the arms embargo issue intensified, and particularly following the trans-Atlantic rift over the problem in early to mid-2005, some in the United States government recognized the need to establish a more regularized dialogue channel with EU partners to discuss broader common issues of concern regarding Asia and China. Washington was very clear, however, that the dialogue mechanism was not intended to "negotiate" positions on lifting the EU arms embargo. The US side has firmly remained in opposition to lifting the arms embargo, and sought to broaden the trans-Atlantic dialogue on Asia and China to other pressing issues. The first meeting of this dialogue was held in May 2005 in Brussels. Following that meeting, Assistant Secretary of State Fried said:

> We decided with our European colleagues that we were simply putting this debate in the wrong order; we should not be debating the arms embargo, we should be having a deeper strategic discussion about Asia and about China and about how Europe and the United States will work with China to make sure that its development ... contributes to international security and prosperity .... [O]ur purpose is to have a common understanding with Europe about Asia and about China so that the discussions with respect to the China arms embargo take place within a framework of shared views. We've been remiss in not having this dialogue early ...[28]

Subsequent meetings of the dialogue mechanisms have been held about every six months, including in December 2005 and June 2006.

Officials in Washington see the dialogue as a success in harmonizing trans-Atlantic views toward Asia and China. During the May 2005 meetings held in Brussels, National Security Council Director for Asian affairs Dennis Wilder was "heartened" by the "shared interests and common values" in trans-Atlantic approaches toward China, including support for the rule of law, free and fair trade, and human rights.[29] In April 2006, referring to trans-Atlantic relations regarding China, Assistant Secretary of State Fried said, "I think we are much better knit-up. We have a dialogue about China .... All of this is better, there is far more understanding on both sides than a year ago."[30]

In addition to the regularized dialogue on political and security issues, there is also increased trans-Atlantic consultation regarding economic and trade policy toward China. Both sides stand firm on not granting China market economy status, which would significantly lessen the antidumping tariffs applied to Chinese goods. This has led officials in Beijing to complain that the trans-Atlantic partnership is "ganging up" on China, a charge one EU official denied; he did acknowledge that the United States and EU "do know a whole lot more about each other's policies on China now."[31]

While US policy has traditionally tended to be more critical of China's economic and trade policies – from the trade deficit, to currency valuation, to protection of intellectual property rights, to unfair trading practices and barriers to the Chinese market[32] – EU Trade Commissioner Peter Mandelson in 2005 launched an EU policy regarding China that is somewhat closer to Washington's approach, but still far from combative. The Commissioner is due to release a report in the second half of 2006, which comes in response to growing concerns among some EU states about increasing competition, recognizing that China "is the biggest single challenge of globalization in the trade field."[33]

Both the United States and the EU pressured China on textile imports in late 2005, reaching their respective agreements after difficult negotiations.[34] In March 2006, the EU imposed stiff duties on imports of leather shoes from China. At the end of March, the United States and the EU joined forces for the first time to issue a rare joint complaint before the World Trade Organization (WTO), accusing China of maintaining illegal trade barriers against imported auto parts. The case claims that China is imposing "local content" rules and unfair import tariffs to force automakers to use domestic rather than foreign auto parts. United States Trade Representative Robert Portman pledged continued and "close coordination" with European counterparts to resolve the dispute.[35] Nevertheless, while the EU took these steps on their trade agenda with Beijing, it is important to note that not all EU member states share the same set of trade interests or intensity of views about this somewhat more assertive approach toward China.

Challenges and opportunities for Europe–China–United States relations

Continuing constraints on trilateral cooperation

Given these views in the United States, and ongoing efforts to strengthen trans-Atlantic exchanges regarding Asia and China, what are the challenges and opportunities ahead for the Europe–China–United States triangle?[36] As this volume amply demonstrates, Europe–China convergence across a range of issues seems well underway. Overall, both sides continue to stress the need to further deepen their relationship, and have agreed to negotiate and conclude a new and more far-reaching framework agreement "that will reflect the full breadth and depth of the strategic partnership between China and the EU."[37] Other prominent, but unofficial, European observers propose an even more ambitious agenda for cooperation, to include formal legislative, judicial, business, monetary and rule of law dialogues, and the establishment of a China–Europe Law School.[38]

The United States and European partners have made progress in mending some of their differences of recent years, and have put in place a dialogue mechanism to address certain concerns regarding Asia and China. Through the work of official and nongovernmental trans-Atlantic exchanges, there is some greater attention on US–China and Europe–China relations, and their implications for the Atlantic alliance (see the chapters in this volume by Algieri and Brødsgaard). The US–China leg of the triangle seems weakest, though the two sides have never been more intertwined and interdependent than they are today. US–China relations remain generally stable as Washington and Beijing seek to expand common ground through their "senior dialogue" and summit-level agreements to enhance military-to-military ties, cooperate in a host of technical, scientific, and medical arenas, and iron out economic differences. The resignation of Deputy Secretary of State Robert Zoellick in 2006, who led the US side of the "senior dialogue," cast doubt on the future prospects of this process.

At the same time, many problems and differences of perception will persist across the legs of this triangular relationship. Many in Europe – especially in national legislatures, in the EU parliament, and on the street – hold negative views toward China's human rights record, especially regarding Beijing's policies toward Tibetans and other ethnic and religious minorities, and toward Taiwan. With each passing year, expectations in Europe will increase that Beijing should ratify and fully implement the International Covenant on Civil and Political Rights, take steps in response to the negative findings about China of the United Nations special investigator on torture, and actively negotiate a new Framework Agreement to govern EU–China relations. Europeans have also begun to feel the pinch of economic relations with China. Growing trade imbalances with China, Chinese competitiveness, as well as China's lax enforcement of intellectual property rights, present serious economic concerns for Europe.

The United States and Europe do not always see eye-to-eye regarding their relationship with China or how best to assure China's rise will be peaceful. Unlike Europe, the United States maintains significant strategic and political interests around China's periphery in the form of alliances and a host of other critical political-military relationships. Perhaps most importantly, Europe's relations with China are unfettered by the complicated and important political and military commitments the United States has made to Taiwan, the principal issue over which the United States and China could come into conflict. The strong American reaction to the possibility of lifting the EU arms embargo – and the lack of preparation on the European side to defuse or deflect it – highlighted the very different approaches to this issue taken in Washington and in key European capitals.

Of course, Beijing's policies on security-related questions will also affect Europe's thinking, and could limit closer ties. For example, with the promulgation of the Anti-Secession Law by China in early 2005, European observers were able to reemphasize the importance of a peaceful resolution of differences across the Taiwan Strait and link that expectation to the arms embargo question. US pressures to maintain the embargo are not likely to diminish in the near-term, placing additional restraints on the kinds of improvements in China–Europe relations which Beijing would hope for. In another area of security interest to both the Europeans and the United States, expectations are on the rise that Beijing will take a more active and constructive stance toward resolving concerns over Iran's nuclear ambitions, through bilateral channels and through United Nations Security Council action.

But by and large, to the degree European policymakers see "threats" emanating from China, they tend to be either on questions of "soft security," such as economic competition, illegal immigration, transnational crime, smuggling of drugs and contraband, environmental issues, and human rights, or on "hard security" issues which have only an indirect impact on European security, such as Chinese proliferation. Indeed, it is clear the EU and individual European capitals see greater threats emanating from *within* China as a result of the country's remarkable but often messy social, economic and political transformation. Hence the strong European concern to assist Beijing's smooth and sustainable transition toward a more open and marketized socioeconomic system while avoiding destabilizing unrest and other domestic challenges.

In spite of a "constructive, cooperative, and candid" relationship between Washington and Beijing, both sides remain wary of one another and find it difficult to dispel lingering strategic distrust. Differences over economic and trade issues, as well as persistent American concerns about China's human rights record, will continue and will likely worsen before they get better. Beijing will watch carefully how Europe–United States consultations evolve, and will bridle at the possibility that Western powers are "ganging up" on China.

In addition to these constraints across the bilateral legs of this triangle, there are other "internal" limits to what these powers can achieve in pursuing a more cooperative, proactive, and globally-oriented agenda. The United States is likely to remain preoccupied with the wars in Iraq and Afghanistan, and with the threats posed by international terrorism more generally. Moreover, the unilateralist strain in US foreign policy, coupled with looming protectionist sentiments at home and continued wariness toward partnerships with continental Europe and China, will persist for the foreseeable future. China's leaders will remain largely focused inward on domestic, internal problems, and will be unable and unwilling to take on a greater global role at this stage. Europe too faces internal political challenges, not least in its ongoing effort to credibly build and implement a Common Foreign and Security Policy (CFSP).

Possibilities for cooperation

In spite of these differences and constraints, these three power centres have a number of strong shared interests. All three power centres share an interest in improving regional stability and economic development, especially in Asia. In addition, all three powers – and US and European partners in particular – share an interest in encouraging a greater and more responsible role for China across a range of global and regional security and development issues. Such an approach would help build in China a greater awareness of its responsibilities as a growing global power, would embed and invest China more deeply in global and regional stability, and would draw Beijing away somewhat from a more insular, narrow and potentially dangerous overemphasis on its regional rivalries and problems – especially with Taiwan, but also with Japan and the United States. Moreover, the three powers also share an interest in seeing China succeed in its ongoing socioeconomic and sociopolitical transition, and emerge in the years to come as more politically open, socially just and economically stable country. Translating these interests into action will require improved understanding and more visionary thinking in China, Europe, and the United States. Within this strategic triangle, the US–China leg would appear to be the weakest in terms of such thinking.

Given both the constraints and shared interests, a cooperative trilateral agenda could focus on six key areas: regional stability, especially regarding unstable and/or difficult regimes; counterterrorism; nonproliferation; emergent transnational challenges; global economic stability; and China's domestic socioeconomic transition.

First, China, European partners and the United States should step up their consultations and cooperation on a number of issues related to regional stability. The United States has long played the role of regional security guarantor, but China may aspire and could contribute to such a role, though not to replace, but to supplement the American position. Beijing's leaders have clearly come to recognize the benefits of becoming more open to and dependent on a globalizing outside world, a view which over time may lead the country to recognize the importance of regional stability for Chinese interests both around China's periphery and even farther afield. In recent years and on certain issues, China has demonstrated a more constructive and active approach toward the global challenges of unstable regions, failing states and terrorism, including dramatically increased contributions to United Nations peacekeeping activities.

The United States, China and European partners might consider further steps regarding regional stability. For example, these partners should work to strengthen the role of United Nations and other multilateral peacekeeping activities, including the encouragement of an even greater role for China in peacekeeping activities; this would also include seeking greater Chinese support for UN and other multilateral action (such as NATO) aimed at stemming regional disputes and instabilities. As a complement, they should also increase their consultations and consensus-building regarding the international response to developments in such countries as North Korea, Burma, Sudan and Iran, including the possibility of United Nations Security Council action. More specifically, Washington and European capitals have a strong interest – as does Beijing – to foster a more constructive and stable approach to differences between China and Japan and between China and Taiwan. In other key regions, the United States, European partners and/or NATO and the Shanghai Cooperation Organization should open a strategic dialogue, and they should work together to move the Association of Southeast Asian Nations (ASEAN) Regional Forum (ARF) toward its stated goals of preventive diplomacy and conflict resolution. All three sides can do more to foster greater military-to-military ties and military confidence-building measures, especially regarding observation of and participation in peacetime military exercises. They should also do more to cooperate on a range of transnational threats, including delivery of humanitarian relief and other disaster responses, as well as exploring a more active role for China in policing sea lanes of communication (SLOCs).

Second, the three power centres can increase their joint efforts aimed at counterterrorism. Again, China is unlikely to proactively and preemptively pursue counterterrorist activities beyond its borders in the same way as Washington and certain European capitals. China has taken some tentative steps to partner with neighbouring countries and regional security organizations on counterterrorism measures, especially in Central Asia. China has likewise issued high-level counterterror declarations with ASEAN, the Asia Pacific Economic Cooperation (APEC) organization and the EU.[39] More substantive cooperation and consultation may be possible, especially regarding terrorist activities in Asia. For example, such steps might include building a stronger and more formal consensus across the United States, China and European countries, through summit statements or in multilateral fora, on stemming Islamic radicalism and terrorist activity, especially in Asia. China and its Shanghai Cooperation Organization (SCO) partners should seriously consider opening the SCO Regional Anti-Terrorism Structure in Tashkent to outside exchanges and consultations with US and European authorities. These partners can also work together in conducting counterterrorism training, exercises, and consultations in preparation for the 2008 Olympic Games in Beijing. They could also explore an expansion in intelligence-sharing on terrorist activity and strengthening the role of regional organizations such as APEC and the ARF to combat such illicit activities as money laundering and weapons smuggling which may contribute to terrorist activities.

Third, China, European countries and the United States could work more closely in combating proliferation. In this area, there has been a greater convergence of interests and action in recent years. China in particular has taken important steps to improve its nonproliferation record and become more active in supporting nonproliferation norms. The United States, European governments and China share seats at the same table in such regimes as the Nuclear Nonproliferation Treaty (NPT), the Chemical Weapons Convention (CWC), the Comprehensive Test Ban Treaty (CTBT), the International Atomic Energy Agency (IAEA), the Zangger Committee, the Nuclear Suppliers Group and the Container Security Initiative. China also demonstrated a greater convergence with US and European views when it backed United Nations Security Council Resolutions 1695 (2006) and 1696 (2006) against proliferation activity by North Korea and Iran, respectively.

China, the United States and European capitals all share a strong interest in bolstering the Nuclear Nonproliferation Treaty both normatively and in its enforcement powers by granting the IAEA and other nonproliferation bodies stronger tools to investigate and enforce the NPT. For example, these parties need to work together in support of tougher sanctions and other measures aimed at gaining nonproliferation compliance from countries such as Iran and North Korea. In addition, all three partners should expand cooperative programmes aimed at strengthening China's export control system and related to China's protection, control, and accounting of its supplies of fissile materials. China should also be further encouraged to support and even participate in the Proliferation Security Initiative (PSI).

Fourth, the three power centres could expand their cooperative approaches toward certain emergent global or transnational challenges. For example, they share an interest to engage more closely with relevant health authorities to ensure China does not become a source for infectious diseases that could spread globally, and encouraging China to take on a greater role as a contributor to, not consumer of, global health resources, improvements and discoveries. Energy and the environment are clearly shared concerns for Europe, China and the United States, and they can do far more to raise the salience and frequency of dialogue and coordination on global energy, resource depletion and environmental degradation. Working together, these three powers should encourage China to take a more active role in United Nations reform, including such questions as greater accountability and transparency of operations, recalibrating the balance of membership dues and contributions, and further empowering the United Nations to address regional security challenges.

Fifth, the United States, Europe and China should expand engagement within regional and global economic institutions. This engagement can be intensified in order to manage continued economic prosperity in the face of looming global economic challenges. Such cooperative measures could include working together to see to the successful conclusion of the WTO Doha round of multilateral trade negotiations, especially in agreeing to further trade liberalization, as well as integrating China more deeply into other institutions of global economic governance, such as the World Bank and the International Monetary Fund. In addition, European and American partners should seriously consider greater Chinese participation in such informal arrangements as the G-8, or establishing new mechanisms which more accurately reflect the global economic structure, such as a "G-4" with the world's largest economies as members: the United States, the European Union members, Japan and China. These three key economic players share an obvious interest to intensify dialogue about America's burgeoning current account and fiscal deficits, concerns over the strength of the US dollar, China's growing global trade imbalances and undervalued currency, and how to manage the interplay of these trends to assure a smooth adjustment of the global fiscal system (perhaps along the lines of a "Plaza Accord-plus").

Finally, Chinese, European and US partners share a strong interest in assuring smooth socioeconomic and sociopolitical development in China. Such cooperative work could focus on such issues as the rule of law, social welfare, good governance, entrepreneurialism, human rights, poverty alleviation, environmental protection, energy efficiency, health care, science and technology development, and education. All sides can consider various efforts to coordinate these programmes in a way that assures their effectiveness and continued success.

Bureaucratically speaking, it will not be a simple task to ramp up substantive cooperation in all or even some of these areas. However, the introduction of some mechanisms might facilitate steps toward greater forms of trilateral and bilateral consultation, coordination and cooperation on these important issues. For example, the United States and European partners should consider strengthening the role of the ongoing trans-Atlantic dialogue on Asia and China in a way that feeds recommendations and action more effectively into their respective policy processes. A part of this process might be to take stock of the range of US–China and Europe–China bilateral cooperative and consultative activities which are already taking place across a host of issues. This might be an activity which could be usefully commissioned for study by partner academic or other nongovernmental groups on either side of the Atlantic with an eye to providing useful background and briefing information in support of the official trans-Atlantic discussions on Asia and China. In the United States, some serious consideration is being given to setting up a senior-level mechanism within the Executive branch to better coordinate US official interaction with China. If such a mechanism is established, trans-Atlantic relations would benefit from having it establish a dialogue channel with a similar mechanism on the EU side and with certain European member states.

In addition, China, the EU and the United States, as well as European member states, share membership in a range of critical international and regional multilateral organizations, such as the United Nations, the World Bank, the International Monetary Fund, the ARF and others. These institutions provide regularized, official channels for the three parties to step up their interaction and take the lead in addressing pressing global and regional issues of common concern. Other, less formal mechanisms could also be created as needed – such as a "G-4" or "Plaza Accord-plus", or bringing China in to a new "G-9" or "G-8+1" process – to boost the capacity of these three key power centres to engage in effective, substantive consultation and cooperation. Beijing and Brussels could also consider arrangements to bring US and possibly other key players (such as Russia and Japan) into mid-level discussions on the margins of the now well-established China–EU summit process.

Conclusions and looking ahead

In sum, and from an American perspective, it is clear these three global power centres are likely to dominate international and regional political, security and economic affairs for many years to come. China in particular is expanding its global and regional presence in a way the world has not seen in centuries. These developments bring along considerable uncertainties, especially considering lingering misgivings in the United States about China–Europe relations and about China's rise, differences between American and European perspectives on how best to engage China and help assure its constructive role in world affairs for the future, and China's continued ambivalence about its growing power and how to use it. The United States and Europe also share serious concerns over China's poor record in dealing with the core trans-Atlantic values of human rights, civil liberties, religious and press freedom, democracy and the rule of law (see discussion of this point in Volker Stanzel's chapter in this volume).

But these uncertainties should not cloud the statesman's judgment about the possibilities for greater consultation, coordination and cooperation amongst Chinese, American and European partners on a range of serious global challenges. This will not be easy, and even if greater cooperation is possible, continuing differences and tensions will likely persist across all three legs of this strategic triangle, especially between the United States and China. Nevertheless, it is in the strategic interest of China, Europe and the United States to seek smooth and constructive relations for the future. To do so, strategists and policymakers should aim for five broad goals in the near- to medium-term, in rough order of priority:

1   Build a more cooperative China–Europe–United States triangle which focuses primarily on global issues of common concern.

2   Work together to assure a smooth transition for China to a more open, just, stable and prosperous society.
3   Expand and improve American understanding of China–Europe relations and their implications for US interests.
4   Continue and deepen regularized trans-Atlantic dialogue on Asia and China which addresses critical security concerns in the Asia-Pacific, how to work with China on the political, economic, security and emerging transnational issues of common concern to Europe and the United States, how to assure China's continued peaceful emergence on the global scene, and how best to strengthen EU export control functions and capacity with an eye to ultimately lifting the arms embargo.
5   Avoid a highly public focus on the arms embargo question, and do not underestimate the depth of concern it generates in the United States, while working to highlight and demonstrate the benefits of broader Europe–China and Europe–China–United States cooperation.

Notes

* The author gratefully acknowledges the assistance of Ms Melissa Murphy, Research Associate with the Freeman Chair, in the preparation of this chapter.

1   Elisabeth Bumiller, "Bush Voices Concern on Plan to Lift China Arms Embargo," *New York Times*, 22 February 2005.
2   R. Nicholas Burns, "The National Security and Foreign Policy Implications for the United States of Arms Exports to the People's Republic of China by Member States of the European Union," testimony before the House Committee on International Relations and the House Armed Services Committee, 14 April 2005, http://www.state.gov/p/us/rm/2005/45146.html, accessed 20 May 2006.
3   Amit Chanda, "US and EU Officials Indicate Continuation of European Weapons Ban on China," *WMRC Daily Analysis*, 15 April 2005, http://0-global.factiva.com.library.lausys. georgetown.edu/aa/default.aspx?pp+print, accessed 20 May 2006.
4   Amit Chanda, "US and EU Officials Indicate Continuation of European Weapons Ban on China," *WMRC Daily Analysis*, 15 April 2005, http://0-global.factiva.com.library.lausys. georgetown.edu/aa/default.aspx?pp+print, accessed 20 May, 2006.
5   US Department of State, Press Release: Tim Receveur, "Lifting Arms Embargo Against China Would Send 'Wrong Signal,'" http://usinfo.state.gov/eur/Archive/2005/Feb/02-821885.html, accessed 20 May 2006.
6   Daniel Fried, Assistant Secretary of State for European Affairs, "The United States and Europe: Addressing Global Challenges Together," Foreign Press Center Briefing, New York, New York, 19 September 2005, http://fpc.state.gov/fpc/53527.htm, accessed 29 May 2006.
7   For text see United States House of Representatives, 109th Cong., H. Res. 57, 2 February, 2005, http://thomas.loc.gov/cgi-bin/query/D?c109:1:./temp/~c109M1x4eZ, accessed 29 May 2006.
8   US Department of State, Press Release: Tim Receveur, "Lifting Arms Embargo Against China Would Send 'Wrong Signal,'" http://usinfo.state.gov/eur/Archive/2005/Feb/02-821885.html, accessed 20 May 2006.
9   Thom Shanker and David Sanger, "U.S. Lawmakers Warn Europe on Arms Sales to China," *New York Times*, 2 March 2005. See also Richard G. Lugar, "Opening Statement for Hearing on Lifting the EU Arms Embargo on China, 16 March, 2005" and

Joseph R. Biden, "Opening Statement for Hearing on Lifting the EU Arms Embargo on China, 16 March 2005," http://www.senate.gov/~foreign/hearings/2005/hrg050316p2.html, accessed 29 May 2006.

10 For text see United States Senate, 109th Cong., S. Res. 59, 17 February, 2005, http://thomas.loc.gov/cgi-bin/query/z?c109:S.RES.59, accessed 29 May 2006.

11 Dan Blumenthal and Thomas Donnelly, "Feeding the Dragon, Hurting the Alliance," *Washington Post*, 20 February 2005.

12 John C. Hulsman, "Prepared Statement" for the House Committee on International Relations, Subcommittee on Europe and Emerging Threats, 16 February 2005, http://wwwc.house.gov/international_relations/euhear.htm, accessed 26 May 2006.

13 Peter Brookes, "The Lifting of the EU Arms Embargo on China," testimony before the Senate Committee on Foreign Relations, March 16, 2005, http://foreign.senate.gov/hearings/2005/hrg050316p2.html, accessed 26 May 2006.

14 Republican Policy Committee Press Release: "Action Has Consequences for U.S. National Security," 4 February 2005, http://rpc.senate.gov, accessed 21 May 2006.

15 John C. Tkacik, "Washington Must Head Off European Arms Sales to China," in *Heritage Foundation Backgrounder*, no. 1739, (18 March 2004), pp. 1–6.

16 John C. Hulsman, "Prepared Statement" for the House Committee on International Relations, Subcommittee on Europe and Emerging Threats, 16 February 2005, http://wwwc.house.gov/international_relations/euhear.htm, accessed 26 May 2006.

17 David Shambaugh, "Don't Lift the Arms Embargo on China," *International Herald Tribune*, 23 February 2005.

18 See, for example, David Shambaugh, "The New Strategic Triangle: U.S. and European Reactions to China's Rise," *Washington Quarterly* (Summer 2005); David Shambaugh, "China and Europe: The Emerging Axis," *Current History* (September 2004); David Shambaugh, *European and American Approaches to China: Different Beds, Same Dreams?*, Sigur Center Asia Papers, No. 15 (Washington, D.C.: Sigur Center for Asian Studies, George Washington University, 2002).

19 Shambaugh, "The New Strategic Triangle," op. cit., pp. 7–23.

20 Bates Gill, *Lifting of the EU Arms Embargo on China*, testimony before the United States Senate Foreign Relations Committee, 16 March 2005, http://www.csis.org/media/csis/congress/ts050316gill.pdf, accessed 22 May 2006.

21 Bates Gill and Gudrun Wacker, eds., *China's Rise: Diverging U.S.–EU Approaches and Perceptions* (Berlin: Stiftung Wissenschaft und Politik, August 2005). See also, Bates Gill and Robin Niblett, "Diverging Paths Hurt U.S. and Europe," *International Herald Tribune*, 6 September 2005.

22 Gill, *Lifting of the EU Arms Embargo*, op. cit.

23 See, for example, Robin Niblett, *China, the EU, and the Transatlantic Alliance*, testimony before the U.S.–China Economic and Security Review Commission, 22 July 2005, http://www.uscc.gov/hearings/2005hearings, accessed 22 May 2006; Michael Yahuda, *Europe and America in Asia: Different Beds, Same Dreams*, Sigur Center Asia Papers no. 18 (Washington, D.C.: Sigur Center for Asian Studies, George Washington University, 2004), especially pp. 8–9. Robin Niblett was, until December 2006, Executive Vice President of the Center for Strategic and International Studies (CSIS), and Director of the CSIS Europe Program. He returned to London at that time to become Director of the Royal Institute of International Affairs (Chatham House). Michael Yahuda is Professor Emeritus of International Relations at the London School of Economics and Political Science and a Visiting Scholar with the Sigur Center for Asian Studies at George Washington University.

24 *Transatlantic Dialogue on China: Final Report*, report No. 43 (Washington, D. C.: Henry L. Stimson Center, February 2003).

25 David C. Gompert, François Godement, Evan S. Medeiros, James C. Mulvenon, *China on the Move: A Franco–American Analysis of Emerging Chinese Strategic Policies and*

their Consequences for the United States (Santa Monica: RAND, 2005), accessed at: http://www.rand.org/pubs/conf_proceedings/2005/RAND_CF199.sum.pdf.

26 Gill and Wacker, eds., *China's Rise,* op. cit.

27 U.S–China Economic and Security Review Commission, *Symposia on Transatlantic Perspectives on Economic and Security Relations with China*, 108th Cong., 2nd Sess. (Washington, D.C.: Government Printing Office, 19 January 2005), pp. iii and vi.

28 Daniel Fried, Assistant Secretary of State for European Affairs, "The United States and Europe: Addressing Global Challenges Together," Foreign Press Center Briefing, New York, New York, 19 September, 2006, http://fpc.state.gov/fpc/53527.htm, accessed 29 May 2006.

29 US Department of State Press Release, "State's Hill Urges Greater European Involvement in East Asia," 23 May 2005, http://hongkong.usconsulate.gov/uscn/state/2005/052301.htm, accessed 22 May 2006.

30 US Department of State Press Release, "U.S.–European Relations," 29 April 2006, http://www.state.gov/p/eur/rls/rm/65879.htm, accessed 23 May 2006.

31 Neil King and March Champion, "EU, U.S. Policy on China Converges on Key Issues," *Wall Street Journal*, 4 May 2006.

32 For an overview of US trade and economic concerns with China, see, for example, Office of the United States Trade Representative, *U.S.–China Trade Relations: Entering a New Phase of Greater Accountability and Enforcement*, February 2006, http://www.ustr.gov/assets/Document_Library/Reports_Publications/2006/asset_upload_file921_8938.pdf, accessed 30 May 2006; United States Department of the Treasury, *Report to Congress on International Economic and Exchange Rate Policies*, May 2006, especially pp. 27–32, http://www.treas.gov/offices/international-affairs/economic-exchange-rates/pdf/international_econ_exchange_rate.pdf, accessed 30 May 2006.

33 "China Is the Biggest Trade Challenge, Says Mandelson," *Europe Information Service*, 8 May 2006, http://0-global.factiva.com.library.lausys.georgetown.edu/aa/default.aspx?pp=print, accessed 30 May 2006.

34 "EU and China Reach Textile Deal," *BBC News,* 9 September 2005, http://newsvote.bbc.co.uk, accessed 30 May 2006. See also: "US and China sign textiles deal," *BBC News,* 8 November 2005, http://news.bbc.co.uk/1/hi/business/4416858.stm, accessed 30 May 2006.

35 David Lenard, "US, EU Take China to WTO on Auto Parts," *Asia Times*, 1 April 2006, http://www.atimes.com/atimes/China_Business/HD01Cb06.html, accessed 30 May 2006.

36 This section in part revises and builds upon earlier work by the author: Bates Gill and Gudrun Wacker, eds., *China's Rise*, op. cit.; Bates Gill, "The Strategic Dynamic of China–Europe–U.S. Relations and the Prospects for Regional Security and Development Cooperation,", presented at the Conference on Global Cooperation in Asia and Beyond: EU, US, and China Relations in Managing Regional Security and Development, Berlin, Germany, 14–15 October 2005.

37 From joint statement issued at the conclusion of the eighth EU–China summit. See "Joint Statement," 5 September 2005, accessed at: http://www.europa.eu.int/comm/external_relations/china/summit_0905/index.htm.

38 See Stanley Crossick, Fraser Cameron, and Axel Berkofsky, *EU–China Relations – Towards a Strategic Partnership* (Brussels: European Policy Centre, July 2005).

39 "Counterterrorism," accessed at the APEC website: http://www.apecsec.org.sg/content/apec/apec_groups/som_special_task_groups/counter_terrorism.html; "Memorandum of Understanding Between The Governments of the Member Countries of the Association of Southeast Asian Nations (ASEAN) And The Government of the People's Republic of China," 10 January 2004, at: http://www.aseansec.org/15647.htm visited on 15 February 2005; "Text of Joint Statement of EU–China Summit," 8 December 2004, published in Foreign Broadcast Information Service, EUP20041208000300.

14 China–EU–US relations

Shaping a constructive future

Ruan Zongze

The ancient Silk Road trading route has been transfigured. One no longer experiences a fatiguing caravan trip, but jet lag, when China and Europe as the two ancient civilizations in the East and West meet. China and the European Union (EU) are active in developing a future-oriented comprehensive and strategic partnership. The two sides have no confrontation on matters of fundamental interests, but share more and more common interests. The Chinese government has stated that: "There is no fundamental conflict of interest between China and the EU and neither side poses a threat to the other,"[1] and "the common ground between China and the EU far outweighs their disagreements."[2]

A prosperous future for China and Europe hinges on wisdom that can steer the course of their bilateral relations. They agreed to work for a comprehensive strategic partnership in 2003. The establishment of Sino-European strategic partnership relations indicates that bilateral relationship has entered a new era. Such a relationship means the two sides would develop bilateral ties in multiple areas from a long-term and strategic point of view. The domain of this relationship is comprehensive – concerning political, strategic, economic, cultural and social areas. No significant problem in any one area will disrupt the entire relationship, given that it is based on the principles of equality, mutual benefit, mutual respect and trust. Considerable interests 0n both sides have gelled around the specific forms of engagement that the two sides have developed.

China–EU–US dynamism is undergoing a dramatic transformation. As the major players in world affairs, China, the EU and the US are at different levels of development. Put another way, China is modernizing, while the European Union is post-modern and the United States is modernized. Recent years have witnessed the intensification of China's interaction with Europe and America. Generally speaking, Europe and America adopt different approaches towards China; the former follows the "liberal" approach, while the latter follows the "realist" approach. In the meantime, China pursues a forward-looking approach to both the EU and the US.

This chapter explores the various aspects of how China's respective relationships with, and policies toward, Europe and the United States are related with each other. How to understand the strategic partnership between China and the EU? Is there a clear line leading from visions and objectives via a common strategy to the means necessary for a credible implementation? Is China trying to "balance" against US "hegemony" by building up relations with Europe? How does China eye its relations with the US vis-à-vis the US policy towards China? How does China perceive the respective roles of each in international governance? How do China–EU–US relations interplay with each other?

Strategic partnership

Formal relations between China and the EU date back to 1975, when their diplomatic relations were established. A bilateral trade and investment agreement was concluded in 1985. Since then, an extensive network has been forged between China and the EU. Following its first long-term strategy concerning China–EU relations in 1995, the European Commission published a series of policy documents including *A Maturing Partnership: Shared Interests and Challenges in EU–China Relations* in 2003, which called for cooperation on questions of global governance and the promotion of global peace and stability and sustainable development. China's publishing of its first comprehensive policy paper on its relations with the EU in 2003 was perceived as a significant contribution to further deepening the ties. This policy paper stated that China was committed to "enhance China–EU all-round cooperation and promote a long-term and stable development of China–EU relations."[3]

Indeed, there are identical areas of Chinese objectives as well as EU objectives. China's objectives are:

- to promote a sound and steady development of China–EU political relations under the principles of mutual respect, mutual trust and seeking common ground while reserving differences, and contribute to world peace and stability;
- to deepen China–EU economic cooperation and trade under the principles of mutual benefit, reciprocity and consultation on an equal basis, and promote common development;
- to expand China–EU cultural and people-to-people exchanges under the principle of mutual emulation, common prosperity and complementarity, and promote cultural harmony and progress between the East and the West.[4]

At the same time, the main aims of the EU to build a comprehensive partnership with China were:

- to engage China further in the international community;
- to support China's transition to an open society; and
- to integrate China further into the global economy. To achieve these aims, the Commission hoped to upgrade the political dialogue, encourage China's interest in ASEM and Asian regional issues, and strike the right terms for China's accession to the WTO. The European Commission would also use the EU's experience and expertise to add value in assisting China's reform

process, and to add human rights, the environment and sustainable development to the agenda.[5]

- to raise the profile of the EU in China.

One of the distinctive features is that Chinese and European leaders exchange frequent visits each year, and the EU has become the number one trading partner of China since 2004. On the whole, future development of EU integration conforms to China's strategic interests. China has been supportive of the integration process of the EU. To some degree this was manifested by Chinese Premier Wen Jiabao's visit to the headquarters of the European Union on 1 May 2004, when the EU formally celebrated its largest ever expansion. Premier Wen held talks with European Commission (EC) President Romano Prodi, vowing to further consolidate and develop the all-around strategic partnership between China and the bloc.

The China–EU Summit is the highest level of the regular political dialogue mechanism between China and the EU. It serves as a platform for them to work together on their shared interests and explore ways to deal with differences and conflicts. Leaders from China and the EU have exchanged frequent visits. In September 2006, the 9th China–EU Summit was held in Helsinki, Finland. Chinese Premier Wen Jiabao, British Prime Minister Tony Blair, whose country was holding the EU presidency, and European Commission (EC) President Jose Manuel Barroso held talks and signed a series of cooperation agreements, including those on climate and space programmes. The summit like the previous ones injected "important impetus" into the development of the all-around strategic partnership between the two sides by confirming the agreement to move towards early negotiations on a new China–EU Framework Agreement with a view to concluding at an early date an agreement that will reflect the full breadth and depth of strategic partnership between China and the EU. During the summit, China and the EU also agreed to set up another regular dialogue mechanism – the vice ministerial-level strategic dialogue. The first such strategic dialogue was conducted in London in December 2005.

The Sino-European relationship has advanced tremendously since the 1990s as both sides have adopted a pragmatic attitude towards each other. To strengthen the ties with the European Union is an important component of China's foreign policy. Chinese Premier Wen Jiabao defines China's comprehensive strategic partnership with the EU in the following way: "By 'comprehensive', it means that the cooperation should be all-dimensional, wide-ranging and multi-layered. It covers economic, scientific, technological, political and cultural fields, contains both bilateral and multilateral levels, and is conducted by both governments and non-governmental groups. By 'strategic', it means that the cooperation should be long-term and stable, bearing on the larger picture of China–EU relations. It transcends the differences in ideology and social systems, and is not subjected to the impact of individual events that occur from time to time. By 'partnership', it means that the cooperation should be equal-footed, mutually beneficial and win-win. The two sides should base themselves on mutual respect and mutual trust, endeavour to expand converging interests and seek common ground on the major issues while shelving differences on the minor ones.[6] Such a strategic framework is meeting with success as China and the EU seek to profit from the extraordinary economic boom now under way in both regions.

The economic and trade linchpin

Clearly, economic interests have served as a major catalyst for a fruitful rapport between China, the world's largest emerging market in need of modern entrepreneurial expertise, and the EU, a sophisticated old hand in terms of corporate development, marketing and resource management.

Since the 1990s, the EU has made a breakthrough in internal integration and external expansion. The smooth launching of the euro, the historic eastward enlargement, the draft of the constitution and progress in formulating common foreign and defence policies have all gone beyond people's expectations. Now the EU represents some 455 million people and a combined GDP of €10 trillion, which is comparable with that of the United States. Although the prospect of the EU developing into a superpower is not yet clear, it will undoubtedly become one of the most decisive forces in the future world. The expansion of the EU offers greater potential for cooperation between China and the EU.

With a bilateral trade volume of US$177.3 billion, the EU remains China's top trading partner and China was the EU's second-biggest trading partner in 2005. The trade between the two sides remains robust. China–EU trade exceeded 200 billion dollars in 2006, according to statistics issued by China's customs authorities.

China–EU bilateral trade had outstanding improvement in trading structure, from such low-grade products of raw materials, light textiles and agricultural products to electromechanical products and high-tech products. Instead of cheap labour and low production costs, which used to be the main attractions for overseas investors, China is now upgrading its workforce and creating a more mature market. Such dynamics have fuelled the great expectation in the potential of bilateral trade with the further expansion of the Chinese market as a result of China's entry into the World Trade Organization (WTO) in 2001.

China's export of high-tech products to the EU increased greatly, surpassing the US as the first export market for China. Fast increasing trade promoted deep development of bilateral economic and trade cooperation. The EU remains the biggest technology provider and the fourth-largest investor in China. By the end of October 2005, China introduced 20,925 technologies from the EU with a contractual value of US$87.1 billion; the EU invested in 22,076 enterprises in China with a contractual value of US$84.7 billion and actual utilized investment was US$46.7 billion.

Besides endeavouring in economic cooperation with coastal areas of China, EU enterprises actively participated in China's "Western development" and "revitalization of the old industrial base of the Northeast". Some EU enterprises moved their production base and research and development centre to the above-mentioned areas, where cost of labour and land are less expensive. Meanwhile, a batch of leading Chinese enterprises, such as Huawei, ZTE, TCL and Haier reached out to invest in the EU and achieved progress.

In addition, China and the EU have made more progress in human exchange, scientific cooperation and cultural exchanges. There is also great interest in tourist travel after the EU countries were approved as tourist destinations for Chinese, assisted by the 2004 Tourism and Approved Destination Agreement. Over 50,000 EU citizens reside in China, and almost 3 million EU visitors came to China in 2005. The number of Chinese trips to the EU was about 674,000 in the same year. More significantly, some 170,000 Chinese students study in the EU. Highlighting the 2005 Sino-European high-tech cooperation is China's active participation in the Galileo satellite navigation system, a major European project. The two sides signed three application contracts, making China the first country outside Europe to join the Galileo Project in 2004.

Meanwhile, trade frictions are on the increase. At the beginning of the 1980s, the EU enjoyed a trade surplus with China. Nowadays, EU–China trade relations are marked by a sizeable and widening EU deficit with China, which reached around €78.5 billion in 2004, its largest trade deficit with any trade partner. China has become the EU's major anti-dumping target. The disagreement over textile imports in 2005 was just another case. The two sides eventually reached an agreement allowing Chinese textile exports to the EU to grow at specified rates. Though the number of disputed areas in the China–EU trade is "very small," China is concerned the disputes will continue to cause irritancies and fuel protectionist calls. Clearly, the EU uses administrative, technological and legal means such as anti-dumping, anti-subsidy, guarantee measures, protection measures and so on to force China to honour its commitments to the WTO and to erase the EU's massive trade deficit. The EU refuses to grant China's complete Market Economy Status and treats this issue just as a technical matter. Since the EU has granted Russia Market Economy Status, many Chinese scholars in economic research regard the EU's refusal as a great obstacle to counter China's rising economic clout.[7]

For the EU, the preoccupation is to strengthen itself and digest new member states. What happened in the referendum on the EU Charter in 2005 threw EU integration into a crisis – which may take years to regain the confidence of a comeback. One side effect, unfortunately, is the rise of protectionism in the EU. It hampers endeavours to further trade and business between China and the EU.

Stakeholder and partner

Having secured a strategic partnership with the European Union, Beijing is struggling to redefine its relations with Washington. In the first term of President George W. Bush, it appeared that Beijing and Washington agreed to characterize their relations as three Cs, referring to candid, constructive and cooperative relations. However, Washington appears to be becoming increasingly concerned that China's rise had received little consideration from the strategic planners, who continue to be more urgently focused on Iraq and the Middle East, particularly given the short-term stakes involved. By contrast, China has bolstered its ties with

Southeast Asia by expanding efforts to increase the sophistication of its foreign policy. China replaced America as the largest foreign trade partner for most countries in the region.

For years the United States has carried out a policy of "engagement" towards China. Washington has hedged its bets to be sure, by maintaining a robust military presence in the Asia-Pacific region through its alliance system to deter China from mounting a challenge. From the perspective of some in Washington, and particularly on Capitol Hill, China is eating America's lunch. Perhaps this sentiment is best exemplified by Robert Zoellick's "stakeholder" legacy. "Uncertainties about how China will use its power will lead the United States to hedge relations with China," observed Mr Zoellick, then Deputy Secretary of State, on 21 September 2005.[8] In fact, Washington never completely lost sight of its strategic focus on China. The past few years witnessed the US strengthening existing relations with its allies in the Asia-Pacific region such as Japan, and bringing India into its security network. Needless to say, the US has expanded US military capabilities in the Asia-Pacific area.

The complexity of Sino-American relations is reflected in the fact that bilateral ties are no longer a topic merely for diplomatic strategy discussions, but are intertwined with fundamental changes taking place within the two countries. Therefore one point of view is far from enough to describe the rich implications of the relationship. It requires analysis from a multitude of angles.

Perhaps more significantly, how to redefine this wide-ranging, complex relationship becomes a pressing issue. The challenge posed by this post-Cold War situation is that when a third party is not available to act as the buffer between Beijing and Washington, the two sides must resolve how to co-exist with each other and identify the other's position in its strategic manoeuvring, from a long-term point of view not attempted before. After all, this means China and the United States need to adapt to each other's presence. It also demands stronger management in actual execution to keep the differences and disputes under control and, under certain instances, reduce friction, cushion conflict and eliminate disruption.

What is most impressive about the recent summit between President Hu and Bush in Washington in April 2006 was that they tried to redefine their relations. In responding to the US call for a "stakeholder," Chinese President Hu said, China and the United States are not only "stakeholders," but also "constructive partners." It also demonstrated that China was taking the initiative to shape the long-term future of Sino-American relations.

Since the beginning of the twenty-first century, bilateral ties between China and the United States have made progress and are maturing in many ways. For a start, Sino-American relations have entered a comparatively long period of relatively steady development. Since the late 1980s and early 1990s, bilateral relations between the two countries have, for the first time, enjoyed four to five years of relatively stable development. On the whole, despite disputes and differences, Sino-American ties are advancing and cooperation in various areas is deepening, helping build a solid foundation for the next phase of development.

Strategic communication between the two countries has achieved unprecedented strengthening. China and the United States have maintained frequent, high-
level contact in recent years, with the leaders of both countries taking a few opportunities every year to meet and exchange ideas. More important, China and the US
have conducted two rounds of strategic talks since 2005. This high-level communication has enabled both sides to exchange views on major issues as they came up,
enhanced mutual strategic understanding and increased mutual trust while clearing
up questions. China and the United States beefed up cooperation at the regional
level, which is particularly prominent in pushing forward the six-party talks on the
Korean nuclear issue in recent years.

The continuous development of Sino-American economic and trade relations
has benefited both sides tremendously. This is the major driving force to bolster
bilateral ties. Of course, the two sides still have disputes over such issues as trade
imbalance, the renminbi exchange rate and intellectual property rights. But it
requires efforts by both countries to solve the problems. Even if they cannot be
solved overnight, the two sides still need to control and manage the disputes
through dialogue so the issues do not grow or get out of hand.

The Sino-American relationship is an irreconcilable match-up of a "you lose, I
win" paradigm and mentality. China's development does not necessarily translate
into the decline of the United States. In fact, while China makes headway in long-
term development, US economic growth is still the fastest in the developed world.
In the past 10 years or so, China joined the United States to become the "twin
engines" driving the growth of the world economy. China has developed under the
general framework of the current international system, which has kept a considerable space for China's development. As a leading builder of the current international system, the United States can benefit from the current international system
as much as China does by keeping it intact.

For the foreseeable future, the China–US relationship will generally remain
stable – yet also uncertain in some areas. China consistently adheres to seeking
cooperation on the issues of common concern while maintaining differing views
from the world's sole superpower in some areas of dispute. As David Shambaugh
observed,

> This complex relationship is currently characterized by substantial coopera-
> tion on bilateral, regional, and global issues. Yet, despite this tangible and
> positive cooperation, there remain evident suspicions and distrust of the
> other's motives and actions … Both sides are engaging to a significant extent,
> yet are hedging against the possibility of a deterioration of ties. Looking to the
> future, the Sino-American relationship is likely to continue to exhibit these
> paradoxical features.[9]

While it is true that the regional security structure based on the US-centric alliance
system has weakened somewhat in the past two decades, the cause of this, however,
has been regional states' decreasing willingness to remain US protectorates, and not
the rise of China. Indeed, regional states' choice reflects, at least partly, their rather

optimistic view of the impact of China's rise on their security. The danger is that the United States may foreclose the possibility that a reunified, prosperous, open and democratic China can become its partner in maintaining peace and stability in East Asia and the world.

Yet, as long as the Taiwan question is not resolved peacefully, there is a real possibility that the United States and China could clash. But even on this issue, there is hope for optimism. Hardliners inside the United States argue that China's reunification, and even China's growth, represents a threat to US interests. They believe that China will inevitably challenge US primacy once it becomes strong enough, thus the US has to do whatever it takes to prevent China from becoming more powerful and achieving reunification.

But more sober voices are increasingly heard, as former US Deputy Secretary of State Robert Zoellick said, before the House of Representatives' International Relations Committee, "Taiwan independence means war."[10] With China continuing its economic growth and political reform, coupled with robust deterrence from the mainland, there is a real possibility for peaceful reunification between the two sides across the Taiwan Straits. It is indeed Washington's interest to end its long-standing "strategic ambiguity" on the Taiwan issue by openly opposing Taiwan independence, and supporting peaceful reunification. Or the US would be drawn into a war between the mainland and the island.[11] Therefore, the United States may take a more relaxed view toward the Taiwan question if it does not consider Taiwan's eventual reunification with the mainland as detrimental to US interests. If so, the US and China can indeed reach an accommodative modus vivendi. Perhaps more notably, recently Beijing and Washington have reached an understanding on maintaining peace and stability across the Taiwan Strait. The US side clearly expressed its opposition to unilaterally changing the status quo. And "Taiwan independence" is exactly what threatens the status quo in the region.

In China, there is a widely shared view that, so long as the United States refrains from jeopardizing China's core national interests, China has largely been content with remaining a regional power, with the US as the ultimate offshore balancer. In fact, China has affirmed that it welcomes the "constructive presence" of the US in the region. To put it differently, should Washington behave like a "benign hegemon," Beijing sees no interest in balancing the US.

No longer a "great game"

The end of the Cold War with the demise of the Soviet Union and the Warsaw Pact led to the end of the "great game" paradigm. *Realpolitik* means steering clear of zero-sum power games. As heavyweight players, China, the EU and the US bear a responsibility together to promote world peace and prosperity since the relations are globally influential. How a modernizing China interacts with a post-modern EU and a modernized America remains to be seen. Clearly there are areas of divergence and convergence, which may guide relations in the coming years.

With respect to the future international order, both China and the EU would like to see a multipolar world, while the US prefers to consolidate its status as the sole superpower as long as possible. China's road of peaceful development is similar to the peaceful rise of the EU since WWII. In the long-term goal, China's modernization process and the EU's integration tally with the trend of multipolarization. Both China and the EU foresee the prospects of the other's growth and keep their eyes on actively developing relations between each other in the future. As new balancing forces of the world, China and the EU have great attraction to each other. The two sides not only strive to enrich and strengthen their strategic relationship, but also dedicate themselves to promoting the process of multipolarization in the world, having more room for flexibility in the international arena and raising their international standing. China and the EU have found the common ground for establishing a more balanced international order on the practical and effective multilateral basis,[12] though there are different views inside the EU, and some countries intend to underplay this notion avoiding offending the United States. For some in Washington, nevertheless, the intensification of China–EU relations seems to create a multipolar world to counterbalance US influence. To balance American hegemony is not, and will not be, the basis for China–EU relations. As the matter of fact, most Chinese and Europeans does not want to weaken their relations with the US. Transatlantic ties and China–US relations are making new headway simultaneously.

With respect to global governance, both China and the EU are in favour of multilateralism and stress the enhancement of the role of the United Nations and the peaceful settlement of international disputes, while the US is ready to use unilateralism if necessary. China and the EU share broad common interests in cooperating in the areas of anti-terrorism, non-proliferation of weapons of mass destruction, cracking down on cross-border crime, poverty relief, environmental protection and sustainable development. China vows to enhance political dialogue and cooperation in all fields with the EU. Many scholars in China tend to view the current setback of the EU integration efforts as a temporary twist and turn, and believe it will steadily move forward to a "global role."[13] The EU regards China more as an opportunity than a challenge, and less as a threat than is the case in the United States. China today also believes the world is moving toward a more civilized era in which the probability of a global war is largely marginal. China's growing confidence in its capability to shape its environment, and belief that the world is getting less dangerous have profound implications for China's diplomatic conduct. Multilateralism, mutually beneficial cooperation and the sprit of inclusiveness is held in realizing security and prosperity and in building a harmonious world. In this respect, the EU is a valuable partner to work with.

Meanwhile, the US and EU share substantial concerns about the implications of China's rise. For them, China's rise poses a number of fundamental challenges. These include the question of how to manage the growing resource demands and environmental impact of a rapidly rising China within a global system, how to cope with the economic consequences of China's rise, which affect employment and trade patterns across the globe. The underlying debate about China in European capitals and Washington is different though. The United States worries over both the economic and military implications of a rising China, while the European countries are more concerned about China's economic clout. Not surprisingly, the United States and the Europeans initiated a strategic dialogue about how to deal with a rising China in 2005 for the first time.

It goes without saying that the EU and the US share identical values and ideology, while there is a wide value gap between China and the EU as well as the US. The future world, however, is no longer defined by ideology. Put succinctly, the optimism that identical ideology means conflict-free relations is not warranted. A growing American concern over the potential challenge from the EU is a wake-up call though. Instead shared interests will definitely play an increasing part in shaping the relations among major powers. China does not necessarily share the same values with either the EU or the US, but does share ever-growing and wide-ranging common interests.

There is a domestic dimension affecting the relations among the three. It is obvious that the EU as a union of sovereign nations rests its decision-making process on capitals such as London, Paris, Berlin and Warsaw – while Brussels manages to compete with its members' policy-making influence. The division of labour between the White House, Congress and Pentagon has complicated the United States' policy making, so to speak. China is also increasingly becoming vulnerable to the competing influences of more diversified interests sectors in China. For example, the Foreign Ministry has to reluctantly compromise its interests with other increasingly influential actors, like the Ministry of Commerce and some large companies, in formulating its policy.

For better or for worse, the implication of China–US relations for China–EU relations is evident. The United States is not only a stimulus or a restraint for China and the EU to get strategically closer, but also the most primary external factor to affect the China–EU strategic partnership. For some Chinese analysts, both China and the EU, as new emerging forces, are facing the pressure of US sole supremacy. They are getting closer strategically and developing substantial cooperation. Both of them advocate multilateralism to pin down US unilateralism, which is in keeping with the objective law of development of international relations. On the other hand, the EU is still in the long course of completely ridding itself of its dependence on the US and realizing its complete political and security independence.[14]

This complex triangular relationship is manifested by the arms embargo issue. There has been a prolonged debate about the European Union lifting its embargo on arms exports to the Chinese military. Washington cut into the debate by lobbying vehemently against the move, which indicates that China–EU relations are causing increasing uneasiness in Washington. The arms embargo issue turned out to be a game that the US is manipulating to put pressure on the EU and check China, to undermine relations between China and the EU. Though the clash between the EU and the US on the issue of lifting the arms embargo on China is much less fierce than that on the issue of the Iraq war in 2003, the impact of the interaction on triangular relations is still far-reaching.[15]

China may have underestimated the complicated dimension transatlantic ties. Most of the EU countries agree that the embargo is out of date and should be repealed and replaced by the EU's own Code of Conduct for arms sales. However, it seems that it is far more difficult to reach a solution on lifting the arms embargo very soon.

In addition, the enlargement of the EU also makes it vulnerable to the intervention of the US. The Franco-German axis has largely been undercut since more independent-minded countries have come aboard. The division of Old and New Europe has become more visible then ever. From the perspective of some European capitals, the US no longer favours European integration as it used to do during the Cold War. Even worse, the tolerance, diversity and sustainable development embodied in the integration of the EU, the first effort in the world to establish "global consensus," is more suitable for the future world than the American model. Instead Washington expressed concerns that a united, stronger EU is likely to become a counterweight against the United States in the world arena. It was particularly true when "old Europe" said "no" to Washington over the Iraq war. The CFSP and autonomous European capabilities will test the resolve of Europe to deliver the newly gained resources to make the crucial step from wishful thinking to reality. However, China will be better off not involving itself with these disputes between the two sides of the Atlantic.

New opportunities

To achieve the ambitious goal of building an affluent society with the minimum of disruption, Beijing is intent on securing smooth and productive relations with the EU and the US in particular. Such a consideration has also become a fabric of China's diplomacy towards both the EU and the US. China is ready to develop China–EU and China–US relations on the basis of mutual respect, equality and mutual benefit and build an even closer partnership.

One of the approaches is to identify and widen the scope of cooperation. Indeed, ample opportunities exist for a constructive relationship among China, the EU and the United States. While most people recognize China as a formidable powerhouse, less appreciated is the fact that China buys as much as it sells. China not only ranked fourth in exports globally, but was also the third-largest importer in 2004. Since China's accession into the WTO, strong domestic demand and market opening-up has led to explosive growth in trade. On average imports have grown almost as rapidly as exports for the past decade. China's growing appetite for foreign goods, coupled with the upcoming 2008 Summer Olympics in Beijing and the 2010 World Expo in Shanghai, would provide greater opportunities for business people from the US and the EU. The new Chinese five-year programme adopted in March 2006 predicts annual growth at 7.5 per cent until 2010. As China maintains its momentum of rapid economic growth, its annual imports will keep on increasing and possibly reach US$1 trillion by 2020 as against 2004's figure of US$500 billion. Both the EU and the US are certainly in a better position to take advantage of extensive networks in China, to maximize the benefit by bolstering market access and investment opportunities.

In the meantime, the EU's enlargement from 15 to 25 becomes an enormous impetus to relations with China. The new members mainly from Central Europe kept traditionally friendly relations with China. They can become a bridge between the EU and China. The new members are undergoing huge transformations with respect to their economy and social changes, which are similar to those undertaken in China. This will contribute to an understanding of China's transformation by the EU as whole.

There are a couple of issues that are high on the agenda in the EU and the US, such as human rights and democracy. China's views on these are of special interest to them. The last three decades brought about the most rapid progress of personal freedom and human rights in modern Chinese history. Indeed, left to the natural course of events, the further progress of the Chinese people's social and political well-being is more likely than otherwise, as China continues to move forward to further economic reform.

Climate change and other environment problems, scarcity of energy resources, global terrorism, and the proliferation of weapons of mass destruction know no border – and hence demand transnational cooperation. There is still more potential room for cooperation in areas such as finance, energy, environment, agriculture, education and rural development. It is in line with their mutual interests to continue the positive policy towards each other and deal with differences with a pragmatic attitude. Undoubtedly, in a world of accelerated globalization, the desire between them to seek common ground and cooperation can only get stronger. Consultation instead of confrontation and dialogue instead of unilateral action provide a good mechanism for the further development of China–EU–US relations. The following areas should be identified for cooperation in this respect:

- maintaining the stability of the international system;
- promoting and contributing to the growth of the world economy;
- access to energy resources and ensuring the security of sea links;
- non-proliferation of WMD;
- environment protection and climate change;
- public health and infectious diseases such as avian flu.

Conclusion

Crucial to Beijing's relations with the rest of the world is the concept of *heping fazhan* ("the peaceful development"). It underscores the fact that far from hurting other nations, China's new-found pre-eminence would bring them sizeable gains. Already China is an indispensable partner for any other country interested in prosperity and peace. The world will look to China with increased interest and anticipation as it develops and implements policies on sustainable development. China's ever-growing interplay with the EU and the US is a reflection of this new paradigm.

Beijing today views itself as a growing power, with limited but increasingly significant capacity in shaping the setting in which it lives. It, however, remains a pressing task for China to make the outside world embrace it as a rapidly rising power. The ideas of China's current strategy are underpinned by the belief that a more cooperative and accommodative China will best serve its interests. It is in China's interests to stick to its basic policy of reform and opening-up and will honour its commitments to the WTO made upon entry into the global trading body. Beijing will continue to improve its foreign-related economic structures, strengthen the protection of intellectual property rights, foster a stable and transparent foreign-related economic management system, create a fair and foreseeable legal environment, and raise the level of freedom and convenience for trade and investment so as to create a better environment for investment. Above all, China will stick to the policies of building a harmonious society internally and a harmonious world externally.

China, the EU and US definitely share a multitude of interests in global governance and in fighting non-traditional threats. Beijing is ready to work with both Brussels and Washington to expand the shared interests and address common concerns. A stable and growing relationship is seen as crucial to nurturing a congenial global climate where China, the EU and US can build up their economic prowess.

A factor that will potentially have the most profound implication for China–EU–US triangular relations is how the United States eyes China's rise, how it responds, how the EU reacts to the US policy, and how China responds to the policy pursued by both the EU and the US vis-à-vis China. The reconfiguration of power in the world has not been as dramatic as many had perceived. The US will remain the only superpower in the decades to come. China–EU relations are not exclusive in nature, and the strategic partnership is by no means a military one. Instead both China and the EU are keen to forge an even closer tie with the US in order to contribute to stability and prosperity in the world.

China's relationship with both the EU and the US is immensely important due to its global impact. China, the United States and the European Union have the most powerful and dynamic economies in the world. This gives them the capability to shape the future world. It's sensible to recognize that the uncertainties are quite substantial. Failure to handle them properly would do a lot of harm to the mutual trust among them. Cooperation and trust are absolutely essential for a constructive relationship among China, the EU and the US. What they need is a common and durable vision, which will put their long-term relations on the right track to the future.

Notes

1   "China's EU Policy Paper," 13 October 2003, http://www.fmprc.gov.cn/eng/wjb/zzjg/xos/dqzzywt/t27708.htm.
2   Ibid.
3   Ibid.
4   Ibid.
5   "Report on the Implementation of the Communication Building a Comprehensive Partnership with China", http://www.delchn.cec.eu.int/en/eu_and_china/Partnership_China.htm.

6 Wen Jiabao, "Jiji fazhan zhongguo tong oumeng de quanmian zhanlue huoban guanxi" [Vigorously Promoting Comprehensive Strategic Partnership Between China and European Union], speech at the China–EU Investment and Trade Forum, Brussels, in *Renmin Ribao* [People's Daily], 7 May 2004.

7 Li Hua, "For More Fruitful China–EU Economic Relations," available at http://www.ciis.org.cn/item/2005-11-15/51182.html.

8 Robert B. Zoellick, "Whither China: From Membership to Responsibility?" Remarks to National Committee on US–China Relations, 21 September 2005, New York, available at: http://www.ncuscr.org/articlesandspeeches/Zoellick.htm.

9 David Shambaugh, "Asia in Transition: The Evolving Regional Order", in *Current History*, April 2006, p. 156.

10 "Mei fu gou wu qing jing gao shuo 'Taiwan du li' yi wei zhe zhanzheng," [US Deputy Secretary of State warns "Taiwan independence" means war], in *Renmin Ribao* [The People's Daily], 12 May 2006.

11 "Don't Sell weapons to Taiwan, US urged", People's Daily Online, http://English.people.com.cn/20065/12.

12 Huo Zhengde, "On China–EU Strategic Relationship," http://www.ciis.org.cn/item/2005-04-07/50919.html.

13 Xin Hua, "Oumeng: cuozhe yu fansi" [EU: Frustrations and Reflections] in *Guoji wenti yaujiu* [International Studies] No. 3 (2006), p. 53.

14 See Hou Zhengde, op. cit.

15 See Hou Zhengde, op. cit.

Part VII

Conclusion and outlook

15 From honeymoon to marriage

Prospects for the China–Europe relationship

David Shambaugh, Eberhard Sandschneider and Zhou Hong

The China–Europe relationship has traversed a long and complicated history. When the then European Community of nine members formally established diplomatic relations with the People's Republic of China in 1975, the relationship was a minor shadow of what it has become today (see Appendix I: Chronology of Relations). Over three decades the relationship has grown to be both extensive and intensive. Consider some examples.

Negligible trade and investment has grown more than forty-fold to the astonishing point of Europe being China's number one trading partner, while China ranks second for Europe. Total two-way trade topped €260 billion in 2006. Europe has also become the largest source of technology and equipment transfer to China, transferring a total of 22,855 "technological items" to China by June 2006.[1] Extensive scientific collaboration also takes place, including energy and space cooperation. In the field of education, there are now more Chinese students (170,000) studying in European institutions of higher education – more than anywhere else in the world. Exchanges between a broad range of European political parties and the Chinese Communist Party (CCP) take place regularly,[2] as the CCP has long been interested in (and has assiduously studied) the experiences of European social democratic parties.[3]

From minimal official interaction, the diplomatic relationship is now broad and deep. This entails annual summits with the EU Presidency, EU Troika Foreign Ministers, and individually with the main member states. Twenty-two sectoral dialogues take place between the European Commission officials and Chinese ministries annually to discuss detailed areas of collaboration,[4] while candidly discussing differences in areas such as human rights. Similar interactions occur bilaterally between China and EU member states. The two sides also collaborate extensively on a range of international issues in the United Nations and other contexts. In 2003 the EU and China proclaimed a "comprehensive strategic partnership." In a May 2004 speech in Brussels, Chinese Premier Wen Jiabao defined the meaning of this partnership:

> It is a shared view of the two sides to work for a comprehensive strategic partnership. By "comprehensive," it means that the cooperation should be all-dimensional, wide-ranging and multi-layered. It covers economic, scientific,

technological, political and cultural fields, contains both bilateral and multilateral levels, and is conducted by both governments and non-governmental groups. By "strategic," it means that the cooperation should be long-term and stable, bearing on the larger picture of China–EU relations. It transcends the differences in ideology and social systems, and is not subjected to the impact of individual events that occur from time to time. By "partnership," it means that the cooperation should be on equal footing, mutually beneficial and win-win.[5]

Beijing has also agreed individual "strategic partnerships" with France, Germany, and the UK.

China is also a significant recipient of European Union overseas "cooperation assistance" (external aid) – with the EU spending €250 million on such cooperation projects during the four-year period 2002–6.[6] In January 2007, when European Commissioner for External Relations Benita Ferrero-Waldner visited Beijing to launch negotiations on a new comprehensive China–EU "Partnership and Cooperation Agreement" (PCA),[7] further agreements were reached totalling €62.6 million in support of a Europe–China School of Law at Tsinghua University, the EU–China Project on the Protection of Intellectual Property, and the Europe–China Business Management Training Project. European foreign direct investment into China has also been substantial, and has supplemented cooperation assistance. According to Chinese sources, by the end of 2006 the EU has invested in 24,033 projects in China, with a contractual value of $92.8 billion and actual realized investment of $50.56 billion.[8]

The foregoing chapters in this volume offer further testimony to these and other areas in this wide-ranging relationship. While the relationship has developed dramatically since establishment of formal relations in 1975, the state of relations today is even more astonishing and impressive when one considers that it is really only since 1995 that it has really blossomed. Prior to that time the relationship was beholden to broader international forces – particularly the Cold War and Sino-Soviet antagonism. China–Europe relations were predominantly derivative of these broader factors. This all began to change, though, around 1995, when three events occurred:

- the EU dropped all sanctions (except military arms sales) dating from the 4 June 1989 incident in Beijing;
- EU and Chinese relations with post-Soviet Russia had become fully normalized;
- the European Commission unveiled the first of its several subsequent policy papers (Communications) on China.[9]

More generally, six other broad factors contributed to the post-1995 surge in the relationship:

- the limiting effects of the Cold War passed and the relationship could finally begin to develop on its own, free of the shadow and influence of the US–Soviet rivalry;

- there is hardly any Taiwan lobby in Europe, as in the United States, to influence the public and politicians – and there is no "Taiwan issue" between European governments and China, as all faithfully subscribe to the "One China Principle";
- Europe has no military presence and few security interests in East Asia (unlike the United States);
- there existed a considerable (but not total) identity of views between Beijing and Brussels concerning the desired nature of the international order and system;
- there exist great complementarities of commercial and economic interests;
- the China strategy/policy mapped out by the European Commission in several policy documents between 1995–2006 offered a benign view of China's rise and identified a range of areas for collaboration.

Taken together, these factors collectively influenced the Sino-European relationship beginning in the mid-1990s and contributed to its dramatic growth over the past decade. The preceding chapters in this volume further illustrate the parameters of development in the relationship during this time.

But what about the future? How are China–Europe relations likely to develop? What are the key variables that will affect the evolution of the relationship going forward?

Exploring the future of China–Europe relations

While the relationship between China and Europe has developed remarkably and broadly in a relatively short period of time, with concomitant enthusiasm being expressed by both sides, it now seems that the relationship may be passing from the "honeymoon" phase into the "marriage" phase – where both parties are beginning to realize the complexities of the relationship, the fact that they do not see identically on many issues, that outside factors and actors contribute to shaping the relationship, but that mutual areas of common interest and cooperation remain substantial and dominant.

The Chinese perspective

During 2006, especially in the second half of the year, the debates over "China's Rise" suddenly heated up in Europe. These debates, carried out in Brussels and also in some major European capitals, led to less favourable publicity about China than previously. Protectionist pressures in European industries adversely affected by the competition from Chinese companies, human rights activists, some parliamentarians, international NGOs operating in Africa, Taiwan sympathizers, and a few China specialists in Europe joined forces in arguing for stronger and more confrontational policies on the part of the European Union toward China.

Such rising intra-European criticisms of China were further reflected, to some extent, in the European Commission's twin "Communication" documents released on 24 October 2006: *China–Europe: Closer Partners, Growing Responsibilities*

(Appendix II) and a separate trade policy paper entitled *Competition and Partnership: A Policy for EU–China Trade and Investment.*[10] These two policy papers were both confirmed by the European Council on 11 December 2006, after some revisions.[11] The documents aroused strong responses on China's part, both from official sources and from European specialists in China, and thus started the first year of the fourth decade of China–Europe relations in bumpy fashion.

After some intensive exchanges on different levels (official diplomacy as well as Track 1½ and Track 2), the Chinese and European sides agreed to restart their negotiations for a new Framework Agreement, thus demonstrating that the new tone expressed in the Communication would not compromise these important negotiations.[12] The day before the talks opened in Beijing, Dr Volker Stanzel, the German ambassador to China (which currently holds the EU presidency), told the news media in Beijing that the EU really wanted to have an "internationally successful China as a partner."[13] By the time China's Foreign Minister Li Zhaoxing and the EU Commissioner for External Relations and Neighbourhood Policy, Benita Ferrero-Waldner, were ready to meet the media in Beijing, both appeared to be positive about the future of China–EU relations. Ferrero-Waldner spoke glowingly about the nature of EU–China relations, saying in Beijing, "Twenty years ago, we were only trade partners, but now we are strategic partners, which means broader and deeper cooperation."[14] Chinese Foreign Minister Li Zhaoxing echoed his European counterpart's description, "China and the EU are not only trading partners, but all-round strategic partners." He further argued that the EU and China "share broad common interests and common positions," and their joint efforts will "be conducive to world peace and common development."[15] Indeed, in addition to trade, the new PCA will cover a wide range of fields for cooperation between China and the EU – including agriculture, transportation, customs, education, science, information, environment and energy, counter-terrorism, as well as security, political dialogues and human rights.

The question now is whether this trend will remain smooth, leading towards better, deeper, broader cooperation between the two parties – or whether the relationship may be subject to changes depending on various predictable and unpredictable variables. In order to forecast or project the future development of Sino-European relations, several variables have to be taken into consideration:

Variable 1: Internal developments of each of the two partners. Both China and the EU are facing great transformations at home. While China finds itself in the midst of building institutions in almost all sectors at different levels to cope with rapid economic growth, together with coping with social challenges such as urbanization, ageing, social stratification, environmental degradation, greater participation by citizens in public policy and decision-making, the EU is also facing institutional as well as normative adjustments in its unprecedented endeavour to build a constitutional polity based on an enlarged common market and diversified populace. While seemingly very different tasks, there actually exist similarities: both are undergoing institutional reforms, albeit incrementally, and both are adjusting their long-established public policies.

The pending issue is whether there are misperceptions and whether strategic mutual trust exits. The EU and China have already established high-level communication and strategic dialogues. However, the European Commission attempted to acquire "more legitimacy" in dealing with China issues starting in May 2006 by inviting a variety of interest groups to offer their opinions and input into the policy formation process. This has the danger of shaking the foundation of mutual strategic trust already established. The setback in the failure to adopt a European Constitution, and diversified national interests involved in the foreign policy-making of the EU, may also be detrimental to the highly strategic nature of EU–China relations. For the Chinese side, the difficulties posed by the issues of lifting the arms embargo and granting Market Economy Status have also attracted more public attention in China, forming a potential pressure on the government and at least contributing to the current complications in bilateral relations.

Variable 2: Outside pressures from the United States and/or globalization. The influence of the US and the differences between the EU and China's development models in an increasingly globalized world undoubtedly put pressure on China–EU relations. The US role in the issue of the arms embargo has already been discussed in great depth and neither China nor the EU are truly optimistic about a rapid solution to the problem.[16] Although there are suggestions that Beijing should focus on Washington for the resolution of the issue, while Europeans use their internal decision-making procedures as an excuse, both sides are fully aware that the issue could become a potential "time bomb" in the bilateral relationship, a perfect example of mistrust contributing to a deterioration of relations. To be sure, if the time bomb blows, it will not only affect one or two parties.

The speed of globalization and the slowness to adjust by the European "welfare states" could be another trap for cooperation between the EU and China. The Europeans have already started criticizing China as the major source of pollution, as using child labour, neglecting basic labour standards, dumping cheap products on the European market, and threatening job security in some sectors in the EU. In other words, many Europeans have benefited from globalization, while many others suffer. If the trend of globalization proved to be too fast for the national welfare states in Europe to cope with, the possibility exists that China, like the US, could be held responsible for the job losses and welfare declines.

Variable 3: The ability of political leaders to make policy adjustments. The leaderships and their visions in the past have served as a very important, sometimes determining, element for the development of the China–EU relationship. At this point, both Chinese and European leaders are thinking strategically and it is a good sign for the relationship. The Chinese, in their traditional way, recommend high-level communications and strategic thinking to lead the trend of bilateral relations. As Chinese Foreign Minister Li Zhaoxing noted, "We should continue to increase political dialogue to enhance mutual trust, and properly handle any differences that arise between the two sides."[17] The Europeans, on the other hand, suggest diverting attention away from home to global issues. When German Ambassador to China Volker Stanzel interpreted the "strategic partnership" as partners who address "global challenges," and China as a partner with whom the EU can "together solve global problems,"[18] he was echoing the policy of some major European strategists.

Chinese Premier Wen Jiabao discussed China–EU relations in a strategic fashion: he told Chinese and European business leaders during the Seventh EU–China Summit that the first principle for China–EU relations should be mutual trust, and this includes respecting each other's choice of development model, transcending ideology and differences in social systems improving understanding; the second principle should be tending to each other's interests while respecting equality and mutual benefit in competition; the third principle should be mutual coexistence and not letting differences disturb the overall relationship; and the fourth principle should be fostering each other's comparative advantages, learning from each other, and prospering together.[19]

The European perspective

There exists a great deal of satisfaction among European governments and within the EU bureaucracy in Brussels that the China–Europe relationship is both a high-priority relationship and it has developed very smoothly and thoroughly over the past decade, and that there exists substantial convergence between the two sides on a wide range of bilateral and international issues. Recognizing this sense of overall satisfaction, it is also evident that beginning around 2005–6 the European side began to recognize both the complexities of the rapidly-developing relationship as well as a number of differences of perspective and policy. While some of these differences had existed for some time in some quarters, they had perhaps not been widely shared across Europe nor articulated very clearly by the EU. The release in October 2006 of the European Commission's latest Communication on China and the accompanying policy paper on EU–China trade and investment, signalled and made explicit many of the concerns about China that had been bubbling beneath the surface in Europe. In the Communication, for the first time in such a policy document, the European Commission made a number of requests of China:[20]

- "open its markets and ensure fair market competition";
- "reduce and eliminate trade and non-tariff barriers";
- "level the [commercial] playing field";
- "fully implement WTO obligations";
- "better protect intellectual property rights";
- "end forced technology transfers";
- "stop granting prohibited subsidies";
- "work on clean energy technologies";
- "be a more active and responsible energy partner";
- "ensure balance in science and technology cooperation";
- "[recognize] the international responsibilities commensurate to its economic importance and role as a permanent member of the UN Security Council";
- "better protect human rights";
- "[ensure] more accountable government";

- be more "results oriented with higher quality exchanges and concrete results" in the human rights dialogue;
- ratify the UN Covenant on Civil and Political Rights;
- enter into formal dialogue with the EU and "improve transparency" concerning aid policies in Africa;
- "maintain peace and stability in the Taiwan Strait";
- improve "transparency on military expenditures and objectives";
- "comply with all non-proliferation and disarmament treaties";
- "strengthen export controls of WMD-related materials.

These requests gave the 2006 Communication a harder edge than any of its predecessors, but it also reflected the new sobriety in Europe (and particularly in Brussels) concerning certain aspects of China's policies and behaviour. The European Council ratified the Communication at its meeting on 11 December 2006, and produced its own 23-point list of observations and concerns about the relationship (Appendix III).[21]

These documents all caused consternation on the Chinese side, who had grown accustomed to the optimistic tone of previous Communications. Some notable Chinese Europe Watchers accused Brussels of adopting confrontational or "containment" policies similar to what some Chinese perceive from the United States. While such accusations are absurd, as neither the EU nor the United States seeks to contain China, nor could they if they desired to do so, they do indicate the surprise that Beijing felt over the tougher language in the new Communication. The Chinese reactions are also a useful reminder of how sensitive and defensive Beijing can be when publicly criticized. Privately, Chinese Foreign Ministry officials apparently assured their official European counterparts that they "understood" European concerns and were not overly alarmed by the tone or the substance of the Communication.[22] The Chinese decision to move ahead with the new Framework negotiations, and the warm reception given EU External Relations Commissioner Ferrero-Waldner in Beijing, are perhaps indicative of the more pragmatic official reaction.

Looking to the future, what variables will likely shape EU policy towards China? Seven sets of variables can be identified.

The first is the impact of trade on the European economies and workforce. With an EU trade deficit with China in excess of €150 billion in 2006, high unemployment rates in several countries (especially France, Germany, and Italy), hollowed-out tertiary industries (particularly in the Mediterranean countries), and relative lack of competitiveness in the "New 12" Central European member states, European economies are increasingly feeling the "China factor." Thus far, it has not got the political traction that it has in the United States, but voices of concern and protectionism can be heard across the continent. European Trade Commissioner Peter Mandelson has publicly indicated, on a number of occasions, that these economic concerns can quickly snowball and possibly have a series of negative consequences – economically and politically.

The second is the degree of Chinese responsiveness to the numerous issues of concern noted above in the 2006 Communication. These are not demands, but they are more than "markers." They are serious requests put forward by the European side, in the spirit of partnership, to advance the China–Europe relationship. To be sure, China has its requests too – notably lifting the arms embargo and granting of Market Economy Status – that the EU needs to take seriously and be responsive to. Candour is a good indicator of a mature relationship. So is responsiveness to each other's concerns. China would be wise not to dismiss, ignore, or otherwise be unresponsive to these genuine concerns put forward by the EU (individual member states have similarly put forward their own sets of concerns to China).

The third variable concerns relations between the EU member states and the European Commission and Council, and between the European Parliament and the Commission/Council. Prior to the release of the 2006 Communication on China it was apparent that civil society, the China expert community, and NGOs in several member states were unsettled and discontent with the European Commission's ambitious and optimistic view of China. Many accused the Commission of being naïve. To be sure, the Commission, via its various Communications, evinced a positive – even visionary – view of EU–China relations. This vision and articulation of policy was, in fact, absent from other member states, which just seemed to be pursuing their own bilateral (and largely commercial) relationships with China – absent a strategic vision or explicit policy framework. The manner in which the EU Commission and Council (mis)handled the arms embargo issue, creating an intra-European and transatlantic policy fiasco, only emboldened the critics of Brussels' China policy. The mishandling was due, in large part, to the Schroeder–Chirac partnership and the fact that they had gown accustomed to being the "motor" of the EU, dictating the agenda and setting the pace for EU decisions.[23] In this case, the two leaders had got way out ahead of other member states and had failed to consult either within the EU or across the Atlantic with Washington. It seems that the European Commission seriously reflected on this subterranean discontent between 2004–6, undertook a rethinking of the relationship and a reexamination of Europe's interests, and incorporated its findings in the new 2006 Communication. This, it would be assumed, will better position the Commission and Council with the member states, but also with voices heard in the European Parliament. China's "free ride" may be over, and the relationship seems to have left its "honeymoon" phase and entered the hard slog of a complex marriage.

A fourth factor that will shape Europe's policy towards, and relations with, China will be the pace and scope of internal reforms in China. The European Union has invested heavily – politically, financially, and rhetorically – in assisting China in a wide range of reforms. In fact, it can be argued that this has been the *core* of the EU's approach to China and what sets the EU apart from the United States and other nations in its dealings with China. The EU (primarily Brussels) has viewed China primarily through the prism of a developing country and transitional nation – in the midst of multiple reforms aimed at marketizing the economy, globalizing the society, and pluralizing the polity. In these reforms, Europeans believe they have much to share with China – given their own histories as welfare states and, more recently, the transition from socialist systems in Central Europe.

This orientation differs markedly from the American approach to the "rise of China" – as Americans tend to be exclusively concerned about the *external* manifestations of China's rise, while Europeans seem more concerned about its *internal* conditions.[24] A reading of the EU Communications on China published since 1995 and an examination of the extensive "cooperation projects" undertaken by the EU in China, and the many training programmes mounted in many European member states for Chinese judges, lawyers, officials, scholars, and civil society participants, all are illustrative of this European approach to "capacity building" in China.

The EU has done a great deal for China through these programmes,[25] and they have been supplemented by numerous training and capacity-building programmes run by the UK, Germany, Denmark, and Sweden in particular. To date the EU and these states have been quite satisfied with the results of the efforts to improve Chinese governance in these areas. However, if some of the reforms stall – particularly in the areas of participatory politics (e.g. village elections), human rights, civil society, rule of law, religion, the death penalty, penal reform, or labour standards – then disenchantment may take hold in Europe. China has to be seen as making continuous progress in these areas in order to sustain these programmes and – more importantly – the generally benign view of China's modernization. Certainly if there is another event like 1989, if even on a more minor scale, that would do much to sour European public and official opinion concerning China. European frustrations in some of these realms are evinced in the section on "Supporting China's Transition Towards a More Open and Plural Society" in the 2006 EU Communication, as noted above.

Fifth, Europe now expects to collaborate more with China in terms of contributing to global governance. This is made clear in the 2006 Communication, but the chapters in this volume by Bates Gill and Volker Stanzel also describe a rich menu for such global multilateral cooperation. The EU welcomes China's recent contributions to UN peacekeeping operations (PKO), to UN reform, to non-proliferation, to resolving the North Korean nuclear crisis, and generally Beijing's new diplomatic activism. But, at the same time, the EU is deeply concerned about China's support for non-democratic states and its "value-free diplomacy" and "no strings attached" aid programmes with such states, particularly in Africa and with Myanmar (Burma). China's relations with Iran and reluctance to press Tehran hard to uphold UN Security Council resolutions (which Beijing voted for) and terminate its nuclear programme is another significant concern. Similarly, the EU is closely monitoring Beijing's worldwide quest for energy resources and raw materials. China may not yet be a global power, but it is increasingly a global actor. As such, Europe (and other nations) will be looking to Beijing to help address many of challenges and crises that afflict the international order.

The sixth variable affecting European policies towards China is the American factor and the new role that relations with China play in the transatlantic relationship. The transatlantic row over the possible lifting of the EU arms embargo on

China (in place since 1989) in 2004–5 lodged the issue squarely in the middle of US–Europe relations. Although the lifting of the embargo was shelved temporarily by the European side, one residual effect has been that China is now a greater factor in transatlantic relations, governmental and non-governmental discussions. A flurry of "Track II" nongovernmental dialogues have been started,[26] while an annual US–EU (Governmental) Dialogue on East Asia has also been initiated (COASI).

The momentum to lift the arms embargo slowed due to five principal factors:

- strong diplomatic representations by US Government officials (including President Bush) and intelligence briefings provided to the European side by the US intelligence community concerning China's military modernization and potential threat to Taiwan;
- the replacement of German Chancellor Gerhard Schroeder by Angela Merkel (he supporting lifting while she opposes);
- the hardening of British opposition to lifting and the admission of the twelve new Central European states into the European Union (most oppose lifting);
- the March 2005 passage of the Anti-Secession Law by China's National People's Congress;
- Increased awareness in Europe of China's military modernization and greater appreciation of the East Asian security situation and US security equities in the region.

Although the December 2006 meeting of the European Council "… reaffirms its willingness to carry forward work towards lifting the arms embargo …," it will remain a long time before total consensus can be reached among the 27 member states to lift it.

One major side-effect of the arms embargo imbroglio, however, was that a greater appreciation of China–Europe relations began to take hold in the US Government and, concomitantly, a greater sensitivity and appreciation of US–China relations and US security commitments in East Asia began to take hold in Brussels and other European capitals. As such, the "China factor" is now lodged more deeply in transatlantic relations and will continue to affect European relations with, and policies toward, China. There exists considerable consensus and broad agreement now between the US and EU on a range of issues pertaining to China.

On the more general level, both the US and EU believe that it is in their respective interests to:

- contribute to a range of China's domestic reforms and "capacity building" in Chinese state and society institutions;
- contribute to China's more active and constructive role on the world stage and jointly contribute to managing issues of "global governance";
- keep their respective societies open to a wide range of Chinese from all walks of life – but particularly students, intellectuals, central-level politicians and

local-level officials, scientists, educators, journalists, and military officers – with an eye towards influencing future generations of Chinese elites;
- work with China to maintain an open global trading and financial system.

More specifically, nongovernmental transatlantic meetings on China have identified a very long list of more than twenty issue areas of mutual interest in and concerning China, to a greater or lesser degree. It is apparent that the commonalities across the Atlantic concerning China far outweigh any differences. These include the desire for improvement in intellectual property rights (IPR); human rights of all kinds; political pluralization; NGO development; improving military transparency; the "One China Policy" and stability across the Taiwan Strait; energy security; resettlement of North Korean refugees; decreasing "economic nationalism" and protected industries; maintaining economic standards according to global criteria; renminbi convertibility and liberalization (floating); more humane Chinese ODA and investment policies (especially in Africa); environmental protection (particularly encouraging clean coal technology and reducing greenhouse gases); climate change; China's contributions to United Nations PKO operations; counter-terrorism; strong corporate governance standards; dialogue on "third areas" (e.g. Central Asia, Middle East, Africa, Latin America).

In each of these, and other, issue areas there exists considerable transatlantic agreement – the task now is to explore in more depth and more precisely both the specifics of these issues and the mechanics of transatlantic cooperation to advance them. To be sure, there exist issues in which there is partial agreement but not total that are of pressing concern and require more detailed discussions. These include the still-existent EU arms embargo issue and duale technology transfer to China.

A final variable that will affect the future development of Sino-European relations lies in the realm of values. While China's position has always been to "set differences in ideology and social and political systems aside," it is not so easy for the European side to do so. In democracies values ground public policies. The EU's 2006 Communication (Appendix II) evinces some of these value differences. Volker Stanzel's chapter in this volume also draws attention to these differences and observes that they are going to have an increasing impact on the relationship over time. This is already evident in European objections to Chinese activities in Africa. More focused discussion between China and Europe on this issue is needed.[27]

In the area of global governance, while it is evident that both sides rhetorically support the strengthening of international institutions and improving multilateral cooperation, it is not clear that they have the same thing in mind when discussing multilateralism. China's view of multilateralism seems to err more towards its long-cherished fidelity to multipolarization and the "democratization of international relations," whereby multiple mechanisms counter a hegemonic global order. To the extent that international institutions can push forward such "democratization" and constrain the United States, that seems to be what Beijing has in mind with "multilateralism" – whereas the EU has a much more specific idea about strengthening global norms, institutions, and international law via "effective multilateralism," as embodied in its Common Foreign and Security Policy (CFSP).

When it comes to issues in the security realm, different orientations, terminology, and values also loom large. Europeans are much more oriented towards "soft power," transnational security threats, and security concerns emanating from "failing states" – while China places more emphasis on building its own "comprehensive and hard power."[28] Europeans and Chinese have, to date, been too easily satisfied with the platitudes of a "strategic partnership," but now need to provide greater meaning to the concept. To this end, various suggestions have been offered for increasing Sino-European security dialogues, China–NATO exchanges, and bilateral military exchanges.[29] The 2006 EU Communication also called for improved expertise on the Chinese military in governmental and non-governmental circles across Europe (which is woefully lacking).

Managing a complex marriage

The excellent chapters contained in this volume, and the preceding discussion in this concluding chapter, are evidence that the China–Europe relationship has, like most marriages, become complex and long-lasting. Divorce is not an option. The two parties are bound together through multiple common interests and linkages, and have ample reason to continue to build and strengthen their relationship. While there is a long history to the relationship, much has been accomplished in a relatively short period of time (since 1995), and there exists great momentum in further building and consolidating those ties. Not only are both China and Europe better off as a result of their relationship and "strategic partnership" – but so is the world. Sino-European relations have become one of the major positive forces in contemporary international relations. It is unquestionably a relationship for the good, and it brings multiple benefits to many. It directly involves a third of the world's population and brings benefits to many more. There is strong political commitment and leadership on both sides to further strengthen communication and ties in all realms. The relationship is also generally free of the suspicions that burden Sino-American and Sino-Japanese relations, as public perceptions of the other remain overwhelmingly positive. The Sino-European relationship is also unburdened by several of the troublesome issues that beset China's relations with the US and Japan – notably security concerns, Taiwan, and the legacy of World War II (in the case of Japan).

Nonetheless, despite all the positives in Sino-European ties, it is also evident that the relationship has, since 2006, begun to emerge from its "honeymoon" phase and settle into a more long-lasting marriage – whereby both sides are beginning to better appreciate some of their differences and are having to adjust to, and live with, them. Thus far, none of these adjustments have been too wrenching, causing more minor tactical adaptations on both sides.

It is also evident that the changed – more sober – climate in relations since 2006 comes primarily from the European side. In fact, when one reviews the rapid progress in relations over the 1995–2005 decade, it is evident that the EU has been the catalytic force in the relationship and played the role of ardent suitor. Brussels pursued Beijing more than vice versa. But, similarly, the lust seems to have begun to wear off more quickly on the European side. This has confused China's government and Europe Watchers, to some extent, as Beijing had grown accustomed to all the sweet words and promises from Brussels.

Going forward, the two sides will need to lower their expectations somewhat; clarify their rosy rhetoric; learn how to live with, narrow or manage their differences; and develop the mechanisms to build a truly sustainable long-term marriage. Occasional frictions are to be expected, but the strong bonds and mutual interests will drive China and Europe closer and closer together over time.

Notes

1 Zhao Junjie, "An Uneasy Balance," *Beijing Review*, Vol. 50, No. 2 (11 January 2007), p. 10.
2 See David Shambaugh, "China's Quiet Diplomacy: The International Department of the Chinese Communist Party," *China: An International Journal*, Vol. 5, No. 1 (March 2007), pp. 26–54.
3 See David Shambaugh, *China's Communist Party: Atrophy and Adaptation* (Berkeley and Washington, D.C.: University of California Press and Woodrow Wilson Center Press, 2007), chapter 3.
4 For a list of these dialogues, see: http://ec.europa.eu/comm/external_relations/china/intro/sect.htm.
5 Wen Jiabao, "Vigorously Promoting Comprehensive Strategic Partnership Between China and the European Union." Speech by the Chinese Prime Minister at the China–EU Investment and Trade Forum, Brussels, 6 May 2004.
6 These monies were expended in three programme areas: economic and social reform (50 per cent); sustainable development (30 per cent); and good governance (20 per cent). See: http://www.delchn.cec.eu.int/en/Co-operation/General_Information.htm.
7 N.A., "China and EU Begin Renegotiating Commercial Treaty," *International Herald Tribune*, 18 January 2007. This is also known as the "Framework Agreement." Negotiations are anticipated to last two years before final conclusion of the new pact.
8 Zhao Junjie, "An Uneasy Balance," op. cit.
9 European Commission, *A Long-Term Policy for China–Europe Relations*, COM (95), 279 final, Brussels, July 1995.
10 See respectively: http://ec.europa.eu/comm/external_relations/china/docs/06-10-24_final_com.pdf; http://ec.europa.eu/trade/issues/bilateral/countries/china/pr241006_en.htm.
11 See: http://register.consilium.europa.eu/pdf/en/06/st16/st16291.en06.pdf.
12 See Chen Jialu, "China, EU Start Talks on New Pact," *China Daily*, 18 January 2007.
13 *China Daily*. http://english.cqnews.net/system/2007/01/16/000729676.html.
14 Ibid.
15 Ibid.
16 Feng, Zhongping, "Ruhe tuidong Zhongguo guanxi shenru fazhan?" (How to Push China–EU Relations Forward?), *Waijiao Pinglun (Foreign Affairs Review)*, No. 91 (October 2006), pp. 16–21.
17 "China Sustainable Industrial Development Network," http://www.csid.com.cn/NewsInfo.asp?NewsId=52000.
18 *China Daily*. http://english.cqnews.net/system/2007/01/16/000729676.html.
19 See footnote 5.

20 These are all selected direct quotations from *EU–China: Closer Partners, Growing Responsibilities*, op. cit.
21 "EU–China Strategic Partnership: Council Conclusions," 2771st Council Meeting, 11–12 December 2006, 16291/06 (Press 353), at: http://register.consilium.europa.eu/pdf/en/06/st16/st16291.en06.pdf.
22 Discussion with high-ranking European diplomat, 1 February 2007.
23 Observation of European Commission official, 26 February 2007.
24 For a more extended discussion of these differences see David Shambaugh, "The New Strategic Triangle: American and European Reactions to China's Rise," *The Washington Quarterly* (Summer 2005).
25 For a full listing of the programmes, see the European Delegation website: http://www.delchn.cec.eu.int/.
26 Various institutions in Europe and the United States have become involved in organizing such dialogues in recent years. On the European side these include the Centre for European Reform (London), SWP (Berlin), Centre for Advanced Policy (Munich), European Centre for Strategic Studies (Paris), and Centre Asia (Paris). On the American side these have included George Washington University, the Henry L. Stimson Center, Brookings Institution, Center for Strategic and International Studies, German Marshall Fund, and Atlantic Council of the United States. In addition, a very small number of "trilateral" US–China–EU meetings have taken place – the organizers have included the Konrad Adenauer Stiftung, European Policy Center (Brussels), DGAP (Berlin), SWP (Berlin), Atlantic Council, George Washington University, University of Denver, Europe Institute of Chinese Academy of Social Sciences, China Institute of Contemporary International Relations. There have also been a large number of bilateral US–China and EU–China dialogues.
27 One effort, to date, was a conference convened in Brussels in July 2006. See Konrad Adenauer Stiftung, *The European Union and China: Strategic Partnership Towards Developing Countries?* (Germany: Konrad Adenauer Stiftung European Dialogue Papers, Volume IV, 2006).
28 See the discussion in May-Britt Stumbaum, "Sino-European Strategic Partnership: Retrospect, Vision and Suggestions for a European Perspective," paper presented at the Fifth Shanghai Workshop on Global Governance "The Current Situation and Future Prospects of Asia–Europe Security Cooperation," Shanghai Institute of International Studies and the Friedrich Ebert Stiftung, 23–4 January 2007.
29 Ibid.; and Nicola Casarini, *The Evolution of the EU–China Relationship: From Constructive Engagement to Strategic Partnership* (Paris: European Union Institute for Security Studies, Occasional Paper No. 64, October 2006).

Appendix I

Chronology of EU–China relations: 1975–2006
(European Commission, 2006)

1975   Establishment of EC–China diplomatic relations in May, after the visit of Sir Christopher Soames, first European Commissioner to visit China.

1978   China and the EC sign a Trade Agreement in Brussels that *inter alia* establishes a Joint Committee in April.

1979   In January, E. Colombo is the first President of the European Parliament (EP) to visit China. In February, Roy Jenkins is the first Commission President to visit China. He meets Deng Xiaoping in July. The first EC–China agreement on textile trade is signed.

1980 The first inter-parliamentary meeting between delegations of the European Parliament and of the National People's Congress is held in Strasbourg in June.

1983 The EC and China launch the first Science and Technology Cooperation Program.

1984 The first political consultations at ministerial level take place, in the context of the European Political Cooperation (EPC).The EC launches the first cooperation projects in China, covering notably such fields as management training and rural development.

1987 The EC co-finances, for the first time, NGO development activities in China.

1988 A Delegation of the European Commission opens in Beijing.

1989 As a reaction to the Tiananmen incidents of 4 June, the EC freezes its exchanges with China and imposes a number of sanctions, including an arms embargo.

1990 In October, the Council and the EP decide to gradually re-establish bilateral relations with China.

1991 The European Commission grants aid to Tibetan refugees for the first time.

1992 EC–China relations are largely normalized, but the arms embargo remains in place. The EC launches its environmental cooperation with China.

1993 An office of the European Commission opens in Hong Kong.

1994 The EU–China Energy Dialogue is established. A new bilateral political dialogue opens between the EU and China.

1995 The European Commission publishes its first Communication on China, "A Long-Term Policy for China–Europe Relations."

1996 January. A specific Dialogue on Human Rights issues is established. In March, China and EU are active participants at the first Asia–Europe Meeting (ASEM).

1997 A Dialogue on Information Society is initiated. The EU–China Academic Network (ECAN) is established. On 23 October the EU–China Dialogue on Human Rights, interrupted in spring 1996, resumes.

1998 The European Commission releases the Communication "Building a Comprehensive Partnership with China." On 2 April the First EU–China Summit convenes in London. In December an agreement on Scientific and Technological Cooperation is signed. On 21 December the Second EU–China Summit convenes in Beijing.

2000 China concludes a bilateral market access agreement with the EU in May, an essential milestone in China's WTO accession process. In July Zhu Rongji is the first Chinese Premier to visit the European Commission in Brussels. In October the first EU–China High-Level Consultations on Fighting Illegal Migration and Trafficking in Human Beings take place in Brussels. On 24 October the 3rd EU–China Summit, Beijing.

2001 On 15 May the European Commission publishes the Communication "EU Strategy Towards China: Implementation of the 1998 Communication and Future Steps for a More Effective EU Policy." On 5 September the 4th EU–China Summit convenes in Brussels. In September a new EU–China Information Society Working Group is launched. In October a Dialogue on Enterprise, Industrial Policy and Regulation is launched in Beijing between DG Enterprise and AQSIQ (the General Administration of Quality Supervision, Inspection and Quarantine of the People's Republic of China). On 11 December China becomes the 143rd Member of the World Trade Organization (WTO).

2002 A Joint Technical Group on Sanitary and Phytosanitary Standards (SPS) is established. On 1 March the European Commission releases its "China Country Strategy Paper 2002–6." In April an exchange of letters between the EU and China formalizes the political dialogue into a regular, structured series of meetings at several levels (EU Troika Foreign Ministers, Political Directors, Heads of Missions, Regional Directors, technical meetings of high officials). On 24 September the 5th EU–China Summit convenes in Copenhagen. In November, a readmission agreement with the Hong-Kong SAR is signed. In December the EU–China Maritime Transport agreement is signed.

2003 The Dialogue on Education, Human Resource Development and Culture is launched. In January China joins the International Thermonuclear Experimental Reactor (ITER) project. In March the European Commission establishes a European Economic and Trade Office in Taiwan. On 3 June China formally requests Market Economy Status under the EU's anti-dumping instrument. On 10 September the European Commission adopts a policy paper entitled "A Maturing Partnership: Shared Interests and Challenges in EU–China relations." On 13 October China releases its first ever policy paper on the EU. A readmission agreement with the Macau SAR is signed. On 30 October the 6th EU–China Summit convenes in Beijing: three major agreements are signed, providing for China's participation in the GALILEO satellite navigation programme, the establishment of an EU–China Dialogue on Industrial Policy, and the setting up of a Dialogue on Intellectual Property. In November The Dialogue on Industrial Policy as well as the Environmental Dialogue are launched. On 24 November The EU–China Competition Policy Dialogue is established.

2004 2004 is the "Year of Europe" in China. In February, an EU–China Seminar on the two Policy Papers issued in October 2003 is held in Beijing, leading to "Guidelines for Common Action." On 12 February China and the EU sign a Memorandum of Understanding, under which the EU will enjoy an "Approved Destination Status" (ADS) (the "Tourism Agreement"). Chinese tourist groups are only allowed to travel to countries which have been granted ADS by China. In March, the European Union becomes the biggest trading partner of China. China is the second-biggest trading partner of the EU. In April, the "Cooperation in

Space Science, Applications and Technology" Dialogue is established. In May, a Dialogue between the Chinese civil aviation authorities and the services of the European Commission is initiated. In May, a Textiles Trade Dialogue is established during the visit of Chinese Premier Wen Jiabao to Brussels. In July the first informal, technical talks on readmission and visa facilitation are held in Beijing. On 8 December the 7th EU–China Summit convenes in The Hague: a joint declaration on non-proliferation and an agreement on peaceful nuclear research are issued; new sectoral dialogues are developed with the signing of an EU–China Customs Cooperation Agreement and the launching of the Dialogue on Macroeconomic Policy; China and the EU agree on the renewal of the 1999 EU–China Science and Technological Cooperation Agreement; financing agreements for four new cooperation programmes with a total value of €61 million are signed (Information Society, Managers Exchange and Training, Social Security Reform, Erasmus Mundus China Window project).

2005 In February the first EU–China Financial Dialogue meeting is held. In July an EU–China Civil Aviation Summit is held in Beijing, and the sectoral Dialogue on Agriculture is established. On 5 September the 8th EU–China Summit convenes in Beijing: a Joint Declaration on Climate Change is issued; A Memorandum of Understanding establishing an EU–China Dialogue on "Energy and Transport Strategies" is signed; another MOU establishing a Dialogue on Employment and Social Affairs is signed. In November DG Internal Market and the Chinese Ministry of Finance sign an exchange of letters establishing the Dialogue on Government Procurement. In December China hosts the WTO ministerial meeting in Beijing. In December the first EU–China Strategic Dialogue at Vice Foreign Minister Level is held in London.

2006 An EU–China MOU on food safety is signed in January. In February, the European Commission and the Chinese Ministry of Science and Technology sign a MOU on cooperation on near-zero emissions power generation technology through carbon capture and storage (CCS). In March, the first EU–China bilateral consultations under the Climate Change Partnership are held. In May the EU–China Dialogue on Regional Cooperation is initiated. On 9 September the 8th EU–China Summit convenes in Helsinki, and the EU and China agree on opening negotiations for a new comprehensive Framework Agreement. Official launch in October of the China–EU Year of Science and Technology, as foreseen at the May 2005 China–EU High-Level Forum on Science and Technology Strategy in Beijing. On 24 October the Commission adopts its Communication "EU–China: Closer Partners, Growing Responsibilities" and a policy paper on trade and investment. In December the first Macroeconomic Dialogue is held.

Appendix II

Commission of the European Communities

Brussels, COM(2006)

Communication from the Commission to the Council and the European Parliament

EU – China: closer partners, growing responsibilities

1. What is at stake?

China has re-emerged as a major power in the last decade. It has become the world's 4th economy and 3rd exporter, but also an increasingly important political power. China's economic growth has thrown weight behind a significantly more active and sophisticated Chinese foreign policy. China's desire to grow and seek a place in the world commensurate with its political and economic power is a central tenet of its policy. Given China's size and phenomenal growth, these changes have a profound impact on global politics and trade.

The EU offers the largest market in the world. It is home to a global reserve currency. It enjoys world leadership in key technologies and skills. The EU plays a central role in finding sustainable solutions to today's challenges, on the environment, on energy, on globalisation. It has proved capable of exerting a progressive influence well beyond its borders and is the world's largest provider of development aid.

Europe needs to respond effectively to China's renewed strength. To tackle the key challenges facing Europe today – including climate change, employment, migration, security – we need to leverage the potential of a dynamic relationship with China based on our values. We also have an interest in supporting China's reform process. This means factoring the China dimension into the full range of EU policies, external and internal. It also means close co-ordination inside the EU to ensure an overall and coherent approach.

To better reflect the importance of their relations, the EU and China agreed a strategic partnership in 2003. Some differences remain, but are being managed effectively, and relations are increasingly mature and realistic. At the same time China is, with the EU, closely bound to the globalisation process and becoming more integrated into the international system.

The EU's fundamental approach to China must remain one of engagement and partnership. But with a closer strategic partnership, mutual responsibilities increase. The partnership should meet both sides' interests and the EU and China need to work together as they assume more active and responsible international roles, supporting and contributing to a strong and effective multilateral system. The goal should be a situation where China and the EU can bring their respective strengths to bear to offer joint solutions to global problems.

Both the EU and China stand to gain from our trade and economic partnership. If we are to recognise its full potential, closing Europe's doors to Chinese competition is not the answer. But to build and maintain political support for openness towards China, the benefits of engagement must be fully realised in Europe. China should open its own markets and ensure conditions of fair market competition. Adjusting to the competitive challenge and driving a fair bargain with China will be the central challenge of EU trade policy in the decade to come. This key bilateral challenge provides a litmus test for our partnership, and is set out in more detail in a trade policy paper entitled "Competition and Partnership" which accompanies the present Communication.

Europe and China can do more to promote their own interests together than they will ever achieve apart.

2. Context: China's revival

Internal stability remains the key driver for Chinese policy. Over recent decades, stability has been underpinned by delivery of strong economic growth. Since 1980 China has enjoyed 9% annual average growth and has seen its share of world GDP expand tenfold to reach 5% of global GDP. China's growth has resulted in the steepest recorded drop in poverty in world history, and the emergence of a large middle class, better educated and with rising purchasing power and choices.

But the story of this phenomenal growth masks uncertainties and fragility. The Chinese leadership treads a complex daily path, facing a range of important challenges, primarily domestic, but which increasingly resonate beyond national boundaries:

- Disparities continue to grow. The wealth gap is significant and growing, as are social, regional and gender imbalances; there is huge stress on healthcare and education systems; and China is already facing significant demographic shifts and the challenges of a rapidly ageing population;
- China's demand for energy and raw materials – China is already the world's second largest energy consumer – is already significant and will continue to grow; and the environmental cost of untrammelled economic and industrial growth is becoming more and more apparent. At the same time growth patterns have not been balanced, with a focus on exports to the detriment of domestic demand.

Growth remains central to China's reform agenda, but increasingly is tempered with measures to address social inequality and ensure more sustainable economic and political development. Paradoxically, in a number of areas, the conditions for stability improve as the Party and State relax control. A more independent judiciary, a stronger civil society, a freer press will ultimately encourage stability, providing necessary checks and balances. Recognition of the need for more balanced development, building a "harmonious society", is encouraging. But further reform will be necessary.

China's regional and international policy also supports domestic imperatives: a secure and peaceful neighbourhood is one conducive to economic growth; and China's wider international engagement remains characterised by pursuit of very specific objectives, including securing the natural resources needed to power growth. At the same time we have seen China's desire to build international respect and recognition. The 2008 Olympic Games in Beijing and the 2010 World Expo in Shanghai will focus the world's attention on China's progress.

China has traditionally described its foreign policy as one of strict non-interference, but as it takes on a more active and assertive international role, this becomes increasingly untenable. The Chinese government is beginning to recognise this, and the international responsibilities commensurate to its economic importance and role as a permanent member of the UN Security Council as illustrated by its increasingly active diplomatic commitments.

The EU and China benefit from globalisation and share common interests in its success. It presents challenges to both and brings further responsibilities. We also share a desire to see an effective multilateral system. But there remain divergences in values, on which dialogue must continue.

As the partnership strengthens, expectations and responsibilities on both sides increase. As China's biggest trading partner, EU trade policy has an important impact on China, as do China's policies on the EU. Increasingly, both sides expect that impact to be taken into account in their partner's policy formulation.

3. The way forward

The EU should continue support for China's internal political and economic reform process, for a strong and stable China which fully respects fundamental rights and freedoms, protects minorities and guarantees the rule of law. The EU will reinforce co-operation to ensure sustainable development, pursue a fair and robust trade policy and work to strengthen and add balance to bilateral relations. The EU and China should work together in support of peace and stability. The EU should increase co-ordination and joint action and improve co-operation with European industry and civil society.

Until now the legal basis for relations has been the 1985 Trade and Co-operation Agreement. This no longer reflects the breadth and scope of the relationship and at the 9th EU–China Summit leaders agreed to launch negotiations on a new, extended Partnership and Co-operation Agreement (PCA) to update the basis for our co-operation. This new agreement presents an important opportunity. It will provide a single framework covering the full range and complexity of our relationship, and at the same time should be forward-looking and reflect the priorities outlined in this Communication.

3.1. Supporting China's transition towards a more open and plural society

The Chinese leadership has repeatedly stated its support for reform, including on basic rights and freedoms. But in this area progress on the ground has been limited. The EU must consider how it can most effectively assist China's reform process, making the case that better protection of human rights, a more open society, and more accountable government would be beneficial to China, and essential for continued economic growth.

Democracy, human rights and the promotion of common values remain fundamental tenets of EU policy and of central importance to bilateral relations. The EU should support and encourage the development of a full, healthy and independent civil society in China. It should support efforts to strengthen the rule of law – an essential basis for all other reform.

At the same time, the EU will continue to encourage full respect of fundamental rights and freedoms in all regions of China; freedom of speech, religion and association, the right to a fair trial and the protection of minorities call for particular attention – in all regions of China. The EU will also encourage China to be an active and constructive partner in the Human Rights Council, holding China to the values which the UN embraces, including the International Covenant on Civil and Political Rights.

The twice-yearly human rights dialogue was conceived at an earlier stage in EU–China relations. It remains fit for purpose, but the EU's expectations – which have increased in line with the quality of our partnership – are increasingly not being met. The dialogue should be:

- More focussed and results-oriented, with higher quality exchanges and concrete results;
- More flexible, taking on input from separate seminars and sub-groups;
- Better co-ordinated with Member State dialogues.

3.2. Sustainable development

One of today's key global challenges is to ensure our development is sustainable. China will be central to meeting this challenge. China's domestic reform policy is important and the Commission will continue to support this through its co-operation programme, including corporate social responsibility. On issues such as energy, the environment and climate change, respect for international social standards, development assistance, as well as wider macroeconomic issues, the EU and China should ensure close international co-operation. Both sides should:

Ensure secure and sustainable energy supplies. As important players in world energy markets, the EU and China share a common interest and responsibility in ensuring the security and sustainability of energy supplies, improving efficiency and mitigating the environmental impact of energy production and consumption. The EU's priority should be to ensure China's integration into world energy markets and multilateral governance mechanisms and institutions, and to encourage China to become an active and responsible energy partner. On that basis both sides should work together to:

- Increase international co-operation, in particular efforts to improve transparency and reliability of energy data and the exchange of information aimed at improving energy security in developing countries, including Africa;
- Strengthen China's technical and regulatory expertise, reducing growth in energy demand, increasing energy efficiency and use of clean renewable energy such as wind, biomass and bio fuels, promoting energy standards and savings through the development and deployment of near zero emission coal technology;
- Commit to enhance stability through a market-based approach to investment and procurement; dialogue with other major consumers; encouragement of transparent and non-discriminatory regulatory frameworks, including open and effective energy market access; and by promoting the adoption of internationally recognised norms and standards.

Combat climate change and improve the environment. We already have a good basis for co-operation on environment issues and on climate change through the Partnership established at the 2005 EU–China Summit.

- The EU should share regulatory expertise, working with China to prevent pollution, safeguard biodiversity, make the use of energy, water and raw materials more efficient, and improve transparency and the enforcement of environmental legislation. Both sides should work together to tackle deforestation and illegal logging, sustainable management of fisheries resources and maritime governance;
- Both sides should build on the Climate Change Partnership, reinforcing bilateral co-operation, and strengthening international co-operation, meeting shared international responsibilities under the Climate Change Convention and Kyoto Protocol and engage actively in the dialogues on international climate change co-operation post-2012. We should strengthen the use of emissions trading and clean development mechanisms.

Improve exchanges on employment and social issues. China is committed to tackle social disparities and promote more balanced development. The EU and China should:

- Intensify co-operation on employment and social issues reinforcing and expanding bilateral dialogue to include issues such as health and safety at work, decent work standards, and meeting the challenges of an ageing population;
- Work together to ensure that international commitments on labour and social issues are upheld.

Improve co-ordination on international development. Closer co-operation on international development issues would benefit the EU, China and partners in the developing world. There are significant downsides if we are not able to co-ordinate effectively, particularly in Africa but also in other developing countries. The EU and China should

- Engage in a structured dialogue on Africa's sustainable development. There should be transparency on the activity and priorities of both sides, providing a basis for full discussion;
- Support regional efforts to improve governance in Africa;
- Explore opportunities for improving China's integration into international efforts to improve aid efficiency, co-ordination and opportunities for practical bilateral co-operation on the ground.

Build sustainable economic growth. China has become a source of growth for the EU and the world, but China's current growth model is also the source of important imbalances in EU–China trade. The Chinese government has recognised the importance of meeting macro-economic challenges, of forward-looking fiscal, monetary and structural policies, boosting consumption and reducing inequalities. Increasing exchange rate flexibility will be an important factor, helping rebalance growth towards domestic demand and increasing Chinese households' purchasing power. Policies which would lead to a reduction of its current account surplus would increase China's control of its economy and contain risks of overheating, and at the same time meet China's shared responsibility to ensure a stable and balanced world economy.

As key economic powers, the EU and China should further develop their partnership and work together to tackle global economic issues; they should:

- Deepen co-operation and share experience in formulating and implementing monetary, fiscal, financial, exchange rate and structural policies;
- Co-operate towards the orderly unwinding of global imbalances;
- Strengthen and upgrade their macro-economic dialogue.

3.3. Trade and economic relations

China's integration into the global trading system has benefited both Europe and China. The EU is China's largest trading partner, representing more than 19% of China's external trade. European companies trading with and investing in China have contributed to China's growth, bringing capital goods, knowledge and technology that have been instrumental to China's development.

An economically strong China is in Europe's interest. China, especially its rapidly increasing middle class, is a growing market for EU exports. EU exports to China increased by over 100% between 2000 and 2005, much faster than its exports to the rest of the world. EU exports of services to China expanded six-fold in the ten years to 2004. European companies and consumers benefit from competitively priced Chinese inputs and consumer goods. Openness brings benefits to both China and the EU.

Nevertheless, in Europe there is a growing perception that China's as yet incomplete implementation of WTO obligations and new barriers to market access are preventing a genuinely reciprocal trading relationship. Imports from China have added to pressure to adjust to globalisation in Europe. This trend is likely to continue as China moves up the value chain.

For the relationship to be politically and economically sustainable in the long term, Europe should continue to offer open and fair access to China's exports and to adjust to the competitive challenge. The EU needs to develop and consolidate areas of comparative advantage in high-value and high-tech design and production and to help workers retrain. China for its part should reciprocate by strengthening its commitment to open markets and fair competition. Both sides should address concern over the impact of economic growth on natural resources and the environment. The EU will:

Insist on openness. The EU will continue working with China towards the full implementation of its WTO obligations and will urge China to move beyond its WTO commitments in further opening its market to create opportunities for EU companies. The EU will accept that it cannot demand openness from China from behind barriers of its own. The EU will urge China to honour its commitment to open accession negotiations on the Government Procurement Agreement in 2008 and work to bring them to a successful conclusion as rapidly as possible.

Level the playing field. Better protection of intellectual property rights in China and ending forced technology transfers are EU priorities, including through implementation by China of WTO obligations and will help create a better investment climate in China. The EU will press China to stop granting prohibited subsidies and reform its banking system, and encourage China to allow market forces to operate in its trade in raw materials.

Support European companies. The Commission will make a major effort to assist companies doing business with China, in particular small and medium sized enterprises while urging them to respect decent work standards. The EU will extend and strengthen the existing information, training and advice on protecting and defending IPR in China. A European Centre in Beijing should be opened. The EU–China Managers Exchange and Training Programme should be extended.

Defend the EU's interests: dialogue first. The EU has a clear preference for resolving trade irritants with China through dialogue and negotiation. The existing EU–China trade related dialogues should be strengthened at all levels, their focus should be sharpened on facilitating trade and improving market access and their scope extended. The EU and China also have an interest in joining their efforts in international rule making and global standard setting bodies. The EU will actively pursue global supervisory and regulatory solutions, promoting open markets and regulatory convergence, and build on co-operation with China through EU–China regulatory dialogues. This will also help to ensure compliance of Chinese imports with EU standards for food and non-food products.

But where other efforts have failed, the Commission will use the WTO dispute settlement system to ensure compliance with multilaterally agreed rules and obligations. Trade defence measures will remain an instrument to ensure fair conditions of trade. The EU is actively working with China with a view to creating the conditions which would permit early granting of MES. Recent progress has been made on some of the conditions. The Commission will continue to work with the Chinese authorities through the mechanisms we have established and will be ready to act quickly once all the conditions are met.

Build a stronger relationship. A key objective of the negotiations for a new Partnership and Cooperation Agreement, which will also update the 1985 Trade and Co-operation Agreement, will be better access to the Chinese market for European exporters and investors, going beyond WTO commitments, better protection of intellectual property and mutual recognition of geographical indications. China is already a major beneficiary of the international trading system and should assume a responsibility commensurate with those benefits, making a substantial contribution to reviving and completing the WTO Doha round.

Many of these steps are not only in EU's interest. They are strongly in China's interest and an integral part of China's progress towards balanced and sustainable growth and development and global leadership and responsibility. The accompanying trade policy paper sets out a comprehensive approach to EU–China trade and investment relations for the medium term.

3.4. Strengthening bilateral co-operation

Bilateral co-operation spans a wide range of issues, including 7 formal Agreements, 22 sectoral dialogues, covering diverse and important issues from aviation and maritime transport to regional and macro-economic policy. Further development of the structured dialogue to exchange experiences and views on competition matters, as well as technical and capacity-building assistance as regards competition enforcement, remains important. Co-operation has been successful and positive. But more must be done to focus co-operation and ensure balance and mutual benefit, in all areas, but particularly on flagship areas such as science and technology co-operation. More should be done to strengthen co-operation on migration issues, people-to-people links, and the structures governing our official relations. Both sides should

Ensure quality and increased co-operation in science and technology. Science and technology co-operation is a priority area for the Chinese government. China spends 1.5% of its GDP on a dynamic and growing research and development programme. Bilateral co-operation is also strong: China is one of the most important third countries participating in more EU research projects under the 6th Research Framework Programme, giving it access to 600 million euros of research, and China is an important partner on key projects such as ITER and Galileo. EU participation in Chinese programmes should be increased.

The Joint Declaration from the Science and Technology Forum in May 2005 set the context for taking co-operation forward, based on mutual benefit and reciprocal access and participation. Both sides should:

- Consolidate and improve the visibility of co-operation. This will allow both sides to focus and set priorities effectively and to respond to dynamic issues such as emerging pandemics or work on clean energy technologies; make it easier to examine scope for increased reciprocity; and provide a basis for more effective co-ordination with Member States;
- Improve joint planning to ensure mutual benefit, and increase flexibility to fund the participation of European researchers in Chinese research programmes. Both sides should facilitate researchers' mobility which in the case of the EU is promoted through specific grants under the Framework Programme.

Build an effective migration relationship. Chinese and other migrants enrich the EU culturally and bring with them important skills and expertise. But there is a significant downside if the process is not managed effectively. There has to be an effective legal framework to facilitate people-to-people exchanges. But we need effective mechanisms to deal with those who abuse the system, with a focus on prevention and return. Both sides should work towards the early conclusion of an effective Readmission Agreement.

- The existing consultation mechanism should continue and be extended to cover both legal and illegal migration, and with renewed political commitment to make progress;
- Both sides should agree and push forward specific co-operation projects on e.g. the exchange of officials and training; and there should be exchanges on biometric technology;
- There should be a dedicated dialogue with the Ministry of Public Security covering migration and the fight against organised crime, terrorism and corruption;
- The EU–China Tourism Agreement (ADS) will need continued proactive and practical co-operation to ensure it functions effectively.

Expand people-to-people links. We should strengthen the full range of people-to-people links which underpin our relations through significant and sustained action on both sides, from cultural exchanges and tourism to civil society and academic links.

- Civil society and institutional links should provide direct support and impetus for political and trade relations. Both sides should facilitate direct links between civil society groups in the EU and China in all areas, and include them in sectoral dialogues where possible. Official non-governmental links should be strengthened and expanded. The European Parliament plays a central role and should expand co-operation with the Chinese National People's Congress. The EU should also strengthen links between ECOSOC and the Chinese Economic and Social Committee, political parties, and between other semi-official bodies.

- Education has been an area of particular success, with 170,000 Chinese students studying in the EU in 2005. We should continue to build on existing co-operation through programmes run by individual Member States and through the China-specific strand of the Erasmus Mundus programme. There have been positive examples of work to set up joint degree courses and joint campuses. We should also implement specific projects such as a European Law School. Both sides will continue to encourage EU students to study in China. To strengthen language capability, the Commission will support a specific programme to train Chinese language teachers to teach in Europe.
- Academic expertise in the EU on China needs to be improved and co-ordinated more effectively. Action is needed by both sides to support effective interaction between European and Chinese academia. The Commission should continue to support an academic network on China, drawing together academic expertise to inform EU policy and co-ordinating information-sharing within the academic community; and there should be a small number of prestigious professorships on Chinese studies created and made available to European universities. There should be a permanent regular dialogue between European and Chinese think tanks.

Make bilateral structures more effective. Both sides should reflect on the structures which govern relations and consider whether they should be streamlined, improved or upgraded. The Commission's 2003 Policy Paper sought to expand sectoral dialogue between the EU and China. This has been very successful, and the majority function well and make an important contribution to our partnership. But progress should be reviewed. Both sides should also consider whether there are new bodies or mechanisms which would further contribute to EU–China relations.

- Annual Summits provide a good framework for maintaining contacts at head of government level. This should be supported by regular cross-cutting exchange and dialogue at technical, ministerial and more senior level. In addition, both sides should explore further options for flexible and informal opportunities to meet and exchange views;
- The recently agreed strategic dialogue at Vice Foreign Minister level should be a key mechanism covering regional and geo-political issues and adding focus, impact and value to the relationship;
- Both sides should undertake a thorough examination of the rationale, interrelationship and performance of the sectoral dialogues with the aim of maximising synergies and ensuring mutual benefit, and ensure interested stakeholders are involved where possible. The Commission will produce a series of Working Documents on specific sectoral challenges;

- A new independent EU–China Forum should be set up. On the EU side it should be at arm's length from the institutions and should draw on civil society, academic, business and cultural expertise, providing policy input to political leaders and impetus to bilateral relations.

The EU should ensure that it speaks with one voice on the panoply of issues related to its relations with China. Given the complexity of the relationship and the importance of continuity, regular, systematic and cross-cutting internal co-ordination will be essential.

The EU's co-operation programme, delivered through the country strategy paper (CSP) and national indicative programmes, should continue to play a role in supporting the partnership between the two sides and China's reform process. But as China moves further away from the status of a typical recipient of overseas development aid, the EU must calibrate its co-operation programme carefully and keep it under review. Co-operation must be in both sides' interests, reflect the EU's own principles and values, and serve to underpin the partnership.

3.5. International and regional co-operation

The EU and China have an interest in promoting peace and security through a reformed and effective multilateral system. They should co-operate closely in the framework of the UN, working to find multilateral solutions to emerging crises, and to combat terrorism and increase regional co-operation, including through involvement by both in emerging regional structures. This common interest, in strong multilateralism, peace and security should also be reflected in closer co-operation and more structured dialogue on the Middle East, Africa and East Asia, and on cross-cutting challenges such as non-proliferation.

East Asia. It is clear the EU has a significant interest in the strategic security situation in East Asia. It should build on the increasing effectiveness of its foreign and security policy and its strategic interest in the region by drawing up public guidelines for its policy.

China has a key role to play in the region and has been working to improve relations with its neighbours, including Russia and India, and with central Asia through the Shanghai Co-operation Organisation. But there remains scope for improvement in Sino-Japanese relations. The EU has an interest in strong relations between the region's major players and in continued regional integration.

Taiwan. The EU has a significant stake in the maintenance of cross-Straits peace and stability. On the basis of its One China Policy, and taking account of the strategic balance in the region, the EU should continue to take an active interest, and to make its views known to both sides. Policy should take account of the EU's:

- Opposition to any measure which would amount to a unilateral change of the status quo;
- Strong opposition to the use of force;
- Encouragement for pragmatic solutions and confidence building measures;

- Support for dialogue between all parties; and,
- Continuing strong economic and trade links with Taiwan.

Transparency on Chinese military expenditure and objectives. There is increasing concern caused by the opacity of China's defence expenditure. As expenditure continues to increase, China needs to be convinced of the importance of improving transparency. At the same time, the EU should improve its analytical capacity on China's military development.

Arms embargo. The arms embargo was put in place as a result of events in Tiananmen Square in 1989. The EU has agreed to continue to work towards embargo lift, but further work will be necessary by both sides:

- Current and incoming Presidencies should finalise technical preparations to ensure lift would not lead to a qualitative or quantitative increase in arms sales, and continue to explore possibilities for building a consensus for lift. The EU should work with China to improve the atmosphere for lift, making progress on China's human rights situation; working to improve cross-Straits relations; and by improving the transparency of its military expenditure.

Non-proliferation. Non-proliferation represents a key area for the strategic partnership. International and bilateral co-operation is based on UNSCR 1540 and the Joint Declaration on Non-Proliferation agreed at the 2004 EU–China Summit. The EU is supportive of China's central role in work on the Korean peninsula and continued Chinese support will be crucial to progress on the Iranian nuclear issue. There has been a good start on dialogue and practical co-operation to strengthen and enforce export controls. The EU should build on this, working with Chinese officials to encourage China to:

- Comply with all non-proliferation and disarmament treaties and international instruments, and to promote compliance with them regionally and internationally;
- Strengthen export controls of WMD-related materials, equipment and technologies as well as of conventional weapons and small arms and light weapons.

Both sides should work together to share practical experience in implementing and enforcing export controls, including through training for Chinese customs officials. They should consider scope for joint EU/Asia initiatives in the context of the ASEAN Regional Forum.

4. Conclusion

China is one the EU's most important partners. China's re-emergence is a welcome phenomenon. But to respond positively and effectively, the EU must improve policy co-ordination at all levels, and ensure a focussed single European voice on key issues.

We have a strong and growing bilateral relationship. But we must continue to build on this. The recommendations in this Communication, which the Council is invited to endorse and complement through Council Conclusions, represent a challenging agenda for the EU to do so, and the Partnership and Co-operation Agreement provides an important practical mechanism to move this agenda forward.

A closer, stronger strategic partnership is in the EU's and China's interests. But with this comes an increase in responsibilities, and a need for openness which will require concerted action by both sides.

Appendix III

2771st Council Meeting
General Affairs and External Relations
EXTERNAL RELATIONS
Brussels, 11–12 December 2006
President Mr Erkki TUOMIOJA
Minister for Foreign Affairs of Finland
Some external relations items were adopted without debate at the 2770th meeting on General Affairs (16289/06).
11.-12.XII.2006
16291/06 (Presse 353) 2
Main Results of the Council
EU–China STRATEGIC PARTNERSHIP – Council conclusions
The Council adopted the following conclusions:

1   The Council is strongly committed to the maturing of the EU's comprehensive strategic partnership with China. For this partnership to develop to its full potential, it must be balanced, reciprocal and mutually beneficial. The partnership is increasingly focused on addressing global challenges, and China plays a key role in the effective international response to these issues. The EU and China have important international commitments and responsibilities, and must both work hard to deliver them, in the interest of wider international security and stability and to strengthen an effective, fair, just and rules-based multilateral international system, with the United Nations at its centre.

2   The Council welcomes the Commission communication "EU–China: closer partners, growing responsibilities" and the Commission working paper "Competition and Partnership" and broadly endorses their recommendations. They are an important contribution to the continuing development of an integrated and coherent EU policy towards China, confirming that the EU should actively support China's emergence as a successful and responsible member of the international community. Taken together, these conclusions, the communication and the working paper constitute a comprehensive review and restatement of EU policy towards China. The Council also welcomes the Commission's communication on Hong Kong and Macao.

3   The Council welcomes the agreement in September 2006 to launch negotiations on a single and over-arching Partnership and Co-operation Agreement as the practical basis for the comprehensive strategic partnership. This agreement must encompass the full scope of the bilateral relationship, including further strengthening of cooperation in political, trade and investment issues, and should be forward-looking and reflect priorities outlined in both these conclusions and the communication. The Council looks forward to the timely conclusion of negotiations of the new comprehensive agreement.

4   The Council reaffirms the great value provided by ongoing dialogue with China at many levels, covering an increasing range of bilateral and international issues, and endorses the recommendation that the Member States and the Commission take stock of existing sectoral dialogues. Dialogues must be focused and deliver practical results, with benchmark setting and with follow-up mechanisms.

5   The Council expresses its appreciation for China's constructive role in regional security and dialogue organisations, as well as its increasing commitments to UN peacekeeping operations. The Council also appreciates the positive role assumed by China on the DPRK nuclear issue, especially China's instrumental role in the resumption of the Six-Party Talks. It welcomes the association of China to the diplomatic efforts initiated by the EU to resolve the nuclear issue in Iran.

6   The Council reaffirms the EU's significant interest and stake in East Asian stability, security and prosperity. It encourages regional dialogue, cooperation and integration in East Asia as conducive to stability and prosperity, as well as further steps towards resolution of the territorial disputes remaining in the region. The Council also welcomes steps taken to lower military and security tensions in East Asia and believes that further security-related confidence building measures might include greater transparency in equipment development and acquisition, doctrine and planning and wider participation in/observation of military exercises. The Council welcomes deepening dialogue and cooperation with China aimed at supporting stability in East Asia including through multilateral arrangements like the ASEAN Regional Forum (ARF) and the Asia–Europe Meeting (ASEM), including China's role as the host of ASEM7 Summit.

7   The Council notes the importance of China as an emerging donor, and of its integration into the international donor community and underlines the need for coordinated action to achieve the Millennium Development Goals and to implement the Paris Declaration on Aid Effectiveness and other relevant multilateral agreements.

8   The Council intends to begin as soon as possible the structured dialogue on Africa with China as agreed at the September 2006 Summit. This is an area of key strategic interest to both the EU and China, demonstrated by the EU's strategy on Africa and the China–Africa Cooperation Forum in Beijing in November 2006. In support of our common interest and Africa's own commitment to poverty reduction and sustainable development underpinned by peace

and security, human rights, good governance, democracy and sound economic management, the EU looks forward to increased cooperation together with China to create new positive realities on the ground. This means working closely with African partners on the basis of national poverty reduction strategies and in accordance with the African Union and New Partnership for Africa's Development principles.

9   Energy security, climate change and protection of environment are top priorities for the EU in achieving sustainable development and are key elements in its relations with China. Collaboration on energy security should be intensified, with a view to creating a stable, secure, efficient and clean energy environment and to promoting open and competitive energy markets. The EU attaches the highest importance to its climate change partnership with China, which should develop its full potential based on the work plan agreed on 19 October 2006. The EU looks forward, in particular, to speeding up cooperation with China on Near Zero-Emissions Coal technology and is committed to intensifying cooperation on other environmental issues, including international cooperation to address illegal logging. China and the EU should also collaborate as closely as possible on multilateral climate change issues, in particular on the further development of the multilateral climate change regime ensuring a broad participation of countries, in accordance with their common but differentiated responsibilities and respective capabilities. The EU also looks forward, as part of UN reform, to continue constructive discussions with China in the process to reinforce international environmental governance, including the possible transformation of UNEP into a UN agency for the environment.

10   The Council recognizes the Chinese government's success in developing the economy and reducing poverty substantially. Noting the important proposals made by the Chinese Government to advance the concept of "harmonious society" and balanced social development, the Council will continue to encourage and support China's internal political and economic reform process. The EU will strengthen cooperation to support social rights, corporate social responsibility and sustainable development including through sustainable production and consumption patterns and more efficient use of natural resources. The EU will also help China to implement its international commitments, including to the ILO and under the Kyoto Protocol. The EU will work with China to combat corruption and transnational crime. Furthermore, the EU encourages China to ratify the UNESCO convention on the Protection and Promotion of Diversity of Cultural Expressions. The EU is convinced of the importance of civil society and its freedom of action to the development of China and will continue to provide support to this important sector.

11   The Council reaffirms the high importance the EU attaches to its exchanges with China on human rights, including through the EU–China Human Rights Dialogue. The Council welcomes progress made by China in giving effect to the economic rights of its citizens and the commitment made to reform its criminal justice system. It also appreciates the commitment made by China to fulfil

international human rights obligations and to cooperate with UN human rights mechanisms, in particular the UN Human Rights Council. The Council looks forward to strengthened communication and coordination with China within the UN Human Rights Council, with a view to supporting its work. However, the Council continues to have serious concerns about the human rights situation in China and deeply regrets the fact that there has been little progress in a number of areas. The EU urges China to release political prisoners, ensure fair trial provisions, to reform the administrative detention system, to lift severe restrictions on freedom of expression, association and religion as well as on access to information, to respect the rights of persons belonging to the Tibetan, Uighur and other minorities. The EU welcomes proposals to improve judicial oversight of death penalty cases but continues to be concerned about widespread application of the death penalty. The EU urges China to enact its commitment to ratify the ICCPR and accede to the Rome Statute of the International Criminal Court at the earliest possible opportunity. The EU will continue to monitor the human rights situation in China and to work with China for positive change through continued and improved dialogue and cooperation. To further strengthen this dialogue, the EU Member States confirm their willingness to share with China their experiences in relation to promoting and protecting human rights.

12 The Council remains committed to its One China policy. The Council is convinced that stability across the Taiwan Straits is integral to the stability and prosperity of East Asia and the wider international community. The Council welcomes initiatives by both sides aimed at promoting dialogue, practical cooperation and increased confidence building, including agreement on direct cross-Straits flights and reductions in barriers to trade, investment and people-to-people contacts. The Council encourages both sides to continue with such steps, to avoid provocation, and to take all possible measures to resolve differences peacefully through negotiations between all stakeholders concerned. The Council encourages both sides to jointly pursue pragmatic solutions related to expert participation in technical work in specialised multilateral fora.

13 The Council reaffirms its willingness to carry forward work towards lifting the arms embargo on the basis of the European Council conclusions of December 2004.

14 The Council welcomes ongoing and increasingly close cooperation and coordination with China on non-proliferation, on the basis of the EU–China Joint Declaration on nonproliferation and arms control agreed at the 2004 EU–China Summit. The Council also appreciates China's ongoing commitment to fighting terrorism, and China's public commitment to respecting, in its counter-terrorism actions, the purpose and principles of the United Nations Charter and the norms of international law, in particular international human rights law, refugee law and humanitarian law. The Council reaffirms its willingness to enhance cooperation with China to promote effective implementation of the UN Global Counter-Terrorism Strategy, adopted by consensus by the UNGA in September 2006.

15   The Council welcomes the Commission's approach to trade and economic relations with China as set out in the Communication and the Working Paper. The Council supports the Commission's strategy of developing the relationship on the basis of open markets, fair competition and compliance with rules. The Council welcomes the fact that the strategy takes into account the different aspects of the relationship, including not only the balance of trade, or exchange rates, but also the comparative advantages available to each side, and social and environmental costs and benefits.

16   The Council acknowledges that trade and economic relations are an increasingly important element of the larger relationship between the EU and China and bring benefit to both. The extraordinary growth of Chinese exports, imports and investments of the past few years is most likely to continue for the foreseeable future. This is a challenge and an opportunity. The challenge for the Union, and also for China, is to manage and deepen the relationship in a sustainable, predictable and balanced way. This is best achieved in partnership, through cooperation, common rules and mutual agreements. The Council emphasises that, building on achievements in the WTO, and in order to remove obstacles to trade and investment, further work on a comprehensive agreement should include ambitious liberalisation of investment and government procurement, facilitation of trade, strong rules on intellectual property, binding commitments to remove technical, sanitary and phytosanitary barriers to trade and the effective protection of geographical indications.

17   The Council reiterates that the rights and obligations of the WTO remain the cornerstone of the EU–China trade relationship. The WTO framework remains the basis for the development of bilateral relations and for solving disputes. Likewise, it is important for China to continue to be engaged in the WTO, implementing fully its obligations and strengthening its support for the multilateral trading system including the Doha Development Agenda, contributing in line with the undoubted benefits it derives from world trade.

18   The Council supports a strong and ambitious European trade policy which will benefit both the EU and China. The Council underlines the need for reciprocity in the EU–China trade and investment relationship. The answer to growing competition with China cannot be to protect the EU from fair competition. Instead the EU should continue to pursue an active policy of openness at home while demanding a similar effort from China. The Council acknowledges that while Chinese access to European markets increases economic growth for both parties, it also brings the need for special attention to help European citizens and business to adapt to these changes. This makes it all the more urgent to make further progress on the Lisbon reform agenda and to pursue the right competitiveness and adjustment policies at home.

19   The Council underlines that reciprocity needs to be achieved by addressing technical, sanitary, phytosanitary, legal and administrative barriers to trade, by addressing non-tariff barriers, notably in goods, services, investment and government procurement. The Council emphasises the importance of actively promoting international environmental, social and safety standards and

sustainable development. The Council shares the view that for European access to the Chinese market to be effective, the EU must tackle a wide range of issues, from ensuring sustainable and secure supply of raw materials and energy to distorting subsidies, from lack of access to Chinese government procurement to transparency and the concrete implementation of regulations, from discriminatory industrial policies to the adoption of international standards.

20 The Council emphasises that effective protection and enforcement of intellectual property rights is an important priority for enabling fair competition in open markets that need protection against piracy and counterfeiting. In current conditions where innovation is a key factor in the success of new business, violations of intellectual property rights, nonpayment of royalties and forced technology transfers deprive European as well as Chinese innovators of their rewards for investment and risk-taking.

21 The Council considers that concrete actions on the ground can also help create opportunities for European exporters. Trade policy should not only address trade barriers but also be broadly based and look at the whole operating environment in which European companies operate in China. In this respect the Council takes note of the Commission's aim of providing advice to European enterprises, in particular small and medium sized enterprises, regarding in particular intellectual property rights.

22 The Council reconfirms that facilitating people-to-people exchange, *inter alia* through tourism, is a priority in EU–China relations. The Council welcomes progress in the implementation of the tourism agreement (Approved Destination Status, ADS) and encourages the further intensification of cooperation at the appropriate levels. At the same time, combating illegal migration, including human trafficking, remains an EU priority. The Council emphasises the importance of progress on the readmission negotiations between the EU and China, as well as concrete cooperation on readmission, which would contribute to continued dialogue with China on visa facilitation.

23 The Council endorses the recommendations of the Commission regarding the importance of greater expertise and knowledge of China in the EU, *inter alia* to enable better policy formulation and decision-making. The Council also encourages greater people-to-people links and supports efforts to give greater visibility in China to EU policies and activity.

11.-12.XII.2006
16291/06 (Presse 353) 13

Index